Managing Risk in Sport and Recreation

The Essential Guide for Loss Prevention

Katharine M. Nohr, JD

Human Kinetics

Library of Congress Cataloging-in-Publication Data

Nohr, Katharine.
  Managing risk in sport and recreation : the essential guide for loss prevention / Katharine Nohr.
      p. cm.
  Includes bibliographical references and index.
  ISBN-13: 978-0-7360-6933-5 (hard cover)
  ISBN-10: 0-7360-6933-X (hard cover)
  1. Liability for sports accidents--United States. 2. Sports--Risk management--United States.   I. Title.
  KF1290.S66N64 2009
  346.7303'22--dc22

                                                              2009008409

ISBN-10: 0-7360-6933-X
ISBN-13: 978-0-7360-6933-5

The Web addresses cited in this text were current as of April 2009, unless otherwise noted.

Acquisitions Editor: Gayle Kassing, PhD; **Developmental Editor:** Ragen E. Sanner; **Assistant Editor:** Anne Rumery; **Copyeditor:** Patricia MacDonald; **Proofreader:** John Wentworth; **Indexer:** Alisha Jeddeloh; **Permission Manager:** Martha Gullo; **Graphic Designer:** Joe Buck; **Graphic Artist:** Denise Lowry; **Cover Designer:** Keith Blomberg; **Photographer (cover):** © Human Kinetics; **Photographer (interior):** See the Photo Credits on page 385.; **Photo Asset Manager:** Laura Fitch; **Photo Production Manager:** Jason Allen; **Art Manager:** Kelly Hendren; **Associate Art Manager and Illustrator:** Alan L. Wilborn; **Printer:** Sheridan Books

Printed in the United States of America   10 9 8 7 6 5 4 3 2 1

The paper in this book is certified under a sustainable forestry program.

Human Kinetics
Web site: www.HumanKinetics.com

United States: Human Kinetics, P.O. Box 5076, Champaign, IL 61825-5076
800-747-4457
e-mail: humank@hkusa.com

Canada: Human Kinetics, 475 Devonshire Road Unit 100, Windsor, ON N8Y 2L5
800-465-7301 (in Canada only)
e-mail: info@hkcanada.com

Europe: Human Kinetics, 107 Bradford Road, Stanningley, Leeds LS28 6AT, United Kingdom
+44 (0) 113 255 5665
e-mail: hk@hkeurope.com

Australia: Human Kinetics, 57A Price Avenue, Lower Mitcham, South Australia 5062
08 8372 0999
e-mail: info@hkaustralia.com

New Zealand: Human Kinetics, Division of Sports Distributors NZ Ltd.
P.O. Box 300 226 Albany, North Shore City, Auckland
0064 9 448 1207
e-mail: info@humankinetics.co.nz

In loving memory of my mom, Janice Haney;
and to my supportive and loving family: Gerry and Monique Nohr;
Kim Nohr, Ed Haney, Merle Christensen, Gerrie Nohr, Jeff Iversen,
and Jay Iversen; Jill, Gordy, and Drew Gradwohl; and Bucky

CONTENTS

CD-ROM Contents   vii

Court Case Finder   xi

Preface   xv

Acknowledgments   xvii

PART I   Fundamentals of Risk Management, Law, and Insurance Claims 1

CHAPTER 1   Introduction to Sport and Recreation Risk Management. 3

CHAPTER 2   Legal Principles 13

CHAPTER 3   Insurance Claims and Litigation 31

CHAPTER 4   Risk Assessment in Sport and Recreation. 43

CHAPTER 5   Risk Control 75

CHAPTER 6   Risk Financing 91

CHAPTER 7   Emergency and Disaster Planning. 99

CHAPTER 8   Transportation 109

PART II   Introduction to Sport-Specific Risk Management Chapters 121

CHAPTER 9   American Football 125

CHAPTER 10   Baseball and Softball 145

CHAPTER 11   Basketball .167

CHAPTER 12   Cycling. .183

CHAPTER 13   Golf 195

CHAPTER 14   Gymnastics .225

CHAPTER 15   Ice Hockey. 237

CHAPTER 16   Soccer. 247

CHAPTER 17   Swimming 261

CHAPTER 18   Tennis 289

CHAPTER 19   Track and Field. .299

CHAPTER 20   Triathlon 319

CHAPTER 21   Volleyball 337

CHAPTER 22   Weightlifting and Weight Training 345

Appendix: General Forms   363
References and Resources   369
Index   375
Photo Credits   385
About the Author   387
How to Use the CD-ROM   390

CD-ROM CONTENTS

The following list of forms can be found in the book and also are available to be printed from the CD-ROM.

CHAPTER 4 RISK ASSESSMENT FORMS

Traffic, Adjacent Activities, and Environmental Elements 56
Locker Rooms 57
Public Restrooms 59
Bleachers, Stands, and Viewing Areas. 60
Entryways and Exits 61
Parking Lots 62
Concession Areas 63
Other Public Areas, Including Ticket Booths and the Press Box 64
Clothing, Protective Gear, and Equipment 65
Athlete Violence and Unruly Behavior 67
Spectator Violence and Unruly Behavior 69
Safety, Supervision, and Health of Players. 70
Supervision of Minors 71
Evaluating the Need for Supervision for Your Activity. 72
First Aid for Players and Spectators 73

CHAPTER 5 RISK CONTROL FORMS

Documenting Inspections 88
Preparation of the Court, Gymnasium, or Field for Play 89
Lightning. 90

CHAPTER 8 TRANSPORTATION FORMS

Vehicle Inspection 117
Emergency Equipment and Other Items in Vehicle 118
Other Transportation Safety Tips 120

CHAPTER 9 AMERICAN FOOTBALL FORMS

Football Fields 134
Inspection of the Football Field. 135
Structures on the Football Field 136
Preparing the Football Field for Play 137
Playing on Fields That Are Used for Other Purposes Besides Football. 138
Lighting of Football Field and Spectator Facilities 139
Football Helmets. 140
Protective Football Equipment 141

Other Football Equipment Issues 142
Inspection of Football Spectator Facilities. 143

CHAPTER 10 BASEBALL AND SOFTBALL FORMS

Inspection of the Baseball and Softball Diamond and Facilities 155
Preparing the Baseball and Softball Field and Facility for Play 157
Playing on Fields That Are Used for Other Purposes Besides Baseball or Softball . . 158
Lighting of Baseball and Softball Field and Spectator Facilities 159
Fences Around the Baseball and Softball Field 160
Protective Baseball and Softball Equipment. 161
Baseball and Softball Bases 162
Baseball and Softball Bats 163
Other Baseball and Softball Equipment Issues 164
Tips for Baseball and Softball Batting Practice Safety 165
Lightning Concerns for Baseball and Softball 166

CHAPTER 11 BASKETBALL FORMS

Inspection of the Basketball Court 178
Preparing the Basketball Court or Gymnasium for Play 181

CHAPTER 12 CYCLING FORMS

Cycling Equipment Safety 188
Cycling Helmet Safety Standards 190
Road Cycling Safety 191
Mountain Biking Safety. 194

CHAPTER 13 GOLF FORMS

Golf Course Design and Safety 211
Inspection of the Golf Course. 212
Golf Course Signage and Warnings 213
Tee Areas 214
Water Hazards on the Golf Course 215
Property Adjacent to Golf Courses and Nongolfers. 216
Golf Cart Paths. 217
Golf Carts 218
Driving Range 219
Golf Scorecards 220
Golfing Equipment and Footwear 221
Alcohol Use on the Golf Course. 222
Severe Weather Conditions and Golf 223
General Golf Course Safety. 224

CHAPTER 14 GYMNASTICS FORMS

Gymnastics Equipment Safety 229
Gymnastics Equipment. 231

Gymnastics Matting 232
Gymnastics Facility Environment 233
Supervision for Gymnasts 234
Responding to Orthopedic and Other Injuries in Gymnastics. 235
Minimizing and Preventing Injuries in Gymnastics 236

CHAPTER 15 ICE HOCKEY FORMS

Inspection of the Ice Hockey Rink, Facilities, and Surrounding Areas 242
Ice Hockey Protective Equipment and Procedure 244
Ice Hockey Safety Tips 245

CHAPTER 16 SOCCER FORMS

Inspection of the Soccer Field 255
Structures on the Soccer Field 256
Preparing the Soccer Field and Facility for Play 257
Playing on Fields That Are Used for Other Purposes Besides Soccer 258
Soccer Protective Equipment 259

CHAPTER 17 SWIMMING FORMS

Inspection of the Swimming Pool 265
Swimming Rules and Regulations 267
Diving Safety. 268
Deck Slides and Swimming Pools. 269
Severe Weather or Lightning and Swimming. 270
Pool Water Quality 271
Swimming Supervision 272
Emergency Plans for Swimming Pools. 274
Practice Drills for Swimming Pools 275
Swimming Emergency Communication and Equipment 276
Swimming Pool Chemical Storage and Handling 277
Lifeguard Training 278
Swimming Pool Incident Reports and Logbooks 279
Swimming Pool Signage 280
Outside Group Use of Swimming Pools 281
Hot Tubs and Spas 282
Fences and Gates Surrounding the Swimming Pool 283
Swimming Pool Electrical Equipment 284
Swimming Pool Covers and Drain Covers 285
Dangerous Objects in the Swimming Pool and Pool Area 286
General Swimming Safety Tips 287

CHAPTER 18 TENNIS FORMS

Eliminating Slip and Fall Hazards on the Tennis Court 294
Eliminating Tennis Court Hazards 295
Tennis Equipment 296

Tennis Supervision 297
Minimizing and Preventing Tennis Injuries 298

CHAPTER 19 TRACK AND FIELD FORMS

General Safety Inspection for Track and Field 305
Shot-Put Safety 306
Discus Safety 307
Hammer Safety 309
Javelin Safety 311
Long Jump and Triple Jump Pits. 313
Long Jump Safety 314
High Jump Safety 315
Safety Considerations for Track and Field Meets. 316
Safety Considerations for Cross Country Events 317

CHAPTER 20 TRIATHLON FORMS

Accounting for Athletes in a Triathlon Using a Computerized Timing System 326
Timing-Chip Scanning for Triathlon Events. 327
Lifeguards and Watercraft at Triathlon Events 328
Triathlon Swim Course Design 329
Preparing for an Open Water Swim Course in Advance of the Triathlon Event 330
Triathlon Bicycle Course Planning. 332
Triathlon Run Course Planning 334

CHAPTER 21 VOLLEYBALL FORMS

Indoor Volleyball Courts (Hard Surface) 340
Beach Volleyball Courts 342
Volleyball Safety Tips. 343

CHAPTER 22 WEIGHTLIFTING AND WEIGHT TRAINING FORMS

Fitness Center Safety. 352
Fitness Center Equipment Safety Tips. 354
Gym Attire 355
Weightlifting Supervision Tips. 356
Ventilation of the Fitness Center Facility. 357
Responding to Weight Training Medical Emergencies and Injuries 358
Medical Risk Factors for Weight Training. 359
Tips for Minimizing and Preventing Weight Training Injuries. 360

APPENDIX: GENERAL FORMS

Incident Report 364
Vehicle Inspection Checklist 365
Equipment Safety Inspection Checklist 366
Maintenance and Repair Log 367
Cleaning Log. 368

COURT CASE FINDER

Subject area	Court case	Page
CHAPTER 9 AMERICAN FOOTBALL		
Facility	Bourne v. Marty Gilman, Inc.	126
	Carbonara v. Texas Stadium Corporation	126
	Griem v. Town of Walpole	127
	Lewin v. Lutheran West High School	127
Hazards	Gardner v. Town of Tonawanda	127
	Goforth v. State	128
	Harris v. Willie McCray, et al.	128
	Henry v. Roosevelt School District	129
	Shain v. Racine Raiders Football Club, Inc.	129
	Stowers v. Clinton Central School Corp.	129
Spectators	Bahrenburg v. AT & T Broadband, LLC	130
Staff	Doe v. Fulton School Dist.	130
Violations	Verni v. Stevens	131
CHAPTER 10 BASEBALL AND SOFTBALL		
Equipment	Baggs ex rel. Baggs v. Little League Baseball, Inc.	146
	Grappendorf v. Pleasant Grove City	146
	McCabe v. City of New York	147
Facility	Cohen v. Sterling Mets, LP	147
	DeRosa v. City of New York	147
	Frazier v. City of New York	148
	Hawkins v. United States Sports Association, Inc.	148
	Haymon v. Pettit	148
Hazards	Avila v. Citrus Community College District	149
	Harting v. Dayton Dragons Professional Baseball Club, LLC	149
	Maisonave v. Newark Bears Professional Baseball Club, Inc.	150
	Reyes v. City of New York	151
	Roberts v. Boys and Girls Republic, Inc.	151
Staff	Elston v. Howland Local Schools	151
	Murphy v. Polytechnic University	152
	Regan v. Mutual of Omaha Ins. Co.	153
CHAPTER 11 BASKETBALL		
Equipment	Mei Kay Chan v. City of Yonkers	168
	Pope v. Trotwood-Madison City School District Board of Education	168
	Ribaudo v. La Salle Institute	168
	Trevett v. City of Little Falls	169
	Yarber v. Oakland Unified School District	169

(continued)

Subject area	Court case	Page
	**CHAPTER 11 BASKETBALL** *(continued)*	
Facility	Casey v. Garden City Park–New Hyde Park School Dist.	169
	Dwyer v. Diocese of Rockville Centre	170
	Edwards v. Intergraph Services Co., Inc.	170
	Pedersen v. Joliet Park District	171
	Poston v. Unified School District No. 387	171
	Springer v. University of Dayton	171
	Thomas v. St. Mary's Roman Catholic Church	172
	Willett v. Chatham County Bd. of Educ.	172
Participant	Dotzler v. Tuttle	172
	Fugazy v. Corbetta	173
	Mastropolo v. Goshen Cent. School Dist.	173
Staff	Grames v. King and Pontiac School District	173
	Kindred v. Board of Education of Memphis City Schools	174
	McCollin v. Roman Catholic Archdiocese of New York	174
	Robinson v. Downs	175
	Schnarrs v. Girard Bd. of Edn.	175
	Yatsko v. Berezwick	175
Violations	Seibert v. Amateur Athletic Union of U.S., Inc.	176
	**CHAPTER 12 CYCLING**	
Facility	Umali v. Mount Snow, Ltd.	184
Participant	Estate of Peters by Peters v. U.S. Cycling Federation	184
	Lloyd v. Sugarloaf Mountain Corp.	185
	Nishi v. Mount Snow, Ltd.	186
	Okura v. United States Cycling Federation	186
Staff	Bennett v. United States Cycling Federation	186
	**CHAPTER 13 GOLF**	
Equipment	MacDonald v. B.M.D. Golf Associates, Inc.	196
	Pine v. Arruda	196
Facility	Barbato v. Hollow Hills Country Club	197
	Finkler v. Minisceongo Golf Club	197
	Freiberger v. Four Seasons Golf Center	198
	Jones v. Kite/Cupp Legends Golf Development	198
	Little v. Jonesboro Country Club	198
	Lombardo v. Cedar Brook Golf & Tennis Club	199
	Manias v. Golden Bear Golf Center	200
	Parsons v. Arrowhead Golf, Inc.	200
	Summy v. City of Des Moines, Iowa	201
	Tiger Point Golf and Country Club v. Hipple	201
	Unzen v. City of Duluth	202
	Williams v. Linkscorp Tennessee Six, LLC	202
	Yoneda v. Tom	202

Subject area	Court case	Page
	CHAPTER 13 GOLF	
Hazards	Bowman v. McNary	203
	MEC Leasing, LLC, v. Jarrett	204
	Sall v. T's, Inc.	204
	Thomas v. Wheat	206
Participant	Hemady v. Long Beach Unified School District, et al.	206
	Mavrovich v. Vanderpool	207
	Shin v. Ahn	207
Staff	Mallin v. Paesani	208
	Wu v. Sorenson	208
Violations	Celano v. Marriott International, Inc.	208
	Morgan v. Fuji Country USA, Inc.	209
	CHAPTER 14 GYMNASTICS	
Equipment	Benbenek v. Chicago Park Dist.	226
	Carmack v. Macomb County Community College	226
Staff	Acosta v. Los Angeles Unified School Dist.	227
	Hayes Through Hayes v. Walters	227
	CHAPTER 15 ICE HOCKEY	
Facility	Brisbin v. Washington Sports and Entertainment, Ltd.	238
	Gernat v. State	238
	Guenther v. West Seneca Cent. School Dist.	238
	Sciarrotta v. Global Spectrum	239
Hazards	Hurst v. East Coast Hockey League, Inc.	240
Violations	Karas v. Strevell	240
	CHAPTER 16 SOCCER	
Facility	Manoly v. City of New York	248
	Morales v. Town of Johnston	248
	Range v. Abbott Sports Complex	249
Hazards	Sutton v. Eastern New York Youth Soccer Ass'n, Inc.	249
Participant	Fabricius v. County of Broome	250
	Jaworski v. Kiernan	250
Spectators	Roberts v. Timber Birch-Broadmore Athletic Ass'n	251
Staff	Stephenson v. Commercial Travelers Mutual Insurance Company, et al.	251
	White v. Mount Saint Michael High School	251
Violations	Henderson v. Walled Lake Consol. Schools	252
	Jennings v. University of North Carolina	253
	McCormick ex rel. McCormick v. School Dist. of Mamaroneck	253
	CHAPTER 17 SWIMMING	
Equipment	Sturdivant v. Moore	262
Facility	Gorbey v. Longwill	262
	Pinckney v. Covington Athletic Club and Fitness Center	263
Staff	Padilla v. Rodas	263

(continued)

Subject area	Court case	Page
	**CHAPTER 18 TENNIS**	
Facility	Atcovitz v. Gulph Mills Tennis Club, Inc.	289
	Augusta Country Club, Inc., v. Blake	290
	Guardino v. Kings Park School District	290
	Marshall v. City of New Rochelle	290
	Sammut v. City of New York	291
	Vecchione v. Middle Country Cent. School Dist.	291
Staff	Livshitz v. U.S. Tennis Ass'n Nat. Tennis Center	291
	Petretti v. Jefferson Valley Racquet Club, Inc.	291
	**CHAPTER 19 TRACK AND FIELD**	
Equipment	Bennett v. City of New York	300
	Mason v. Bristol Local School Dist. Bd. of Edn.	300
	Moose v. Massachusetts Institute of Technology	301
	Morales v. Beacon City School Dist.	301
	Morr v. County of Nassau	301
	Siau v. Rapides Parish School	301
Hazards	Kreil v. County of Niagara	302
	Rankey v. Arlington Bd. of Edn.	302
Staff	Feagins v. Waddy	303
	Poelker v. Warrensburg Latham Community Unit School Dist. No. 11	303
	**CHAPTER 20 TRIATHLON**	
The Swim: Hazards	Hiett v. Lake Barcroft Community Ass'n, Inc.	320
Bicycle Course: Hazards	Banfield v. Louis	323
	Johnson v. Steffen	323
	**CHAPTER 21 VOLLEYBALL**	
Facility	Eisenberg v. East Meadow Union Free School Dist.	338
	Ryder v. Town of Lancaster	338
Participant	Barretto v. City of New York	339
	**CHAPTER 22 WEIGHTLIFTING AND WEIGHT TRAINING**	
Equipment	Calarco v. YMCA of Greater Metropolitan Chicago	346
Hazards	American Powerlifting Ass'n v. Cotillo	347
Participant	Orlando v. FEI Hollywood, Inc.	347
Staff	Evans v. Pikeway, Inc.	347
	Holmes v. Health & Tennis Corp. of Am.	348
	Lund v. Bally's Aerobic Plus, Inc.	349
	Murphy v. Fairport Cent. School Dist.	349

PREFACE

Risk management plays a fundamental role in any sport and recreation program. If risks are not assessed, controlled, and properly financed, an organization will likely experience increased lawsuits and insurance claims and may also find that it is not financially prepared for the consequences. This is particularly important in poor economic times when economic motivation leads people with mounting credit card debt and unemployment to pad insurance claims or to develop insurance fraud schemes. Organizations, even in good times, must protect themselves and maintain a safe place for all participants.

This book offers comprehensive information on risk management that combines insurance, law, and sports in a unique and useful way that will assist athletic directors, coaches, administrators, athletes, risk managers, claims adjusters, attorneys, and anyone else interested in sport and recreation safety. The risk management process is explained, and potential loss exposures are identified. Legal principles that relate to loss most often experienced by sport and recreation organizations are explained so they can be easily understood. Detailed information regarding the insurance claims and litigation process is provided based on the author's more than 20 years of experience representing insurance companies and their insureds in tort claims. The book then gives a comprehensive explanation and analysis of risk management and its components: risk assessment, risk control, and risk financing. Enterprise risk management is explained so large organizations that might want to combine business and hazard risks will have an understanding of this holistic risk management technique.

Chapters on emergency disaster planning and transportation are also included. These are particularly important in a world faced with the consequences of global warming, high energy costs, and catastrophic motor vehicle accidents.

The second part of the book provides a summary of published appellate court decisions as well as lists of safety questions and tips for the following sports: American football, baseball and softball, basketball, cycling, golf, gymnastics, ice hockey, soccer, swimming, tennis, track and field, triathlon, volleyball, and weightlifting and weight training. The introduction portion of this section provides a detailed explanation of how to understand and apply these appellate court decisions. This section is important to anyone interested in understanding sport and recreation law and its applicability to particular sports.

The checklists and forms included in the risk assessment, risk control, and sport-specific chapters can assist sport and recreation organizations in reducing injuries and decreasing insurance claims and lawsuits. All of the book's checklists and forms can be found on the CD-ROM, ready to print on 8.5 × 11 paper. This will help you to print and organize your own risk management tools. A CD-ROM icon has been included as a visual trigger to remind you of which materials are available on the CD-ROM (see figure 1). The risk financing portion of the book will assist with decision making related to insurance purchases. The emergency disaster planning chapter provides assistance with improvement of existing disaster plans or starting one from scratch. The transportation chapter sets forth guidelines for transporting athletes and others.

Figure 1 This symbol appears on materials in the book that can also be found for printing on the CD-ROM.

The information contained in this book will provide any sport and recreation organization with the tools needed to develop a top-notch comprehensive risk management plan.

ACKNOWLEDGMENTS

Thank you to My Heavenly Father for His constant blessings.

Special thanks to my editors, Gayle Kassing and Ragen Sanner of Human Kinetics, whose infinite patience, expertise, and support brought this project to completion. I'm so grateful for the guidance of my mentors and friends: Culle Reid, Esq., Stuart Hinckley, Esq., and Ian McGregor, PhD. Thank you to my intern, Sarah Gigantino, one of my biggest cheerleaders. I'm so appreciative to my friends and employees: Heather Murphy, Lenore Ogawa, and Ruth Chun.

I'm especially thankful for the constant support and love of my friends: Cindi John; Lisa Moore; Tamara Gerrard, Esq.; Donna Good; Mary Alexander; Prebah Covetz; Fran Nichols; Dianne Johannson; Brian Rosa; Amy Nelson; Deborah Blackman; Lisa Kelliher; Colleen Crismon; Jenny Douglas; Kristina Selsct, Esq.; Ramona Emerson, Esq.; Lee Jay Berman; Lesia Ferriero; Marylyn Sye; Michael Doerning; Brian Kelly; Rory McGorty; Carol Himalaya-Fidele; Daria Gagnon; Carol Hoshino; Lilian Kanai, MD; Cindy Peterson; Janice Marsters; Cindy Kubas; Chet Nierenberg, MD; Mel Choy; Milton Tani, Esq.; Luis Larcina; Bette Stebbins; Jeff Rhodes; Chris Dilliner; Kanoi Dilliner; Dave Mickits; George Hom, Esq.; John Cregor, Esq.; John Price, Esq.; Jim Myhre, Esq.; Michael Tsuchida, Esq.; Peter Fong, Esq.; Jan Reischel; Tracy Adams; Wendy Humphrey; Val Moss; Robin Fawkes; Charlie Crawford; Dannette Harrington; JJ Johnson; Bill Burke; Steve Foster; Harrison Kiehm, Esq.; Judy Mick; Melissa Deats; Kat Callahan; and Pat Lee.

A special thanks to the people at USA Triathlon, Honolulu Association of Insurance Professionals, and National Association of Insurance Women.

Thank you to my very special clients and employees of AIG Hawaii Insurance Company, USAA, DTRIC, Island Insurance Company, Fairmont Specialty Group, GEICO, Progressive Insurance Company, and ELCO, and to Ralph Rosenberg Court Reporters, IMS, Inc., and to David Carr.

PART I

Fundamentals of Risk Management, Law, and Insurance Claims

Baseball is almost the only orderly thing in a very unorderly world. If you get three strikes, even the best lawyer in the world can't get you off.

Bill Veeck

The first part of this book addresses topics that are important for risk management of all sport and recreation organizations. Although many people have heard terms such as *contracts*, *statutes*, and *torts*, the legal principles chapter explains concepts that are relevant to the duties owed by individuals and entities to sport and recreation participants and patrons. If you've had any difficulty understanding legal concepts before, or simply need a refresher course, chapter 2 will provide that information. The insurance claims and litigation chapter provides a practical explanation of the claims and litigation process, starting with the incident or injury. The claims adjusting and litigation processes are explained so you will know what to expect if an injured person makes an insurance claim or files a lawsuit.

Part I also breaks down the fundamental elements of risk management, explaining in detail how to assess, control, and finance risks. This information provides the basics for any risk management plan that is specific to sport and recreation. In the risk assessment chapter, general checklists are provided for facilities and environmental concerns; clothing and equipment safety; violent and unruly behavior; and the safety, supervision, and health of athletes. The risk control chapter discusses attitudes related to safety in an effort to reduce injuries. The chapter also addresses the issues of safety plans, rules, and emergency procedures; inspection, cleaning, maintenance, and repair of facilities; crowd control, safety procedures, and plans for lightning; and protective gear and other equipment. The risk financing chapter explains the concepts of risk transfer and retention as well as selecting risk financing techniques, including insurance and self-insurance in accordance with the goals of an organization. The chapter also provides an explanation of enterprise risk management.

All organizations should engage in emergency disaster planning, an ongoing process. Chapter 7 discusses the types of disasters that should be planned for and the elements of disaster planning that should be established in order to respond when a disaster occurs. Chapter 8 addresses one of the riskiest activities faced by any organization: transportation. The chapter discusses the types of travel available but primarily focuses on automobile operation, inspection, maintenance, emergency equipment, insurance, and safety.

Once you have learned the principles of law, insurance claims, litigation, risk assessment, control, finance, emergency disaster planning, and transportation, the remaining half of this book addresses specific sports.

1

Introduction to Sport and Recreation Risk Management

*Twenty years from now you will be more disappointed
by the things you didn't do than by the ones you did do.
So throw off the bowlines. Sail away from the safe harbor.
Catch the trade winds in your sails. Explore. Dream. Discover.*

—Mark Twain

Every sport and recreational pursuit is risky. Athletes, coaches, officials, spectators, and even innocent bystanders can be injured by balls, slippery ground, ill-fitting equipment, lightning, and many other hazards. Despite these risks, sports and recreation bring great joy and health to participants and fans. Risk management is the process of decision making and implementation so as to minimize injuries and loss and their effects on your sport organization, facility, or event. Developing a risk management program will reduce the risks involved, whether you are an event director, facility manager, coach, athletic director, official, athlete, or spectator.

Your organization will probably want to appoint a risk manager to oversee your risk management program and establish a risk management team or committee that can divide up the tasks involved in this process. Usually people within your organization will not have the expertise to develop a comprehensive risk management program on their own. It may be a good idea to seek assistance from a sport risk management consultant or legal counsel that might have experience and training in sport law. Your organization will also benefit from continually seeking training in this area by sending employees to seminars or classes in sport law and risk management. Employees should read books and newsletters on sport risk management for background information and to receive continual updates of court decisions and changes in the industry.

The following are some excellent resources:

- Ammon, R., R.M. Southall, and D.A. Blair. (2004). *Sport Facility Management: Organizing Events and Mitigating Risks*. Morgantown, WV: Fitness Information Technology.
- Appenzeller, H. *From the Gym to the Jury*. www.gym2jury.com.
- Appenzeller, H. (2005). *Risk Management in Sport Issues and Strategies*. Durham, NC: Carolina Academic Press.
- Fried, G. (1999). *Safe at First*. Edited by H. Appenzeller. Durham, NC: Carolina Academic Press.
- Griffiths, T. (2003). *The Complete Swimming Pool Reference* (2nd ed.). Champaign, IL: Sagamore.
- McGregor, I. *Risk Management for Campus Recreation*, March 2006 to present.
- Pittman, A.T., J.O. Spengler, and S.J. Young. (2008). *Case Studies in Sport Law*. Champaign, IL: Human Kinetics.
- Spengler, J.O., D.P. Connaughton, and A.T. Pittman. (2006). *Risk Management in Sport and Recreation*. Champaign, IL: Human Kinetics.
- Tarlow, P. (2002). *Event Risk Management and Safety*. New York: Wiley.

Your risk management program will involve risk assessment, risk control, and risk financing. This book primarily addresses the risk assessment phase of a risk management program by providing lists of questions you should consider when evaluating a particular sport. When answering those questions, you will discover weaknesses and strengths of your program, and by doing that you will be able to develop and implement risk control techniques and formulate a risk financing structure that is suitable for your individual circumstances.

RISK ASSESSMENT

In the risk assessment phase, you identify and analyze the risks or loss exposures that are involved in your sport or recreation program. Loss exposures are covered in greater detail in chapter 4. You also consider ways to reduce those loss exposures. For example, if you manage a swimming pool, one of the biggest risks is that people using the pool might drown. In doing your risk assessment, you will look at your facility's experience. Has anyone drowned in the past? What caused the drowning? Could the drowning have been prevented? To reduce the risk of drowning, you will probably analyze how the lifeguards on duty could do a better job of scanning the pool and responding to emergencies. You may also look at the signage at the pool to see if there are warnings of risks associated with using the swimming pool.

RISK CONTROL

Once you have assessed the risks of your organization, which may be a lengthy and tedious process, you will want to utilize risk control techniques. The goal is to select the techniques most appropriate for the circumstance and implement their use. If your risk assessment reveals that three people have had heart attacks in the past 12 months in your football stadium, which attracts many older spectators, an example of a risk control technique would be to make automated external defibrillators (AEDs) available throughout the facility. If this risk control technique is implemented, you would likely establish a plan to train designated staff members in AED use. Other risk control techniques that might be considered in response to the number of heart attacks in your facility are to have more ambulances on site, employ a physician and nurses, improve communication so that medical emergencies

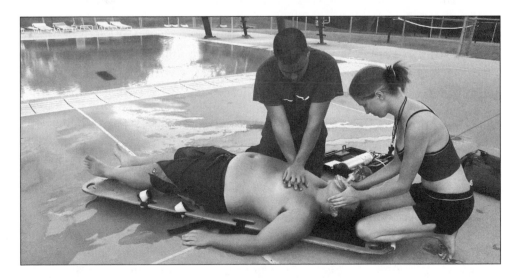

Your facility may wish to obtain automated external defibrillators and train employees to use them.

can be responded to quickly, make sure employees have CPR training, and provide better signage as to the location of your first aid rooms.

Once you have decided on the techniques you plan to implement in response to potential risks, you need to monitor the measures that have been taken. If you purchased AEDs and installed them in public locations, monitoring this risk control technique requires that you continually evaluate their location, their frequency of use, their maintenance, signage, and the availability of trained users.

RISK FINANCING

Another phase of the risk management process involves risk financing. No matter what you do to try to prevent injuries, people will be hurt and losses will occur. Lawsuits may be filed against your organization arising from those injuries. You need to be prepared to financially handle losses and lawsuits by either retaining the risk, transferring the risk, or some combination of both. Insurance brokers and agents should be consulted about these issues. Brokers act on the client's behalf to obtain insurance that is in the client's best interest. An insurance agent works for a particular insurance company, which may facilitate an organization's quest for more affordable comprehensive coverage. An independent agent has several company affiliations and so will be able to match a client with the insurance coverage that is most appropriate for its needs. Your sport risk management consultant should also be able to give you guidance on risk financing, particularly if the consultant does enterprise risk management (i.e., looks at both the hazard risks and business risks of your organization).

Rather than pay costly insurance premiums to insure the entire potential risk that you face, you may decide to retain some risk. Risk retention means using your organization's funds to pay for your losses or a portion of your losses. An example of risk retention that most people are familiar with is the deductible associated with an automobile insurance policy. If a car accident occurs and there is a $1,000 deductible, for example, the insured will have to pay $1,000 before the insurance company will make any payments toward the loss. The higher this deductible, the lower the insurance premiums.

Risk retention might be planned or unplanned. If your organization decides in advance that it can afford to pay a certain amount on each claim and insures the remaining portion, that would be planned risk retention. Alternatively, if it turns out that your company does not have sufficient insurance and there is a large judgment against you, then your company will have retained a portion of that loss. For example, a patron of a health club falls off a treadmill, hitting her head on the ledge of a window that is located within a foot of the machine. She is rendered unconscious from the fall and suffers brain damage. The patron sues the organization, alleging it was negligent in locating the treadmill so close to the window. The evidence at trial reveals that several other people had fallen off that treadmill and injured themselves on that windowsill. Despite notice of the danger, management of the health club elected to keep the treadmill in that location so that television sets would not have to be relocated. A jury awards the plaintiff $1.5 million. The health club's total insurance policies that provide coverage add up to $1 million, leaving the organization with $500,000 to pay. In this scenario, the insured health club partially retains the loss because it did not anticipate that its loss exposure would exceed $1 million.

An organization may prefer to transfer its risks rather than retain them. An example of risk transfer is buying an insurance policy. Rather than pay for a loss, an organization pays insurance premiums; when a loss occurs, the insurance company pays for it instead of the organization.

RISK MANAGEMENT PROCESS

To make risk management easier for you, the following list breaks the process down into eight steps that should be taken:

1. Develop and identify your organizational goals.
2. Identify the risks of the sport and recreational pursuits involved.
3. Analyze those risks.
4. Examine possible techniques that your organization could use to control risks.
5. Select the most appropriate techniques for risk control.
6. Implement those techniques.
7. Monitor the results of using those techniques.
8. Revise your risk management plan as needed in order to better meet your organizational goals.

Steps 2 and 3 are the risk assessment steps that are explained in more detail in chapter 4. Steps 4, 5, and 6 are the risk control steps discussed in chapter 5. As an overview of the risk management process, an example regarding "Joe Smith" is provided here so you will better understand how risk assessment, risk control, and risk finance work in the sport and recreation setting. Once the steps are completed, it would be prudent to repeat them on a regular basis in order to keep your risk management planning up to date.

SUMMARY

Risk management is the process of decision making and implementation so as to minimize injuries and loss and their effects on sport organizations, facilities, or events. Any sport organization will benefit from appointing a risk manager to oversee a risk management program and establish a risk management team or committee that can divide up the tasks involved in this process. A risk management program involves risk assessment, risk control, and risk financing. Risk assessment involves identifying and analyzing the risks or loss exposures that are present in a particular sport or recreation program. Risk control techniques should be selected and implemented that are most appropriate for the circumstances. Risk financing techniques are important so that an organization will be prepared to financially handle losses and lawsuits by either retaining the risk or transferring the risk.

You should follow eight steps when developing your organization's risk management plan:

1. Develop and identify your organizational goals.
2. Identify the risks of the sport and recreational pursuits involved.
3. Analyze those risks.
4. Examine possible techniques that your organization could use to control risks.
5. Select the most appropriate techniques for risk control.
6. Implement those techniques.
7. Monitor the results of using those techniques.
8. Revise your risk management plan as needed to better meet your organizational goals.

In addition to safety issues when operating your sport and recreation programs, there are many other loss exposures that should be considered when developing a comprehensive risk management plan.

Risk Management Scenario: Joe Smith

To illustrate how to perform the eight steps of the risk management process, the example of a race director putting on a triathlon is used.

DEVELOP AND IDENTIFY ORGANIZATIONAL GOALS

Joe Smith has been a triathlete for many years in a small town. He noticed that there are very few triathlons offered in the town, and so local athletes have to drive at least 100 miles (160 km) to enter races. Joe decided to become a race director and put on several small triathlons of either sprint or intermediate distances each year. In developing and identifying his organizational goals, Joe decided that they were as follows:

- Make the events fun for athletes of all abilities.
- Keep people safe while they are swimming, biking, and running.
- Make a small profit so that races can continue from year to year.

IDENTIFY THE RISKS OF THE SPORT

Joe knew there were many risks associated with running the triathlons. The following are some of the risks he identified:

Risk assessment may expose the concern of stolen equipment, such as a triathlete's bicycle.

- People drowning in the lake where they would be swimming
- People contracting water-borne illnesses if the lake was contaminated
- Bicycles stolen out of the transition area
- Cyclists being hit by cars during the biking portion of the events
- Cyclists getting hurt in biking accidents
- Athletes becoming dehydrated
- Runners getting hit by cars or bikes
- Not enough people signing up for the event, resulting in a loss of money
- Weather conditions preventing the event from proceeding or making it more dangerous

ANALYZE THE IDENTIFIED RISKS

Joe analyzed all the identified risks. The following is his analysis of the risk of bicycles being stolen out of the transition area.

Joe observed that many people brought expensive bikes to triathlons. The competitors had to leave the bikes in the transition area under the supervision of the race director while they listened to the prerace speech, when they swam, when they ran, and during the postrace party and awards ceremony. The bikes needed to be identified in a way that made it clear who owned the bikes and so that no one but the owners could leave the transition area with a bike. The bikes also needed to be secured so that no one could steal them. If someone did take a bike while it was under Joe's supervision, he might be liable for the cost of the bike. If there were 100 bikes in the transition area during a race and the average value of the bikes was $2,000 each, Joe could be responsible for $200,000 worth of bicycles.

EXAMINE POSSIBLE TECHNIQUES TO CONTROL THE RISKS

When Joe examined how to control his risk of exposure from having $200,000 worth of bicycles in his care, he considered security, identification, and insurance among other possible techniques. Joe made sure that a sturdy fence surrounded the transition area so it was not accessible to any people who were not participating in the event. He examined the possibility of having security guards or volunteers at the entrances and exits who would not allow anyone in the transition area that did not have a race number, official's shirt, or volunteer's shirt. If someone took a bike out of the transition area, a security guard or volunteer would have to check to see if the person's race number matched the number on the bike. Joe made sure he had a numbering system that could be used for bike security as well as racer identification for timing purposes. Joe made sure he had purchased sufficient insurance to cover him in case a bike was stolen or damaged while in his care.

SELECT THE MOST APPROPRIATE TECHNIQUES FOR RISK CONTROL

Joe had to decide whether he should hire security guards or have his race volunteers perform the function of keeping the transition area secure. In Joe's experience, he has had some problems with reliability of volunteers, but he was concerned about the cost of security guards. If he hired two security guards to be at the race from 4:00 a.m. to 11:00 a.m., it would cost him $140. There was no charge for volunteers. Joe decided that since his profit margin was small and he could not afford security guards, he would use two of his most reliable volunteers and train them so they would be able to do a good job of keeping the bicycles secure.

IMPLEMENT THE CHOSEN RISK CONTROL TECHNIQUES

Joe contacted the volunteers he wanted at the transition area on the day of the triathlon. He made sure he had backup volunteers in case his first choices could not make it or did not show up. Joe decided to have four volunteers so they could relieve each other for periodic breaks. He trained the volunteers and intermittently checked with them before, during, and after the event to make sure they were doing their job and that no bicycles were damaged or stolen.

MONITOR THE RESULTS OF USING THE CHOSEN RISK CONTROL TECHNIQUES

After the first triathlon of the season, Joe needed to examine whether the volunteers he used to keep the bicycles secure worked well and whether any changes needed to be made. It was brought to Joe's attention during the race that some of the athletes parked their bicycles along the fence in the transition area rather than in the bike racks. This increased the risk that those bikes could be stolen, as they could be lifted out of the transition area by someone leaning over the fence. Joe also discovered that his volunteers let a few family members and friends of athletes into the transition area who did not have race numbers. After the race was over and during the awards ceremony, he noticed that the volunteers had left the transition area even though 14 bikes had not yet been picked up by their owners. Joe noted all this information so he could revise his plan for the next race.

REVISE THE RISK MANAGEMENT PLAN AS NEEDED TO BETTER MEET ORGANIZATIONAL GOALS

After noting the problems with his transition risk management plan, Joe was concerned that if bicycles were stolen it could eat into his goal of making a small profit from the race. He decided to make a few revisions to his plan. He made several rules and decided that these rules would have to be emphasized to his volunteers. Those rules were as follows: (1) No bicycles are allowed to be parked against the fence; (2) no family or friends of athletes are allowed in the transition areas unless they are wearing a race number; and (3) at least two volunteers have to stay in the transition area until all bikes have been picked up by their owners. Joe decided to continue using volunteers in the transition area because he considered it a low-cost means of securing the bikes, and he believed it was a better means by which he could meet his organizational goal of making a small profit.

RISK MANAGEMENT SCENARIO SUMMARY

The Joe Smith scenario is an example of how the steps of risk management can be used to assess risks and implement risk control techniques. Risk management in sport and other industries is broader in scope than just addressing safety concerns. Risk to organizations spans a wide range of subjects and concerns. For further discussion of these concerns, see chapter 4.

2

Legal Principles

A little neglect may breed great mischief. For want of a nail the shoe was lost; for want of a shoe the horse was lost, and for want of a horse the rider was lost, being overtaken and slain by the enemy; all for want of a little care about a horse-shoe nail.

—Benjamin Franklin

Thorough risk management planning and execution will likely reduce the number of lawsuits against an organization and its employees, sponsors, and vendors. To fully understand the risk management process, it is important to grasp legal principles. The legal education process is complex, requiring three years of law school and application in the practice of law. Understanding the basic concepts in this chapter will assist you in communicating with attorneys your organization hires to defend you in the event of a lawsuit or to assist with sport risk management issues. Learning as much as you can about the legal system and legal terminology should also better prepare you to comply with laws and prevent injuries and litigation.

CIVIL AND CRIMINAL LAW

There are two types of laws: civil and criminal. Civil law essentially is when one person files a lawsuit against another because that person breached a duty that was owed and caused that person damages or injury. Criminal law is when someone violates a law that was made because the action harmed others. Criminal cases involve prosecution by the state or federal government rather than an action taken by another individual or company. Most lawsuits that involve sport organizations arise out of civil law. Civil cases result in monetary damages being paid by the person at fault. Criminal cases might also mean that a person has to pay money in the form of fines or restitution to victims, but those convicted of crimes might also lose their freedom and go to prison.

An example of a criminal case in sports is *United States v. Comprehensive Drug Testing, Inc.*, 473 F.3d 915 (9th Cir. 2006), which arose out of the federal investigation of a drug laboratory and its alleged distribution of illegal steroids to professional baseball players. This published court decision addresses issues related to turning over drug-testing information to the government. Whenever you see a court case that has a government entity as the plaintiff, as in this case, this provides a reasonable clue that the case is criminal rather than civil in nature.

An example of a civil case is *Weinert v. City of Great Falls*, 97 P.3d 1079 (Mont. 2004). In this case, the plaintiff was a 15-year-old boy who was injured when sledding at a city park, at which the defendant, City of Great Falls, installed a safety net at the bottom of the hill to assist sledders who could not stop on their own. The plaintiff claimed that the safety net that stopped him caused injury, and so he filed a lawsuit against the City of Great Falls, claiming it was negligent. The city prevailed in this case. Note that even though one of the parties to this lawsuit was a government entity, the plaintiff was an individual. If the person filing the lawsuit is an individual or company, it is very likely that the lawsuit is civil in nature, with the plaintiff seeking monetary damages.

There are three different ways that you or your organization might be held legally responsible or liable for your actions or failure to act. Legal liability can arise out of (1) contracts, (2) statutes, or (3) torts. Although torts are the most important for the purposes of sport risk management and will be discussed at length, you should also concern yourself with contracts and statutes.

CONTRACTS

You can be found liable under a contract if you breach the contract (i.e., if you do something in violation of an agreement you made with someone else). A case involving breach of contract occurred when Vibra-Whirl, Ltd., entered into a contract with Longview Independent School District in Texas. Vibra-Whirl agreed to install a synthetic turf football field at a school in return for payment by the school district. When the school district refused to pay the company, Vibra-Whirl filed a lawsuit alleging breach of contract.

Normally a public school is immune from suit because it is a governmental entity. In this case, the court determined that by entering into a contract with Vibra-Whirl, the school district waived its immunity from liability with respect to Vibra-Whirl's breach of contract claim against them (*Longview Independent School District v. Vibra-Whirl, Ltd.*, 169 S.W.3d 511 [Tex. App. 2005]). If your organization is a governmental entity and anticipates being immune from lawsuits, this case provides a good argument for the alternative if the plaintiff to the lawsuit sued under a contract.

Another way a party to a contract might find itself liable is through a hold harmless agreement—when one party to the contract promises to pay another party if there is a loss to that party. An example of this is found in a case in which Sagamore Club, LLC, entered into a contract with Ratio Architects, Inc., to provide architectural and engineering services for building the Sagamore Golf Clubhouse in Indiana. Ratio Architects hired LHB as a consultant to provide structural engineering services, and Wurster Construction was hired as the general contractor. Wurster subcontracted with Main Street to install and erect wood trusses on the project. During the course of the construction, two employees of Main Street who were working off the ground on trusses fell to the ground when a girder beam broke, causing injury to themselves and one Main Street employee on the ground. The injured employees sued LHB for damages. Since there was a contract between LHB and Main Street that had a hold harmless agreement in it, LHB filed a lawsuit against Main Street, claiming that Main Street had an obligation under the contract to indemnify and defend LHB. Although Main Street prevailed in this action, this case illustrates how a hold harmless agreement might come into play [*Pekin Insurance Co. v. Main St. Construction, Inc.*, Slip Copy, WL 1597924 (S.D. Ind. 2007)].

STATUTES

Each state's legislature makes the laws governing that state. The United States Congress enacts federal law, which is applicable to the entire country. State and federal laws are commonly known as statutes, under which a sport organization can find itself liable. A good example of this is state and federal workers' compensation law. Simply stated, workers' compensation statutes require employers to put money into a fund that will pay benefits to workers who are injured on the job. The workers get paid out of the fund without having to file lawsuits against their employers.

In the example described earlier, the Main Street employees who were injured while constructing the golf clubhouse were most likely covered by workers' compensation insurance through their employer, Main Street. Note that the employees filed the lawsuit against LHB and not their employer. Very commonly, professional athletes who are injured on the job file workers' compensation claims and receive benefits. An example of this involved a professional hockey player who was injured during a game, which arose out of his employment with the St. Louis Blues Hockey Club. The player's employer provided him with a portion of his salary in weekly benefits. The case ended up in court when there was a dispute regarding the total amount owed to the player and attorney's fees [*Dubinsky v. St. Louis Blues Hockey Club*, 229 S.W.3d 126 (Mo. App. 2007)].

A common statute that sport programs in educational institutions receiving federal funding must follow is Title IX of the Education Amendments of 1972, which is often simply referred to as Title IX. This federal statutory

Title IX has worked to ensure that educational institutions receiving federal financial assistance cannot deny anyone education programs or activities because of gender.

provision's name has been changed to the Patsy T. Mink Equal Opportunity in Education Act. The law states that "no person in the United States shall, on the basis of sex, be excluded from participation in, be denied the benefits of, or be subjected to discrimination under any education program or activity receiving Federal financial assistance."

Another federal statute that sport organizations must adhere to is the Americans with Disabilities Act of 1990, commonly called ADA. This civil rights law prohibits discrimination of persons with disabilities. ADA defines disability as "a physical or mental impairment that substantially limits a major life activity."

TORTS

Up until now, you may have thought that a torte was a pastry. Tort is also an important concept in civil law, although spelled differently, referring to a wrongful act or omission. A person found liable for a tort would likely be told by the court to pay money to the person who was injured. The person who committed the tort is the tortfeasor, or wrongdoer. If more than one person commits a tort, they are joint tortfeasors.

There are three types of torts:

1. Negligence torts
2. Intentional torts
3. Strict liability torts

Negligence Torts

The most important type of tort to understand in sport risk management is negligence. Negligence is conduct that falls below a reasonable standard. In other words, it is the failure to exercise reasonable care that a reasonably prudent person would have exercised in the same or similar circumstances. This standard applies to acts as well as omissions.

A plaintiff in a lawsuit must prove certain elements in order for a defendant to be found negligent. The elements of negligence are as follows:

1.   Duty or duty of care—There is a relationship between the defendant and the plaintiff such that the defendant owes a duty to exercise reasonable care to the plaintiff. This duty could arise out of a relationship, such as between a general manager of a sports team and a spectator. It could arise out of a voluntary assumption of a duty, such as a coach giving a player a ride home from a game. Or the duty could be imposed by statute, such as a law requiring that spectators' bags be searched before entering a sports stadium. In these relationships, the defendant has a duty to anticipate foreseeable dangers and take necessary precautions to protect the plaintiff.

2.   Breach of duty—The defendant breached the duty of care that he or she owed to the plaintiff. In other words, the defendant's actions or failure to act fell below the standard of care applicable to the given situation. If a safety rule is in place, that rule might be determined to be the standard of care. For example, if there is a rule requiring a soccer field to be inspected for potentially hazardous objects before play can begin, then such inspection may be determined to be the standard of care. If there is no such rule and a standard of care cannot easily be discerned, the question is how a reasonably prudent person would have behaved in the same or a similar situation.

3.   Proximate cause—There must be a proximate causal connection between the negligent conduct and the resulting injury. For example, the netting that protects spectators behind home plate at a baseball stadium had a hole in it. A spectator got hit in the face by a foul ball that went through the hole, causing a serious eye injury. Evidence at trial established that the manager of the stadium knew the hole in the netting was there but failed to fix it, and so the court found that his negligence was the proximate cause of the spectator's injury. If the court found that the spectator had a preexisting

eye injury and the errant ball was not the cause of her injury, the element of proximate cause would not have been met.

4. Damages—The plaintiff has to suffer an actual injury or damages. If in the previous example, the spectator could not prove that she was injured by the ball that hit her, then the fourth element would not have been met.

There are a number of duties, also known as duties of care, that might exist in an athletic setting. The following list explains possible duties and gives an example of a scenario in which the duty might have been breached:

- Duty to plan for potential hazards and develop a plan to respond. Example: A university lies in an area prone to hurricanes but has no emergency plan in place.

- Duty to assess abilities of athletes and their physical fitness level. Example: A personal trainer at a gym pushes an out-of-shape 50-year-old female, on her first session, to bench press 100 pounds (45 kg) of weight.

- Duty to provide proper equipment. Example: A high school, short on funding, requires students to provide their own football helmets without inspecting them for compliance with safety standards.

- Duty to maintain safe conditions. Example: A golf and country club does not sweep its pathways of fallen branches, pine cones, and seedpods, which causes a tripping hazard.

- Duty to provide safe transportation to and from an event. Example: A high school allows its cheerleaders to ride with their boyfriends or strangers to and from basketball games.

- Duty to supervise. Example: A physical education teacher leaves her fourth-grade tumbling class alone while she steps outside to take a call on her cell phone.

- Duty to select, provide, and train coaches. Example: A youth soccer organization is made up of volunteer coaches who have not undergone background checks or any training.

- Duty to instruct properly. Example: A baseball coach directs two batters to stand next to each other, while two pitchers located next to each other on the pitcher's mound take turns pitching to one of the batters.

- Duty to appropriately match athletes when they compete against each other. Example: A 14-year-old female who weighs 130 pounds (59 kg) is directed to wrestle a 15-year-old male who weighs 160 pounds (73 kg).

- Duty to warn of unsafe practices. Example: Fans are allowed to tear down the university's goalposts after football games when the team wins.

- Duty to warn of inherent dangers in practice and competition. Example: A high school football coach does not warn his players that helmet-to-helmet contact is dangerous and could cause injury.

- Duty to make sure that athletes are covered by injury insurance when participating. Example: A gymnastics club located in an area where few people have their own health insurance does not provide any insurance for its members, nor does it inquire as to whether its young members have insurance that will cover them if they are injured.

- Duty to develop and implement an emergency response plan. Example: A youth baseball club has not developed a plan in the event that lightning is forecast or close by.

- Duty to provide emergency care. Example: An elderly man has a heart attack at a fitness club that is equipped with an AED. No one who is working at the club uses the AED or CPR in response.

Although these are hypothetical examples of possible violations of duties, there are many legal cases that address the issue of whether a duty is owed in the area of sport and recreation. An example is the Texas appellate case of *Chrismon v. Brown*, 246 S.W.3d 102, WL 2790352 (Tex. App. 2007), which involves a lawsuit filed by a volunteer assistant coach on a girls' softball team against the volunteer head coach and softball association. The assistant coach sued for damages arising from an injury that occurred when the head coach hit her in the face with a bat that slipped out of his hands while he was swinging it during a drill. The court determined that a sport participant owes no duty to another sport participant regarding risks that are inherent in the sport they are engaged in. However, the participant does owe a duty to other participants of the sport for risks that are not an inherent part of the sport or if the conduct is grossly negligent or intentional.

It is important to pay close attention to the example raised in the *Chrismon v. Brown* case. Courts will commonly rule that there is no duty where sport participants have assumed the risks inherent in the sport they are engaged in. Often, the only way a person or entity will be found liable is if the injured person is able to prove that the conduct of the defendant was intentional or grossly negligent. More often than not, courts rule in favor of defendants where there is an allegation of simple negligence. However, this should not in any way encourage lack of safe practices and sound risk management.

Damages

If a defendant is sued and is found liable because of negligence, a court might award the plaintiff damages in order to provide compensation for an injury. The underlying purpose of an award of damages is to put the plaintiff back in the position he would have been in if the tort had not taken place.

Compensatory damages are the payments made for the actual loss that the plaintiff has experienced. Damages awarded in tort cases are classified as either special or general damages. Special damages compensate the plaintiff for actual monetary losses that have been sustained, such as medical expenses or wage loss. General damages may be awarded to an individual plaintiff who has suffered harm, compensating for pain and suffering and emotional distress that do not have an economic value.

Another form of damages that can be awarded are punitive damages, also referred to as exemplary damages. These damages are not awarded to compensate a wronged plaintiff, but rather to deter future conduct from the defendant and others as well as to punish a defendant who might have acted recklessly or maliciously. Courts are expected to exert restraint in awarding punitive damages, which are subject to the due process clauses of the Fifth and Fourteenth Amendments of the United States Constitution.

Courts may overturn jury awards of punitive damages if the element of outrage similar to that usually found in a crime is not present. For example, a volunteer at the Tiger Point Golf & Country Club, Mr. William J. Hipple, sustained a broken toe when a handrail at the golf club fell on his foot. Mr. Hipple was forcibly removing the defective handrail with two other people when the incident happened. The golf club had been notified 10 to 12 days before the incident that the handrail was in very bad disrepair. The appellate court overturned the punitive damage award in the amount of $85,000 against the golf club, concluding that simply neglecting to repair the handrail even though the golf club knew it was defective for several weeks did not demonstrate the culpability that is required to support an award for punitive damages. It is important to note that this explanation considers the issue of punitive damages only and not compensatory damages. Simply because the court overturned the damages designed to punish the golf club does not mean the golf club did not have to pay damages awarded to compensate the plaintiff for his injury [*Tiger Point Golf and Country Club v. Hipple*, 977 So. 2d 608 (Fla. App. 1 Dist. 2007)].

Defenses in Negligence Actions

The primary way to defeat a negligence action is to show that one or more of the four elements of negligence have not been met. A defendant can demonstrate that she did not owe a duty of care to the plaintiff. She can establish that the duty of care that was owed was not breached. Even if it was breached, the defendant might show that her act or omission was not the proximate cause of the plaintiff's injury. She could also attempt to show that there was no actual harm or injury suffered by the plaintiff.

If the defendant is not able to establish that the elements of negligence have not been met and there are no other viable defenses available, the defendant will try to show that the injuries were minor so as to reduce the amount of potential damages that have to be paid. The defendant will also investigate whether the plaintiff had a preexisting injury so that only a portion of the value of the injury will have to be paid by the defendant.

Another defense is that of comparative or contributory negligence on the part of the plaintiff. In a situation where the plaintiff is partly at fault for the injury, the plaintiff may receive a proportionate reduction in damages in a state where comparative negligence is the law. In a state in which contributory negligence is the law, a plaintiff who is even partly at fault cannot recover any damages from the defendant.

Statute of limitations is another possible defense if the plaintiff takes too long to file a lawsuit against the defendant. There are statutes that limit the amount of time for filing so that evidence will not be lost and witnesses unavailable. Statutes of limitations for tort actions vary from state to state, so it is important to check with an attorney in your state so that you understand the time frames. Statutes of limitations apply differently to minors. If a minor is injured because of negligence, the statute does not begin to run until the minor reaches majority age. For example, if a boy is injured while playing football when he is 14 years old, he will be able to file a lawsuit until his 20th birthday if majority is considered to be 18 and the statute of limitations is 2 years in the state in which the injury occurred.

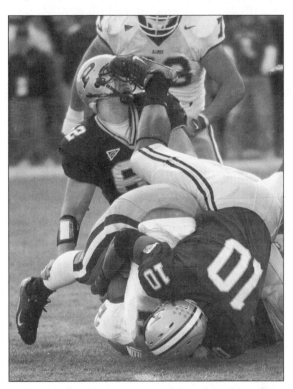

A court may determine that a player who voluntarily participates in an activity or sport assumes the risks involved in participating, such as injury that may happen to football players when they are tackled.

Assumption of risk is another defense that is often raised in sport and recreation lawsuits. A plaintiff who has assumed the risk of participating in a sport would not be able to recover damages from a negligent defendant. For example, if a football player is injured during a tackle, the defendant football organization usually argues that the player knew that football is a dangerous sport and that he could be injured when tackled, and so he voluntarily assumed the risk by participating. The defendant would argue that the plaintiff cannot recover damages for the injury because he assumed the risk.

Release or waiver is a common defense used in sport and recreation cases. Sport organizations often have participants sign a document that specifies the potential dangers of the sport or activity and that the participant understands and accepts the risks. The document will also explicitly release the organization and others from liability if the participant should be injured. Some jurisdictions have said that these documents are against public policy, and even if they are signed, the participant can recover against the organization if there is negligence. Other states allow releases and waivers as long as they are carefully drafted and signed and understood by the participant.

Governmental immunity, known as sovereign immunity, is also a defense that may be available to local, state, or federal governmental agencies that might be immune from lawsuits unless they consent. However, there are some statutes under which tort actions can be brought, such as the Federal Tort Claims Act, which waives immunity in some circumstances. There are also immunity exceptions where an entity purchases liability insurance, waiving sovereign immunity.

A defense that might be used in the sport context is that the defendant had no supervisory responsibility over the person who is claiming injury. For example, if a soccer player leaves practice and is injured while driving home, the soccer coach may claim that any supervisory responsibility ended when the player left the field or school, and so the coach owed no duty to the player at the time she was injured.

Another defense that can be used is that the incident that caused injury was unforeseeable, and so there was no negligence on the part of the defendant. For example, a spectator at a basketball game slipped and fell in the foyer immediately outside the gymnasium. She filed a lawsuit against the owner of the building alleging that he was negligent for failure to warn and for the allegedly unreasonably dangerous condition. Since the owner had no previous notice that there was anything wrong with the floor and no one had slipped there before, the injury was unforeseeable, and so there was no negligence on the part of the owner.

Lack of causation is another possible defense. Injured parties often file lawsuits for injuries that were caused by something other than the incident in question. For example, an athlete was traveling on a bus with her volleyball team, and the bus jerked forward when suddenly stopping to avoid an accident. The athlete was thrown out of her seat and hit her knee on the back of a chair. She claimed to have injured her knee from that incident, but medical records established that she had a knee injury before that incident, and the court found that the bus incident was not the legal cause of her injury.

Alternative Ways to Prove Negligence

To avoid liability, it is important to be aware of other ways a plaintiff might be able to prove negligence, which are as follows:

- Negligent entrustment
- Vicarious liability
- Joint and several liability
- Negligence per se
- Res ipsa loquitur

Negligent entrustment is often raised in a situation where someone lends a car to another and there is an accident. The plaintiff claims that the person who lent the car is liable because she allowed an incompetent or unfit person to use a dangerous object, the car. The plaintiff will try to prove that the person who used the car had a bad driving record, was known to drive carelessly, used drugs or alcohol, was not licensed, or some other facts that will establish the driver to be incompetent or unfit. The plaintiff will also try to establish that the person who lent her the vehicle knew or should have known of the driver's incompetence or unfitness. Negligent entrustment involves the entrustment of not only an automobile but also any other dangerous object. Some courts award punitive damages in these cases.

Organizations should be aware that they may be found vicariously liable for the actions of their agents, employees, volunteers, or any others who are acting on their behalf. Vicarious liability means being legally responsible for those persons acting on your behalf. If an employee is acting within the scope of his employment when committing a tort, an employer might be held liable under the master–servant rule, also known as the respondeat superior doctrine. Under this doctrine, a lawsuit might be filed against the employee, alleging negligence, and against the employer, alleging vicarious liability.

The relationship between the organization and the individual might be that of principal and independent contractor rather than employer and employee. This situation arises when an organization contracts with someone to obtain a result, and the organization does not exert any control over how that result is accomplished. If that is the case, the principal might be able to escape liability, by virtue of the common law rule that a principal is not vicariously liable for acts of its independent contractor. However, U.S. courts have carved out exceptions to this rule over the years. A principal may be held liable for an independent contractor's actions for nondelegable duties, or those duties that cannot be entrusted to another. For example, if a spectator falls in the stands at a football game, the spectator may have a cause of action against the owner of the stadium, even though an independent contractor created a hazard that caused the spectator to fall. It may be determined that the duty to keep the stadium safe was nondelegable, and so the doctrine of respondeat superior is applicable.

Another situation in which a principal might be held liable for an independent contractor's negligence is when the activity involved is inherently dangerous. For example, Climb High Mountain Company is in the business of leading expeditions up Mount Everest. It hires an independent contractor to build a tent system at base camp, but because of the independent contractor's negligence, the tent collapses and kills four people. It might be determined that because of the inherently dangerous nature of erecting a tent system at base camp on Mount Everest, elevation more than 17,000 feet (5,000 m), the principal cannot escape vicarious liability.

Joint and several liability is important to understand if you or your organization is one of multiple defendants in a lawsuit. If joint and several liability is applicable in your jurisdiction, that means if you are found to be at all liable, even 1 percent responsible, and the other defendants are not able to pay their portion of the judgment, you may be responsible for the whole amount of damages. For example, your insurance coverage is $1 million, and the other two defendants each have coverage for $100,000. If the damages are valued at $1 million, you may want to contribute a larger portion to possible settlement even if you think your potential liability will be less than 50%. After trial, if the judgment turns out to be $900,000, and you are found to be 25 percent liable and the other defendants are found to be 50 percent liable and 25 percent liable and both pay their $100,000 (and they do not have any assets or other moneys available), you will have to pay $700,000. This scenario should be considered before trial when evaluating settlement.

Negligence per se is when simply committing an act is inherently negligent because of a statute or ordinance that prohibits that act. If this occurs, the plaintiff will not have to prove there was a breach of duty of care. For example, a local ordinance states that any swimming pool open to the public must either display a sign warning that there is no lifeguard on duty or have a lifeguard on duty during all hours of operation. XYZ swimming pool's warning sign that there is no lifeguard on duty fell off and was lying facedown on the ground for weeks. A woman drowned in the XYZ swimming pool during the time the sign was down. In a wrongful death action brought against XYZ, Inc., the owner of XYZ swimming pool, the woman's estate is alleging that defendant XYZ, Inc., was negligent per se because the ordinance requiring the sign was violated.

Res ipsa loquitur is another means by which negligence might be proven. The phrase is Latin for "the thing speaks for itself." This legal doctrine is applicable when negligence is inferred simply by an accident occurring. The cause of the accident must be in the exclusive control of the defendant, the accident would not ordinarily happen, and the accident was not caused by the plaintiff's own negligence. For example, a plaintiff who is injured in an elevator in a recreational facility might invoke the doctrine of res ipsa loquitur in an action against the owner. She would have to prove that the elevator was in the exclusive control of the owner of the facility, that the accident would not happen in the ordinary course of events, and that she did not contribute to the cause of the accident.

Intentional Torts

Thus far, the discussion has related to torts that are done unintentionally. There is also a class of torts that are purposefully done, which are called intentional torts. An intentional tort is a civil wrong resulting from an intentional act on the part of the person committing the tort. A party may be held liable for an intentional tort if there is substantial certainty that the result of the action will occur. Essentially, there may be intent to cause harm or at least to perform an act that likely will cause harm.

Intentional torts against a person include the following:

- Assault
- Battery
- False imprisonment
- False arrest
- Defamation
- Invasion of privacy
- Malicious prosecution
- Malicious abuse of process
- Intentional infliction of emotional distress

Intentional torts involving property include the following:

- Trespass to land
- Trespass to chattels—A tort in which a person has intentionally interfered with another person's lawful possessions of personal property. For example, someone stealing athletic equipment.
- Conversion—When someone takes away or wrongfully assumes the right to goods which belong to another. For example, a delivery person refuses to deliver athletic equipment to a school after a demand for delivery has been made.
- Nuisance
- Interference with a copyright, trademark, or patent

Many of these intentional torts occur in the sport industry and should be guarded against. Assault and battery may occur in the context of violence

Intentional torts involve intent to cause harm or at least to perform an act that likely will cause harm. This has become an increasingly frequent problem among parent spectators at children's sport events or disappointed fans at important games.

involving spectators, officials, coaches, security guards, and others. False imprisonment, which is restraining or confining a person without his consent, or false arrest, which is restraining a person without legal authority, could occur when an organization is attempting to respond to a spectator or customer who has committed a crime, injured another, or violated rules. Invasion of privacy could occur in a sport setting by unauthorized search of bags, improper behavior in locker rooms, or unauthorized release of private facts. Interference with copyright or trademark should always be guarded against with use of printed material and when establishing an organization name and in advertising.

In light of the emergence of the Internet, one intentional tort that should be addressed in some detail is defamation. Widespread use of the Internet—including blogs, e-mail, and Web sites—and other high-tech media has increased the incidents of defamation in sport. Although defamation, slander, and libel are common terms among laypeople, they have legal meanings and elements that must be proven in court by a plaintiff seeking an award of damages for injury. Defamation means making a false statement about another person that causes that person to suffer harm. Libel means that the defamatory statement is made in a printed or fixed medium, usually a magazine or newspaper. Slander involves making the defamatory statement orally.

In most jurisdictions, the elements that have to be proven in order to establish defamation include

1. a false and defamatory statement about another person;
2. the publication (does not have to be in print) of that defamatory statement by a third party;
3. negligence on the part of the publisher of the statement; and
4. damages (mental anguish, reputation) to the plaintiff that were caused by the defamatory statement.

Because jurisdictions differ as to the laws of defamation, it is important to seek legal counsel when addressing this issue.

Other interpersonal concerns that should be guarded against in sport organizations are sexual and workplace harassment and "cyberstalking." In many sport organizations, employees have access to the Internet and are free to e-mail others inside and outside the organization. Consequently, it is important that management take steps to eliminate employees' reasonable expectation of privacy when using the organization's e-mail system. An organization should provide employees with an electronic communications policy before monitoring their e-mail. Such a policy should inform employees of the absence of any privacy right when they use the organization's e-mail and Internet systems. The policy should also set forth the employer's right to monitor, record, review, and intercept all communications that are sent through the organization's Internet and e-mail systems. These policies will preserve the organization's reputation and image; help prevent sexual and workplace harassment; and diminish the incidence of cyberstalking, which is harassing, threatening, or annoying people using multiple e-mails. The policy should also assist in prevention of defamation actions and copyright violations that an organization might otherwise be exposed to with unlimited employee use of e-mail and the Internet.

Strict Liability

So far, the discussion has been focused on negligence and intentional torts. The third type of tort is strict liability. The legal doctrine of strict liability means a person is liable for her actions regardless of whether the person was at fault. This occurs in a situation where someone engages in inherently dangerous activities. For example, an organization decides to put on a carnival and give elephant rides using an elephant leased from the local zoo. The elephant runs amok and kills several people. The organization may be held strictly liable because of the inherently dangerous nature of elephants.

One type of strict liability is products liability. Generally, products liability claims are based on strict liability rather than on negligence. Under a theory of strict liability, a manufacturer can be held liable even if it did not act negligently. Since strict liability is a harsh outcome, it is generally only applied to manufacturer defects. Because of the use of products and equipment in sport, it is important to understand the legal concept of products liability. If an injury is caused by defective equipment, the injured party might bring a lawsuit against someone who sold the product or the manufacturer. The product might be defective if it was negligently designed or manufactured, has insufficient warnings, lacks instructions for proper use, or incorporates a hidden danger. For example, a bicycle tire might be designed improperly so that when used in environments with temperatures higher than 90 degrees Fahrenheit (32 degrees Celsius), it blows up. Another example is that the tire was designed properly but manufactured so that it cannot retain air, and a flat tire results after 50 miles (80 km) of riding. A lawsuit might be brought if there was no warning about the temperature limitation of the tire or if the instructions for use did not explain the proper amount of air that should be pumped into and maintained in the tire.

Manufacturers have a duty to make sure products are safe for use by those who buy them. Equipment that has been found to be defective includes skateboards, helmets, bicycles, trampolines, snowmobiles, playground equipment, in-line skates, exercise equipment, and soccer goals.

Products liability encompasses the causes of action of negligence, breach of warranty, and strict products liability. In a negligent products liability claim, the plaintiff will allege that the manufacturer made a mistake, defectively designed the product, or failed to give adequate instruction for use or warn of a danger related to product use. The example about the bicycle tire could have resulted in a negligent products liability claim.

In a breach of warranty claim, the plaintiff will allege that the product did not meet standards of the implied warranty or it breached the warranty. For example, a manufacturer of a rubber material for use as protection under playground equipment might provide a warranty that the material will cushion falls from a height of 5 feet (1.5 m). However, in use of the material, multiple children at an elementary school have sustained fractures from falls of less than 5 feet (1.5 m). The school might file a lawsuit against the manufacturer alleging breach of warranty.

In strict products liability, there is no need to prove negligence. Instead, if the product is defective, the manufacturer or supplier may be found strictly liable and have to pay damages for any injuries caused by the defect. This occurs when a product is determined to be unreasonably dangerous or defective, reaching the consumer without being substantially changed.

Products liability claims are brought against anyone who is in the distribution chain, which could be the manufacturer, distributor, wholesaler, or retailer. Such claims could also arise out of renting, servicing, maintaining, selecting, assembling, installing, or adjusting sport or recreational equipment. Touching a product will possibly subject an organization to a products liability claim. However, servicing the product only and not engaging in the sale of the product will likely insulate an organization from such a claim.

If your organization is part of the distribution chain of products, there may be some products liability exposure. Some examples of this in sport are renting bowling shoes, selling football helmets to players, or selling bicycle tubes to athletes.

SUMMARY

There are three different ways that you or your organization might be held legally responsible or liable for your actions or failure to act. Legal liability can arise out of torts, contracts, and statutes. There are three types of torts: negligence, intentional torts, and strict liability torts. To prove negligence, there has to be a duty owed to another, a breach of that duty, a causal connection between the breach and the injury suffered, and damages. There are a number of circumstances in which sport organizations and their agents owe duties to others. Damages may be special or compensatory, general or punitive. Defenses to negligence claims include comparative or contributory negligence, statute of limitations, assumption of risk, release or waiver, government immunity, no supervisory responsibility (no duty), unforeseeable incident, or lack of causation. Alternative ways to prove negligence are negligent entrustment, vicarious liability, joint and several liability, negligence per se, and res ipsa loquitur.

Intentional torts against a person include assault, battery, false imprisonment, false arrest, defamation, invasion of privacy, malicious prosecution, malicious abuse of process, and intentional infliction of emotional distress. Intentional torts involving property include trespass to land; trespass to chattels; conversion; nuisance; and interference with a copyright, trademark, or patent. Products liability encompasses the causes of action of negligence, breach of warranty, and strict products liability.

A basic understanding of the legal principles outlined in this chapter will help you understand the summaries of sport legal cases that follow. Grasping legal principles will also assist you in developing risk management plans and communicating with legal counsel and insurance claims adjusters.

3

Insurance Claims and Litigation

No brilliance is required in law, just common sense and
relatively clean fingernails.

—John Mortimer

When is the last time you heard someone threaten to file a legal action or make an insurance claim? Unfortunately, this is commonplace in modern society. Most sport organizations and events will face lawsuits or become involved with the filing of insurance claims. When this occurs, it is helpful to have a practical understanding of the process. This chapter provides detailed information that will assist you with each step.

INJURY

When an injury arises out of a sport or recreation activity, the first step is for the injured person to receive medical care. This does not always happen right away. A person often does not feel the full effects of an injury for up to several days after the incident. The injured person may not seek medical treatment for days or weeks after an injury. There can also be significant delays before an incident or accident is reported to personnel at a sport or recreation organization or facility. When an injury becomes known, the first step for the organization is to have the injured person, or in the case of a minor, the child's parent or guardian, fill out an incident report.

INCIDENT REPORT

Every organization should have an incident report form available for personnel to fill out shortly after a person reports an injury. Incident reports should contain the following information:

- Name of person injured
- Name of parent or guardian if person injured is a minor
- Address and telephone numbers
- Date of birth and age of person injured
- Social security number of person injured (or, at least, the last four digits)
- Name of employer
- Health insurance coverage information (name of insurer and policy number)
- Date and time of incident or injury
- Location of incident
- Description of how incident occurred, in narrative detail
- Description of status of person injured (e.g., athlete, spectator, volunteer, employee)
- Information regarding club or team membership, if applicable
- Information regarding the event during which the injury took place and whether that event was sanctioned by the applicable national governing body
- Police report number, if applicable
- Description of the nature of the injury
- Identification of body parts injured
- Description of medical or health care received in response to injury
- Whether transported by ambulance to a medical facility
- Whether seen in an emergency room of a hospital, and identification of that medical facility
- First date of health care
- Identification of health care providers seen
- Whether the injured person had ever had a previous, similar injury or condition
- If the person has had a previous, similar injury or condition, the date and health care providers seen for that injury or condition

- Identification of any witnesses to the incident
- Addresses and telephone numbers of witnesses
- Signature of injured person (or parent or guardian, if a minor)

Incident report forms should be kept secured in a filing cabinet or database so they can be located in the event that a lawsuit arises. If there is an insurance claim, the insurance carrier may request that you provide a copy of the incident form. However, the injured person may also be required to fill out a claim application in order to receive payment of insurance benefits. It may be years before litigation or claims arising out of an injury resolve, so it is best to keep incident forms for a period beyond the expiration of your state's statute of limitations. Remember that statutes of limitations of minors do not begin until after they reach majority.

INSURANCE CLAIMS REPORTING

Prompt notification of claims to your insurance carrier allows for easier and more thorough investigation. Before any accidents or injuries occur, it is important to understand the claims reporting process with your insurance carrier. Claims reporting telephone numbers should be easily accessible, and a person in the organization should be charged with initiating such reports. There should also be a process by which your organization keeps tracks of insurance claims. This is important for risk assessment, risk control, and risk financing purposes.

Claims reporting requires that someone provide all the relevant information to the insurance company. This will likely be done by telephone, and forms may need to be completed thereafter. It is very important to fully and timely comply with the filling out of any forms. Insureds have an obligation to cooperate with the insurance company during the claims stage as well as with any legal defense counsel provided by the insurance company. Pay close attention to deadlines placed on you by the insurance company. For example, if an investigator or claims adjuster instructs you to return a form in 30 days or to immediately provide a copy of any court documents, that is what you must do.

CLAIMS ADJUSTING AND INVESTIGATION

Once a claim is made, a claims adjuster will likely be assigned to the claim. Claims adjusters investigate, evaluate, and settle insurance claims. An adjuster or investigator may visit the scene of the incident to investigate

Claims adjusters may need to take photographs of damages, so be sure to check if those are needed before you start cleaning up.

the claim. Photographs and measurements may be taken. A diagram of the area might be drawn. If there is property damage involved, then an appraisal might be done, especially if the property damage claim is to a motor vehicle.

An investigator or claims adjuster might also take recorded statements of witnesses to the incident. This can be done over the telephone or in person. Witnesses are telephoned, often when they least expect it, and asked to give a recorded statement. Once they consent, the statement is taken. The witnesses will usually not see a transcription of the recording until litigation arises. Recorded statement transcriptions may be used as a means to cross-examine witnesses who change their story about the incident over time. Sometimes more than one insurance company will call a witness and request a recorded statement, resulting in multiple transcripts. The plaintiff's attorneys may also hire investigators to talk with witnesses, sometimes recording these encounters. Not all recorded statements taken by insurance carriers are transcribed. If the case never proceeds to litigation, there will likely be little use for a transcription.

If a death or very serious injury arises out of an incident or accident, the insurance carrier might hire an expert to examine the scene, take photographs and measurements, and render an opinion. Usually experts are not retained until litigation ensues. Because that might take time, it is possible that an insurance claims adjuster will decide to have an expert examine the scene while it is still in the same condition as when the incident occurred. The expert may prepare a report that will be given to the claims adjuster to assist with claims evaluation and possible settlement.

Investigation is conducted when it appears that a lawsuit could be filed arising out of the incident or accident. A file is opened and a claim number assigned. The claims adjuster monitors the file for the possibility of a legal action and instructs the insured to alert her when he is served with a complaint. As soon as service is accomplished, the organization should promptly provide the complaint to the insurance carrier, informing it of the date of service. In many jurisdictions, the defendant has as few as 20 days to answer the complaint, and so time is of the essence. Once the insurance company receives the complaint, it will likely assign it to approved defense counsel to represent the defendant organization at its expense.

INSURANCE COVERAGE QUESTIONS

The first step of the liability claims adjusting process is to determine if the policy provides coverage for the allegations alleged in the complaint. The allegations in the complaint determine whether coverage will be afforded, even if such allegations are disputed or are later found to be false. Under a commercial general liability (CGL) policy, the insurance contract generally states that the insurance company will pay the amounts the insured becomes legally responsible for paying in damages. Exclusions in the policy might be applicable, and so the claims adjuster will address those early on in the litigation process. Sometimes a portion of the claims are covered, and some claims are not, so the adjuster will have to explain this to the insured in writing. For example, many insurance policies do not provide coverage for punitive damages but do provide coverage for compensatory damages. In this instance, the adjuster will send a letter to the insured explaining this and advising the insured that she may wish to retain her own counsel for representation on that issue.

Sometimes, there is a question as to whether there is coverage for the entire claim. In this event, the insurance adjuster will write a letter to the insured reserving the right to deny coverage if the facts later establish that the policy does not provide coverage. The insurance company will then investigate the matter and promptly make a coverage decision. A letter will then be sent to the insured either stating that coverage applies or denying coverage.

If there is a question of coverage that the insurance carrier must ask a court to decide, it will hire counsel separate from the defense counsel to file a declaratory judgment action and ask the court to decide the coverage issue. Essentially, the court is making a declaration of the rights of the parties. Declaratory judgment actions are expensive and could possibly take years and so are generally not brought if the financial exposure on the case is small. If a declaratory judgment action is brought, the insurance carrier has to pay for an attorney to defend the organization during this process, and the carrier might even have to pay to settle the claim.

THE LITIGATION PROCESS

The litigation process can be intimidating to anyone who is not an attorney, expert witness, or frequent party to lawsuits. Much of the literature in risk management that addresses this process is more academic than practical. The following description is based on actual litigation experience. Please note that this process may vary from state to state.

Discovery

Discovery is the portion of the pretrial litigation process during which the parties request from each other relevant information and documents so they can "discover" the pertinent facts of the case.

Once an insurance defense attorney is hired, the insurance carrier has likely completed much of its own investigation on the claim. Additional information gathering is done through discovery conducted by the attorneys in the course of litigation, pursuant to the rules of the court. After the defense attorney files the answer to the complaint, the parties can request the other parties to answer a series of questions (requests for answers to interrogatories) and produce documents. The rules of the particular jurisdiction will govern how many questions can be asked and the scope of the documents that can be requested. Once this information is received, the attorney (or paralegal) reviews the information and summarizes it for the claims adjuster, who is constantly monitoring the litigation.

It is important to note that even though the insurance company has hired the attorney, the insurance carrier is not the attorney's client. The attorney–client relationship is between the attorney and the person or organization that is being defended. Anything that is said between the attorney and client is confidential pursuant to the attorney–client privilege. Nevertheless, since the insurance company is paying for the defense, the reality is that the insurance company must authorize the discovery being conducted by defense counsel. Costs are necessarily kept as low as possible while providing the best defense possible.

If the matter involves allegations of physical or psychological injuries, the defense attorney will either request medical and psychological records by subpoena or simply have the plaintiff sign a release authorization so that the health care provider will release the documents directly to the attorney. A subpoena is usually issued using a court reporting company, which prepares a legal document and arranges for the records to be turned over by the provider. A notary will ask the custodian of records questions regarding the records being turned over, such as if those records are complete.

Since the Health Insurance Portability and Accountability Act of 1996 (HIPAA), it is more challenging for defense attorneys and insurance carriers to obtain records needed to evaluate medical claims. HIPAA is a law that was enacted to ensure the privacy of patients' medical information. Providers will often not turn over records unless original release authorizations are signed that are current. The plaintiff's attorneys may also require that the defense attorney sign a stipulation for protective order or some other document designed to limit how the information is used.

Once documents and basic information are obtained, depositions of witnesses, the plaintiff, and defendants may be taken. A deposition is a formal proceeding in which an attorney asks questions of a person before a court reporter. The court reporter is authorized to put the deponent under oath to tell the truth and uses a machine to take down everything that is said verbatim. The information is put in booklet form in a question and answer format, and the witness will have the opportunity to review the transcript to make changes if the transcript is inaccurate. The attorney can ask any questions that are relevant and could lead to discoverable information. During the course of the proceeding, attorneys may make objections for the record that can be ruled on by a judge at a later date. The information obtained through deposition further assists the defense attorney and claims adjuster in evaluating the case on liability issues and damages.

Expert Witnesses

Through the course of litigation, experts might be retained by both parties in order to prove various issues of fact. If the way a motor vehicle accident happened is at issue, the parties might hire accident reconstructionists, who are usually engineer experts who can use information, such as measurements, property damage, and skid marks, to reconstruct the accident and testify accordingly. If there is a question as to whether a person could have sustained a particular injury in a car accident, a biomechanical engineer might be retained. The defendant may request that the plaintiff submit to an independent medical examination, which involves reviewing records, physically examining the plaintiff, and rendering opinions. A plaintiff might hire an economist to value the economic losses that he suffered because of the accident. In turn, the defense might hire its own economist to combat the opinions of the plaintiff's economist. There are many types of experts that can be hired during the course of litigation for the purpose of testifying about a myriad of topics. These experts will have to testify about their credentials in order to be qualified as an expert in their particular field. Only after being so qualified will they be able to testify about their opinions, which will be limited to their expertise.

Alternative Dispute Resolution

Because litigation costs have risen, most jurisdictions advocate use of alternative dispute resolution (ADR) rather than have cases proceed directly to trials, which are held at taxpayers' expense. ADR can be arbitration or mediation. Arbitration is where an arbitrator, usually an attorney, serves in the same capacity as a judge. The arbitrator may be assigned to govern the discovery process as well as hear the evidence and render a decision on the case. Sometimes arbitrations are binding, and the parties have to comply with the decision. These binding arbitrations can be required under an insurance contract, agreed on by the parties, or required by law. Arbitrations may be appealable in court, so that if one of the parties does not agree with the arbitration award, she can appeal it and proceed to a jury trial.

Mediation is another means of resolving cases without going to trial. A mediator is appointed by a court or agreed to by the parties. The mediator may or may not be an attorney but is usually someone trained in mediation techniques. Rather than hear the evidence, the mediator will assist the parties in coming to a compromise resolution. Although mediators can be expensive, the process saves time and attorneys' fees and costs.

In most jurisdictions, courts attempt to settle cases before they proceed to jury trial. A settlement judge is assigned to the case. When the case gets close to trial, a settlement conference will be held and the judge will talk to both parties in turn, assisting in the resolution of the matter. The judge will often require that the claims adjuster, who has ultimate authority for issuing payment, be present. The plaintiff will also be required to attend so that settlement can occur. The judge may exert pressure on one or both parties to settle so that court resources can be saved. The judge will do this by telling the parties what the potential outcome will be based on the facts presented. A large number of cases are settled in this manner.

During the pretrial processes, insurance adjusters and defense attorneys must constantly evaluate the claim and consider the best strategy for paying only what the claim is worth. The chance of the defendant being found liable and the amount of damages that the plaintiff has sustained are factored into the equation. Settlement offers may be made periodically to resolve the matter. Usually an offer is made before the lawsuit has even been filed. Presuit offers may be attractive, as the plaintiff's attorney has spent little time and money on the case. Once experts are hired and depositions have been taken, the money stakes go up—the plaintiff must receive a higher offer in order to pay these costs.

Motions for Summary Judgment

At any stage of the litigation process, a party may wish to file a motion for summary judgment. A summary judgment is a decision made by the court based on statements of the evidence presented to the court in the form of a motion. The evidence is presented for the court record without a trial. This is used when there are no disputed material issues of facts in the case. The court will decide if one of the parties is entitled to judgment as a matter of law.

Such motions are extremely common in sport and recreation cases. If the material facts of the case are not in dispute, a party will request that the court, as a matter of law, rule that summary judgment be entered in his favor. For example, if a spectator is hit by a ball in a stadium and sues the ballpark for negligence, the ballpark defendant may ask the court to rule as a matter of law that the spectator assumed the risk by sitting in the stands in the unprotected area. The court will review the law in the particular jurisdiction and apply it to the facts of the case. Appellate court decisions, statutes, affidavits, deposition transcripts, and other documentary evidence might be reviewed. The parties' attorneys will also likely make oral arguments. The judge will decide by written order which party prevails. If, as a matter of law, the court decides that the party against whom the motion has been brought cannot prevail at trial, the entire case might be dismissed. It is also possible that a partial summary judgment will be entered if it does not dispose of all issues in the case or dismiss all of the parties. Either party may appeal a summary judgment granted by a lower court. If a partial summary judgment is issued, leave of the court may be required before appeal can be taken.

Jury Trials

Most people have a good idea of what goes on in a trial from what they see on television, in movies, and on the news. Jury trials are much less common than most people think. Less than 4 percent of civil cases proceed to jury trial. In many states, the rate is closer to 1 percent. The reason is primarily economic. It makes sense to resolve matters quickly, save money on attorneys' fees and costs, and use less expensive means earlier in the litigation process to resolve a case. Since most tort cases involve insurance, this process is driven partly by insurance carriers, who attempt to keep costs down in response to their duties to their policy holders and shareholders. Another reason for the rise in alternative dispute resolution is the high cost to taxpayers for judges, staff, courtrooms, jurors, bailiffs, and court reporters. Because of these financial realities, the cases that go to trial have generally exhausted other avenues of pretrial resolution.

If the case does proceed to trial, the first step is pretrial motions that are heard by the judge, before a jury is selected. Motions in limine (*in limine* is a Latin phrase meaning "at the threshold" or "at the outset") will be filed, asking the court to exclude certain evidence from being considered by the jury. The court is essentially deciding before the trial begins what evidence it will not allow to be presented to the jury because it will be prejudicial against a party. For example, a party might ask the court to exclude any mention of insurance, as such mention will alert the jury to the fact that the defendant has insurance and might result in a higher award being rendered.

Next, jury selection begins. The attorneys will be able to ask the jurors questions in voir dire (which refers to an oath to tell the truth) so they can make assessments as to which jurors might be biased against their client. When attorneys engage in voir dire, they ask the jurors questions to elicit possible bias. For example, an attorney might ask if the jurors know any of the parties or their attorneys. If a juror knows a party, the juror might have a bias in favor of that party. Each party will have the right to dismiss a certain number of jurors. Once a jury has been empanelled, opening statements will be made by each party's attorney, explaining what they expect the evidence to establish.

The plaintiff, through his attorney, then puts on his case, calling witnesses for direct and cross-examination as well as submitting documentary evidence. After the plaintiff's case, the defense counsel might make a motion for directed verdict, arguing that no matter what other facts are presented, as a matter of law, the plaintiff cannot prevail. If the motion is granted and it addresses all issues before the court, the defendant has prevailed and the case is over. If the motion is denied, the case proceeds forward. The defense then puts on its case.

Once all the evidence has been received, the attorneys make closing statements, which recap the evidence and explain how the law applies to the evidence. The jury will then deliberate and render a verdict.

Anytime during the trial, the parties may make an offer of settlement. It is not unusual for cases to settle while a trial is in progress. If a party becomes concerned that the verdict will be against him, he has a chance to get out of the case at anytime if he is able to enter into a settlement agreement. A defendant might increase his offer, or a plaintiff might be willing to take a lesser amount.

APPELLATE PROCESS

If a case proceeds to a jury verdict, either party might elect to file an appeal with the appellate court. Just as the pretrial and trial process can be lengthy, an appeal can take several years. First, the party files a notice. The appealing party files an opening brief, explaining how the court erred in making a decision and identifying the law that supports its position. The nonappealing parties will have the opportunity to file answering briefs, arguing that there was no error and that the lower court was correct in coming to its decision. The appealing party will then follow up with its reply brief, providing the opportunity to combat the points made in the answering brief. The appellate court may allow oral argument, particularly if the justices have questions. Some appellate courts rarely invite oral argument. Eventually, the appellate court will render a written decision, which will either be published or unpublished, depending on the preference of the court. If it is published, it becomes the law of the jurisdiction of the court and will serve as precedent for other cases. If the decision is unpublished, it is significant only to the parties to the case. However, unpublished decisions may provide information to other parties as to how the court might rule when addressing a similar factual scenario.

SUMMARY

When an injury occurs, the first step is to request that an incident report be completed. If the incident will likely result in an insurance claim, the organization's insurance carrier should be notified promptly. Investigation of the claim may ensue, consisting of photographing, measuring, and diagramming the scene and taking witness statements. If a lawsuit is filed, the insurance company will determine if coverage exists under the applicable insurance policy. If there is a duty to defend under the policy, the insurance company will hire a defense attorney at its expense. Discovery will take place in order for the parties to evaluate the case, which may consist of written interrogatories, production of documents, and depositions. Experts may be hired by either party. The plaintiff may have to submit to an independent medical examination. The claims adjuster and defense attorney will evaluate the case for possible settlement before trial. Commonly, alternative dispute resolution is attempted by arbitration, mediation, or settlement conferences. Parties also might file motions for summary judgment in an effort to dispose of legal issues. If resolution is not successful, the case may proceed to a jury trial. A losing party to a motion for summary judgment or trial may file an appeal. An appellate court will issue a decision that may serve as precedent to future cases in the jurisdiction.

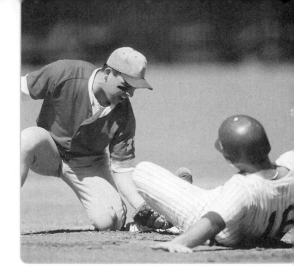

Risk Assessment in Sport and Recreation

Progress always involves risks. You can't steal second base and keep your foot on first.

—Frederick B. Wilcox

As explained briefly in chapter 1, risk assessment in sport and recreation means identifying and analyzing loss exposures that are present in a particular sport. This chapter provides a detailed description of what a risk assessment entails so your organization can identify and analyze the risks and loss exposures you face.

LOSS EXPOSURES

Identifying the loss exposures in a particular sport or recreation organization means determining which exposures will undermine the organization's goals. Essentially, loss exposures can be placed in four categories: (1) property, (2) liability, (3) personnel, and (4) net income. This book, for the most part, addresses potential liability loss exposures to a sport organization. The following is a list of those topics your organization should include in a comprehensive risk management plan.

Property loss exposure arises out of the possibility of damage, destruction, or disappearance of property resulting from a peril or cause of loss.

Examples of losses would be to unimproved land, buildings, and other structures; tangible personal property (securities and money; inventory; computer and media equipment; valuable records and papers; records of accounts receivable; furniture, supplies, and machinery; mobile property); intangible personal property (patents, trademarks, copyrights, goodwill, and trade secrets); and legal interests in property (owner's interest; buyer's and seller's interest, landlord or tenant's interest, secured creditor's interest, and bailee's interest).

Liability loss exposure results from an organization having a legal responsibility to pay a claim for bodily injury or property damage sustained by another party. These loss exposures arise out of torts (negligence, intentional torts, and strict liability torts); contracts (breach of contract and hold harmless agreements); and by statutes (e.g., worker's compensation). Categories of liability loss exposures include

- Premises and operations
- Environmental
- Products liability
- Professional
- Completed operations
- Employment practices
- Watercraft
- Automobile
- Director's and officer's
- Worker's compensation
- Fiduciary responsibilities arising out of benefit plans

Personnel loss exposure occurs when an employee, manager, or owner with special knowledge or skill retires, resigns, or dies.

Net income loss exposure arises when some circumstance affecting the organization causes reduction of net income, which could occur as a result of property, liability, or personnel loss exposures. This could happen in poor economic times when revenues are down. For example, stadiums may have reduced ticket sales; gyms may have a reduction in members; and schools may have a reduction in tuition or higher costs, leading to cuts to athletic program funding.

The 11 topics of loss exposure are complex, and a thorough analysis of each is beyond the scope of this book. However, reduction of loss exposures cannot be accomplished if they are not identified. For example, you will not be able to erect warning signs or establish rules of behavior in order to reduce injuries unless you notice where they are needed. Sometimes identification of loss exposures is simple and obvious. But even those circumstances lead to a multitude of lawsuits. Court actions involving slips and falls would not be so prevalent if organizations were able to readily identify areas where people are prone to fall. It often takes a lawsuit before conditions are made safe.

To identify liability loss exposures, your organization has a number of options that can be used instead of taking on the task of doing an in-house audit. A consultant who specializes in performing sport risk management audits and risk assessments can be retained. A consultant will identify potential liability exposures, using an independent, unbiased perspective and applying his own expertise and experience. Another source of assistance is your insurance carrier. Although the insurance carrier may not perform an audit, you may wish to speak to your broker or agent about assistance on risk management issues. Your insurance carrier may be able to provide you with loss control education or assistance that could lead to decreased liability loss exposure and reduced premiums. National governing bodies of sports and sports associations are another source of sport risk management resources and expertise that can assist you in identifying and assessing risks. Their Web sites can be an excellent resource for staying abreast of important issues.

The sections that follow include brief descriptions of loss exposures and an explanation of their relevance in the sport industry. As you will see, the potential loss exposures in the sport field are many and significant. For each loss exposure described, an organization's risk management team will have to make a complete assessment and then implement proper risk management controls and utilize appropriate risk financing. Incomplete risk assessment, controls, and financing can mean losses that could potentially destroy an organization.

Property Loss Exposures

Sport organizations and events often own or lease both real and personal property. Real property is the land and the buildings and structures on the land. This might be the stadium, playing field, or gymnasium. Personal property is all property that is not real property and can be tangible or intangible. Tangible property in a sport environment might be the equipment used to play the sport but could also be the property in the office or other facilities, such as furniture, computer equipment, and machinery. Money, accounts receivable records, and valuable papers are also included. Intangible personal property includes copyrights, trademarks, trade secrets, patents, and goodwill. A sport organization may have copyrights, trademarks, and goodwill to protect.

Possible natural causes of loss to property are windstorm, flood, earthquake, fire, smoke, lightning, hail, snow, sleet, ice, water, and sinkhole collapse. Humans also pose a threat to property, such as by terrorism. Other human-caused losses include crime, vandalism, riot, violence, explosion, or vehicles. Economic causes include war, strikes or boycotts, and changes in spectator or consumer preferences.

Premises Liability Loss Exposures

An organization might be held liable for a bodily injury that occurs on the organization's premises or possibly on other property that the organization is using. In the sport industry, premises liability actions could occur in situations as follows: a spectator slips or trips and falls in the stands, in the restroom, or in another public area; a gym member or guest hurts himself in a fitness class or in the weight room; an athlete trips over equipment in a field or runs into an object; or a spectator gets hit by a ball where no protective netting was in place. There are many more scenarios that might give rise to premises liability loss exposure in a sport and recreation setting.

Automobile Liability Loss Exposures

If your organization owns, maintains, or uses any motor vehicles, it has automobile liability loss exposure. Motor vehicles are common causes of accidents and injuries. If a motor vehicle accident occurs, there may be liability exposure to the driver and possibly the owner of the vehicle who entrusted the driver with the vehicle. The exposures of automobile liability are bodily injury, loss of companionship claimed by the injured person's spouse (loss of consortium), wage loss arising from the injury, medical and rehabilitation bills, pain and suffering, and emotional distress. There is also property damage (damage to the vehicles) loss exposure.

Watercraft Liability Loss Exposures

If an organization owns or uses watercraft, then there will be watercraft liability loss exposure. The loss exposures include bodily injury or death, property damage, and pollution liability. Remember that when boats are used for a sport, even if they are not used by athletes, there will be watercraft liability loss exposure. For example, boats used to monitor a long-distance ocean swim might expose an organization to liability.

Workers' Compensation Liability Loss Exposures

If your organization has employees, there will be a legal obligation to those employees for injuries or diseases that arise from the job. Workers' compensation statutes govern rules regarding injured workers and monetary awards for such injuries or death. Workers' compensation is a no-fault system that is in place so workers will have their medical and rehabilitative treatment and wage loss paid without having to sue their employers. People are just as likely to be injured in the sport industry as in other industries, and so workers' compensation is an important liability loss exposure to consider.

Intellectual Property Loss Exposures

Intellectual property includes products of human intelligence that have value and can be protected under federal law, such as copyrightable works, ideas, discoveries, and inventions. In the sport industry, the most common intellectual property loss exposures are to copyrights, trademarks, and patents. Copyright is the legal right granted by the U.S. government to use a written document or other form of expression. A health club might issue a monthly newsletter to its patrons, which could be copyrighted. A trademark is a legal right granted by the U.S. government to use a distinctive design or set of words that identifies an organization's product or service. Most people are familiar with the Nike "swoosh" trademark. A patent refers to the legal right granted by the U.S. government to exclusively use a new, useful, and nonobvious invention. Inventors of new gym equipment might choose to obtain patent protection for their invention. Sport organizations could have loss exposure if they infringe on the use of copyrights, trademarks, patents, and other intellectual property.

Criminal Loss Exposures

A number of crimes could possibly expose a sport organization to loss. Those crimes include burglary, robbery, shoplifting (e.g., at a golf course pro shop that sells retail items), fraud, embezzlement, counterfeiting, forgery, terrorism, arson, vandalism, computer crime, and espionage. Many of these crimes would be directed to the front office or accounting segment of the sport operation. Some of the crimes could take place during a game or match, such as terrorism or arson. Other crimes could be perpetrated by people who work for the organization, such as embezzlement.

Disaster Loss Exposures

Most organizations and people are aware that they are exposed to potential disaster in the form of natural disasters, actions taken by other people, or economic disasters. Some potential disasters are fire, explosion, flood, windstorm, hurricane, tornado, severe cold weather, flood, snowstorm, hailstorm, ice storm, lightning, earthquake, and avalanche. Some land-related disasters could possibly affect a sport organization as well, such as blasting, soil deterioration, sinkholes, and volcanic action. With the likely impending consequences of global warming, disaster loss exposures should be considered a priority for sport risk managers.

Natural disasters can injure people and cause significant property damage, such as the damage to this gymnasium done by Hurricane Katrina, and should be considered a priority for sport risk managers.

Personnel Loss Exposures

Personnel loss exposure relates to the potential loss to an organization when its employees retire, suffer disability, resign, or die. The productivity of the organization can be detrimentally affected by such losses, and economic consequences may ensue. This potential loss exposure occurs with any company, and sport organizations are not immune. If your team has suffered the loss of a coach, you will be familiar with this loss exposure.

Net Income Loss Exposures

Unexpected losses of an organization's net income are a loss exposure that could occur in any company. A sport organization may experience such losses when attendance to events are down, participation in a sport decreases, memberships to gyms decrease, school enrollment declines, and costs of operation increase or through many other factors. For example, gasoline price increases may cause consumers to elect not to drive to sports practices and events, causing a decline in net income.

FACILITY AND ENVIRONMENTAL SAFETY

There are organizations that, because of the particular business that they are in, have significant environmental liability loss exposures. For example, a business that manufactures chemicals would have concerns about liability arising from pollution of the environment. Generally, sport and recreation organizations do not have these types of exposures.

Sport organizations and facilities face environmental and safety considerations depending on the venue. However, some safety considerations should be considered for any facility or sports venue. The following are some questions about loss history that you should ask when assessing the risk of your sport venue or facility.

- What is the history of accidents and injuries that are related to the physical structure and environment? If this assessment reveals that multiple injuries have occurred in a particular area of the facility, this information should be used to repair or change that part of the structure. If changes cannot be made, consider posting warning signs or cordoning off an area.

- Have you reviewed data of accidents and injuries for the past 5 to 10 years? Doing so will reveal any weaknesses in your operation. If the injuries are related to aspects of your facility, those may be addressed with repair, alteration, or signage.

- Have there been any lawsuits filed that relate to injuries sustained on the field, at the venue, or in the facility? If lawsuits have been filed, it would be prudent to review the complaints and read the allegations of the plaintiffs. Lawsuits often lead to repair, change, or notice in relation to a hazardous condition.

- If there is a history of injuries on the field, at the venue, or in the facility, have corrections been made to prevent future, similar injuries? If an organization has knowledge of injuries that occur at a particular location, this will negatively affect its legal position if another injury takes place. The organization could be found negligent for not repairing the dangerous condition and not providing warning of the known defect.

- What is the proximity of the field or venue to medical facilities? How long will it take for an ambulance or the fire department to arrive if called? If a facility is remote, it makes more sense to be well equipped with AEDs, first aid supplies, and medically trained personnel. If medical facilities or ambulances are minutes away, help may arrive before in-house equipment and training are utilized.

If a particular venue has a history of accidents or problems, you will want to know how those occurred and what must be done to prevent future, similar occurrences. You may consider choosing a safer venue if possible future loss cannot be prevented efficiently or economically. You will also want to know how far your facility is from emergency services. Remote locations will pose particular problems when emergencies occur. Venues that are prone to natural disasters may also cause you to reconsider the location or at least plan on developing a comprehensive plan for responding, if and when natural disasters occur.

Traffic, Adjacent Activities, and Environmental Elements

Traffic, other athletic games, weather, and pollutants may be hazardous and should be addressed, regardless of the sport. If you have a choice between facilities, venues, or playing fields, use the venue with the fewest external dangers. In assessing relevant external influences, some questions that should be asked can be found in "Traffic, Adjacent Activities, and Environmental Elements" on page 56.

Locker Rooms

Locker rooms are a common place for injuries to occur. Floors can be slippery, creating slip and fall hazards. Use of hair dryers and other electrical appliances can lead to electrocution with the possibility of standing water from various sources. Privacy of patrons can be compromised by cell phone cameras or by other means. Locker rooms can be the site of violence or hazing if there is insufficient security and supervision. Some questions that should be asked about any facility's locker rooms can be found in "Locker Rooms" on page 57.

Public Restrooms

Public restrooms at any sport facility have to be inspected and maintained before, during, and after events and practices. If a facility is open to the public for long hours most days, a regular inspection and cleaning schedule should be utilized. Water from sinks and toilets may cause patrons to slip and fall, and clogged toilets and unsanitary conditions can also be problematic. Unlocked and deserted restrooms could also pose a safety risk. See "Public Restrooms" on page 59 for questions that should be addressed.

Bleachers, Stands, and Viewing Areas

Spectator safety is dependent on safe bleachers or stands. Spectator injuries and lawsuits can largely be prevented if bleachers and other public areas are safe. The questions in "Bleachers, Stands, and Viewing Areas" (see page 60) should be asked when inspecting bleachers.

Entryways and Exits

Entryways and exits are easily overlooked when assessing the risk of a sport facility. However, if they are not cleared of debris and well marked, serious injury could result, especially if there is a fire or other disaster requiring quick evacuation. The questions in "Entryways and Exits" (see page 61) should be addressed when inspecting the entryways and exits of your facility.

Parking Lots

Parking lots are common locations for low-velocity motor vehicle accidents and car hijackings or other violence. Patrons can also slip, trip, or fall if there is wet, icy, or uneven ground. Parking lots are also the venue for tailgating parties, which have been the site of violence and other challenges. Parking lots and surrounding grounds should be inspected regularly and the questions in "Parking Lots" (see page 62) asked.

Concession Areas

Concessions that sell food and drink, including alcohol, create risks such as food poisoning, slips and falls, and service of alcohol to already intoxicated patrons who could become unruly or drive while intoxicated. Concessions that use deep fryers or stoves may also increase fire hazards. Because of these concerns, the questions in "Concession Areas" (see page 63) should be asked.

Other Public Areas, Including Ticket Booths and the Press Box

All public areas should be inspected to make sure there is nothing dangerous that could cause someone to be injured. The questions in "Other Public Areas, Including Ticket Booths and the Press Box" (see page 64) should be asked when inspecting other public areas.

Clothing, Protective Gear, and Equipment

Sport participants' safety may depend on their clothing, protective gear, and equipment. Most sports have rules, procedures, and customs that dictate the clothing and safety protection worn. Make sure athletes understand the requirements for clothing and protective gear. Your organization might also consider making certain safety items mandatory (e.g., bright swim caps in ocean or lake races; helmets in snow sports).

It is important to be thoroughly knowledgeable about the protective clothing, gear, and equipment that is necessary for your sport or recreational activities.

Usually, protective gear would not have been manufactured if there were no serious injuries that the designer of the gear was motivated to address. Protective gear that is ill fitting, not in good repair, or inappropriate for the particular sport might provide little or no protection. It is best to select the right gear and make sure it fits well and is in excellent condition. Equipment used should be in good repair and be inspected and maintained in accordance with the manufacturer's recommendations.

Questions you should consider when addressing this subject can be found in "Clothing, Protective Gear, and Equipment" on page 65.

VIOLENCE AND UNRULY BEHAVIOR

It may be reasonably foreseeable that there will be violence at a sporting event, especially when the opposing teams have a history of hotly contested games or are traditionally considered to be rivals. Violence takes place at all levels of play, from children's games with unruly parents to professional sporting events, with player and fan violence broadcast on television.

Athlete Violence and Unruly Behavior

Questions related to violence and sport participants should be asked when formulating your risk management plan (see "Athlete Violence and Unruly Behavior" on page 67). It is often difficult to predict when violence might erupt between two opposing teams. Usually, the history of their behavior when playing against each other is the only information that will be available. It is reasonable to take action to diffuse the situation if violence is a concern, such as by separating the teams as much as possible and counseling the players as to how they are expected to behave. It is a good idea to enforce behavior and safety rules strictly and consistently if you wish to maintain a safe environment that is free of violence between teams and players.

Spectator Violence and Unruly Behavior

Spectators may also be the source of unruly behavior, violence, or even terroristic actions. Spectator violence can occur before the game, at tailgating parties in a stadium parking lot, during the game in the stands or other public areas, after the game when players storm the field, or in public areas at or away from the game venue. Some organizations engage in a public relations campaign well before events in order to curb violence. They may broadcast their concerns and rules related to behavior via television, radio, print media, and the Internet. To curb tailgating-related violence, universities have limited the time and location for such parties and have prohibited people who do not have game tickets from participating.

Any event that allows the serving of alcohol to spectators will face a variety of potential safety concerns. Patrons who drink alcohol may become disruptive or violent. They could become ill because of overconsumption, and they might get behind the wheel of a motor vehicle and drive home. The latter has caused many deaths and lawsuits, with sporting organizations sometimes being named as defendants.

Other concerns are spectators bringing weapons, illegal substances, or dangerous items that could cause harm to athletes or other spectators. Controlling spectators' behavior requires anticipation and special planning. When addressing concerns of spectator violence and unruly behavior, the questions in "Spectator Violence and Unruly Behavior" (see page 69) should be asked.

SAFETY, SUPERVISION, AND HEALTH OF PLAYERS

Common allegations in lawsuits involving sport injuries are that there was improper supervision of minor athletes; players were mismatched according to skill and size; and coaches failed to explain safety rules related to each drill and activity. Injuries can occur when players are not physically or medically able to play, and so risk managers should receive assurance from the athletes or their parents that they have been released by their doctors to play the particular sport and that they do not have any serious medical problems that might be aggravated. Behavioral problems from use of alcohol or drugs could cause injury. Injuries might also be caused by jewelry or inadequate shoes. Because of these concerns, the questions in "Safety, Supervision, and Health of Players" (see page 70) should be addressed.

SUPERVISION OF MINORS

Children participating in sports should be supervised, and so when a child is injured in a sport setting, there is usually an allegation that the coach, event director, manager, teacher, facility owner, or others were negligent because they failed to properly supervise the child. Whenever someone is placed in the care of others, the duty to supervise arises. The questions in "Supervision of Minors" (see page 71) should be addressed when considering what is reasonable for the supervision of children participating in sports.

When evaluating the need for supervision for your activity, consider these questions and what reasonable supervision of your activity or event would look like. You will also need to consider the questions found in "Evaluating the Need for Supervision for Your Activity" (see page 72).

It is advisable to have a sufficient number of supervisors available relative to the number of children. It may be possible to enlist parents to assist with the supervisory function at certain events, as parents are likely to be there to watch their children anyway. This will require communication with the parents. The most important thing when running sporting events with children is making sure the children are safe and free from harm. Along these lines, all coaches and volunteers that are involved with children should undergo a criminal background check.

FIRST AID FOR PLAYERS AND SPECTATORS

Players are frequently injured while playing sports, requiring first aid such as ice on a swollen knee, shoulder, or ankle or even an automatic external defibrillator (AED) if they have a heart attack. Spectators may also require first aid while using your facility. In light of this anticipated concern, the questions in "First Aid for Players and Spectators" (see page 73) should be asked when developing your risk management plan.

RISK ANALYSIS

Once risks have been identified using risk management assessment and audits, those risks should be analyzed. A common means of analysis is the Prouty approach chart or risk matrixes that analyze risk exposures based on severity versus frequency. Such charts provide guidance for classifying risks as severe, moderate, or slight in severity and slight, moderate, or definite as to frequency. Analyzing loss exposures in this way will help an organization make decisions regarding risk financing (transferring or retaining), which will be discussed in a subsequent chapter, and risk control. In situations in which loss severity is slight to significant and loss frequency is slight to moderate, it may be reasonable to take actions to reduce or prevent the losses from occurring. For example, at a sport facility, slips and falls are common occurrences that vary in severity. These may deserve more risk management attention than the possibility of a large fire, which might occur every 25 years. An organization would, of course, have a fire prevention plan in place and transfer the risk by purchasing insurance, but the organization would likely put more resources into slip and fall reduction and prevention.

Essentially, an organization has to make a decision as to which of the identified risks require action on the part of the organization to reduce or prevent. It may be discovered through this analysis that some risks should be avoided altogether. For example, an athletic club may elect not to install a climbing wall so that the liability exposure of that activity can be avoided. In certain situations, it will make sense to transfer the risk by purchasing insurance rather than actively instituting any action to avoid the risk. For example, an organization may decide to purchase flood insurance and not take any actions with regard to potential floods (such as purchasing sand bags and shovels). The risk analysis phase can best be accomplished with professional guidance by a consultant or insurance underwriter or broker who is trained in this area.

SUMMARY

Identifying loss exposures in sport and recreation can be done by performing a risk management assessment or audit, performed in-house or with assistance from professionals. The lists of questions in the following checklists provide an excellent starting point to assess issues about the following topics:

- Facility and environmental safety
- Traffic, adjacent activities, and environmental elements
- Locker rooms
- Public restrooms
- Bleachers, stands, and viewing areas
- Entryways and exits
- Parking lots
- Concession areas
- Other public areas, including ticket booths and the press box
- Clothing, protective gear, and equipment
- Athlete and spectator violence and unruly behavior
- Safety, supervision, and health of players
- Supervision of minors
- First aid for players and spectators

By reviewing and answering the questions posed, an organization will have a good start toward assessing liability risks. Once liability risks are identified, those risks should be analyzed as to their likely severity and frequency. By performing this analysis, it can be decided which risks should be transferred or avoided and what efforts can be made to reduce or prevent. Once analysis has taken place, this information can be used to institute risk control techniques, which are discussed in the next chapter.

TRAFFIC, ADJACENT ACTIVITIES, AND ENVIRONMENTAL ELEMENTS

Traffic, other athletic games, weather, and pollutants may be hazardous and should be addressed, regardless of the sport. If you have a choice between facilities, venues, or playing fields, use the venue with the fewest external dangers. In assessing relevant external influences, the following questions should be asked.

Common to all sports is the need to examine the facility, field, or venue for defects before play. The inspection should be documented. If there are safety concerns, you may wish to select an alternative venue or address those concerns before play. If any repairs need to be made, such repairs should be made before use and documented.

Considerations	Yes or No (check one)	Notes for follow-up
Does your field or venue overlap with other fields or venues?	❑ Yes ❑ No	
Are there sufficient barriers between the field or venue and vehicular traffic?	❑ Yes ❑ No	
Have apparatuses used in other sports been left on the playing field or venue or in the immediate vicinity?	❑ Yes ❑ No	
Are there any environmental concerns, such as proximity to pollutants or environmental hazards?	❑ Yes ❑ No	
Are there other considerations particular to your venue?	❑ Yes ❑ No	

From Katharine M. Nohr, 2009, *Managing Risk in Sport and Recreation: The Essential Guide for Loss Prevention* (Champaign, IL: Human Kinetics).

LOCKER ROOMS

Locker rooms are a common place for injuries to occur. Floors can be slippery, creating slip and fall hazards. Use of hair dryers and other electrical appliances can lead to electrocution with the possibility of standing water from various sources. Privacy of patrons can be compromised by cell phone cameras or by other means. Locker rooms can be the site of violence or hazing if there is insufficient security and supervision. The following are questions that should be asked about any facility's locker rooms.

Considerations	Yes or No (check one)	Notes for follow-up
Do locker rooms have slippery surfaces or other defects or hazards?	❏ Yes ❏ No	
Is there sufficient lighting?	❏ Yes ❏ No	
Is the drainage system in good repair?	❏ Yes ❏ No	
Is the plumbing system in good repair?	❏ Yes ❏ No	
Have rusty lockers and other hazardous items been removed?	❏ Yes ❏ No	
Is there rubber matting in appropriate places to prevent slipping on wet surfaces?	❏ Yes ❏ No	
Is there sufficient ventilation?	❏ Yes ❏ No	
Are the locker rooms of sufficient size?	❏ Yes ❏ No	
Are soap dispensers of the type that do not drip?	❏ Yes ❏ No	
Are electrical outlets and devices located away from water?	❏ Yes ❏ No	
Are ground-fault interrupters used on appliances that are operated close to water?	❏ Yes ❏ No	
Are saunas, steam rooms, or hot tubs locked when not in use?	❏ Yes ❏ No	
Is there adequate supervision?	❏ Yes ❏ No	
Is there sufficient security so that unauthorized persons do not enter locker rooms?	❏ Yes ❏ No	

(continued)

From Katharine M. Nohr, 2009, *Managing Risk in Sport and Recreation: The Essential Guide for Loss Prevention* (Champaign, IL: Human Kinetics).

Locker Rooms *(continued)*

Considerations	Yes or No (check one)	Notes for follow-up
Are individuals allowed privacy in locker rooms?	❑ Yes ❑ No	
Are cell phone cameras and other photographic devices banned from locker rooms?	❑ Yes ❑ No	
Are locker rooms cleaned and sanitized?	❑ Yes ❑ No	
Are patrons warned not to share towels or other personal items so that diseases such as MRSA are not spread?	❑ Yes ❑ No	
Are there other considerations particular to your locker rooms?	❑ Yes ❑ No	

From Katharine M. Nohr, 2009, *Managing Risk in Sport and Recreation: The Essential Guide for Loss Prevention* (Champaign, IL: Human Kinetics).

PUBLIC RESTROOMS

Public restrooms at any sport facility have to be inspected and maintained before, during, and after events and practices. If a facility is open to the public for long hours most days, a regular inspection and cleaning schedule should be utilized. Water from sinks and toilets may cause patrons to slip and fall, and clogged toilets and unsanitary conditions can also be problematic. Unlocked and deserted restrooms could also pose a safety risk. The following are questions that should be addressed.

Considerations	Yes or No (check one)	Notes for follow-up
Are the floors clear of debris and moisture?	❑ Yes ❑ No	
Are the restrooms clean, consistent with a regular cleaning schedule?	❑ Yes ❑ No	
Are the restrooms locked when not in use or otherwise secured so that only those using the facility have access to the restrooms?	❑ Yes ❑ No	
Are sinks and toilets in good repair?	❑ Yes ❑ No	
Have toilet paper and paper towels been stocked?	❑ Yes ❑ No	
Are there other considerations particular to your public restrooms?	❑ Yes ❑ No	

From Katharine M. Nohr, 2009, *Managing Risk in Sport and Recreation: The Essential Guide for Loss Prevention* (Champaign, IL: Human Kinetics).

BLEACHERS, STANDS, AND VIEWING AREAS

Spectator safety is dependent on safe bleachers or stands. Spectator injuries and lawsuits can largely be prevented if bleachers and other public areas are safe. The following questions should be asked when inspecting bleachers.

Considerations	Yes or No (check one)	Notes for follow-up
Do the bleachers have loose nuts and bolts, cracks, splinters, debris, or dangerous protrusions?	❑ Yes ❑ No	
Do the bleachers have nonskid steps and well-marked and clear pathways?	❑ Yes ❑ No	
Have bleachers been cleaned? If so, have they been dried sufficiently so that they are not slippery?	❑ Yes ❑ No	
Have mobile bleachers that are being used been put in place and set up properly?	❑ Yes ❑ No	
If mobile bleachers are not being used, have they been stored so they will not be a hazard to athletes while playing?	❑ Yes ❑ No	
If mobile bleachers are stored, have they been stored in a secure location so they are inaccessible to children?	❑ Yes ❑ No	
Will spectators be located in a safe place that has good visibility of the playing court or field?	❑ Yes ❑ No	
Are cheerleaders, photographers, and band members located a reasonable distance from the playing court or field?	❑ Yes ❑ No	
Are safety railings or barriers in place to prevent people from falling off stands or bleachers?	❑ Yes ❑ No	
Are there other considerations particular to your bleachers, stands, and viewing areas?	❑ Yes ❑ No	

ENTRYWAYS AND EXITS

Entryways and exits are easily overlooked when assessing the risk of a sport facility. However, if they are not cleared of debris and well marked, serious injury could result, especially if there is a fire or other disaster requiring quick evacuation. The following questions should be addressed when inspecting the entryways and exits of your facility.

Considerations	Yes or No (check one)	Notes for follow-up
Are entryways and exits marked clearly and visibly?	❑ Yes ❑ No	
Are entryways and exits clear of all objects so that patrons are able to enter and exit easily?	❑ Yes ❑ No	
Are entryways and exits in conformance with the applicable fire code?	❑ Yes ❑ No	
Is security present at entryways and exits?	❑ Yes ❑ No	
Are there other considerations particular to your entryways and exits?	❑ Yes ❑ No	

From Katharine M. Nohr, 2009, *Managing Risk in Sport and Recreation: The Essential Guide for Loss Prevention* (Champaign, IL: Human Kinetics).

PARKING LOTS

Parking lots are common locations for low-velocity motor vehicle accidents and car hijackings or other violence. Patrons can also slip, trip, or fall if there is wet, icy, or uneven ground. Parking lots are also the venue for tailgating parties, which have been the site of violence and other challenges. Parking lots and surrounding grounds should be inspected regularly and the following questions asked.

Considerations	Yes or No (check one)	Notes for follow-up
Is security adequate in parking lots and surrounding grounds?	❑ Yes ❑ No	
Is there proper lighting in parking lots and surrounding grounds?	❑ Yes ❑ No	
Are parking lots well marked so that traffic is flowing safely?	❑ Yes ❑ No	
Are there adequate personnel to assist with parking?	❑ Yes ❑ No	
Are parking personnel wearing bright and reflective vests or clothing with safety flashlights?	❑ Yes ❑ No	
Have parking personnel received training as to how to safely perform their functions?	❑ Yes ❑ No	
Are there slippery areas or objects that might cause a person to slip or fall?	❑ Yes ❑ No	
Have warning signs been erected to inform visitors and others of slippery areas and obstructions?	❑ Yes ❑ No	
Where parking lots are used for tailgating parties, are specific hours for this use specified?	❑ Yes ❑ No	
Is participation at tailgating parties limited to persons with a ticket to the event?	❑ Yes ❑ No	
Is alcohol use limited or prohibited at tailgating parties?	❑ Yes ❑ No	
Are there other considerations particular to your parking lots?	❑ Yes ❑ No	

From Katharine M. Nohr, 2009, *Managing Risk in Sport and Recreation: The Essential Guide for Loss Prevention* (Champaign, IL: Human Kinetics).

CONCESSION AREAS

Concessions that sell food and drink, including alcohol, create risks such as food poisoning, slips and falls, and service of alcohol to already intoxicated patrons who could become unruly or drive while intoxicated. Concessions that use deep fryers or stoves may also increase fire hazards. Because of these concerns, the following questions should be asked.

Considerations	Yes or No (check one)	Notes for follow-up
Are concession operators properly licensed?	❏ Yes ❏ No	
Are concession operators sufficiently insured?	❏ Yes ❏ No	
Do concession operators have insurance that names the facility and your organization as additional insureds?	❏ Yes ❏ No	
Are concession areas clean, dry, and free of tripping hazards?	❏ Yes ❏ No	
Are spills surrounding the concession area cleaned up promptly?	❏ Yes ❏ No	
Are there rules in place that are strictly followed that prohibit the sale of alcohol to minors and already intoxicated patrons?	❏ Yes ❏ No	
Have concession employees been trained in how to identify intoxicated persons?	❏ Yes ❏ No	
Are there limits as to how many alcoholic beverages may be purchased by an individual?	❏ Yes ❏ No	
Is there a cutoff time for service of alcoholic beverages?	❏ Yes ❏ No	
Are there other considerations particular to your concession areas?	❏ Yes ❏ No	

From Katharine M. Nohr, 2009, *Managing Risk in Sport and Recreation: The Essential Guide for Loss Prevention* (Champaign, IL: Human Kinetics).

OTHER PUBLIC AREAS, INCLUDING TICKET BOOTHS AND THE PRESS BOX

All public areas should be inspected to make sure there is nothing dangerous that could cause someone to be injured. The following should be asked when inspecting other public areas.

Considerations	Yes or No (check one)	Notes for follow-up
Are the areas clean?	❑ Yes ❑ No	
Are the areas free of tripping hazards?	❑ Yes ❑ No	
Are entryways and exits properly marked?	❑ Yes ❑ No	
Are entryways and exits clear?	❑ Yes ❑ No	
Do chairs and structures have any broken parts?	❑ Yes ❑ No	
Are there other considerations particular to your other public areas, including ticket booths and the press box?	❑ Yes ❑ No	

From Katharine M. Nohr, 2009, *Managing Risk in Sport and Recreation: The Essential Guide for Loss Prevention* (Champaign, IL: Human Kinetics).

CLOTHING, PROTECTIVE GEAR, AND EQUIPMENT

Sport participants' safety may depend on their clothing, protective gear, and equipment. Most sports have rules, procedures, and customs that dictate the clothing and safety protection worn. Make sure athletes understand the requirements for clothing and protective gear. Your organization might also consider making certain safety items mandatory (e.g., bright swim caps in ocean or lake races; helmets in snow sports). Usually, protective gear would not have been manufactured if there were no serious injuries that the designer of the gear was motivated to address. Protective gear that is ill fitting, not in good repair, or inappropriate for the particular sport might provide little or no protection. It is best to select the right gear and make sure it fits well and is in excellent condition. Equipment used should be in good repair and be inspected and maintained in accordance with the manufacturer's recommendations. The following questions should be addressed when considering this subject.

Considerations	Yes or No (check one)	Notes for follow-up
Is there customary clothing for the sport? If yes, please list in the Notes column.	❑ Yes ❑ No	
Does the governing body of the sport or any other organization prescribe or recommend protective gear?	❑ Yes ❑ No	
Is there protective gear available for the sport? If yes, please list in the Notes column.	❑ Yes ❑ No	
Is protective gear required in order to participate in the sport? If Yes, please list in the Notes column.	❑ Yes ❑ No	
Is there the potential for injury suffered by participants of this sport? If yes, please list in the Notes column.	❑ Yes ❑ No	
Will the use of protective gear or clothing decrease the likelihood or severity of injury?	❑ Yes ❑ No	
Does the protective gear fit properly?	❑ Yes ❑ No	
Has the protective gear been altered in any way so that it might not function properly?	❑ Yes ❑ No	
Has the protective gear and equipment been properly cleaned, maintained, or repaired?	❑ Yes ❑ No	
Are equipment and protective gear regularly inspected?	❑ Yes ❑ No	
Are inspections documented?	❑ Yes ❑ No	

(continued)

From Katharine M. Nohr, 2009, *Managing Risk in Sport and Recreation: The Essential Guide for Loss Prevention* (Champaign, IL: Human Kinetics).

Clothing, Protective Gear, and Equipment *(continued)*

Considerations	Yes or No (check one)	Notes for follow-up
Is there a regular schedule for cleaning equipment?	❑ Yes ❑ No	
Is there a regular schedule for maintenance on the equipment?	❑ Yes ❑ No	
Are cleaning and maintenance documented?	❑ Yes ❑ No	
Are repairs documented?	❑ Yes ❑ No	
Is equipment that requires repairs taken out of use?	❑ Yes ❑ No	
Is equipment stored properly when not in use?	❑ Yes ❑ No	
Is equipment assembled and set up in accordance with the manufacturer's recommendations?	❑ Yes ❑ No	
Is equipment moved by people trained and capable to do so?	❑ Yes ❑ No	
Is equipment stored so that it will not invite children to play on it?	❑ Yes ❑ No	
Is equipment stored so that it cannot be used without supervision and authorization?	❑ Yes ❑ No	
Are there appropriate warnings on potentially dangerous equipment?	❑ Yes ❑ No	
Is use of equipment monitored?	❑ Yes ❑ No	
Is use of equipment limited to the purposes it is designed for?	❑ Yes ❑ No	
Are there other considerations particular to the clothing, protective gear, and equipment required?	❑ Yes ❑ No	

From Katharine M. Nohr, 2009, *Managing Risk in Sport and Recreation: The Essential Guide for Loss Prevention* (Champaign, IL: Human Kinetics).

ATHLETE VIOLENCE AND UNRULY BEHAVIOR

Questions related to violence and sport participants should be asked when formulating your risk management plan. It is often very difficult to predict when violence might erupt between two opposing teams. Usually, the history of their behavior when playing against each other is the only information that will be available. It is reasonable to take action to diffuse the situation if violence is a concern, such as by separating the teams as much as possible and counseling the players as to how they are expected to behave. It is a good idea to enforce behavior and safety rules strictly and consistently if you wish to maintain a safe environment that is free of violence between teams and players.

Considerations	Yes or No (check one)	Notes for follow-up
Have you been put on notice that violence may occur at a specific game or match?	❑ Yes ❑ No	
Are players warned that a certain amount of roughness and trash talking is expected in the ordinary play of the game?	❑ Yes ❑ No	
Have you adopted safety rules that are communicated to everyone involved and regularly enforced?	❑ Yes ❑ No	
Are the teams that are playing each other long-standing rivals?	❑ Yes ❑ No	
In the case of a game between rivals, will the game be played on a neutral site in order to reduce the chances of violence?	❑ Yes ❑ No	
Are there players that have a history of violence in the past?	❑ Yes ❑ No	
Has there been consistent trash talking or other behavior that has been of concern?	❑ Yes ❑ No	
Have officials been harassed by specific players or coaches?	❑ Yes ❑ No	
Do you have trained security guards present?	❑ Yes ❑ No	
Have you excluded potential troublemakers, whether spectators, teams, or players, from the event?	❑ Yes ❑ No	
Have you provided warnings to players, officials, spectators, and others involved in the event of potential violence?	❑ Yes ❑ No	
Have you implemented and followed a policy related to your response to acts of violence, and has this policy been communicated to players, officials, spectators, and others involved in the event?	❑ Yes ❑ No	

(continued)

From Katharine M. Nohr, 2009, *Managing Risk in Sport and Recreation: The Essential Guide for Loss Prevention* (Champaign, IL: Human Kinetics).

Athlete Violence and Unruly Behavior *(continued)*

Considerations	Yes or No (check one)	Notes for follow-up
Is the threat of violence significant enough to cancel the game?	❑ Yes ❑ No	
When violence erupts, do you institute a cool-off period, remove the hostile persons, or cancel the game?	❑ Yes ❑ No	
Are players separated when problems arise?	❑ Yes ❑ No	
Are arrival and departure times of rival teams staggered?	❑ Yes ❑ No	
Are movements of teams in and out of locker rooms staggered?	❑ Yes ❑ No	
Is there strict supervision in locker rooms?	❑ Yes ❑ No	
Are the locker rooms of rival teams separated?	❑ Yes ❑ No	
Are there other considerations particular to your situation regarding athlete violence and unruly behavior?	❑ Yes ❑ No	

From Katharine M. Nohr, 2009, *Managing Risk in Sport and Recreation: The Essential Guide for Loss Prevention* (Champaign, IL: Human Kinetics).

SPECTATOR VIOLENCE AND UNRULY BEHAVIOR

Spectators may also be the source of unruly behavior, violence, or even terroristic actions. More problems can be brought about by the consumption of alcohol. Other concerns are spectators bringing weapons, illegal substances, or dangerous items that could cause harm to athletes or other spectators. Controlling spectators' behavior requires anticipation and special planning. When addressing concerns of spectator violence and unruly behavior, the following questions should be asked.

Considerations	Yes or No (check one)	Notes for follow-up
Are spectators allowed to consume alcohol? If Yes, to what extent?	❑ Yes ❑ No	
Are spectators who demonstrate drunken behavior ejected?	❑ Yes ❑ No	
Are concession stands that serve alcohol prohibited from serving visibly intoxicated spectators?	❑ Yes ❑ No	
Are there limits placed on the amount of alcohol that can be served to one person?	❑ Yes ❑ No	
Will concession stands serving alcohol close at a particular time, allowing time to pass before spectators drive their motor vehicles?	❑ Yes ❑ No	
Are spectators prohibited from bringing any specific items into the viewing area?	❑ Yes ❑ No	
Are there security guards and police officers monitoring the behavior of spectators?	❑ Yes ❑ No	
Are ushers or other personnel stationed around the viewing area in order to assist and monitor spectators?	❑ Yes ❑ No	
Is there an emergency action plan established to evacuate spectators in the event of a natural disaster, bomb threat, or other catastrophic event?	❑ Yes ❑ No	
Are there other considerations particular to your situation regarding spectator violence and unruly behavior?	❑ Yes ❑ No	

From Katharine M. Nohr, 2009, *Managing Risk in Sport and Recreation: The Essential Guide for Loss Prevention* (Champaign, IL: Human Kinetics).

SAFETY, SUPERVISION, AND HEALTH OF PLAYERS

Common allegations in lawsuits involving sport injuries are that there was improper supervision of minor athletes; players were mismatched according to skill and size; and coaches failed to explain safety rules related to each drill and activity. Injuries can occur when players are not physically or medically able to play, and so risk managers should receive assurance from the athletes or their parents that they have been released by their doctors to play the particular sport and that they do not have any serious medical problems that might be aggravated. Behavioral problems from use of alcohol or drugs could cause injury. Injuries might also be caused by jewelry or inadequate shoes. Because of these concerns, the following questions should be addressed.

Considerations	Yes or No (check one)	Notes for follow-up
Is proper supervision provided for minor athletes?	❑ Yes ❑ No	
Have players been matched according to skill and size?	❑ Yes ❑ No	
Have coaches explained the safety rules related to each drill and activity involved in the course of play?	❑ Yes ❑ No	
Are players sufficiently physically fit and medically able to play the game?	❑ Yes ❑ No	
Are players prohibited from consuming alcohol during the game or practice?	❑ Yes ❑ No	
Are players who demonstrate drunken or other inappropriate behavior ejected?	❑ Yes ❑ No	
Is wearing jewelry while playing prohibited?	❑ Yes ❑ No	
If a player is observed to be playing unsafely, is he or she removed from practice or the game?	❑ Yes ❑ No	
Are drills eliminated or modified when there is insufficient space?	❑ Yes ❑ No	
Are athletes (or their parent or guardian) required to attest in writing that they are in good physical health and that they have a doctor's clearance to participate in the activity?	❑ Yes ❑ No	
Have athletes (or their parent or guardian) read and signed all consents, waivers, and releases of liability required by your organization to participate?	❑ Yes ❑ No	
Have athletes provided emergency contact information?	❑ Yes ❑ No	
Have athletes provided information regarding special needs, medical conditions, medication, and other health information that has been requested?	❑ Yes ❑ No	
Are there other considerations particular to your situation regarding safety, supervision, and health of players?	❑ Yes ❑ No	

From Katharine M. Nohr, 2009, *Managing Risk in Sport and Recreation: The Essential Guide for Loss Prevention* (Champaign, IL: Human Kinetics).

SUPERVISION OF MINORS

Children participating in sports should be supervised, and so when a child is injured in a sport setting, there is usually an allegation that the coach, event director, manager, teacher, facility owner, or others were negligent because they failed to properly supervise the child. Whenever someone is placed in the care of others, the duty to supervise arises. The following questions should be addressed when considering what would be reasonable for the supervision of children participating in sports.

How old are the children who will be participating? _____

What is the experience level of the participants? _____

What is the maturity level of the participants? _____

Considerations	Yes or No (check one)	Notes for follow-up
Are the activities appropriate for the children's ages, maturity levels, and experience?	☐ Yes ☐ No	
Do the children have any special needs?	☐ Yes ☐ No	
Will equipment be used? If Yes, list what type of equipment in the Notes column.	☐ Yes ☐ No	
Have the children used that type of equipment before?	☐ Yes ☐ No	
Will the children's parents be present?	☐ Yes ☐ No	
Will parents have any supervisory responsibility?	☐ Yes ☐ No	
Will there be times when the children are watching others and not participating in the activity? If Yes, what will the children be doing when they are not participating?	☐ Yes ☐ No	
Will the children who are not participating be supervised?	☐ Yes ☐ No	
Is there any dangerous equipment or conditions that will be present, such as a nearby swimming pool or a vacant gymnasium with gymnastics apparatuses?	☐ Yes ☐ No	
Are there times when the supervisor may have to leave others unsupervised, such as in the event of an emergency?	☐ Yes ☐ No	
Are there other considerations particular to your situation regarding the supervision of minors?	☐ Yes ☐ No	

From Katharine M. Nohr, 2009, *Managing Risk in Sport and Recreation: The Essential Guide for Loss Prevention* (Champaign, IL: Human Kinetics).

EVALUATING THE NEED FOR SUPERVISION FOR YOUR ACTIVITY

It is advisable to have a sufficient number of supervisors available relative to the number of children. It may be possible to enlist parents to assist with the supervisory function at certain events, as parents are likely to be there to watch their children anyway. This will require communication with the parents. The most important thing when running sporting events with children is making sure the children are safe and free from harm. Along these lines, all coaches and volunteers who are involved with children should undergo a criminal background check. When evaluating the need for supervision for your activity, consider what reasonable supervision of your activity or event would look like. You will also need to consider the following questions.

Considerations	Yes or No (check one)	Notes for follow-up
Do supervisors need to be provided for the event? If Yes, list how many supervisors will be needed in the Notes column.	☐ Yes ☐ No	
Do you have enough supervisors per child? Record the ratio that you need to maintain in the Notes column.	☐ Yes ☐ No	
Do the supervisors need training and experience before they can supervise? If Yes, list the training and experience each should have in the Notes column.	☐ Yes ☐ No	
Have all coaches and volunteers undergone background checks?	☐ Yes ☐ No	
Will the children's parents be involved in the supervision of their children? If Yes, list to what extent in the Notes column.	☐ Yes ☐ No	
Are there any policies, procedures, or regulations in place that dictate the ratio of supervisors to children for the event?	☐ Yes ☐ No	
Are there any policies, procedures, or regulations that provide any requirements regarding supervision of children that should be followed?	☐ Yes ☐ No	
Are there other considerations that would affect the need for supervision for your activity?	☐ Yes ☐ No	

From Katharine M. Nohr, 2009, *Managing Risk in Sport and Recreation: The Essential Guide for Loss Prevention* (Champaign, IL: Human Kinetics).

FIRST AID FOR PLAYERS AND SPECTATORS

Players are frequently injured while playing sports, requiring first aid such as ice on a swollen knee, shoulder, or ankle or even an automatic external defibrillator (AED) if they have a heart attack. Spectators may also require first aid while using your facility. In light of this anticipated concern, the following questions should be asked when developing your risk management plan.

Considerations	Yes or No (check one)	Notes for follow-up
Is first aid available to players and spectators? If so, record who is providing first aid in the Notes column.	☐ Yes ☐ No	
Do the first aid providers need training? If Yes, list what training is needed in the Notes column.	☐ Yes ☐ No	
Are there persons trained in CPR?	☐ Yes ☐ No	
Do you have areas set aside for first aid stations? List their locations in the Notes column.	☐ Yes ☐ No	
Are there signs to notify spectators and players of the availability of first aid stations?	☐ Yes ☐ No	
What supplies and devices are available in the first aid stations?	☐ Yes ☐ No	
What medical supplies and devices are available in places other than the first aid stations?	☐ Yes ☐ No	
Are supplies and medical devices such as AEDs clearly marked and located in convenient locations?	☐ Yes ☐ No	
Are persons trained in the use of AEDs available?	☐ Yes ☐ No	
Are all training and certifications for first aid, CPR, and AEDs kept current?	☐ Yes ☐ No	
Are training certificates for first aid, CPR, and AEDs kept on file?	☐ Yes ☐ No	
Are there telephones available to call 911?	☐ Yes ☐ No	
Are there medical facilities located nearby?	☐ Yes ☐ No	
Have facility personnel been trained as to what to do in the event of a medical emergency?	☐ Yes ☐ No	
Are there other considerations particular to your needs for first aid for players and spectators?	☐ Yes ☐ No	

From Katharine M. Nohr, 2009, *Managing Risk in Sport and Recreation: The Essential Guide for Loss Prevention* (Champaign, IL: Human Kinetics).

5

Risk Control

Living at risk is jumping off the cliff and building your wings on the way down.

—Ray Bradbury

Once an organization has completed a thorough risk assessment or audit and has had the opportunity to analyze the liability risks, the organization will be in a better position to control risks. In chapter 1, risk management steps 1 through 8 are listed. Risk control covers steps 4, 5, and 6 of that process: examining the feasibility of various risk management techniques and then selecting and implementing the appropriate ones.

To understand this phase better, it is important to recognize that the opposite of risk control is when an organization experiences losses that are unplanned, sudden, and sometimes violent or catastrophic. Implementing risk control means making a conscious decision to take action or not to take action with respect to a risk. For example, managers of a health club are concerned that someone might have a heart attack in the facility. Because of this concern, they install AEDs in strategic locations and institute an AED training plan, or they consciously decide not to do so because a fire department is located only one block away. Such measures constitute risk control because they involve decision making. On the other hand, if the health club managers do not even consider the possibility of someone suffering a heart attack in the facility, and someone does so and dies, risk control has not taken place.

RISK CONTROL TECHNIQUES

Risk control techniques include avoidance, loss prevention, loss reduction, duplication, separation, and diversification. The technique of avoidance means an organization decides to stop a particular activity or not start it in the first place. For example, a high school in Colorado might decide to eliminate its snowboarding club because there have been too many injuries. Or a high school in California may decide not to start a surfing club because of the potential for injuries. The technique of loss prevention implements measures to reduce the frequency of loss. For example, a baseball stadium might extend the protection afforded spectators in certain areas to decrease the number of spectators hit by baseballs. Loss reduction is a loss control technique that is designed to decrease loss severity. An example of this is football players wearing padding and helmets. They may still injure themselves when being tackled, but this protection will reduce the severity of injuries.

The other risk control techniques—duplication, separation, and diversification—do not affect liability loss exposures as avoidance, loss prevention, and loss reduction do. Duplication means having spare parts or equipment so you can continue business as usual if a loss occurs. Separation means dispersing assets or activities so that if a natural disaster occurs, for example, it will not wipe out all of an organization's assets or activities. Diversification primarily deals with business risk, meaning the spread of loss exposures among various business activities or investments so that one event will not provide a significant impact.

The following topics address some means of loss prevention and loss reduction in sport and recreation. Essentially they pertain to hazard control. A hazard is a condition that increases the severity and frequency of losses. By taking the steps outlined, an organization will likely decrease the frequency of losses. If losses occur, hopefully they will be less severe. The topics addressed include the following:

- Organizational attitudes toward safety
- Facility inspection
- Facility cleaning, maintenance, and repair
- Preparation of the court, gymnasium, or field for play
- Crowd management
- Lightning
- Protective gear
- Equipment inspection, maintenance, and repair

Although the topics of emergency disaster planning and transportation could be included in this chapter under the heading of risk control, they will be addressed in subsequent chapters in greater detail.

ORGANIZATIONAL ATTITUDES TOWARD SAFETY

An organization's attitudes toward safety will influence liability loss exposures. Frequency and severity of loss can be influenced favorably if safety precautions are a high priority. The airline industry provides a good example of this. Whenever you fly on an airplane, there is an expectation that safety is the number one priority of the airline, and odds are that the plane will reach its destination safely. The pilot is in charge of safety, and customers are told that the flight attendants are there for the passengers' safety first. Without fail, safety rules and procedures are explained in great detail by flight attendants or on television monitors. Passengers can read about safety procedures on cards that are placed in each seat pocket. Oxygen masks, flotation devices, and other safety equipment arc always present; and passengers can count on being told that their seatbelt has to be buckled, their seats upright, and the window shades open for takeoff and landing. Customers on airplanes tolerate delays so that mechanical repairs can be made, and they endure hearing the same instruction about how to fasten a seatbelt over and over again because they demand safe air travel. It is expected that when passengers get on a plane, they will arrive at their destination safely, and they probably will.

The safety model used in air travel could be applied to sport participation and viewing if athletes, parents, fans, coaches, administrators, and officials demanded and expected safety at the level that the airlines provide. For sport organizations to step up to the plate and provide this kind of safety, a number of things would have to happen with each organization.

Take Charge of Safety

Just like the pilot, someone has to take charge and direct the safety of the sporting activity or event. This could be the coach, athletic director, owner, or manager. The person in charge puts safety first—above winning, above profits, and above discomfort or embarrassment. For example, lightning is imminent, and the baseball game has proceeded through eight innings. The score is tied, and the fans are excited. The ballpark owner has to make a decision to evacuate the outdoor ballpark or to risk playing the ninth inning with the potential of lightning, which has been known to strike the ballpark before. Using the airline example, the decision would be automatic. The owner would suspend play and evacuate the park. Many people in the sport industry would likely be disinclined to evacuate a ballpark in these circumstances. Certainly, the decision of continuing play can be taken. This action simply increases the risk of loss and is not consistent with a safety-first attitude.

Personnel Must Have Safety-First Attitudes

Everyone who is running a sport event or training session, just like the flight attendants, should be there first for the safety of the athletes and others. Second, they are there for all other objectives. This means the personnel's first priority is safety above all else. For example, during a running race, an assistant to the race director is told there is a problem on the course with traffic direction and at the same time is asked by the timer to help sort out problems with several athletes' numbers. Which task should he attend to first? Since the traffic direction problem could mean potential deaths or injuries, he must address that first. He is there for the athletes' safety first. Second, he can try to make sure the correct athletes receive awards and that all participants have a good time at the race.

Adopt Safety Plans, Safety Rules, and Emergency Procedures

To reduce and prevent losses, just like the airlines, every sport facility, organization, and event should have safety plans, safety rules, and emergency procedures. These plans, rules, and procedures should be well thought out, be written down, and address all potential safety concerns.

The content of safety plans, safety rules, and emergency procedures will vary with each sport and recreational pursuit. Before reinventing the wheel, check with the applicable NGB (national governing body) for your sport and with other organizations to see if they have established standards. For example, USA Swimming has safety action plan samples on its

A sport or recreational event often comes with multiple problems or issues that need to be prioritized so that safety issues are handled first.

Web site: http://usaswimming.org. The Red Cross provides safety plans that can be helpful, such as its "Plan on Lightning Safety," found at www.redcross.org. Local fire departments are helpful to assist with fire safety plans as well.

Communicate and Practice Safety Plans, Safety Rules, and Emergency Procedures

Safety plans, rules, and emergency procedures mean nothing if they are not communicated, understood, and practiced. Sport organizations and events should communicate this information in multiple ways so that safety becomes part of the culture of the event or facility. Some effective means of communication are Web sites, e-mail, fliers, information sheets, DVD presentations, scorecards, prerace meetings, orientation, signs, newsletters, and bulletin boards. Your organization or facility should consider using multiple means of communication. Emergency procedures and plans should be practiced on a regular basis. Without practice, people will not understand the actions to be taken, and problems and weaknesses in the plan cannot be sorted out.

Safety Rules Must Be Enforced

Safety rules have no meaning or value if they are violated without repercussion. For example, if a football player does not wear his shoulder pads to practice, he should not be permitted to play. Enforcement should be consistent.

FACILITY INSPECTION

Another means of loss prevention and reduction is inspecting facilities. Inspections can take place at regular intervals, such as daily or weekly, or they can take place before, during, and after practices or events, whichever is most reasonable for the particular sport or activity. For example, before a soccer game or practice begins, the field should be inspected for holes, foreign objects, or defects.

Documentation of each inspection is important in the event a lawsuit is filed. Regular, thorough documented inspections may assist you in defense of a lawsuit. Alternatively, if there is a lack of documentation, it will be harder to prove that inspections were actually done. Forms can be used to document each inspection (see the appendix on page 363). The information that should be documented can be found in "Documenting Inspections" on page 88.

FACILITY CLEANING, MAINTENANCE, AND REPAIR

Each area of the facility should have a documented cleaning and mainte-nance schedule. Regular inspections as previously outlined should reveal additional cleaning, repair, and maintenance that must be accomplished in a timely manner and documented.

Cleaning should be done before and after events at regularly scheduled intervals that do not disrupt use. During events, cleaning personnel should intermittently restock restrooms with paper, empty trash throughout the facility, and clean up spills. The area of play should be monitored at all times for slipping and tripping hazards during play. Maintenance should take place on a regularly scheduled basis, utilizing manufacturers' recommended main-tenance schedules. Repairs should be made promptly. If an item is found to be in disrepair, it should be taken out of service immediately. If it cannot be stored, a sign should be displayed warning that it is out of service and should not be used.

Documentation of cleaning, repair, and maintenance is also crucial to your defense of a lawsuit. Cleaning logs should be kept on a daily basis. Maintenance logs should document all the details of regular maintenance, and repair logs should describe the nature of repairs that are made. Again, if there is a lack of documentation, it will be harder to prove that cleaning, maintenance, and repairs have actually been done. Forms can be used for such documentation (see the appendix on page 363). The following informa-tion should be documented:

- Who performed the cleaning, repair, or maintenance
- When the cleaning, repair, or maintenance was done
- A description of the cleaning, repair, or maintenance

PREPARATION OF THE COURT, GYMNASIUM, OR FIELD FOR PLAY

After inspections have been performed and documented, defects and hazards should be repaired before play begins. The questions in "Preparation of the Court, Gymnasium, or Field for Play" (see page 89) should be addressed.

CROWD MANAGEMENT

Your organization or event may never have to address issues of crowd man-agement. However, if your organization hosts events in which large crowds gather, an important part of risk control is establishing and implementing a crowd management plan. Large sporting event facilities have been the site of thousands of preventable deaths and injuries caused by crowd crushing; collapsing of railings, stands, fences, barriers, roofs, balconies, walls, and gates; riots; fires; stampedes; and police shootings. The following elements should be present in a crowd management plan:

- Competent staff trained in crowd management
- Emergency and disaster planning and implementation
- Procedures to eject unruly, intoxicated, or disruptive spectators
- Implementation of an effective communications network
- Use of signage to promote crowd management

A crowd manager is generally employed for the purpose of overseeing the facility's crowd management. The crowd manager's duties should be some or all of the following:

- Coordinating events and managing the facility
- Understanding and implementing the crowd management, risk management, and disaster plans
- Assessing and managing crowd behavior
- Providing good service to patrons of the facility
- Responding to complaints and concerns
- Implementing applicable policies and procedures
- Assessing and responding to problem behavior of patrons
- Reacting appropriately to problem behavior
- Resolving ticketing, credential, and seating problems
- Facilitating the adherence to applicable laws regarding persons with disabilities
- Coordinating the assistance of persons with disabilities in exiting the facility or otherwise responding to disasters or other emergencies

There are certainly many sporting activities that do not draw crowds and have no need for crowd management staff. However, with recent terrorism in the United States and throughout the world, as well as riots and bedlam erupting at many sport venues on a fairly regular basis, crowd management is essential.

LIGHTNING

Lightning strikes can cause serious injuries or death. Most lightning injuries occur during the daytime and during spring or summer months. If lightning is a risk to your organization, it is imperative that a comprehensive plan for lightning emergency response be developed (see "Lightning" on page 90).

PROTECTIVE GEAR

A sport or recreation organization may wish to require and enforce use of certain protective gear as part of its loss prevention and reduction plan, even if the participants are responsible for providing their own gear. Use of helmets, mouth guards, and protective padding will reduce the frequency of injuries and their severity. Several national organizations have developed sport equipment safety standards, including the following:

American National Standards Institute (ANSI)
25 West 43rd St.
New York, NY 10036
212-642-4900
www.ansi.org

American Society for Testing and Materials (ASTM)
100 Barr Harbor Dr.
West Conshohocken, PA 19428
610-832-9500
www.astm.org

National Operating Committee on Standards for Athletic Equipment (NOCSAE)
P.O. Box 12290
Overland, KS 66282
913-888-1340
www.nocsae.org

Snell Memorial Foundation
3628 Madison Ave., Ste. 11
North Highlands, CA 95660
916-331-5073
www.smf.org

Helmets

Helmets are required equipment for many sports because they are effective in preventing or reducing the severity of head injuries. Because helmets are designed to address the specific biomechanical forces that occur in particular sports, it is important to wear the type of helmet that was designed for that sport. Helmets are either required or recommended for use in the following sports:

- Baseball
- Bicycling

- Boxing
- Football
- Ice hockey
- Field hockey
- Horseback riding
- In-line skating
- Lacrosse
- Motor sports
- Rugby
- Skateboarding
- Skiing
- Snowmobiling
- Softball
- Wrestling

Mouth Guards

Mouth guards are another standard piece of equipment used in many sports. They are designed to prevent or reduce injury to the mouth, teeth, tongue, cheeks, and lips. The risk of teeth being knocked out in contact sports is significant, and so mouth guards are often required or recommended for practice and competition.

The American Dental Association has recommended that athletes participating in the following sports wear protective mouth guards:

- Acrobatics
- Basketball
- Boxing
- Discus throwing
- Field hockey
- Football

In many sports, protective gear extends beyond obvious padding and helmets to include keeping participants' teeth safe with mouth guards.

- Gymnastics
- Handball
- Ice hockey
- Lacrosse
- Martial arts
- Racquetball
- Rugby
- Shot putting
- Skateboarding
- Skiing
- Skydiving
- Soccer
- Squash
- Surfing
- Volleyball
- Water polo
- Weightlifting
- Wrestling

This list is probably a surprise to you if you participate in, coach, manage, or view some of these sports. It is rare to see athletes surfing, weightlifting, playing racquetball, and doing many of these sports while wearing mouth guards. However, the dentists at the American Dental Association who established this list have determined that lost and damaged teeth are prevalent in such sports.

Padding and Other Protective Gear

A number of contact sports require padding and protective gear. Athletes participating in some sports choose to wear padding or protective gear because it improves their performance or makes the sport more comfortable. Many of the sports listed here also include helmets, mouth guards, and athletic protectors among their protective equipment. Sports in which padding or protective gear is used include the following:

- American football: face mask, neck pad, shoulder pads, hip pads, lumbar pad, forearm pads, rib pad, thigh pads
- Baseball catcher: face mask, chest protector, catcher's mitt, knee pads, shin guards
- BMX: knee pads, elbow pads, shin guards

- Boxing: gloves, abdominal protector, hand bandages
- Cricket: batting glove, leg protectors
- Cycling: gloves, padded shorts
- Fencing: gloves, breast protector, Kevlar fencing outfit
- Golf: glove
- Gymnastics: hand protectors
- Ice hockey: shoulder pads, throat protector, elbow pads, knee pads, shin pads, chest pad, gloves
- In-line skating: knee pads, elbow pads, wrist guards
- Powerlifting: protective belt
- Soccer: shin guards
- Speedskating: neck guard with bib, knee guards, shin guards, gloves
- Tae Kwon Do: breast guard, trunk protector, groin guard, shin guards, forearm guards
- Volleyball: knee pads
- Weightlifting: abdominal and lumbar support belt, wrist and knee bandages

EQUIPMENT

Equipment used in sports is extensive, including various sizes and types of balls, pucks, batons, javelins, discuses, hammers, poles, bicycles, weights, skateboards, clubs, bats, skis, sleds, rackets, paddles, bows, arrows, stones, brooms, sticks, carabiners, ropes, harnesses, crosses, skates, stair steppers, treadmills, and so on. Athletes and others can be injured when using sports equipment. Some universal issues related to sports equipment should be addressed in relation to loss reduction and prevention, including inspection, maintenance, and repairs.

Inspection and Maintenance of Equipment

Equipment should be regularly inspected and tested to determine if it is defective or in need of repair. Maintenance should be done regularly as appropriate to all equipment. After each use, equipment should be cleaned in accordance with the manufacturer's recommendations. It is important when purchasing or using equipment for any sport that the manufacturer's recommendations regarding use, maintenance, and repair be followed. If you do not have this information, it can probably be obtained from the company that sold the equipment, from the manufacturer directly, or on the Internet from the seller's or manufacturer's Web site.

Repairs

Repairs should be requested and completed within a reasonable time of the need for repair. All repairs should be made by persons who are skilled in doing so. Replacement parts should be used with care. It is a good idea to obtain replacement parts from the manufacturer specifically made for the equipment being repaired. If random spare parts are used, the equipment might not function properly. Until repairs are made, the item in need of repair should not be used. An example of litigation in this area relates to football helmets. Helmets repaired using face masks from different manufacturers have allegedly caused injuries or increased their severity.

Documentation of Cleaning, Repair, and Maintenance of Equipment

Documentation of cleaning, repair, and maintenance is important if a lawsuit ever arises over equipment that causes injury. Maintenance logs should be kept documenting all the details of regular maintenance. Repair logs should be kept describing the nature of repairs that are made. If there is a lack of documentation, it will be harder to prove that cleaning, maintenance, and repairs have actually been done. Forms can be used for such documentation (see the appendix on page 363).

The following information should be documented:

- Who performed the cleaning, repair, or maintenance
- When the cleaning, repair, or maintenance was done
- A description of the cleaning, repair, or maintenance

Implementing a thorough equipment safety inspection, cleaning, maintenance, and repair program that is well documented is a fundamental element of a risk management program. It will not only help prevent injuries but also provide evidence of an organization's reasonableness in the event of a lawsuit.

SUMMARY

Risk control means examining the feasibility of various risk management techniques and then selecting and implementing the appropriate ones. Implementing risk control means making a conscious decision to take action or not to take action with respect to a risk. Loss exposures can be managed through risk control, risk finance, or a combination of these two methods. Risk control techniques include avoidance, loss prevention, loss reduction, duplication, separation, and diversification. Developing risk management plans regarding the following will further an organization's risk prevention and reduction: improving organizational attitudes regarding safety; inspecting facilities; cleaning, maintaining, and repairing facilities; preparing courts, gymnasiums, and fields for play; managing crowds; developing safety plans in the event of lightning; requiring players to wear protective gear; and inspecting, maintaining, and repairing equipment.

DOCUMENTING INSPECTIONS

Documentation of each inspection is important in the event a lawsuit is filed. Regular, thorough documented inspections may assist you in defense of a lawsuit. Alternatively, if there is a lack of documentation, it will be harder to prove that inspections were actually done. Forms can be used to document each inspection (see the appendix on page 363). The following information should be documented during an inspection.

Considerations	Notes for follow-up
Date and time of the inspection.	
Who performed the inspection?	
What was inspected?	
What was the outcome of the inspection (i.e., was there anything in disrepair)?	
What actions were taken to correct the problem?	
When were those actions taken?	
Who corrected the problem?	
Are there other considerations particular to the inspection?	

From Katharine M. Nohr, 2009, *Managing Risk in Sport and Recreation: The Essential Guide for Loss Prevention* (Champaign, IL: Human Kinetics).

PREPARATION OF THE COURT, GYMNASIUM, OR FIELD FOR PLAY

After inspections have been performed and documented, defects and hazards should be repaired or removed before play begins. The following questions should be addressed in preparing an area for play.

Considerations	Yes or No (check one)	Notes for follow-up
If a hazard cannot be corrected before play, has it been determined whether the area is safe for play or whether to cancel the practice or game?	❏ Yes ❏ No	
If the area is safe for play but a hazard exists, have clear and adequate warnings been provided to all players and other persons who will be utilizing the area of play (e.g., officials and coaches)?	❏ Yes ❏ No	
Are extra balls removed during play?	❏ Yes ❏ No	
Are all protruding wall fixtures and switches padded or painted a bright color so as to warn players?	❏ Yes ❏ No	
If the area of play is inside and there is insufficient ventilation on a hot and humid day, have you relocated or canceled the game or practice in order to prevent heat-related illnesses?	❏ Yes ❏ No	
Are there other considerations particular to preparing the court, gymnasium, or field for play?	❏ Yes ❏ No	

From Katharine M. Nohr, 2009, *Managing Risk in Sport and Recreation: The Essential Guide for Loss Prevention* (Champaign, IL: Human Kinetics).

LIGHTNING

Lightning strikes can cause serious injuries or death. Most lightning injuries occur during the daytime and during spring or summer months. If lightning is a risk to your organization, it is imperative that a comprehensive plan for lightning emergency response be developed.

Considerations	Yes or No (check one)	Notes for follow-up
Are weather conditions monitored before and during the game or practice?	❑ Yes ❑ No	
Have coaches and staff been trained to recognize nearby lightning activity and to determine the distance of lightning from the field and the potential danger?	❑ Yes ❑ No	
Have criteria been established for when evacuation of the field should occur, when play should resume, or whether a game or practice should be canceled?	❑ Yes ❑ No	
Has an evacuation plan been made, using nearby shelters, that also includes spectators?	❑ Yes ❑ No	
Have players and other personnel been instructed as to how evacuation will take place, and do they practice the evacuation?	❑ Yes ❑ No	
Is the evacuation plan monitored and changed where necessary?	❑ Yes ❑ No	
Are there other considerations particular to lightning?	❑ Yes ❑ No	

From Katharine M. Nohr, 2009, *Managing Risk in Sport and Recreation: The Essential Guide for Loss Prevention* (Champaign, IL: Human Kinetics).

Risk Financing

If it weren't for baseball, many kids wouldn't know what a millionaire looked like.

—Phyllis Diller

The next step after assessing risks is risk financing, an important means of controlling risks. Risk financing requires consciously deciding whether or not to generate funds to pay for potential losses, by means of transfer or retention. When addressing risk financing issues, it is important to consider organizational risk management goals and financial goals. This requires decision making from an organization's board of directors, chief financial officer, and others, as well as persons involved in risk management.

RISK TRANSFER

A sport organization may choose to transfer risks rather than retain them. Transfer can be done by purchasing insurance or by using noninsurance techniques. Most people are familiar with the process of transferring possible financial consequences to an insurance company. The organization pays a certain small amount in the form of an insurance premium in return for the insurance carrier paying for a possible large amount if a loss should occur. In return for the premium, the insurance carrier will pay those losses that are covered by the insurance contract as well as provide claims handling services and hire an attorney to defend the organization in the event of a lawsuit.

A noninsurance risk transfer is where an organization uses a method to transfer all or a portion of the financial consequences of a loss to another party. One way of doing this is using a hold harmless agreement in a contract. For example, an organization may insist that the concessionaire for its stadium agree to hold the organization harmless or indemnify it for any liability that arises out of the concession stands. This means that if the organization is named as a defendant in a lawsuit filed by someone injured by a drunk driver who was served alcohol by the concessionaire at the stadium, the concessionaire would have to pay any portion of a judgment rendered against the stadium.

RISK RETENTION

An organization may use the risk financing technique of risk retention by using its own funds to pay for losses. This can be planned or unplanned. If risk retention is planned, the organization deliberately assumes a loss exposure because it is the most convenient and efficient means to fund the loss, or it has no other option. Risk retention is unplanned when the organization does not take any steps to plan funding in advance, such as when a hurricane destroys its property and there is no insurance or funds allocated to pay for the damage.

An organization that chooses risk retention can opt for partially or completely retaining the risk. Sometimes it makes more financial sense to buy insurance for a portion of the risk and plan to pay losses out of the organization's funds in order to save money on premiums. Risk retention can also involve pre-loss funding, by setting aside money that will be used in the event of a loss. Current-loss funding means waiting until the loss occurs and then using moneys out of the organization's budget to cover it. Post-loss funding means that when a loss occurs, the organization finances it, paying for the loss over time.

SELECTING RISK FINANCING TECHNIQUES

A sport organization benefits from seeking professional risk management advice when determining which risk financing techniques are most appropriate and economical, considering the organization's financial position and goals. As discussed in chapter 1, it is important to ascertain the loss or accident history in order to establish the loss frequency and severity. It is also important to understand how often accidents happen and their level of severity. For example, an organization's gymnasium, where basketball and volleyball practices and games are held, has had an average of 10 minor injuries reported per year for the past 5 years. The history also shows that the gymnasium experienced significant flooding 15 years ago. There was one lawsuit that arose out of an injury when someone fell off the bleachers at a game. The insurance carrier settled that lawsuit for $20,000, and the organization had to pay a deductible of $1,000. This example illustrates the characteristics of the frequency and severity of several losses. The high-severity loss was the flood, which occurred only once and so would be categorized as low frequency. The bleacher accident would likely be considered to be of moderate severity, and its occurrence would be categorized as likely to occur more frequently than a flood for that location. The 10 minor injuries would be considered low severity and higher frequency (see figure 6.1).

It is important to analyze the level of severity of possible losses and their likely frequency in order to decide whether to transfer or retain losses or do a combination of both. Generally, organizations transfer the high-severity losses, such as fires and natural disasters. Low-severity losses that occur more frequently are more likely to be retained because organizations can afford to handle them. Medium-severity losses often result in mixed retention and transfer. An organization may opt to retain a portion by having a higher deductible on their insurance policy, for example.

RISK FINANCING GOALS

An organization should consider its risk financing goals before making decisions about retention and transfer. An important goal is an organization's availability of money to pay for losses. If an organization does not have extra cash for this purpose, it may be more interested in transferring the risk.

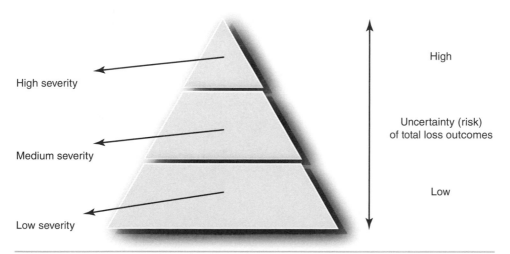

Figure 6.1 Analyzing the frequency and severity of losses assists an organization in deciding whether to retain or transfer risks.

Another important goal related to risk financing is to keep the cost of risk as low as possible. When an organization decides to retain hazard risks, it also must incur the cost of administration, which includes handling claims. There are administrative expenses associated with any risk financing plan as well. Risk control and risk assessment expenses are part of this issue. If you hire a risk management consultant to perform a risk review, that will factor into the cost of risk.

Another goal of your organization might be to maintain liquid assets. If an organization decides it wants to retain a large portion of losses, then it will need to have more liquid assets available in order to do this.

All potential risk financing goals should factor into how an organization finances risk, whether by retention, transfer, or a combination of both. On the surface, it might appear more reasonable to transfer risks, but in reality, the cost might be so significant that it makes more financial sense to create a combination of transfer and retention.

INSURANCE

It is very likely that your organization has purchased multiple types of insurance to transfer its hazard risk. The purpose of insurance is to spread the risk of loss among a large number of organizations that have similar loss exposures. Insurance companies provide risk management services as well,

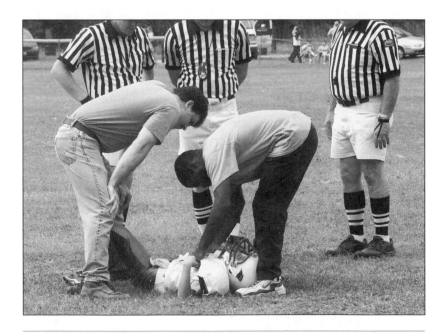

Purchasing insurance is a common way to transfer hazard risk.

including expertise in providing risk assessments and risk control. They provide claims adjustment services, including administration of claims payments, settling claims, fraud investigation, retention of attorneys, and overseeing legal defense. Insurance companies also pay for and retain legal services.

A sport and recreation organization likely has various types of commercial insurance, including general liability insurance, property insurance, auto insurance, business income insurance, workers' compensation insurance, flood insurance, directors and officers liability insurance, umbrella liability insurance, crime insurance, and possibly equipment breakdown insurance. Many other types of commercial insurance are available, but this list represents the most common for sport organizations.

There are many advantages to purchasing insurance rather than employing alternative risk financing techniques. Insurance reduces uncertainty; provides claims handling and risk control services; and may satisfy creditor, legal, and business requirements. There might be tax benefits associated with paying premiums, and if need be, the policy can be easily canceled. Disadvantages of insurance include the cost of premiums and the fact that it usually does not completely transfer risks and may fluctuate in price and availability.

Self-Insurance Plans

An organization may decide to use a self-insurance plan to retain risks and avoid the transaction costs associated with purchasing insurance from an outside company. Usually self-insurance is selected as a risk financing technique for losses that are low severity and high frequency. An example in a sport organization might be minor injuries that occur on the premises, such as slips and falls. This retention can be capped by purchasing excess liability insurance in the event that a severe loss occurs. For example, a slip and fall might cause a fractured spine. High-severity losses are generally not part of a self-insurance plan; they are usually transferred. These are too large for most organizations to retain and are generally unpredictable, such as natural disasters.

Self-insurance only makes sense for organizations with well-developed risk control programs and sufficient financial resources for risk administration and financing. Self-insurance plans can be used for auto liability and physical damage, general liability, workers' compensation, floods, earthquakes, and health care benefits. It is also possible to become involved in a group self-insurance plan for health care benefits or workers' compensation.

Captive Insurance Plans

If a sport and recreation organization is large, it may want to form a subsidiary company known as a captive insurer for the purpose of insuring its loss exposures. Captive insurance companies perform the same functions as an insurance company in that they issue insurance policies, collect premiums, and pay losses that are covered under the policies. Captive insurers may retain a certain amount of loss and then transfer a certain amount by purchasing what is called reinsurance or excess insurance. Certain states have favorable statutory laws for creation of captives. If your organization is interested in forming a captive, it is best to seek expert advice in exploring and executing this risk finance option.

ENTERPRISE RISK MANAGEMENT

Large sport and recreation organizations may benefit by taking a more global approach to their risk management concerns by including business risk as well as hazard risk. Enterprise risk management (ERM) combines the two with the strategy of increasing the value of the business to shareholders or owners. Some organizations appoint a chief risk management officer (CRMO) to oversee all risks that the organization faces and to work closely with other corporate officers and the board of directors in managing risks in the most cost-effective manner. Usually any discussion or actions relating to sport and recreation risk management organizations concern only hazard risk or accidental loss, which, as discussed previously, includes liability, property, net income, and personnel loss exposures. These loss exposures constitute pure risk in that there is only a possibility of loss or no loss. There is no possibility of gain. Business risks, on the other hand, include the possibility of gain as well as the possibility of loss or no loss.

With ERM, business risks are included in a more global approach so that an organization can manage all its risks: strategic, operational, financial, and hazard. Strategic risks relate to an organization's management and long-term goals. For example, a fitness club might consider merging with another fitness club to increase the number of locations. Operational risks relate to an organization's ability to operate. For example, a golf course requires water to keep the grass alive and green. In certain locations, a golf course faces operational risks of not being able to obtain sufficient water. Other utilities, such as electrical power or petroleum, or the ability to obtain necessary supplies, are operational risks as well. Financial risks relate to an organization's financial activities. For example, if an American basketball team is scheduled to play only in Europe and the U.S. dollar is devalued in comparison to the euro, this could affect the team's profitability. As discussed previously, hazard risks relate to risks associated with accidental losses, such as damage to property, bodily injury suffered by players or spectators, or a key manager leaving the organization.

Other risk categories that organizations might include with the ERM model are contractual risk, reputation risk, information risk, and regulatory risk. The point is that ERM is a more holistic approach to risk management that addresses more than just hazard risk, the traditional form of risk management.

SUMMARY

Sport and recreation organizations need to make decisions regarding risk financing that are consistent with their financial position and goals. Risk financing will likely include a combination of retention and transfer. Transfer can be accomplished by purchasing insurance. Retention can be accomplished simply by having large deductibles associated with insurance policies or by creating a self-insurance plan. Large organizations may choose to form their own insurance company subsidiary, which is called a captive insurance company. It is important that large sport and recreation organizations are aware of the enterprise risk management approach and consider this strategy if they are seeking to combine all risks under one umbrella of operation.

7

Emergency and Disaster Planning

I beg you take courage; the brave soul can mend even disaster.

—Catherine the Great

Every sport organization should be well prepared for disasters that could strike at any time. Sport organizations, like any other businesses or non-profits, need to safeguard their businesses from all types of natural or intentionally caused disasters. Planning for such a disaster could mean saving lives and businesses. Each organization has critical resources that disaster planning should protect. Consider the impact a disaster will have on the following:

- Human lives—Athletes, coaches, employees, customers, vendors, suppliers, clients, management, and all other people who are involved in some way in an organization could be affected by a disaster.

- Physical resources—Physical resources include facilities, equipment, offices, furniture, computers, important papers, and any other structure or personal effects. These can all be damaged or destroyed in a disaster and should be protected.

- Continuity of the sport programs and organization—In the face of a disaster, an organization may not experience significant loss of human lives or physical structure damage. Nevertheless, there can be loss of use or attendance when surrounding areas are destroyed or damaged. The economy could be affected such that sport and recreation programs lose customers.

CONSIDER THE RISKS

Natural disasters occur in every region of the world. Certain areas are vulnerable to certain disasters and not to others. The impact of global warming will likely increase the frequency and severity of natural disasters. It is also possible that regions that have never experienced certain natural disasters may begin experiencing them. For example, on March 15, 2008, a tornado, with winds estimated at 130 miles per hour (210 km/h), struck Atlanta, Georgia, while thousands watched basketball games in the Georgia Dome and the Philips Arena. The tornado was the first on record to strike downtown Atlanta and the first inside the city since 1975.

The following is a list of potential natural disasters. An organization should assess the chance of each disaster hitting its area before formulating a disaster risk management plan.

- Avalanches
- Coastal erosion
- Droughts
- Earthquakes
- Extreme heat
- Floods
- Freezing
- Hailstorms
- Hurricanes
- Ice storms
- Land subsidence
- Landslides
- Severe thunder and lightning
- Severe winter storms
- Storm surges
- Tornadoes
- Tsunamis
- Volcanoes
- Wildfires
- Windstorms

Other acts and circumstances should also be considered as part of your disaster planning:

- Arson
- Bomb explosion

- Bomb threat
- Chemical exposure
- Computer crimes
- Criminal activity
- Fire
- Hazardous material
- Hostage situation
- Medical emergency
- Pandemic, such as avian flu
- Power failure
- Riot
- Terrorism
- Transportation accident
- Violence
- War
- Water supply interrupted

Every sport organization should have a disaster and emergency planning team that designs a disaster plan specifically for the organization. How an organization reacts and recovers from a disaster will depend on the extent of planning.

DEVELOPING AN EMERGENCY PLAN

In developing an emergency plan, an organization first has to establish how to protect the people in its facilities at the time of the occurrence. Second, an organization needs to protect its facilities or athletic venues and their contents. Third, an organization strives to protect its business continuity.

Protecting People

The number one priority in developing an emergency plan is protecting human lives. Usually, evacuation is necessary in order to accomplish this. Evacuation may involve removal from a building or even from an area or region. In the event of a tornado, evacuation means having people go to an underground shelter designed particularly for that purpose, or if no such shelter is available, to a shelter that would provide protection. A tsunami requires moving people to higher ground. A fire, bomb threat, explosion, or other internal disaster means moving people out of a building and away from a threat. Chemical exposure may require use of protective gear. A pandemic, such as avian flu, may mean quarantine for a period of time and administration of vaccines. Whatever the threat, prompt action to save lives should be planned for and practiced.

The Department of Homeland Security offers downloads of business emergency disaster plans that would greatly assist sport and recreation organizations in preparing for disasters. Information is available at www .ready.gov. The Federal Emergency Agency (FEMA) also provides disaster preparedness information regarding numerous hazards. Such information can be found at www.fema.gov. An organization should also check with state agencies about the availability of disaster planning assistance.

Protecting Buildings and Their Contents

When facilities are built, materials should be fire resistant and wind resistant. The buildings should have good insulation and solid foundations and footings to withstand any natural disaster that is likely to occur in the area. If there is a likelihood of windstorms, hurricanes, or earthquakes, consideration should be given to having the building constructed to withstand those disasters. Firewalls can be built and sprinkler systems can be installed to minimize damage from fire. All building codes in the area should be complied with when building or remodeling. It may be prudent to have a building inspector determine whether there has been compliance. When selecting a location, flood zones and other dangerous areas might be avoided in order to lower the risk of flooding, mudslides, or coastal erosion. It is a good idea to consult maps that illustrate the effect of global warming on coastal areas if applicable.

Protecting an Organization's Business Continuity

In the event that a disaster destroys a facility, an organization will want to be prepared by having backed up all computer files and having such backups located at an alternative site. It is also important to consider where teams or athletes will play or practice in the event that a facility is no longer available. Is there another location out of which your organization can operate if your facility is destroyed? This is of particular concern for schools.

PREPARING AN EMERGENCY DISASTER PLAN

After an organization has analyzed the potential risks involved, research should be done to determine how to respond to each emergency and checklists developed for dealing with them. This may seem like a daunting task, but it will likely mean peace of mind, less risk in the event of a disaster, and greater confidence by others in the organization.

The steps to be accomplished in preparing an emergency disaster plan are as follows:

- Create a team of people who are charged with this task.
- Designate those people who will execute the plan when it goes into effect.
- Provide copies of the plan when it is complete to all appropriate personnel.
- Communicate the plan by written material and signage.
- Practice the plan.
- Modify the plan as needed.

Disaster planning is an ongoing process. As personnel in an organization change, plans will have to be updated as well to reflect assignments of personnel charged with executing the plan. When choosing a person to be in charge of the plan, it is important to select someone who will likely be available should a disaster strike. The head of an organization could have a heavy travel, meeting, or event schedule that requires that he be away from the facility. The designated person in charge should have the personality and characteristics of someone who is capable of executing an emergency plan. Alternates should be selected in the event that the designated person is not available.

The plan should be put in a binder and be given to all appropriate personnel. Copies should be kept off site in the event the facility is destroyed. It is a good idea for copies to be kept at the homes of key personnel who will be executing the plan. You may think it is a good idea to keep the plan digitally on a computer. However, it is unlikely that there will be power during a disaster, and so the plan would not be accessible.

It is important to have an emergency disaster plan already in place so that the procedures can be followed if a disaster does hit.

Regular meetings should be held to discuss an organization's disaster plan and to communicate its contents. Portions of the plan should be communicated on signs so that people will have ready access to the information. Signage is appropriate for information concerning evacuation and location of exits, fire extinguishers, first aid supplies, CPR instructions, location of and instructions for an AED, and so on.

Organizations should have emergency and disaster drills in order to practice the plan. Personnel should be informed that there will be a drill on a certain day, or it can be a surprise. It is a good idea to involve government agencies in drills and planning. Fire departments, police departments, EMS organizations, civil defense organizations, and Homeland Security might be willing to participate and can provide some assistance with disaster and emergency planning.

With each practice of the plan or institution of it, weaknesses will be discovered, allowing for modification as necessary. People may not understand what they are supposed to do. In that event, more training is needed. Through the process of practice, it may be discovered that appropriate equipment is lacking or that there are problems with the evacuation plan. All these things can be addressed before a disaster or emergency occurs.

A disaster plan should include sections that detail lines and methods of communication during the emergency; emergency evacuation procedures; plans for basic survival necessities and equipment; lines of authority, assignments, and recalling staff; securing the facility; caring for and discharging minors; medical care; addressing emotional impacts; and public relations.

Maintaining Communication

It should be anticipated that there may be limited access to telephones and that computer access will not be possible. You may wish to establish a calling tree so that certain people are charged with calling others. For example, each person may be given a portion of the team members or parents to be called.

The following telephone numbers should be included:

Emergency Phone Numbers

- Fire department
- Police department
- Hospitals
- Ambulance
- Hazardous materials specialists
- Key personnel (including cell phones and home phone numbers)
- Security

Other Phone Numbers

Make sure to include cell phone numbers, and consider text messaging as a means of prompt communication.

- Suppliers
- Vendors
- Coaches
- Administrators
- Employees
- Customers
- Athletes
- Team members
- Parents

Developing Emergency Evacuation Procedures

It is important to include a current floor plan of the facility when planning for emergency evacuation. Develop a plan for all types of scenarios. Consider that a fire could be confined to a certain part of the building and that evacuation will have to proceed in another part. Alternatively, exits could be blocked or a bomb could have exploded. Plan for evacuating people who are physically challenged, the elderly, and children. Certain classes of people will have a difficult time moving quickly, moving at all, hearing or seeing, or understanding what is going on. Make sure your evacuation procedure accommodates those people. If an athletic event attracts elderly spectators or your players are children, your focus in planning should be on that group.

Providing Food, Water, Shelter, and Fuel for 72 Hours

Generally, people should provide for themselves and their families so they have food, water, shelter, and fuel for 72 hours after a disaster. An organization may wish to keep such supplies at its facilities in the event that some personnel, clients, athletes, coaches, or spectators are stranded and use the facilities for shelter during a disaster.

Providing Generators, Emergency Lights, and Medical Equipment

A sport organization should plan on being able to provide light, heat, or air conditioning with generators if necessary. If electricity goes out during a game, it is important to at least provide sufficient lighting so that spectators can exit the facility safely. Medical emergencies should always be prepared for, and an organization should continually assess its ability to respond.

Medical equipment such as AEDs, basic first aid supplies, and other equipment should continually be inspected, replaced, and reassessed.

Designating Lines of Authority, Assignments, and Staff

After a disaster, there is a good possibility that communication by telephone or cell phone will not be available. Staff should have a clear understanding of the lines of authority and who is to report to work in the event of an emergency. For example, if your organization employs security personnel, there is a reasonable chance you will want them working at your facility in the event of an emergency.

Securing the Facility

An organization's disaster plan should address the security of its venues and facilities. Without electricity, alarms may not be functional. Facilities could become vulnerable to vandalism and burglary during power outages and when there are few if any personnel present. If a facility is the only one with lights on and heat, there may be an influx of people who try to gain access. These considerations should be planned for.

Caring for and Discharging Minors

If an organization is involved with providing sport and recreation to minors, it will need to have a plan of how to care for the children in its charge. The organization will also have to plan for how to discharge the minors to their parents or guardians and how to communicate with them in the event of an emergency.

Providing or Obtaining Medical Care

The disaster at hand might involve a medical emergency to one or hundreds of people. An organization should be familiar with the medical emergency facilities that are located in its vicinity, how to contact them, and how to transport patients there. It may be prudent to contact such facilities in advance of an emergency and discuss whether they will be able to accommodate a large number of people. For example, if you run a sport stadium, the number of casualties in a disaster may be great, and so they may have to be taken to a number of local hospitals.

Dealing With the Emotional Impacts of the Disaster

Disasters can be devastating physically, financially, and emotionally to an organization's employees, volunteers, coaches, athletes, clients, and others. It is important to plan on dealing with the emotional aspects of a disaster.

A public relations representative for an organization should be charged with providing information to the public in response to a disaster.

This can be done by being understanding and patient to those people who have been affected or even by providing counseling services or suggesting such services.

Assigning a Public Relations Liaison

Organizations will benefit from having only one or a few people deal with the media and the public in response to a disaster. The organization's spokesperson should be selected carefully and should be skilled in dealing with the media. Press releases and public statements can be issued at intervals in order to provide information that will give the public confidence in your response to events. This will help ensure the continuing goodwill of a business and its successful continuity.

RISK FINANCING FOR NATURAL DISASTERS

In chapter 6, Risk Financing, the concept of transferring and retaining risk is explained. A fundamental element in preparing for potential natural disasters is determining whether to self-insure, transfer the risk by purchasing insurance, or use a combination of insurance and self-insured retention. Insurance brokers and agents are good sources of information as to the type of insurance coverage available for the specific disasters you are concerned about. Availability and cost will differ depending on the exposure. For example, if your organization is located in New Orleans, Houston, or coastal Florida, where a significant number of hurricanes have hit in recent years, hurricane and flood insurance will likely be costly and difficult to obtain. Government resources, such as the Federal Emergency Management Agency (FEMA), may be helpful if you are having difficulty obtaining insurance or information regarding risk financing for natural disasters.

SUMMARY

Disasters can have a tremendous impact on human lives, physical resources, and business continuity. An organization should consider the risks of natural disasters and other disasters in light of its physical location and other factors. An emergency plan should be developed that is communicated, practiced, and revised on a regular basis. The emergency disaster plan should include procedures regarding communication, evacuation, supplies, power, lines of authority, security, caring for and discharging minors, medical care, emotional impacts, public relations, and any other relevant topics.

Transformation

We willingly pay 30,000–40,000 fatalities per year for the advantages of individual transportation by automobile.

—John von Neumann

One of the riskiest activities that most people participate in every day is getting in their motor vehicles and driving. Consequently, one of the primary risks that has to be considered in developing a sport risk management plan is the use of motor vehicles and other forms of transportation to transport athletes, coaches, officials, spectators, press, VIPs, and others to and from athletic events. For the most part, if an organization is putting on an event and the participants and attendees who will be attending the event are responsible for their own transportation to and from the event, the organization will not have any duty that they arrive safely. However, if an organization is in a position in which it owes a duty to transport athletes or others to an event, it may have exposure for negligence if an accident should happen. This occurs most often in school and university settings or with teams that are to be transported to a game together. This also may occur when an organization transports spectators or others by bus or shuttle from a distant parking lot or location to a stadium. In those circumstances, lawsuits likely will arise if accidents occur.

A number of measures can be taken in order to decrease the risk of accidents and to limit potential exposure or liability. There are also means by which the risk can be transferred, such as by purchase of insurance as discussed in the previous chapter regarding risk financing. This chapter addresses risk control techniques as well as possible financing of transportation risks.

VEHICLE OPERATORS

If you have ever wondered why most rental car companies will not rent to drivers under the age of 25, it is because younger drivers cause a proportionately large number of car accidents. Rental car companies have found it cost effective to eliminate the riskiest group of drivers completely from their patrons. Sport organizations should take a lesson from the rental car companies and prohibit anyone under age 25 from driving athletes or others to and from events, unless waivers are signed completely releasing the organization from liability for any potential injuries. This arrangement may not be practical because of a limited pool of drivers, but it should significantly limit liability exposure.

Another issue with motor vehicle operators is their skill at driving a car or a particular vehicle, such as a van or bus. Fundamentally, a driver who is operating a vehicle that is transporting athletes or others to and from an event should be licensed to drive the particular vehicle. Preferably, the driver will have undertaken some special driver's training, such as commercial driver training. The driver should also have a safe driving record; wear eyeglasses or contacts if required; practice safe driving habits; refrain from using a cell phone while driving; use seat belts; and not drive under the influence of alcohol or drugs or drive when fatigued.

If an organization does not have vehicle operators it can rely on to safely transport people to an event, it is far better to hire a professional driver to perform that function. The cost of a professional driver should be offset by the risk of using an unsafe driver.

TYPES OF TRAVEL

Transportation is most commonly done in motor vehicles, such as private passenger cars, SUVs, minivans, 12-passenger vans, 15-passenger vans, or buses. Planes, trains, ferries, and boats might also provide transportation. Vehicles operated commercially by professionals are far safer than those operated privately. Unfortunately, the cost is often prohibitive, and so organizations opt for less expensive private vehicles. There have been incidents of rollovers when 12- and 15-passenger vans have been used to transport athletic teams. One factor that can increase the likelihood of rollover is passenger load. Unfortunately, larger vehicles are often needed to transport teams. Following are some of the issues that need to be considered when providing transportation.

- Transporting spectators—Generally, organizations do not undertake the task of transporting spectators. If there is a need to do so, the best means is probably to contract with a professional company. That way you will be transferring the risk to the other company. Because the cost will probably be more significant, you may wish to pass this cost on to the spectators.

- Transporting event staff—The same considerations that are applicable to transporting athletes are applicable to transporting event staff to a venue. Workers' compensation coverage may be applicable as well as automobile insurance coverage when doing so.

- Traveling with more than one vehicle—There may be times when you are transporting more than one group to an event, using more than one vehicle. In this situation, you may consider traveling in a caravan or at least being in cell phone contact in the event of an emergency.

- Other modes of travel—Travel by airplane, boat, or train is statistically safer than travel by automobile. Unfortunately, such modes of travel may not be available or are prohibitively expensive. This chapter does not address nonautomobile travel because it is much less likely to cause injury or loss to an organization.

VEHICLE INSPECTION

Most drivers of vehicles transporting passengers to and from athletic events are not mechanics. In an ideal situation, a mechanic would inspect a vehicle before each use. Since that is not likely to happen in the real world, before using a vehicle to transport people to and from an athletic event, a reasonable inspection of the vehicle should be made. The items outlined in "Vehicle Inspection" (see page 117) should be working properly.

The driver should make sure there is sufficient gas and oil in the automobile as well as windshield wiper fluid, antifreeze, and other fluid levels. The driver should also check to see if the vehicle has had recent maintenance and has had an up-to-date safety inspection if required by law.

EMERGENCY EQUIPMENT AND OTHER ITEMS IN VEHICLE

Vehicle registration, an insurance card, safety inspection documents, and any other required documents as well as the vehicle manual should be kept in the automobile—usually in the glove compartment. There should also be a cell phone in the vehicle for emergency purposes and the telephone number of an automobile club that can be called if there is an emergency. For a checklist of emergency equipment and other items that should be in a vehicle, see "Emergency Equipment and Other Items in Vehicle" on page 118.

Be sure to have all emergency equipment on hand when you are responsible for transporting athletes or recreation participants.

Most of these items will not be used when traveling to and from sporting events. However, in an emergency they may come in handy or even save a life. The driver, when doing his inspection of the vehicle, should make sure it is equipped with necessary emergency items. If the trip is long or there is a risk of inclement weather, it would be helpful to include most or all of the identified emergency items.

MAINTENANCE

Most vehicles manufactured today have recommended maintenance schedules and procedures. The vehicle manual should provide this information, or it can be obtained from the dealership where the vehicle was purchased or on the Internet. Following the manufacturer's suggested maintenance protocol is a reasonable way to maintain any automobile that is used to drive athletes and others to and from athletic events. In doing so, it is important to use a reputable mechanic or garage that can be entrusted to thoroughly inspect and repair the vehicle. If there are any signs that something is wrong between its regularly scheduled maintenance checks, the vehicle should be examined immediately. Records should be kept of all maintenance that each vehicle undergoes and should be available if any questions should arise about the fitness of a particular vehicle to undertake a trip.

On a more frequent basis, when the vehicle is refueled with the type of fuel recommended by the manufacturer, tires should be checked and filled with the amount of air recommended, windshield wiper blades and fluid should be checked, and oil as well as any other fluids that could be running low should be checked. Warning lights on the dash should be heeded, and there should be immediate follow-up.

Maintenance to a vehicle should also include close attention to the tires. Tires should be rotated on a regular basis and checked for signs of wear. Tires should be replaced at regular intervals and also after nonrepairable flats. Tire pressure should be regularly checked with a gauge kept in the automobile. It is important to not overfill tires and to follow the tire manufacturer's recommendations.

MOTOR VEHICLE INSURANCE

Every automobile that is used to transport athletes and others to athletic events or facilities should be fully insured in compliance with local law. Most people cannot easily understand motor vehicle insurance policies even though the trend is for automobile insurers to provide easy-to-read policies. It is a good idea to talk with your insurance agent or broker about the insurance policies that have been purchased for the vehicles that will be transporting athletes and others. You will want to make sure there is coverage and that exclusions will not apply if used for a particular purpose excluded under the policy. You will also want to make sure that policy limits are high enough to cover your organization in the case of a catastrophic accident.

A number of states require by law that each vehicle carry no-fault insurance. No-fault insurance is first-party insurance and generally covers those people who are in an insured vehicle. This insurance pays for medical care and possibly wage loss and other benefits immediately, without regard to fault. The eligible injured persons do not have to file a lawsuit against the at-fault party in order to get paid. For example, if you were injured in an automobile accident that was caused by the driver who rear-ended your vehicle, your own no-fault insurance will pay for your medical bills right away. You may wish to later bring a lawsuit against the at-fault party. If a recovery is made, your insurance company might be able to get the money back that it had paid on your behalf from the person who caused the accident (usually her insurance carrier).

There should also be bodily injury liability coverage on vehicles used by an organization. In the event that the driver of the vehicle negligently causes an accident, the bodily injury liability coverage should cover an organization up to the limits of the policy. For example, coverage could be for $100,000 per person and $500,000 per occurrence. That means if someone sues an organization under the policy, he can only receive up to $100,000. Any liability beyond that will have to be paid by another policy that is either secondary or excess or will have to be paid by the organization directly. If multiple people die in the accident, clearly there will not be enough insurance coverage available in this scenario if that is the only policy available.

Underinsured motor vehicle coverage (UIM) can also be purchased to cover a person if it turns out that the driver who was at fault in the accident does not have enough insurance. This insurance is called UIM insurance and is also first-party coverage, purchased from a person's own insurance company. For example, you suffer a serious back injury in an accident, but the other driver has bodily injury insurance limits of only $20,000. The other driver pays that amount to you, but this does not fully compensate you for your injuries. You have $100,000 of UIM coverage, and so you request your own insurance company to pay you the balance of the value of your injury claim under that insurance policy. If your injury claim is valued at $80,000 and you already received $20,000 from the other driver, you would receive $60,000 under your own policy.

Uninsured motor vehicle insurance coverage (UM) can also be purchased from a person's own insurance carrier. This insurance will provide coverage if the at-fault driver is not insured. In that event, an injured person would seek insurance coverage directly from her own insurance company under a UM policy.

It is a good idea for individuals who transport athletes to and from events to discuss with their insurance agents or brokers the possibility of obtaining umbrella or excess coverage. Usually these policies are the least expensive way to increase insurance coverage for catastrophic accidents.

If employees of an organization will be driving the vehicles used to transport athletes and others, they will likely be covered by the company's workers' compensation policy if an accident occurs while they are in the course and scope of their employment.

Property damage insurance or collision coverage should also be part of any motor vehicle policy. This insurance coverage pays for the damage to any vehicles that occur because of the fault of the driver. Usually, the insurance company will ascertain whose fault the accident was, and if it was the insured's fault, it will pay for the damage to both vehicles up to the policy limits of the collision coverage. Sometimes an insurer will pay for its insured's property damage and then will seek repayment of the amount paid from the at-fault driver's insurance company. Before repairs are made, the insurer will seek a property damage appraisal and may require that an authorized body shop perform the work. If the damage to the car exceeds the value of the car, then the car will be considered "totaled," and the insurance company will make a cash payment to the vehicle's owner. The insurance company may retain the car and sell it for salvage value.

It is important that you make sure all vehicle insurance is in effect and provides sufficient coverage in order to protect your organization.

Reductions in insurance premiums may be obtained by showing good driving records, by instituting safe driving policies, by undertaking certain safe driving practices, or by having a large deductible or retention. An insurance agent or broker can provide information about how an organization can reduce its insurance premiums. Essentially, the less risk of loss there is to the insurance carrier, the lower the premium. Whatever you can do to reduce your insurance carrier's risk will translate to lower premiums.

TRANSPORTING ATHLETES

When an organization undertakes to transport minor athletes from one location to another, permission slips from their parents should be signed. All athletes (or, if minors, their parent or guardian) should sign releases and waivers of liability and should provide emergency contact information. It is important that supervision is provided on a bus or van transporting a number of athletes so that the athletes do not disrupt the driver and interfere with the safe operation of the vehicle.

Drivers who are assigned to transport an athletic group should be trained to handle emergency situations. They should be subject to strict rules such as the ones listed in "Other Transportation Safety Tips" on page 120.

SUMMARY

Travel by motor vehicle is an inherently risky means of travel for an organization's athletes, staff, and spectators. Because of this, care should be taken to make travel as safe as possible. Vehicle operators who transport others should be at least 25 years of age and be trained and experienced in driving the vehicle in question. Special considerations should be given when transporting athletes, spectators, and event staff. If your organization can afford to travel by airplane, boat, or train, such means of travel are statistically safer than travel by automobile and should be considered. Vehicles should be regularly inspected and maintained. All repairs and inspections should be documented and those records kept and made available if necessary. Vehicles should be equipped with emergency supplies appropriate for the conditions and length of the trip planned. Motor vehicle insurance with coverage limits high enough in accordance to the exposure should be purchased.

VEHICLE INSPECTION

Most drivers of vehicles transporting passengers to and from athletic events are not mechanics. In an ideal situation, a mechanic would inspect a vehicle before each use. Since that is not likely to happen in the real world, before using a vehicle to transport people to and from an athletic event, a reasonable inspection of the vehicle should be made.

The driver should make sure there is sufficient gas and oil in the automobile as well as windshield wiper fluid, antifreeze, and other fluid levels. The driver should also check to see if the vehicle has had recent maintenance and has had an up-to-date safety inspection if required by law.

Considerations	Yes or No (check one)	Notes for follow-up
Are the brakes working properly?	❑ Yes ❑ No	
Are the headlights working properly?	❑ Yes ❑ No	
Are the brake lights working properly?	❑ Yes ❑ No	
Are the turn signals working properly?	❑ Yes ❑ No	
Is the horn working properly?	❑ Yes ❑ No	
Are the windshield wipers working properly?	❑ Yes ❑ No	
Is there enough windshield wiper fluid?	❑ Yes ❑ No	
Are the tires in good condition, and do they have enough air in them?	❑ Yes ❑ No	
Are all mirrors in place and correctly adjusted?	❑ Yes ❑ No	
Is the steering working properly?	❑ Yes ❑ No	
Is the battery fully charged and in working order?	❑ Yes ❑ No	
Does the vehicle need gas?	❑ Yes ❑ No	
Does oil need to be added or changed?	❑ Yes ❑ No	
Does the vehicle need antifreeze?	❑ Yes ❑ No	

From Katharine M. Nohr, 2009, *Managing Risk in Sport and Recreation: The Essential Guide for Loss Prevention* (Champaign, IL: Human Kinetics).

EMERGENCY EQUIPMENT
AND OTHER ITEMS IN VEHICLE

Vehicle registration, an insurance card, safety inspection documents, and any other required documents as well as the vehicle manual should be kept in the automobile—usually in the glove compartment. There should also be a cell phone in the vehicle for emergency purposes and the telephone number of an automobile club that can be called if there is an emergency.

Considerations	Yes or No (check one)	Notes for follow-up
Vehicle registration?	❑ Yes ❑ No	
Insurance card?	❑ Yes ❑ No	
Safety inspection documents and stickers?	❑ Yes ❑ No	
Current registration sticker, if applicable?	❑ Yes ❑ No	
Vehicle manual?	❑ Yes ❑ No	
Cell phone and charger?	❑ Yes ❑ No	
Phone number of automobile club in case of an emergency?	❑ Yes ❑ No	
Blankets?	❑ Yes ❑ No	
Fresh drinking water?	❑ Yes ❑ No	
Car jack?	❑ Yes ❑ No	
Spare tire?	❑ Yes ❑ No	
Emergency road flares?	❑ Yes ❑ No	
First aid kit?	❑ Yes ❑ No	
Flashlight?	❑ Yes ❑ No	
Jumper cables?	❑ Yes ❑ No	

(continued)

From Katharine M. Nohr, 2009, *Managing Risk in Sport and Recreation: The Essential Guide for Loss Prevention* (Champaign, IL: Human Kinetics).

Emergency Equipment and Other items in Vehicle *(continued)*

Considerations	Yes or No (check one)	Notes for follow-up
Map or GPS system?	☐ Yes ☐ No	
Tire gauge?	☐ Yes ☐ No	
Fire extinguisher?	☐ Yes ☐ No	
Food?	☐ Yes ☐ No	
Waterproof matches and candle?	☐ Yes ☐ No	
Whistle?	☐ Yes ☐ No	
Towel?	☐ Yes ☐ No	
Collapsible shovel?	☐ Yes ☐ No	
Rope?	☐ Yes ☐ No	
Knife?	☐ Yes ☐ No	
Duct tape?	☐ Yes ☐ No	
Tool kit?	☐ Yes ☐ No	
Gloves, hats, and boots?	☐ Yes ☐ No	
Chains or traction devices for tires?	☐ Yes ☐ No	
Are there other considerations for emergency equipment and other items in the vehicle?	☐ Yes ☐ No	

From Katharine M. Nohr, 2009, *Managing Risk in Sport and Recreation: The Essential Guide for Loss Prevention* (Champaign, IL: Human Kinetics).

OTHER TRANSPORTATION SAFETY TIPS

Drivers who are assigned to transport an athletic group should be trained to handle emergency situations. They should be subject to strict rules such as the following.

Considerations	Yes or No (check one)	Notes for follow-up
Have vehicle operators used alcohol or drugs before or during the trip?	❑ Yes ❑ No	
Have vehicle operators gotten sufficient sleep and rest before driving?	❑ Yes ❑ No	
Has appropriate conduct been defined and communicated to the athletes before the trip?	❑ Yes ❑ No	
Is misconduct immediately addressed and not tolerated while the vehicle is in motion?	❑ Yes ❑ No	
Are speed limits strictly followed?	❑ Yes ❑ No	
Are all traffic laws strictly followed?	❑ Yes ❑ No	
Is first aid available in the vehicle?	❑ Yes ❑ No	
Are head counts made when stopping for a rest break, and are all persons accounted for before the vehicle continues on the trip?	❑ Yes ❑ No	
Do vehicles carry safe loads of passengers? For example, if an organization uses SUVs and vans (particularly designed for 12 or 15 passengers), loads should be carefully considered to reduce the possibility of a rollover.	❑ Yes ❑ No	
Is cell phone use by the driver, including texting and video game playing, strictly prohibited while driving?	❑ Yes ❑ No	
Are there other considerations for transportation safety?	❑ Yes ❑ No	

From Katharine M. Nohr, 2009, *Managing Risk in Sport and Recreation: The Essential Guide for Loss Prevention* (Champaign, IL: Human Kinetics).

PART II

Introduction to Sport-Specific Risk Management Chapters

"I'm tired of hearing about money, money, money, money, money. I just want to play the game, drink Pepsi, wear Reebok."

Shaquille O'Neal

Each sport has its own hazards that should be addressed specifically when an organization attempts to control risks. Coaches, administrators, players, and others involved in a particular sport have a good idea what the safety concerns are. National sport governing bodies, youth associations, collegiate associates, and other organizations generally provide assistance with safety issues by developing guidelines and implementing safety rules. They may also provide education, publications, and safety certification programs in furtherance of promoting a safe sport. Anyone involved with a sport must be familiar with this information and adhere to rules and guidelines as much as possible.

The following sport-specific chapters are not designed to establish guidelines or standards in any particular sport. The information provided consists of summaries of the most recent reported appellate court decisions in each sport. In some sports, such as triathlon, the chapter summarizes all available reported appellate court decisions because there are so few. In addition to the court case summaries are lists of questions that cover many safety issues in the particular sport, which should augment the risk control information in chapter 5. Some chapters include lists of safety tips that should be helpful to coaches, administrators, and athletes.

It may be tempting to skip over the sport-specific chapters that are not applicable to sports you are involved in. However, it is recommended that you read all the court case summaries because they address the analysis that courts of many jurisdictions have applied to all types of sport and recreation issues. The analysis and conclusions apply to the specific sport addressed by the court, but they may have factual scenarios that are common in other sports as well.

For example, if you are interested in whether a spectator of a baseball game who is hit by an errant ball will prevail in a lawsuit against the stadium, you should also turn to the ice hockey chapter and read about spectators hit by hockey pucks. If you are interested in the issue of government or statutory immunity, you will find cases in various sports chapters that address that issue. If your concern is liability arising out of a hole in a grass soccer field, check the other sports chapters concerning baseball, football, and golf, which use grass playing surfaces as well.

It is important to understand what the summaries of reported appellate court cases represent and the legal impact of these decisions before you review them. Very few sport and recreation cases reach appellate courts, and even fewer cases lead to reported case law. The reason is that the vast majority of lawsuits filed in civil court are settled, proceed to arbitration, or are dismissed by summary judgment. As stated in chapter 3, a summary judgment is a decision made by the court based on statements of the evidence presented to the court in the form of a motion. The evidence is presented for the court record without a trial. This approach is used when there are no disputed material issues of facts in the case. The court will decide if one of the parties is entitled to judgment as a matter of law.

Appellate court decisions, also called case law, constitute binding law in the jurisdictions in which they are decided. We must look to case law along with statutory law to determine what the applicable law is for any given set of facts. The U.S. Congress and most state legislatures do not draft laws relating to most issues concerning sport and recreation. Consequently, we look to reported appellate court decisions for legal guidance.

The process of sorting out the applicable law is even harder when you consider that only the cases in the particular jurisdiction where the accident or injury occurred serve as precedence. This means that if the particular jurisdiction is California, the court need only follow California law. Even if a similar factual situation is set forth in a case by an appellate court in Nevada or New York, the California court does not have to follow it. Cases that are decided outside of the jurisdiction are used only to persuade the court.

Another important point that must be understood when reading case law is that the court addressed a particular factual situation when making its decision. If the facts in your case are different in any important or material way, then the court may not come to the same decision on your case. For example, an appellate court in Texas ruled that a soccer player was entitled to summary judgment where the facts established that he accidentally tripped another player, causing injury. In another Texas case, the facts might be that a soccer player (or basketball, baseball, or football player) purposefully tripped another player, causing injury. The court may have considered the tripping to be an inherent part of the sport in the first case when it was done accidentally. However, the court might find that in the second case, where the player acted willfully, the player could be found liable, and so summary judgment would not be appropriate. In this situation, the cases are factually distinguishable, and so the first case does not serve as precedent, or, in other words, is not controlling on the second case.

After reading this explanation, you might wonder what the value of reading any case law could be. It is helpful in understanding what a court might rule in a similar factual situation. Judges are very interested in hearing what another jurisdiction decided in a virtually identical factual situation. They may decide to go in a different direction if they believe the reasoning of the court was not sound or if statutes or case law in their jurisdiction require that they decide differently. Reading case law is also helpful for the purpose of understanding what facts led the plaintiff to file a lawsuit. If you understand how the plaintiff became injured, then actions can be taken in your organization that could help prevent a similar injury.

The summaries provided give the legal citation for the particular appellate case. With this citation, you can go to almost any law library in the United States and obtain a full copy of the case. Appellate court decisions can also be obtained from legal databases such as Westlaw or LexisNexis, which are available in many law libraries and law firms. Another way you might obtain a copy of a legal decision is to "Google" the names of both parties. More and more legal decisions are available on the Internet. If you do research on a legal database, you may be surprised at the number of decisions that are unpublished or not reported. Only published decisions can be cited as precedence. Unpublished decisions are binding only on the parties to the particular case.

The appellate court case summaries outline the key facts that were reported in the decision. Keep in mind that some courts provide lots of detail, and some courts provide so little information that it is hard to understand what really happened. The summaries also provide information as to what the final outcome was and the reason for that outcome.

As you read these summaries, you might get the impression that you are missing information about how the case was decided. This impression will be correct in that the summaries do not address the points of error that were brought before the court, which are interesting to trial lawyers but will not be very helpful in the field of sport and recreation risk management. What happens when an appeal is filed from a summary judgment or a jury verdict is that the appealing party has to point out to the court how the trial court committed error when deciding the case. For example, there might be an error as to the applicability of a jury instruction. This information is not included.

Another point that should be understood about the summaries is that the injured party is always called the plaintiff or by his or her name in order to make the case easier to understand. In reality, in an appellate court case, parties are called the appellant (the party who appeals a losing decision to a higher court, requesting that the decision be modified or reversed) and the appellee, the party against whom the appeal is taken. This can be confusing, and so these designations have been left out.

After you review all the appellate case summaries, you may come to the reasonable conclusion that defendants are often successfully dismissed via motions for summary judgment on various theories, including assumption of risk, no duty, lack of foreseeability or knowledge of a condition, government immunity, and so on. Even though this is the reality in sport and recreation, the cost of bringing these motions and the discovery required to file such motions is significant. Insurance companies are usually paying for these defense costs under their duty to defend, which will drive up the cost of insurance to the insured as well as other policyholders. It is much less costly to avoid litigation altogether and provide a safe environment for sport and recreation.

An important fact that will not become apparent from reading the appellate case summaries is that certain types of tort cases are not likely to be resolved by summary judgment. These cases tend to involve premises liability, in which someone was injured in an area outside the field of play, and motor vehicle accidents.

Cases that have material issues of fact to be decided by a finder of fact (judge or jury) will proceed by alternative dispute resolution (arbitration or mediation), trial, or settlement.

With this in mind, pay careful attention to the lists of safety questions and tips. If your organization is careful to perform regular inspections to identify hazards; correct or warn against dangerous conditions; require all appropriate safety gear be worn; communicate and enforce safety rules; and keep all areas of play and public access clean, well maintained, and free of hazards, you may avoid losses and litigation.

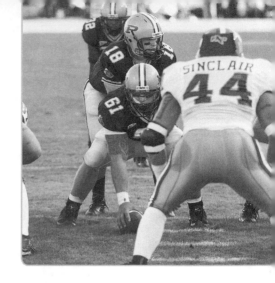

American Football

Football is, after all, a wonderful way to get rid of your
aggressions without going to jail for it.

—Heywood Hale Brown

Football has a reputation for being a dangerous sport in which players can suffer severe injuries. Consequently, issues of safety are addressed by most football organizations at every level—youth, high school, college, and professional. When considering issues of safety and risk management, it is a good idea to consider the level of the sport being played. Obviously, youth should be treated differently than adults. Many reported appellate court cases have addressed injuries to youth and adults that have arisen out of football. The cases described here do not address professional football. The reason is that most lawsuits filed by professional players relate to workers' compensation issues, since the injuries usually arose out of the course and scope of the players' work for a pro team.

FOOTBALL LAWSUITS AND SETTLEMENTS

There have been some large settlements and jury verdicts in football cases that involved serious injuries. Following are examples of these:

- A 15-year-old boy settled a case for $2 million in which he fell while swinging from a goalpost during a football game. The plaintiff suffered a fractured skull, facial nerve damage, and total hearing loss as a result of the fall. The lawsuit alleged that the school was negligent because of its failure to secure the goalpost properly and in failing to maintain the premises in a safe condition. The defendant denied these allegations.

- A 14-year-old boy was awarded $6.25 million by a jury in Snohomish, Washington, for a football injury that left the boy paralyzed. The plaintiff alleged that his coach was negligent in telling him to tackle another player.
- A 16-year-old high school football player who was paralyzed while playing football was awarded $5.3 million in a products liability case brought against the football helmet manufacturer.
- A 17-year-old high school football player settled a lawsuit for $12.5 million arising out of being tackled into a steel post that was located 11 feet 5 inches (3.5 m) from the sideline of the field on which the plaintiff was practicing.

A number of reported appellate court decisions address various causes of injuries in football. The football cases discussed in this chapter address circumstances in which plaintiffs were injured because of heatstroke, adjacent fields, a torn-down goalpost, field conditions, an object on the field, and conditions of public areas; from alcohol served by the stadium concessionaire; and in the locker room.

Facility

Bourne v. Marty Gilman, Inc.   In *Bourne v. Marty Gilman, Inc.*, 452 F.3d 632 (7th Cir. 2006), the plaintiff was a 21-year-old Ball State student who joined a crowd that rushed the football field, celebrating Ball State's victory. A goalpost, torn down by the crowd, fell on the plaintiff's back, rendering him paraplegic. Ball State encouraged the crowd's action by flashing a sign on the scoreboard. In light of this action, Ball State settled the lawsuit with the plaintiff for $300,000. The remaining party was the manufacturer of the goalpost. The plaintiff claimed the goalpost was unreasonably dangerous and defective because it was foreseeable that fans would tear down the goalposts without understanding the risk, and so the risk should have been reduced using alternative designs. The court concluded the goalpost was not unreasonably dangerous or defectively designed.

Football stadiums should provide sufficient security so that spectators do not rush the fields after the games, and if this is allowed, goalposts should be protected. Goalposts that are well designed might also be erected so as to prevent this problem. Certainly, inviting fans to tear the goalposts down was a problem here.

Carbonara v. Texas Stadium Corporation   In *Carbonara v. Texas Stadium Corporation*, 244 S.W.3d 651, 2008 WL 192345 (Tex. App. 2008), the plaintiff, who attended a Dallas Cowboys football game, fell while descending on an escalator in Texas Stadium, sustaining head trauma. The plaintiff alleged that a trash can was improperly placed, which caused him to fall. There was also evidence that the plaintiff was sitting on the escalator rail and that his leg bumped another person riding the escalator, causing the plaintiff to fall over the side. The stadium operator was able to prevail on motion for summary judgment under the premises liability claim.

Escalators used in stadiums should be properly installed and maintained, with appropriate safety markings, in accordance with all applicable regulations. People who wear Crocs, flip-flops, and similar types of footwear run the risk of serious foot injury should the shoe become caught in the escalator.

Griem v. Town of Walpole

In *Griem v. Town of Walpole*, Not Reported in N.E.2d, WL 2678488 (Mass. Super. 2006), 10-year-old Douglas Griem was seated in the bleachers at a high school football game with his parents. After leaving his seat, Douglas was running on a walkway under the bleachers when he turned his head to see if his friends were following him. He suffered a severe neck injury when he collided with an angled support beam. The plaintiff, through his parents, sued the Town of Walpole for negligence; nuisance; willful, wanton, or reckless conduct; and loss of parental consortium. The court dismissed the nuisance claim by motion, but not the other allegations. The court noted that the case would proceed to trial on such allegations, or a settlement could be reached beforehand.

Perhaps the support posts could have been painted a bright color? If someone is running and not paying attention to where he is going, he is bound to become injured. This seems like a case in which the plaintiff assumed the risk and was negligent for his own actions.

Lewin v. Lutheran West High School

In *Lewin v. Lutheran West High School*, Slip Copy, WL 2269502 (Ohio App. 2007), the grandmother of one of the players at a high school football game sustained injury when she fell in a hole while walking from the football stadium to the parking lot after the game. The court determined that there was a dispute as to how the plaintiff fell, and so there was an issue of fact for a jury to decide. Hence, the high school was not entitled to summary judgment.

The grounds of any sport and recreation facility should be inspected and well maintained. If a hole is discovered, it should be repaired, warned against by use of cones or signage, or cordoned off.

Hazards

Gardner v. Town of Tonawanda

In *Gardner v. Town of Tonawanda*, 850 N.Y.S.2d 730, 850 N.Y.S.2d 730 (2008), the plaintiff was injured when he slipped on a baseball glove in an indoor recreational flag football game. The evidence established that the plaintiff was aware that cones and plastic flags were used as sideline markers but was not aware that a baseball glove was being used. There was no evidence presented that the baseball glove was more dangerous than the cones and plastic flags. The court concluded that the plaintiff assumed the risk, and the owner of the facility in which the game was played prevailed.

It is probably not a good idea to use objects other than cones and plastic flags as sideline markers, as this case illustrates.

Goforth v. State   In *Goforth v. State*, Slip Copy, WL 541820 (Tenn. Ct. App. 2007), the plaintiff filed a lawsuit arising out of injuries he sustained at football practice while on scholarship at East Tennessee State University. The field was muddy on the day of practice, and the plaintiff slipped and fell when he tackled another player. Testimony established that the team often plays on a muddy field, as well as in other adverse weather conditions. The evidence also revealed that the players were taught proper tackling techniques in that they were to keep their heads and eyes up. The plaintiff was not able to prove that the coaches of the team were negligent for continuing practice in the mud.

Many football and other sports fields would not see much use if mud was a deterrent. Players clearly assume the risk that they will slip and fall while playing football.

Harris v. Willie McCray, et al.   In *Harris v. Willie McCray, et al.*, 867 So. 2d 188 (Miss. 2003), Victor Harris, a football player for Jefferson County High School in Mississippi, was practicing with the team on a hot summer day. The coach, Willie McCray, allowed only one water break during the team's

Players generally assume the risk that they will slip and fall when playing on a slippery outdoor football field.

two-hour practice. Harris asked the coach if he could rest but was not allowed to do so. Harris suffered permanent injuries as a result of heatstroke, which he claimed the school district and coach were responsible for, in a lawsuit filed on his behalf. The defendants were successful in raising immunity defenses under a Mississippi statute because the acts of the coach were discretionary. It was noted that a coach exercises his discretion even when denying a player water on a hot summer day.

Coaches, athletic trainers, and other personnel should be trained to recognize and prevent heatstroke. As global warming causes increased temperatures, it is imperative to ensure athletes are well hydrated and monitored for heatstroke.

Henry v. Roosevelt School District

In *Henry v. Roosevelt School District*, 29 A.D.3d 954, 815 N.Y.S.2d 472 (2006), the plaintiff, an eighth-grade student, slipped and fell on a wet grass field while playing football in physical education class. The defendant prevailed in the action. The court did not provide the rationale for its conclusion that the school district was entitled to summary judgment.

It would have been interesting to understand the court's rationale in this case, as the plaintiff probably was required to participate in physical education and arguably did not assume the risk.

Shain v. Racine Raiders Football Club, Inc.

In *Shain v. Racine Raiders Football Club, Inc.*, 297 Wis. 2d 869, 726 N.W.2d 346 (2006), Shain, the coach of a youth football team, sustained a knee injury during a scrimmage. What is unusual about the incident is that it occurred during halftime at a minor league football game. Six youth football teams played in three scrimmages side by side on the football field. The field was divided into three fields, with the middle field sharing out-of-bounds lines with the other fields. Coach Shain was standing on the sidelines, between two of the games, when players behind him hit him during a tackle, knocking him down. The court concluded that a coach knows the risks of being on the sidelines during a football game. Defendants prevailed by motion for summary judgment because of Coach Shain's contributory negligence.

In this circumstance, it may not have been reasonable to have anyone stand on the sidelines between two games, making it difficult to coach the athletes without risking injury.

Stowers v. Clinton Central School Corp.

In *Stowers v. Clinton Central School Corp.*, 855 N.E.2d 739 (2006), 17-year-old high school junior Travis Stowers died from heatstroke after participating in football practice on a hot and humid day. The evidence established that practice was modified because of the weather conditions, and the players were urged to drink water and to inform the coaching staff if they were not feeling well. Travis had vomited during practice and was monitored and questioned about his health after he resumed play. His response was that he was fine. Toward the end of practice, Travis lost consciousness, which was never regained. The school prevailed at trial. On appeal, the court affirmed part of the decision and reversed the verdict as it related to a proposed jury instruction regarding the release form signed by the plaintiff and his mother. Essentially, the court did not properly instruct the jury that the release forms had to explicitly release the particular party (the high school) from negligence in order for the release form to be applicable.

In this case, the coaching staff seemed to take reasonable precautions to make sure that players were well hydrated and monitored for heatstroke.

Spectators

Bahrenburg v. AT & T Broadband, LLC   In *Bahrenburg v. AT & T Broadband, LLC*, 425 F. Supp. 2d 912 (N.D. Ill. 2006), a camera woman, hired as an independent contractor to film a high school football game, was standing by the end zone when a player collided with her, causing her to hit her head on the track next to the football field. The plaintiff sustained a brain injury and filed a lawsuit against Comcast, alleging she was not provided with the proper equipment, instructions, training, or warnings in relation to the assignment. Comcast filed a lawsuit against the school district for contribution, alleging that placing the football field and track close together, allowing the plaintiff to stand near the end zone, and failing to warn her was willful and wanton. The school district was not successful in having the matter dismissed by motion because of the allegations that they acted willfully and wantonly. If proven, they would fall under an exception of the state tort immunity statute.

In this case, it appears the allegation that the school district behaved willfully and wantonly prevented the case from being dismissed. The facts will likely reveal that there was no willful and wanton behavior on their part. The high cost of providing a defense to this lawsuit and the potential for an unfavorable verdict at trial will probably make settling the case out of court before trial reasonable.

Staff

Doe v. Fulton School Dist.   In *Doe v. Fulton School Dist.*, 35 A.D.3d 1194, 826 N.Y.S.2d 543 (2006), the plaintiff filed a lawsuit against Fulton School District, alleging it inadequately provided supervision in the locker room, which led to their eighth-grade son being sexually assaulted by teammates on his football team. Evidence was presented that the players were not supervised in the locker room for a period of 20 to 30 minutes, and during that time period, the boys engaged in aggressive and reckless horseplay.

The court determined that a jury would have to decide whether the school district should have reasonably foreseen the consequence of failing to provide locker room supervision at the time of the incident.

Locker room supervision would likely have prevented the incident in this case. It is important to consider whether there is sufficient locker room supervision and whether there are backup supervisors in the event someone becomes ill or has another reason for leaving the area.

Violations

Verni v. Stevens   In *Verni v. Stevens*, 387 N.J. Super. 160, 903 A.2d 475 (2006), several plaintiffs were injured in a car accident, apparently caused by a drunk driver, Daniel Lanzaro, who had been drinking beer at Giants Stadium before the accident. The plaintiffs filed suit against the New Jersey Sports and Exposition Authority, the New York Giants, Giants Stadium, Aramark Sports and Entertainment Group, the bars that served Lanzaro alcohol after the game, and others. Lanzaro started drinking when he was tailgating before the game. Lanzaro admitted that he guzzled beer he purchased from the stadium concession stand and by the first quarter was drunk. Before halftime, he purchased at least four beers by tipping the server in order to circumvent the stadium limit of two beers. At the beginning of the third quarter, Lanzaro left the stadium. He drank a beer in the parking lot before

Rules about alcohol consumption must be in place to help protect spectators, staff, and players.

driving to a bar, where he stayed for 40 minutes. After a stop at a fast food restaurant, Lanzaro caused the accident that led to the lawsuit.

During the course of trial, it was established that there is a two-beer limit at Giants Stadium and that alcohol servers are prohibited from serving alcohol to visibly intoxicated patrons. The servers were provided training about alcohol awareness, which included identifying intoxicated individuals. The jury verdict awarded compensatory damages of more than $53 million and punitive damages of $65 million. On appeal, it was determined that there were multiple errors at trial, so the judgment was reversed and remanded for a new trial. A number of the defendants were able to enter settlement agreements with the plaintiffs before trial.

This case illustrates the importance of regulating alcohol consumption at games. Although it is desirable to make money selling beer and allowing patrons to enjoy their experience, heavy consumption of alcohol leads to security issues, violence, and motor vehicle accidents, increasing loss exposure.

FOOTBALL SAFETY CONSIDERATIONS

These reported appellate cases span a wide area of risk management and safety concerns as they relate to football, but they could occur in other sports as well. Understanding the potential for injury allows safeguards to be taken in order to prevent problems in the future. To facilitate your organization's safety standards for American football, please use all the forms on pages 134 to 143.

An important note should be made about football safety. All players must be taught the proper tackling techniques and understand how to use them so they can avoid head and neck injuries. The National Athletic Trainers' Association produced a 14-minute DVD titled *Heads Up: Reducing the Risk of Head and Neck Injuries in Football*, funded by the Andrews Institute for Orthopaedics & Sports Medicine. This DVD teaches proper techniques for players initiating contact with their opponents: head up and shoulders down. The DVD can be downloaded for free at http://nata.org/consumer/headsup.htm.

SUMMARY

Football is known to be a dangerous sport, resulting in significant injuries that might sideline players temporarily or prevent players from ever playing again. The violent nature of the game is part of what makes it exciting, and football would certainly not be the same if physical contact between players was diminished or eliminated. Despite the potential for injury, with sufficient care in maintaining the facility and equipment and monitoring safe play and behavior, fewer injuries are possible and lawsuits can be prevented.

FOOTBALL FIELDS

When assessing the risk of a football field, the layout and configuration should be evaluated as set forth below.

Considerations	Yes or No (check one)	Notes for follow-up
Is there a track surrounding the field?	❑ Yes ❑ No	
Will there be runners using the track during football practice?	❑ Yes ❑ No	
Are there other track and field events being practiced in close proximity to the football field?	❑ Yes ❑ No	
Does your field overlap with other fields?	❑ Yes ❑ No	
Are there sufficient barriers between the field and vehicular traffic?	❑ Yes ❑ No	
Have apparatuses used in other sports been left on the playing field or in the immediate vicinity?	❑ Yes ❑ No	
Are there any environmental concerns, such as proximity to pollutants or environmental hazards?	❑ Yes ❑ No	
Are there other considerations for football fields?	❑ Yes ❑ No	

From Katharine M. Nohr, 2009, *Managing Risk in Sport and Recreation: The Essential Guide for Loss Prevention* (Champaign, IL: Human Kinetics).

INSPECTION OF THE FOOTBALL FIELD

Inspecting the football field for defects requires evaluation and examination of the ground, fencing, grass or turf, lines used to mark the field, lighting, drainage system, and sprinkler system. Defects in these areas have been known to cause injury. You will need to address the following questions.

Considerations	Yes or No (check one)	Notes for follow-up
Are there holes in the ground or protruding objects that are obvious or concealed by grass or synthetic turf?	❏ Yes ❏ No	
Does the field have an adequate drainage system?	❏ Yes ❏ No	
Will sprinkler heads on a grass field pose a hazard?	❏ Yes ❏ No	
Are the pylons in the end zones made of material that will not cause injury if a player runs into them?	❏ Yes ❏ No	
Are the lines marking the field made out of any substance that could cause injury to a player's eyes or respiratory system?	❏ Yes ❏ No	
Has the football field been inspected in 10-yard increments before the practice or game by walking across the grass and looking for balls, equipment, garbage, glass, rakes, shovels, or any other objects that should be picked up and cleared away before play begins?	❏ Yes ❏ No	
Have objects been cleared from the field before play begins?	❏ Yes ❏ No	
If the field is made of artificial turf, has it been checked for exposed and unmatched seams and any other irregularities in the turf?	❏ Yes ❏ No	
Has the grass been mowed before the event?	❏ Yes ❏ No	
Have sprinkler heads, irrigation stand pipes, and drainage hole covers been inspected to make sure they will not pose a hazard to players?	❏ Yes ❏ No	
Have rocks and clumped mud been removed from the field to eliminate tripping hazards?	❏ Yes ❏ No	
Have all tripping hazards been eliminated before play begins?	❏ Yes ❏ No	
Are there other considerations for inspection of the football field?	❏ Yes ❏ No	

From Katharine M. Nohr, 2009, *Managing Risk in Sport and Recreation: The Essential Guide for Loss Prevention* (Champaign, IL: Human Kinetics).

STRUCTURES ON THE FOOTBALL FIELD

Goalposts and sideline markers can pose a hazard to players. The following questions should be asked in this regard.

Considerations	Yes or No (check one)	Notes for follow-up
Are the goalposts in good condition?	❑ Yes ❑ No	
Are the goalposts sturdy and well anchored?	❑ Yes ❑ No	
Can the goalposts be secured so they cannot be torn down or tampered with when not being used?	❑ Yes ❑ No	
Are the goalposts located in the back of the end zone so as to prevent injury from players running into them?	❑ Yes ❑ No	
Have the goalposts been sufficiently padded to protect players?	❑ Yes ❑ No	
Are the sideline markers made of material that will likely cause injury to players?	❑ Yes ❑ No	
Are the sideline markers padded and made of a thin material with flat (rather than spiked) bottoms?	❑ Yes ❑ No	
Are there other considerations for structures on the field?	❑ Yes ❑ No	

From Katharine M. Nohr, 2009, *Managing Risk in Sport and Recreation: The Essential Guide for Loss Prevention* (Champaign, IL: Human Kinetics).

PREPARING THE FOOTBALL FIELD FOR PLAY

After inspections have been performed and documented, defects and hazards should be repaired or removed before play begins. The following questions should be asked when preparing the field for play.

Considerations	Yes or No (check one)	Notes for follow-up
Have lines on the field been marked with slaked lime that could cause serious eye damage to players when tackled?	❏ Yes ❏ No	
Have you made sure the substance (chalk or paint) used to mark lines on the field will not be hazardous to players?	❏ Yes ❏ No	
If a hazard cannot be corrected before play, has it been determined whether the field is safe for play or whether to cancel play?	❏ Yes ❏ No	
If the field is safe for play but a hazard exists on the field, have clear and adequate warnings been provided to all players and other persons who will be utilizing the area of play (e.g., coaches, referees, and other officials)?	❏ Yes ❏ No	
Are extra balls and other equipment removed from the field during play?	❏ Yes ❏ No	
If the weather is excessively hot and humid or if there is lightning or rain, has the game or practice been relocated or canceled to prevent injuries or illnesses?	❏ Yes ❏ No	
Are there other considerations for preparing the field for play?	❏ Yes ❏ No	

From Katharine M. Nohr, 2009, *Managing Risk in Sport and Recreation: The Essential Guide for Loss Prevention* (Champaign, IL: Human Kinetics).

PLAYING ON FIELDS THAT ARE USED FOR OTHER PURPOSES BESIDES FOOTBALL

Sometimes injuries occur when a field is used for a sport it is not intended for. If the structure of the field or objects or infrastructure that is part of the field can cause injury when it is being used for football, you should consider moving your game or practice to a more appropriate field. The following questions should be addressed.

Considerations	Yes or No (check one)	Notes for follow-up
Is the field designed and intended for football? If No, list what other sports or activities the field is used for in the Notes column.	❏ Yes ❏ No	
Has the field been properly designed for dual purposes? If No, list what hazards might exist if you use the field for football.	❏ Yes ❏ No	
Have all dangerous items or equipment been removed or separated from the field?	❏ Yes ❏ No	
Are there other considerations for fields that are used for other purposes besides football?	❏ Yes ❏ No	

From Katharine M. Nohr, 2009, *Managing Risk in Sport and Recreation: The Essential Guide for Loss Prevention* (Champaign, IL: Human Kinetics).

LIGHTING OF FOOTBALL FIELD
AND SPECTATOR FACILITIES

If football is played in the dark, it is important to make sure there is sufficient illumination. The following questions can be asked on this topic.

Considerations	Yes or No (check one)	Notes for follow-up
Are the lights illuminating the field turned on before dusk?	❑ Yes ❑ No	
Do the lights provide proper illumination of the field (i.e., not too bright or too dim)?	❑ Yes ❑ No	
Have light poles been inspected for stability and safety?	❑ Yes ❑ No	
Are the bleachers or stands and other spectator areas sufficiently illuminated?	❑ Yes ❑ No	
Are there other considerations for the lighting of field and spectator facilities?	❑ Yes ❑ No	

From Katharine M. Nohr, 2009, *Managing Risk in Sport and Recreation: The Essential Guide for Loss Prevention* (Champaign, IL: Human Kinetics).

FOOTBALL HELMETS

Football helmets are made of hard plastic that is lined with absorbent material, such as air cells or foam. Each helmet should have a removable face mask that will protect the player's face from injury. The quarterback's helmet will likely have an earpiece, allowing the coach to communicate plays to him. The following questions address helmet fit and safety.

Considerations	Yes or No (check one)	Notes for follow-up
Are there helmets available to fit each player?	❑ Yes ❑ No	
Have the helmets been adjusted so they fit each player properly?	❑ Yes ❑ No	
Has the person adjusting the helmets been sufficiently trained in doing so?	❑ Yes ❑ No	
Do helmets have an NOCSAE or equivalent safety seal?	❑ Yes ❑ No	
Do the helmets provide full coverage to the ears and jaw?	❑ Yes ❑ No	
Do the helmets have face guards?	❑ Yes ❑ No	
Are the helmets light enough so as not to cause injury?	❑ Yes ❑ No	
Have players been instructed as to how to care for their helmets?	❑ Yes ❑ No	
Have players been instructed not to throw or sit on their helmets?	❑ Yes ❑ No	
Have players been instructed not to modify their helmets in any way?	❑ Yes ❑ No	
Is an air pump or other device available during games and practices to reinflate air bladders in the helmets?	❑ Yes ❑ No	
Are helmets inspected on a regular basis by a helmet reconditioning company or comparable experts to determine if they are in good condition?	❑ Yes ❑ No	
Are the helmets designed for the age and experience level of athletes using them (e.g., junior high school, high school, college or professional)?	❑ Yes ❑ No	
Are there other considerations for helmets?	❑ Yes ❑ No	

From Katharine M. Nohr, 2009, *Managing Risk in Sport and Recreation: The Essential Guide for Loss Prevention* (Champaign, IL: Human Kinetics).

PROTECTIVE FOOTBALL EQUIPMENT

Football players have to protect themselves from injuries that might be sustained while tackling and being tackled. Because of the full body contact and potentially violent nature of the game, it is important that each player be fully equipped with well-fitted protective equipment that is free from defects. The following questions should be asked in relation to protective equipment.

Considerations	Yes or No (check one)	Notes for follow-up
Are there shoulder pads, neck support pads, shin guards, mouth guards, rib pads, hip pads, lumbar pads, forearm pads, knee pads, thigh pads, and athletic supporters available to fit each player?	❑ Yes ❑ No	
Has the equipment been adjusted so that it fits each player properly?	❑ Yes ❑ No	
Has the person adjusting the equipment been sufficiently trained in doing so?	❑ Yes ❑ No	
Are there other considerations for protective equipment?	❑ Yes ❑ No	

From Katharine M. Nohr, 2009, *Managing Risk in Sport and Recreation: The Essential Guide for Loss Prevention* (Champaign, IL: Human Kinetics).

OTHER FOOTBALL EQUIPMENT ISSUES

All equipment that is used in football should be subject to scrutiny. Make sure players are using safe balls, wearing proper cleats, and not wearing anything, such as jewelry, that could injure themselves or other players. You should ask the following questions.

Considerations	Yes or No (check one)	Notes for follow-up
Will players need to wear cleats? If Yes, list what type of cleats the players will need to wear in the Notes column.	❏ Yes ❏ No	
Are the cleats appropriate for the age level and field surface?	❏ Yes ❏ No	
Are players instructed to remove jewelry and watches?	❏ Yes ❏ No	
Are there other considerations for other equipment issues?	❏ Yes ❏ No	

From Katharine M. Nohr, 2009, *Managing Risk in Sport and Recreation: The Essential Guide for Loss Prevention* (Champaign, IL: Human Kinetics).

INSPECTION OF FOOTBALL SPECTATOR FACILITIES

Before football games, parking lots may be used for tailgating parties, where spectators consume alcoholic beverages and food. People may be grilling food, which could cause a fire or burn injuries. Special attention should be given to areas where tailgating parties are held. Your parking lot and surrounding grounds should be inspected and monitored and the following questions asked.

Considerations	Yes or No (check one)	Notes for follow-up
Is security adequate in the parking lot and surrounding grounds?	❑ Yes ❑ No	
Is there proper lighting in the parking lot and surrounding grounds?	❑ Yes ❑ No	
Is the parking lot well marked so that traffic is flowing safely?	❑ Yes ❑ No	
Are there adequate personnel to assist with parking?	❑ Yes ❑ No	
Are parking personnel wearing bright and reflective vests or clothing with safety flashlights?	❑ Yes ❑ No	
Have parking personnel received training as to how to safely perform their functions?	❑ Yes ❑ No	
Are there slippery areas or objects that might cause a person to slip or fall?	❑ Yes ❑ No	
Have warning signs been erected to inform visitors and others of slippery areas and obstructions?	❑ Yes ❑ No	
Is consumption of alcohol allowed in the parking lot?	❑ Yes ❑ No	
Are there any city or county laws or ordinances that pertain to the consumption of alcohol in the parking lot?	❑ Yes ❑ No	
If consumption of alcohol is allowed, have the necessary permits been acquired?	❑ Yes ❑ No	
May patrons bring coolers or alcohol into the facility?	❑ Yes ❑ No	
Is cooking or grilling allowed in the parking lot?	❑ Yes ❑ No	
Are there any city or county laws or ordinances that pertain to cooking or grilling in the parking lot?	❑ Yes ❑ No	

(continued)

From Katharine M. Nohr, 2009, *Managing Risk in Sport and Recreation: The Essential Guide for Loss Prevention* (Champaign, IL: Human Kinetics).

Inspection of Football Spectator Facilities *(continued)*

Considerations	Yes or No (check one)	Notes for follow-up
If cooking or grilling is allowed, have the necessary permits been acquired?	❑ Yes ❑ No	
Is tailgating limited to ticket holders?	❑ Yes ❑ No	
Is tailgating restricted to certain hours?	❑ Yes ❑ No	
Are there other considerations for inspection of spectator facilities?	❑ Yes ❑ No	

From Katharine M. Nohr, 2009, *Managing Risk in Sport and Recreation: The Essential Guide for Loss Prevention* (Champaign, IL: Human Kinetics).

10

Baseball and Softball

A baseball game is simply a nervous breakdown divided into nine innings.

—Earl Wilson

Baseball is well known for injuries to spectators and players when they are hit by balls traveling at high velocity. Baseball bats have also been known to cause injury when people step in their paths. Litigation has arisen out of these hazards but also from slips and falls in ballparks and other incidents.

BASEBALL AND SOFTBALL LAWSUITS AND SETTLEMENTS

There have been a few reported baseball and softball cases in which the plaintiffs received significant settlements for injuries. The following are some examples of jury verdicts:

- A young child sitting on his mother's lap suffered a skull fracture when he was hit by a baseball while watching a baseball game. The plaintiff sued a public entity, claiming the fence was too low to protect spectators from being hit by baseballs. Although the child experienced a good recovery, the parties settled the case for $900,000.

- A jury awarded $2.7 million to stockbroker Linda Postlethwaite, 48, who was hit between the eyes with a wild pitch thrown by Mitch Williams of the Philadelphia Phillies during a Phillies–Marlins game on August 8, 1993. Williams had been warming up in the bullpen when he threw the pitch that hit the plaintiff, who was not protected by a net; the net had been lowered from 13 feet (4 m) to 8 feet (2.4 m) to give the fans a better view. The plaintiff was sitting on the third-base side near the bullpen and so was not protected by the net. As a result of the errant pitch, she sustained a broken nose. She still suffers from headaches and lack of concentration and has not been able to work since the incident. The Marlins' owner, who ordered that the net be lowered further, was found to be 36.5 percent liable; Robbie Stadium Corp. was found to be 31.5 percent liable; the Marlins were assessed 27.5 percent liability; and the Phillies were found to be 4.5 percent liable. The case was confidentially settled for a lower amount.

- A settlement of $13,500 was reached between an 11-year-old boy who was struck by baseballs in the defendant's batting cage. The boy sustained facial contusions, a fractured jaw, and loss of teeth as a result of the alleged negligence of the defendant, who, according to the plaintiff's allegations, did not provide helmets or operate the batting cage safely and reasonably.

A number of published appellate court decisions address various causes of injuries in baseball and softball. The following baseball and softball cases address circumstances in which plaintiffs were hit by a car while chasing a foul ball, hit by a baseball as a spectator or a player, pummeled by an aggressive fan in a T-shirt launch, injured from slipping and falling in a stadium, hit by a flying pitcher's mound, struck by a bat or a fast-moving ball launched by an aluminum bat, injured when sliding into base, hurt while traveling with the team, or injured because of a defect in the field.

Equipment

Baggs ex rel. Baggs v. Little League Baseball, Inc.

In *Baggs ex rel. Baggs v. Little League Baseball, Inc.*, 17 Misc. 3d 212, 840 N.Y.S.2d 529 (2007), the plaintiff, a 12-year-old boy, sustained facial fractures when he was struck in the head by a line drive after he pitched a ball to a 13-year-old boy who was using an aluminum bat at a Little League baseball tournament. The plaintiff alleged that the defendant was negligent in allowing use of an aluminum bat without increasing the distance between the pitcher's mound and the home plate and for allowing a 13-year-old to play in his division. The court addressed the jurisdiction of the case, denying the defendant's motion for summary judgment.

The facts in this case are illustrative of the issue concerning use of aluminum bats rather than wooden bats in baseball.

Grappendorf v. Pleasant Grove City

In *Grappendorf v. Pleasant Grove City*, 173 P.3d 166 (Utah 2007), a 13-year-old boy died from massive brain injuries caused by a movable pitcher's mound that struck him in the head when it was projected into the air by a gust of wind. The court determined that the defendant was not immune from the lawsuit under the applicable governmental immunity statute.

Any objects that could easily be launched by wind should be secured to prevent injury. If a windstorm is anticipated, loose items should be secured.

McCabe v. City of New York

In *McCabe v. City of New York*, 45 A.D.3d 541, 847 N.Y.S.2d 92 (2007), the plaintiff was practicing with his Little League baseball team and injured his ankle when sliding into second base, which he claimed was not movable. Testimony was established that the base was movable. The defendant was dismissed by summary judgment motion.

This case illustrates the potential danger of bases that are not movable.

Facility

Cohen v. Sterling Mets, LP

In *Cohen v. Sterling Mets, LP*, 17 Misc. 3d 218, 840 N.Y.S.2d 527 (2007), a concessions vendor employed by Shea Stadium was injured by a spectator who dove for a T-shirt launched into the stands as part of a promotional activity. The court reasoned that the T-shirt launch was similar to a ball being tossed into the stands. It was not considered a necessary part of the game, but was customary. The defendant's motion for summary judgment was granted.

There are clearly risks to throwing T-shirts and other items into the stands. Before doing this, it would be reasonable to caution the spectators not to dive for items and to pay attention when items are thrown. Make sure the items are not heavy and will not likely cause any injury if they hit a spectator who is not paying attention.

DeRosa v. City of New York

In *DeRosa v. City of New York*, 30 A.D.3d 323, 817 N.Y.S.2d 282 (2006), the plaintiff was injured when he fell down stairs that led to Monument Park in Yankee Stadium. At the time of the incident, the plaintiff was carrying a mug with one hand and could not grip the handrail because it was too close to the wall. The plaintiff's expert testified that the stairway violated applicable building codes. The director of stadium operations for Yankee Stadium testified that there had been no previous complaints or incidents related to the handrails. He also stated that there were no repair or maintenance records in relation to the stairs. A stadium security guard testified that he observed the incident and believed the plaintiff's knee gave out and did not see him reach for the handrail as alleged. The defendants succeeded in a motion for summary judgment. It was determined they did not have notice of a dangerous condition and that the portion of the building code the plaintiff relied on did not apply to the stairwell because the stairs did not lead outside.

Wherever there are stairs, people will fall. However, it is important to make sure that all applicable building codes are adhered to and that stairs are inspected and kept clean, dry, and free of trip and slip hazards.

Frazier v. City of New York

In *Frazier v. City of New York*, 47 A.D.3d 757, 850 N.Y.S.3d 552 (2008), the plaintiff was attending a baseball game at Shea Stadium when he was injured from a slip and fall on a ramp. According to the testimony of the plaintiff's wife, the plaintiff may have stepped on a crushed hotdog, complete with bun and condiments, which may have been on the ramp for at least one hour before the incident. The court concluded that there was insufficient evidence to support this. The defendant established that they did not know of the slippery condition and did not create it and so were granted summary judgment.

Sport and recreation facilities should maintain cleaning and sweeping schedules, especially where food from concessions is likely to land on the floor. In some locations, security cameras may be used and could be helpful as evidence when a fall is captured on camera.

Hawkins v. United States Sports Association, Inc.

In *Hawkins v. United States Sports Association, Inc.*, 633 S.E.2d 31 (W. Va. 2006), the plaintiff, while playing in a softball tournament, injured his knee on a 12-inch (30 cm) long, 2 inch (5 cm) diameter PVC pipe while sliding toward first base. The pipe had been installed by coaches, employed by the Marion County Board of Education, to anchor bases for girls' softball, without informing anyone or warning players it had been buried on the field. Hawkins' medical expenses exceeded $56,000. He filed suit against the United States Sports Association, Inc.; Marion County Board of Education; Marion County Slow Pitch Softball Association; Marion County Softball Association; and the City of Fairmont, claiming negligence for failure to discover the pipe and make the field safe for play. Discovery revealed that the field had been inspected before the game, and the field had been swept and raked in advance of the competition. During the inspections and field preparation, the plastic pipe went unnoticed. The court dismissed all the defendants from the case except Marion County Board of Education, because the others did not know the pipe was buried in the ground. There was also no evidence that they were negligent in preparing the field for play or in not finding the pipe during their pregame inspections.

This case illustrates the importance of warning athletes of hazards on or near the playing field.

Haymon v. Pettit

In *Haymon v. Pettit*, 37 A.D.3d 1194, 829 N.Y.S.2d 766 (2007), the plaintiff was a 14-year-old boy who was standing outside a baseball stadium for the purpose of catching foul balls hit out of the ballpark. The plaintiff was hit by a car and injured when he ran into the street after a ball. The plaintiff filed a lawsuit against the owner of the stadium. The court concluded that the owner did not have a duty to prevent the plaintiff from running into the street after foul balls, and so summary judgment was granted in his favor.

If children are known to catch foul balls outside a stadium where there is motor vehicle traffic, the stadium management may wish to have security guards monitor the area or have signs erected prohibiting such conduct. This is also true for other sport and recreation facilities where children may skateboard or engage in other potentially dangerous activity.

Hazards

Avila v. Citrus Community College District   In *Avila v. Citrus Community College District*, 38 Cal. 4th 148, 131 P.3d 383 (2006), the plaintiff played baseball for his community college team, the Rio Hondo Roadrunners. In 2001, the Roadrunners were playing a game against the Citrus Community College Owls. One of the Roadrunners pitchers hit a Citrus College batter. During the next inning, when Avila was up to bat, a Citrus College pitcher cracked Avila's batting helmet when he hit Avila in the head with a pitch. As a consequence of his head injury, Avila was in pain, felt dizzy, and staggered. Nevertheless, the team manager instructed Avila to run to first base and then told him to stay in the game even after he complained of pain. A pinch runner was used when Avila made it to second base, allowing Avila to leave the game. His injuries were not attended to during the game. The plaintiff sued his manager, both schools, the helmet manufacturer, and other entities. The court concluded that (1) the college was not protected by governmental immunity statutes; (2) the college owed the plaintiff a duty not to increase the inherent harm of the sport; and (3) there was no breach of duty. The plaintiff assumed the risk of being intentionally hit while at bat as an inherent risk of baseball. The court found that the college satisfied its duty by replacing Avila with a pinch hitter.

Team managers, coaches, and other personnel should be cautious when players have sustained potential head injuries. Even if the injury does not appear to be serious, seeking a doctor's care before allowing the athlete to continue play is the best way to avoid aggravation of an injury and a lawsuit.

Harting v. Dayton Dragons Professional Baseball Club, LLC   In *Harting v. Dayton Dragons Professional Baseball Club, LLC*, 171 Ohio App. 3d 319, 870 N.E.2d 766 (2007), the plaintiff was attending a baseball game at which a chicken mascot was entertaining the spectators. The plaintiff was hit in the head and rendered unconscious by a foul ball when her attention was focused on the chicken. The baseball park had made warnings to spectators about the dangers of foul balls over the loudspeaker during the game. Tickets for the game also contained a warning that the ticketholder assumed the risk of injury from batted balls as well as other specified risks. The court did not absolve the plaintiff from her own responsibility to pay attention to the game because of the distraction caused by the chicken mascot. The court concluded that the plaintiff assumed the risk of the baseball game, and the defendant was dismissed by summary judgment.

If the tickets to your events do not already provide a warning that the ticketholder assumes the risk of injury, adding this language could serve as a viable defense in future litigation.

Maisonave v. Newark Bears Professional Baseball Club,

Inc. In *Maisonave v. Newark Bears Professional Baseball Club, Inc.*, 185 N.J. 70, 881 A.2d 700 (2005), the plaintiff was injured in the eye when a foul ball struck him while he was standing in Riverfront Stadium's mezzanine while

Spectators should be warned about the dangers of foul balls so they can make an informed decision about assuming the risks involved with their presence at a game.

attending a minor league baseball game. The incident occurred while the plaintiff was standing at a beverage cart adjacent to the first-base line, which was beyond the protection of protective netting. The plaintiff's right eye socket was fractured in numerous places, resulting in numbness, drooping of the eye, scarring, and sinus problems. The plaintiff sued the Newark Bears Professional Baseball Club, Inc., and Gourmet Dining Services, which provides food and beverage services for the stadium. The court addressed the application of the limited duty rule, which is a specialized negligence standard protecting stadium owners and operators. Courts had previously required that stadium operators offer protected seating areas and that a spectator who chose an unprotected seat assumed the risk since errant balls are an inherent part of the game. The court in this case concluded that the limited duty rule applies only to injuries occurring in the stands. When guests leave the stands they let down their guard, no longer watching the game or looking for foul balls, and so the owner has a duty of reasonable care, just as any other business would.

Are concession stands situated so that those purchasing food and beverages could be hit by errant baseballs? Moving concession stands to an area where balls are not likely to land or adding protective netting could prevent injuries to patrons.

Reyes v. City of New York

In *Reyes v. City of New York*, 15 Misc. 3d 690, 835 N.Y.S.2d 852 (2007), the plaintiff was struck in the face and injured by a foul ball in the third-base dugout while coaching a high school baseball team at a city park. The defendant was able to prove that the plaintiff, who was an experienced coach and baseball player, understood the risk of being in the dugout. However, according to expert affidavits, the fencing to protect the dugout was in a state of disrepair and violated safety standards, creating a hazardous condition that contributed to the coach's injury. This disrepair was not inherent in the game of baseball, and so the court denied the defendant's motion for summary judgment. The case was ordered to proceed to trial to determine if the City of New York was negligent.

Fencing used for protection of any spectators or players should be regularly inspected and kept in good repair.

Roberts v. Boys and Girls Republic, Inc.

In *Roberts v. Boys and Girls Republic, Inc.*, 850 N.Y.S.2d 38 (2008), the plaintiff was watching her son play baseball when she walked near a player taking a practice swing outside the baseball diamond. The plaintiff was injured when she was struck by the bat. The question posed by the court was whether the plaintiff assumed the risk of being injured. The court concluded that the plaintiff did assume the obvious risk of being hit by the baseball bat. She was also precluded from recovery based on her theory that the defendant was negligent in marking or designing the baseball field.

Spectators can pose a problem when they enter playing areas. As much as possible, spectators should be kept out of the field of play by signage, barriers, security, and other personnel for their own protection.

Staff

Elston v. Howland Local Schools

In *Elston v. Howland Local Schools*, 113 Ohio St. 3d 314, 865 N.E.2d 845 (2007), a 15-year-old boy was struck in the head by a baseball while engaged in a short-toss practice drill using an L-screen, which is a protective device used to protect a pitcher from being hit directly with a batted ball. The boy applied ice to his head and boarded the bus to the team's baseball game. His parents decided to take him to a hospital, where he underwent brain surgery; four titanium plates and screws were implanted in his head. The plaintiff filed a lawsuit against his coach and his school for negligence and failure to supervise. The school filed a motion for summary judgment, which was granted. The plaintiff appealed, and the appellate court reversed the lower court's decision so that the matter would have to proceed to trial.

In this case, it appears that the coach, trainer, or other team personnel allowed the boy to board the team bus to go to the game rather than immediately seek medical assistance. Whenever there is a suspected head injury, medical treatment should be sought, as the parents did here.

Medical treatment should be sought for all suspected head injuries.

Murphy v. Polytechnic University   In *Murphy v. Polytechnic University*, 18 Misc. 3d 623, 850 N.Y.S.2d 339 (2007), the plaintiff sustained injuries when the university softball team head coach struck her in the face while demonstrating a batting skill. The defendant's motion for summary judgment was denied because the plaintiff may not have foreseen the risk of being hit by a coach swinging a bat. She likely would conclude that the coach would ensure he could safely swing the bat, especially since he had 25 years of experience.

Whether a coach or other personnel is swinging a bat, a golf club, or a tennis racket, it is important to exercise care to make sure no one is in striking distance. Novice players, children, and spectators are particularly susceptible to injury because they may not fully understand the need to keep their distance.

Regan v. Mutual of Omaha Ins. Co.   In *Regan v. Mutual of Omaha Ins. Co.*, 375 Ill. App. 3d 956, 874 N.E.2d 246 (2007), a university baseball team took a trip to Florida to participate in a baseball tournament. On the team's only day off, the plaintiff dove into a wave in the ocean adjacent to the team's hotel, sustaining a spinal cord injury. This lawsuit arose out of an insurance coverage issue. The plaintiff was seeking coverage under a catastrophic athletic injury insurance program provided to members of the National Association of Intercollegiate Athletics. The question was whether the incident was covered under the definition of "covered travel." The court concluded that there was coverage under the policy.

People who are not familiar with the power of waves and the dangers of swimming and surfing in the ocean face potential catastrophic injury. Even supervision in this type of situation would not necessarily have prevented the injury. Education about the power of the ocean and inquiry of local water safety experts about a particular area are helpful. Before entering the ocean, it is a good idea to watch the local people to see how they behave in relation to the particular spot and to ask lifeguards if there are any dangers to be aware of. Watching for and heeding warning flags and signs regarding jellyfish, breaks, drop-offs, and other dangers are imperative.

BASEBALL AND SOFTBALL SAFETY CONSIDERATIONS

These reported appellate cases span a wide area of risk management and safety concerns as they relate to baseball and softball, but they could occur in other sports as well. Understanding the potential for injury allows safeguards to be taken to prevent problems in the future. To facilitate your organization's safety standards in baseball and softball, please use all the forms on pages 155 to 166.

SUMMARY

The published appellate court decisions illustrate the many ways a player or spectator can be injured in relation to the game of baseball or softball. Many injuries, especially caused to spectators, can be avoided by careful attention to the game and location of the ball. Spectators can be warned about the possibility of balls being hit in the stands. However, even players paying careful attention to the game are hit by very fast-moving balls, leading to significant injuries. By establishing a comprehensive risk management plan, a baseball or softball team or organization can hopefully avoid injury and resulting insurance claims and lawsuits.

INSPECTION OF THE BASEBALL AND SOFTBALL DIAMOND AND FACILITIES

Before using a baseball or softball diamond, it is prudent to inspect it to ascertain whether there are any defects that can be corrected or should at least be avoided during the course of play. It may be prudent to consider another location if defects are particularly hazardous. Inspection for defects requires evaluation and examination of the backstop, ground, dugouts, fencing, dirt and grass, lighting, drainage system, and sprinkler system. You will need to address the following questions.

Considerations	Yes or No (check one)	Notes for follow-up
Is the backstop in good condition?	❑ Yes ❑ No	
Are there holes in the ground or protruding objects that are obvious or concealed by grass?	❑ Yes ❑ No	
Is the batting cage in good condition?	❑ Yes ❑ No	Where is the batting cage located?
Does the type of dirt used in the field pose any hazards?	❑ Yes ❑ No	
Does the dirt contain rocks or hardened dirt and clumped mud?	❑ Yes ❑ No	
Is the dirt so soft that players will sink into it?	❑ Yes ❑ No	
If you will be playing at night, are the lights bright enough to illuminate the infield and outfield?	❑ Yes ❑ No	
Does the field have an adequate drainage system?	❑ Yes ❑ No	
Will sprinkler heads pose a hazard?	❑ Yes ❑ No	
Are dugouts located a reasonable distance from home plate and the playing field?	❑ Yes ❑ No	
Are dugouts protected by fencing?	❑ Yes ❑ No	
Has someone performed an inspection of the field before the practice or game by walking across the grass and looking for bats, balls, garbage, glass, rakes, shovels, or any other objects?	❑ Yes ❑ No	
Have all bats, balls, garbage, glass, rakes, shovels, and other objects been cleared from the field before play begins?	❑ Yes ❑ No	

(continued)

From Katharine M. Nohr, 2009, *Managing Risk in Sport and Recreation: The Essential Guide for Loss Prevention* (Champaign, IL: Human Kinetics).

Inspection of the Baseball and Softball Diamonds and Facilities *(continued)*

Considerations	Yes or No (check one)	Notes for follow-up
Have sprinkler heads, irrigation stand pipes, and drainage hole covers been situated to make sure they will not pose a hazard to players?	❑ Yes ❑ No	
Have rocks and clumped mud been removed from the field to eliminate tripping hazards?	❑ Yes ❑ No	
Has dirt been raked so as to loosen it and dirt checked for tripping and falling hazards?	❑ Yes ❑ No	
Have all tripping hazards been eliminated before play begins?	❑ Yes ❑ No	
Has the pitcher's mound been inspected for depressions that could pose a tripping hazard?	❑ Yes ❑ No	
Has a rake been made available for each pitcher?	❑ Yes ❑ No	
Have pitchers been informed that a rake is available so they can alter the mound in accordance with their need?	❑ Yes ❑ No	
Do you suspend play if the pitcher's mound requires more substantial repair?	❑ Yes ❑ No	
Has the batter's box been inspected for depressions that could pose a tripping hazard?	❑ Yes ❑ No	
Is a rake available for each batter?	❑ Yes ❑ No	
Have batters been informed that a rake is available so they can alter the batter's box in accordance with their needs?	❑ Yes ❑ No	
Is play suspended if the batter's box requires more substantial repair?	❑ Yes ❑ No	
Have the bleachers (and other areas where spectators will sit or congregate) and public areas been inspected for slippery surfaces, holes in netting or fences, broken benches, or other hazards?	❑ Yes ❑ No	
Has the fencing surrounding the playing field and the backstop been inspected for any holes or defects?	❑ Yes ❑ No	
Has the dugout been inspected for slippery surfaces, holes in protective fencing, or other hazards?	❑ Yes ❑ No	
Has the screening or netting in place to protect spectators been inspected for holes or defects and to make sure it will perform as intended?	❑ Yes ❑ No	
Are there other considerations for inspection of the baseball and softball diamond and facilities?	❑ Yes ❑ No	

From Katharine M. Nohr, 2009, *Managing Risk in Sport and Recreation: The Essential Guide for Loss Prevention* (Champaign, IL: Human Kinetics).

PREPARING THE BASEBALL AND SOFTBALL FIELD AND FACILITY FOR PLAY

After inspections have been performed and documented, defects and hazards should be repaired or removed before play begins. The following questions should be asked before play begins.

Considerations	Yes or No (check one)	Notes for follow-up
If the field is watered down before play to prevent dust (to protect players' eyes), have you made sure the field does not become muddy so as to pose a slipping or falling hazard?	❑ Yes ❑ No	
Have lines on the field been marked with slaked lime that could cause serious eye damage to players sliding into a base headfirst?	❑ Yes ❑ No	
Have you made sure the substance (chalk or paint) used to mark lines on the field will not be hazardous to players who slide or run into bases?	❑ Yes ❑ No	
If a hazard cannot be corrected before play, has it been determined whether the field is safe for play or whether to cancel play?	❑ Yes ❑ No	
If the field is safe for play but a hazard exists on the field, have clear and adequate warnings been provided to all players and other persons who will be utilizing the area of play (e.g., umpires and coaches)?	❑ Yes ❑ No	
If defects, holes, tears, or other problems have been identified, have you blocked off those areas to spectators before beginning play if the defects are not able to be repaired beforehand?	❑ Yes ❑ No	
Have dugout fences that have holes and defects been repaired prior to play?	❑ Yes ❑ No	
Have measures been taken to temporarily remedy defects or close dugouts where defects are present?	❑ Yes ❑ No	
Are extra balls, bats, and other equipment removed from the field during play?	❑ Yes ❑ No	
If the weather is excessively hot and humid or if there is lightning or rain, have you relocated or canceled the game or practice to prevent injuries or illnesses?	❑ Yes ❑ No	
Are there other considerations for preparing the field and facility for play?	❑ Yes ❑ No	

From Katharine M. Nohr, 2009, *Managing Risk in Sport and Recreation: The Essential Guide for Loss Prevention* (Champaign, IL: Human Kinetics).

PLAYING ON FIELDS THAT ARE USED FOR OTHER PURPOSES BESIDES BASEBALL OR SOFTBALL

Sometimes injuries occur when a field is used for a sport it is not intended for. If the structure of the field or objects or infrastructure that is part of the field can cause injury when it is being used for baseball or softball, you should consider moving your game or practice to a more appropriate field. The following questions should be addressed.

Considerations	Yes or No (check one)	Notes for follow-up
Is the field designed and intended for baseball or softball? If No, list what other sports or activities the field is used for in the Notes column.	❑ Yes ❑ No	
Has the field been properly designed for dual purposes? If No, list what hazards might exist if you use the field for baseball or softball.	❑ Yes ❑ No	
Have all dangerous items or equipment been removed or separated from the field?	❑ Yes ❑ No	
Are there other considerations for fields that are used for other purposes besides baseball or softball?	❑ Yes ❑ No	

From Katharine M. Nohr, 2009, *Managing Risk in Sport and Recreation: The Essential Guide for Loss Prevention* (Champaign, IL: Human Kinetics).

LIGHTING OF BASEBALL AND SOFTBALL FIELD AND SPECTATOR FACILITIES

Baseball and softball games are often played at dusk or in the dark. Balls thrown and hit where there is insufficient lighting could pose a risk to players and spectators. Consequently, it is important to consider the following questions about lighting.

Considerations	Yes or No (check one)	Notes for follow-up
Are the lights illuminating the field turned on before dusk?	❑ Yes ❑ No	
Do the lights provide proper illumination of the field (i.e., not too bright or too dim)?	❑ Yes ❑ No	
Have light poles been inspected for stability and safety?	❑ Yes ❑ No	
Are the bleachers or stands and other spectator areas sufficiently illuminated?	❑ Yes ❑ No	
Are there other considerations for the lighting of field and spectator facilities?	❑ Yes ❑ No	

From Katharine M. Nohr, 2009, *Managing Risk in Sport and Recreation: The Essential Guide for Loss Prevention* (Champaign, IL: Human Kinetics).

FENCES AROUND THE BASEBALL
AND SOFTBALL FIELD

Fences surrounding baseball and softball fields serve several purposes. They protect players from being injured by running into traffic or other dangerous areas; they protect motor vehicles and people from being hit by balls that might be stopped by the surrounding fence; and they prevent people and animals that are not involved in play from entering the field and potentially being injured. The following questions should be considered when evaluating the fencing around a baseball or softball field.

Considerations	Yes or No (check one)	Notes for follow-up
Is there a fence surrounding the outfield?	☐ Yes ☐ No	
Is the fencing high enough?	☐ Yes ☐ No	
Is the fencing in good repair?	☐ Yes ☐ No	
Is the fencing sufficient to close off areas to outsiders and traffic?	☐ Yes ☐ No	
Is the fence made of material that could cause injury to a player running after a ball?	☐ Yes ☐ No	
Is there any flexibility built into the fence or cushioning on the fence to prevent or diminish injury?	☐ Yes ☐ No	
Is there a warning track, warning lines, or other warning devices on the ground before the fence (e.g., short-cut grass)?	☐ Yes ☐ No	
Is the fence painted a bright color, or are there bright advertisements on the fence that will serve as warnings to players?	☐ Yes ☐ No	
Are there other considerations for fences around the field?	☐ Yes ☐ No	

PROTECTIVE BASEBALL AND SOFTBALL EQUIPMENT

Baseball and softball players have to protect themselves from fast-moving balls and bats. Depending on whether players are batting, catching, pitching, or playing in the outfield, specific protective gear should be worn. The following questions should be asked relative to protective equipment.

Considerations	Yes or No (check one)	Notes for follow-up
Does the catcher have proper safety equipment, including a face mask and helmet, a protective cup, a chest protector, shin guards, knee pads, and a well-padded catcher's mitt?	❑ Yes ❑ No	
Are there batting helmets available to fit each player?	❑ Yes ❑ No	
Do helmets have an NOCSAE or equivalent safety seal?	❑ Yes ❑ No	
Do the helmets have face guards with full coverage to the ears and jaw?	❑ Yes ❑ No	
Are the helmets light enough so as not to cause injury?	❑ Yes ❑ No	
Are players wearing baseball caps that protect their eyes from the glare of sun or lights?	❑ Yes ❑ No	
Are players using protective gloves or mitts so they can catch balls without injuring their hands?	❑ Yes ❑ No	
Are there other considerations for protective equipment?	❑ Yes ❑ No	

From Katharine M. Nohr, 2009, *Managing Risk in Sport and Recreation: The Essential Guide for Loss Prevention* (Champaign, IL: Human Kinetics).

BASEBALL AND SOFTBALL BASES

There are a number of types of bases you can select from as well as manufacturers of bases. You will want to select the appropriate bases and install them properly in accordance with the manufacturer's specifications. When considering the bases you use, the following questions should be asked.

Considerations	Yes or No (check one)	Notes for follow-up
Are you using bases for game play? If so, list in the Notes column what kind of bases you are using: anchored bases, rubber unanchored bases (impact bases), or Break Away bases.	❑ Yes ❑ No	
Are you familiar with the safety data published in relation to the bases used?	❑ Yes ❑ No	
Have the bases been installed properly in accordance with the manufacturer's specifications?	❑ Yes ❑ No	
Are you familiar with the strengths and weaknesses inherent with the base type you are using?	❑ Yes ❑ No	
Is the base type you are using recommended by the applicable official sanctioning body?	❑ Yes ❑ No	
Is the base type you are using appropriate for the age range and ability of the players who are using them?	❑ Yes ❑ No	
Are there other considerations for bases?	❑ Yes ❑ No	

From Katharine M. Nohr, 2009, *Managing Risk in Sport and Recreation: The Essential Guide for Loss Prevention* (Champaign, IL: Human Kinetics).

BASEBALL AND SOFTBALL BATS

Baseball and softball bats have been known to cause injury if they are not in good condition or if they are the wrong size or shape for the player or ball used. There has been particular concern about the safety of using aluminum bats. The following questions should be considered to assess the safety of the bats used.

Considerations	Yes or No (check one)	Notes for follow-up
Are all bats in good condition, with knobs at the grip end and not cracked or splintered?	❑ Yes ❑ No	
Do bats have a sufficient grip, either tape or roughened, so the batter does not lose his or her grip?	❑ Yes ❑ No	
Are the bats the right size for the players?	❑ Yes ❑ No	
Is the appropriate bat being used for the sport (i.e., baseball bat for baseball and softball bat for softball)?	❑ Yes ❑ No	
Is the type of bat being used approved by the appropriate governing body of the sport?	❑ Yes ❑ No	
Are there other considerations for baseball and softball bats?	❑ Yes ❑ No	

From Katharine M. Nohr, 2009, *Managing Risk in Sport and Recreation: The Essential Guide for Loss Prevention* (Champaign, IL: Human Kinetics).

OTHER BASEBALL AND SOFTBALL EQUIPMENT ISSUES

All equipment that is used in baseball and softball should be subject to scrutiny. Make sure players are using safe balls, wearing proper cleats, and not wearing anything, such as jewelry, that could injure themselves or other players. You should ask the following questions.

Considerations	Yes or No (check one)	Notes for follow-up
Are metal cleats allowed to be worn by players below the collegiate level?	❑ Yes ❑ No	
Are players wearing the proper type of cleats? If Yes, list what type of cleats the players are wearing in the Notes column.	❑ Yes ❑ No	
Are the cleats appropriate for the age level and field surface?	❑ Yes ❑ No	
Are players instructed to remove jewelry and watches?	❑ Yes ❑ No	
Are Reduced Injury Factor balls used by younger players?	❑ Yes ❑ No	
Are the balls used appropriate for the age level and type of game played?	❑ Yes ❑ No	
Are there other considerations for other equipment issues?	❑ Yes ❑ No	

From Katharine M. Nohr, 2009, *Managing Risk in Sport and Recreation: The Essential Guide for Loss Prevention* (Champaign, IL: Human Kinetics).

TIPS FOR BASEBALL AND SOFTBALL BATTING PRACTICE SAFETY

Bats swinging and balls being hit at high velocity are likely to cause injury if reasonable care is not taken. The following questions should be asked in this regard.

Considerations	Yes or No (check one)	Notes for follow-up
Has the batting cage netting been inspected for holes and defects?	❑ Yes ❑ No	
Has loose netting been installed to reduce deflected balls into the batting cage?	❑ Yes ❑ No	
Is the pitcher protected by a chain-link pitching screen?	❑ Yes ❑ No	
Is the pitcher wearing colored clothing so that a white ball is more visible, or are you using red or orange baseballs for greater visibility?	❑ Yes ❑ No	
Are all participants involved in batting practice wearing batting helmets?	❑ Yes ❑ No	
If a pitching machine is used, has appropriate training been provided for its use?	❑ Yes ❑ No	
Is there constant supervision provided during the use of the pitching machine?	❑ Yes ❑ No	
Is the pitching machine maintained in accordance with its manufacturer's standards?	❑ Yes ❑ No	
Have warnings been issued, verbally and in writing, about dangers arising from using the pitching machine?	❑ Yes ❑ No	
Are there other considerations for tips for batting practice safety?	❑ Yes ❑ No	

From Katharine M. Nohr, 2009, *Managing Risk in Sport and Recreation: The Essential Guide for Loss Prevention* (Champaign, IL: Human Kinetics).

LIGHTNING CONCERNS FOR BASEBALL AND SOFTBALL

Lightning strikes can cause serious injuries or death. Since most lightning injuries occur during the daytime and during spring or summer months, it is imperative that your risk manager or risk management committee develop a comprehensive plan for lightning emergency response. The emergency plan should address the following questions.

Considerations	Yes or No (check one)	Notes for follow-up
Are weather conditions monitored before and during the game or practice?	❏ Yes ❏ No	
Are coaches and staff trained to recognize nearby lightning activity and to determine the distance of lightning from your ballpark and the potential danger?	❏ Yes ❏ No	
Have criteria been established for when evacuation of the field should occur, when play should resume, or whether a game or practice should be canceled?	❏ Yes ❏ No	
Has an evacuation plan been made, using nearby shelters, that also includes spectators?	❏ Yes ❏ No	
Have players and other personnel been instructed as to how evacuation will take place, and has the evacuation been practiced before the season's first lightning storm?	❏ Yes ❏ No	
Is the evacuation plan monitored and changed where necessary?	❏ Yes ❏ No	
Are there other considerations for lightning?	❏ Yes ❏ No	

From Katharine M. Nohr, 2009, *Managing Risk in Sport and Recreation: The Essential Guide for Loss Prevention* (Champaign, IL: Human Kinetics).

11

Basketball

The rule was "No autopsy, no foul."

—Stewart Granger, on the pickup games of his childhood

Reported appellate court decisions in basketball have arisen out of injuries caused by a number of safety and risk management issues. Hazards on and around the court can be padded or eliminated in order to prevent injuries. Players are often hurt during the course of the game from body contact and falls, but those injuries are generally considered to be inherent in the sport and do not usually result in litigation.

BASKETBALL LAWSUITS AND SETTLEMENTS

There have been a few reported basketball cases in which the plaintiffs received significant settlements for injuries. The following are some examples of jury verdicts:

- A court awarded $45,000 to a student who was injured during a school basketball practice when she fell on a scissors lift that was next to the basketball court. She attempted to catch a ball out of bounds when she ran into the lift.

- A court awarded $2.25 million to a 34-year-old man who was rendered quadriplegic when injured in an outdoor basketball game.

A number of reported appellate court decisions address various causes of injuries in basketball. The following basketball cases address ADA violations as well as circumstances in which plaintiffs were injured while playing, due to violence or unsportsmanlike conduct, unpadded walls and fixtures, floor conditions, glass adjacent to the court, the backboard or pole, and facility defects; or were injured in the bleachers, parking lot, and in motor vehicle accidents.

Equipment

Mei Kay Chan v. City of Yonkers

In *Mei Kay Chan v. City of Yonkers*, 34 A.D.3d, 824 N.Y.S.2d 380 (2006), the plaintiff was playing basketball during physical education class when he collided with a classmate, causing him to impact with an unpadded concrete wall. The plaintiff sustained injuries and sued the school, alleging negligent supervision as well as negligence in failing to pad the gymnasium walls. In response to both parties' motions for summary judgment, the court concluded that there were material issues of fact as to whether the gym teacher provided sufficient safety instruction in light of the teacher's concern about the unpadded walls and whether the school was negligent because it did not install padding.

In this case, it appears that safety instructions were given to students in lieu of padding the walls. It is probably less expensive for facilities to pad walls than to defend potential lawsuits that will likely arise from consequent injuries.

Pope v. Trotwood-Madison City School District Board of Education

In *Pope v. Trotwood-Madison City School District Board of Education*, 162 F. Supp. 2d 803 (S.D. Ohio 2000), an eighth-grade student was playing basketball on a half-court in the school's gymnasium. He tripped and fell as he ran toward another player, which caused him to stumble and hit his head on the gymnasium wall, which was covered by a mat. The student fractured his neck and was unable to breathe despite rescue efforts. He remained on life support for five months, until the system was disconnected and he died.

It was determined that the school district was immune from liability under an applicable governmental immunity statute.

This case illustrates the risk of injury that could arise when a wall is padded but very thinly. With the large number of players, 10 playing on each half-court, the risk of injuries was certainly increased.

Ribaudo v. La Salle Institute

In *Ribaudo v. La Salle Institute*, 45 A.D.3d 556, 846 N.Y.S.2d 209 (2007), the plaintiff, an experienced high school basketball player, ran into an unpadded concrete wall while running at full speed in his attempt to prevent a ball from going out of bounds. The plaintiff was injured and so brought suit against the high school where the incident occurred. The defendant prevailed based on a primary assumption of risk theory in that the risk of running into a wall is an inherent part of basketball and that the unpadded concrete wall was open and obvious. It was noted that the plaintiff did not present any evidence that the school violated any standards applicable to basketball courts.

It is fortunate for the defendant in this case that it prevailed using primary assumption of risk and open and obvious defenses. However, it still is a good idea to pad walls in areas where players are running at full speed and likely will run into the walls.

Trevett v. City of Little Falls

In *Trevett v. City of Little Falls*, 6 N.Y.3d 884, 849 N.E.2d 961 (2006), the plaintiff sued the city for injuries sustained by his son when, in attempting a layup, he collided with the basketball pole supporting the backboard and rim. The court dismissed the complaint because colliding with the pole, which was open and obvious, is an inherent risk in the game of basketball, and so the plaintiff's son assumed the risk.

One of the primary arguments that defendants make in premises liability cases, such as this, is that the object or defect that caused injury was open and obvious rather than hidden or latent. The other theory applied—assumption of risk—protects defendants in sport and recreation cases, allowing for frequent successes in having cases dismissed before trial. This case is a good example.

Yarber v. Oakland Unified School District

The setting for *Yarber v. Oakland Unified School District*, 6 Cal. Rptr. 2d. 437 (Cal. 1992) is an adult after-school basketball game in a junior high school gymnasium. While shooting the ball, Yarber was hit by another player, causing him to run into an unpadded concrete wall that was 4 feet (1.2 m) from the out-of-bounds line. Yarbor sustained a head and cervical spine injury. The court held that the school district was immune from liability under an applicable statute.

Most basketball facilities have padded walls to prevent such injuries. It is important to assess whether there is padding in your organization's facilities and to make sure padding is sufficient to prevent injury if a player should collide with the wall while running at full speed.

Facility

Casey v. Garden City Park–New Hyde Park School Dist.

In *Casey v. Garden City Park–New Hyde Park School Dist.*, 40 A.D.3d 901, 837 N.Y.S.2d 186 (2007), a ninth-grade boy sued the school district because of injuries sustained when he fell in a large hole on a basketball court in the schoolyard. He played basketball there on a regular basis and had been playing for 40 minutes before the incident occurred. The court concluded that since the plaintiff voluntarily participated in the game and the hole was open and obvious, he consented to the risk, which is inherent in the sport of basketball.

Regular inspection of the court should have revealed the large hole, and it could have been repaired, preventing injury. If the hole was discovered, the area could have been cordoned off, cones could have been placed around the hole, or the court could have been closed until repairs were made.

Dwyer v. Diocese of Rockville Centre

In *Dwyer v. Diocese of Rockville Centre*, 45 A.D.3d 527, 845 N.Y.S.2d 126 (2007), a high school student filed a lawsuit against the school that operated the gymnasium in which he was injured while playing basketball. The plaintiff's hand was cut when it hit the glass pane on a door, causing it to shatter. The plaintiff presented an expert opinion that safety glass should have been installed. The defendant prevailed after submitting evidence showing that the door complied with the building codes in effect when the school was built.

Even if the building codes allow for glass in the vicinity of a basketball court, it seems reasonable that a facility replace such glass if it is likely that a player could be injured.

Edwards v. Intergraph Services Co., Inc.

In *Edwards v. Intergraph Services Co., Inc.*, __ So. 2d__, WL 162245 (Ala. Civ. App. 2008), the plaintiff, a SWAT team member, suffered a ruptured Achilles tendon when his tennis shoe got caught in a small perforation in the flooring on a basketball court at the defendant's gymnasium. The evidence established that there had been no complaints of injury for the 14 years the flooring had been used before the incident. An affidavit of a flooring expert expressed the opinion that the

Glass near a basketball court can be dangerous.

flooring was better suited for a locker room or swimming pool area than a gymnasium. The plaintiff was not able to establish that his injury was caused by any negligence of the defendant. There was no evidence that the defendant could have discovered the defect by inspection. The defendant prevailed in its motion for summary judgment.

It is important to use the appropriate flooring materials for sport and recreation activities. In this case, it appears the owner of the gymnasium thought the gym floor was safe, as there had been no complaints in 14 years. People fall playing basketball and other sports all the time. Organizations cannot prevent all such injuries.

Pedersen v. Joliet Park District

In *Pedersen v. Joliet Park District*, 483 N.E.2d 21 (Ill. 1985), a student slipped and fell on an allegedly slippery and dusty tile floor when attempting to catch a pass while playing in a school basketball game, causing a torn knee ligament. The plaintiff was not able to show that the owner of the gymnasium's alleged negligence was the proximate cause of the injury.

Although the plaintiff did not succeed in this case, it is prudent to keep floors clean, dry, and in good repair.

Poston v. Unified School District No. 387

In *Poston v. Unified School District No. 387*, 37 Kan. App. 2d 694, 156 P.3d 685 (2007), the plaintiff went to a middle school, where his stepson was playing basketball. The plaintiff entered the doors to the common area, motioning to his stepson that he was there to pick him up, when a loose door hinge fell on the plaintiff's head, causing injury. The question for the court was whether the school district was immune from suit under the applicable recreational use immunity statute, even though the incident did not occur in the gymnasium but in a doorway to a common area leading to the gym. Because the common area was an appurtenance to the gym, the court found that the school district was immune from suit.

This case illustrates the need to keep all parts of a facility in good repair.

Springer v. University of Dayton

In *Springer v. University of Dayton*, Slip Copy, WL 1717906 (Ohio App. 2006), the plaintiff was attending a basketball tournament at the University of Dayton Arena. After the game, the plaintiff was jogging to his car in a dark parking lot when he tripped over a wire traffic cable. Although the plaintiff did not see the cable when he was jogging, it was visible to him after he fell. The plaintiff filed a lawsuit against University of Dayton, alleging negligence. The defendant prevailed as the court found the university did not have a duty of care to the plaintiff where the condition was open and obvious and not hidden from view. If the plaintiff had watched where he was jogging, he would have seen the wire.

Dark parking lots are scenes of various safety issues. The cost of lights could pay off by preventing injuries and criminal acts.

Thomas v. St. Mary's Roman Catholic Church

In *Thomas v. St. Mary's Roman Catholic Church*, 283 N.W.2d 254 (S.D. 1979), a high school varsity basketball player's artery was severed and he sustained extensive lacerations on both arms when he crashed through glass after tapping a ball back into the playing area. The player's momentum carried him through glass paneling located within 6 feet (1.8 m) of a boundary line of the basketball court and adjacent to the entryway of the gymnasium. The plaintiff's doctor testified that the plaintiff had 25 percent disability in both arms because of diminished sensation, coordination, and strength. The jury rendered a verdict in favor of the plaintiff in the amount of $125,000.

This is an unusual case because most basketball courts do not have glass windows in their vicinity. If there are glass windows near a basketball court, this case illustrates the potential danger if they are not made with safety glass. Mirrors could also pose a danger, which should be considered if a dance studio with mirrors is used for sports such as basketball.

Willett v. Chatham County Bd. of Educ.

In *Willett v. Chatham County Bd. of Educ.*, 176 N.C. App. 268, 625 S.E.2d 900 (2006), the plaintiff sued the Chatham County Board of Education for injuries he sustained when the bleachers in the gym, where he was watching a basketball game, folded. He claimed that the applicable governmental immunity statutes did not apply. The court determined that they did and granted the board of education's motion for summary judgment.

Bleachers should be regularly examined for possible defects. If the bleachers used are portable, they must be set up properly to prevent situations such as the one that occurred in this case. With the large number of people who use bleachers, the loss exposure is high.

Participant

Dotzler v. Tuttle

In *Dotzler v. Tuttle*, 234 Neb. 176, 449 N.W.2d 774 (1990), an adult basketball player, Dotzler, was playing in a pickup basketball game at the Omaha Southwest YMCA when another player allegedly shoved or pushed him, causing him to fly backward 19 or 20 feet (about 6 m) onto the floor, fracturing both his wrists.

The court concluded that the other participant was liable only if his conduct was willful or with reckless disregard for the safety of the injured player. The reason is that in sport, players agree to a certain amount of physical contact that could be considered assault and battery without their consent. Courts generally do not impose tort liability on athletes because this could restrict athletic competition.

It is important to post rules against rough and violent play and enforce them. In this case, it might have been difficult to prevent the incident unless a YMCA employee was monitoring the game.

Basketball players assume the risk of a certain amount of physical contact during play that could inadvertently lead to an injury.

Fugazy v. Corbetta   In *Fugazy v. Corbetta*, 34 A.D.3d 728, 325 N.Y.S.2d 120 (2006), the plaintiff was hit in the face during an altercation after a youth basketball game. He filed an action against a player on the opposing team, alleging negligence and assault and battery. He filed another action against the player's father, alleging negligent supervision. The court determined there were issues for the jury to decide regarding the alleged assault and battery by the other player. The negligent supervision charges were dismissed against the player's father because the plaintiff failed to establish that he had a duty to supervise his son or his son's teammates.

Lawsuits arising out of youth sport injuries generally include claims of lack of supervision, whether there is any factual basis or not. Providing supervision for youth sports is a high priority. However, simply because lack of supervision is alleged does not mean the plaintiff will succeed with such a claim.

Mastropolo v. Goshen Cent. School Dist.   In *Mastropolo v. Goshen Cent. School Dist.*, 40 A.D.3d 1053, 837 S.2d 236 (2007), the plaintiff filed a lawsuit against the school district, alleging injury that was caused when he swung from the pipes that supported a basketball backboard. The school district prevailed by summary judgment, establishing that the plaintiff's actions were the sole cause of his injury and that he knowingly violated school rules.

This case illustrates the importance of safety rules, which should be established and enforced.

Staff

Grames v. King and Pontiac School District   In *Grames v. King and Pontiac School District*, 332 N.W.2d 615 (Mi. 1983), a female basketball player claimed injury after she was assaulted in a high school locker room after a basketball game by members of the opposite team.

The plaintiff and her parents filed a lawsuit against the school district and several school district employees, alleging that they were negligent in their failure to provide sufficient supervision of the locker room. The court did not allow the lawsuit because the defendants were protected by governmental immunity.

In circumstances involving rival teams, it is important to keep the teams separated. Security or other adult supervision may assist in preventing this type of incident.

Kindred v. Board of Education of Memphis City Schools

In *Kindred v. Board of Education of Memphis City Schools*, 946 S.W.2d 47 (Tenn. 1996), a student, collecting admissions at a school basketball game, was fatally shot by a former student. The incident occurred in 1987, when Marcus Briggs, the son of the plaintiff was a student at a junior high school in Memphis. Briggs volunteered to take admission charges at the door of the gymnasium for a basketball game between students and some faculty members. Coach Anderson was charged with supervising the admissions and game. Defendant Randy Oliver, a high school student at another school, refused to pay. He grabbed Briggs, threatening to fight. Coach Anderson escorted Oliver off campus, and Oliver called, "I'll be back," a common threat that hadn't resulted in serious problems previously. Oliver returned to the school with his aunt's pistol and shot Briggs.

The court explained that in order for negligence to be imposed on the defendants, the plaintiff would have to establish that the harm was reasonably foreseeable. The court did not find the defendant board of education negligent because it was not foreseeable that an act of such violence would occur. There was no evidence the defendants would have notice that a shooting would arise out of the incident between Oliver and Briggs.

Coaches, administrators, and those personnel in charge of sporting events should consider calling local police when serious incidents arise and seeking the assistance of trained security personnel. Where firearms and other weapons are a foreseeable threat, use of metal detectors could save lives.

McCollin v. Roman Catholic Archdiocese of New York

In *McCollin v. Roman Catholic Archdiocese of New York*, 54 A.D.3d 478, 846 N.Y.2d 158 (2007), an eighth-grade student at a private school filed a lawsuit against the operator of the school, the archdiocese, for injuries the student suffered when an older student who was assisting the coach at basketball practice kicked the younger student in the face. The defendant's motion for summary judgment was granted because the actions of the older student were unforeseeable, and nothing showed that the attack could have been prevented with greater supervision.

This case includes the issues of foreseeability and supervision. Sometimes, the type of problems that occur cannot be reasonably foreseen, and so there is not much a supervisor can do to prevent the incident from occurring.

Robinson v. Downs

In *Robinson v. Downs*, 39 A.D.3d 1250, 834 N.Y.S.2d 770 (2007), the plaintiff sued on behalf of her daughter, a basketball player, who was injured in an automobile accident while an assistant coach, a high school senior, was driving the coach's car. The appellate court concluded that the lower court had properly granted the defendant's motion for summary judgment on the counts alleging negligent supervision, hiring, instructing, assigning, and training the coach. However, the court concluded that the issue regarding vicarious liability for the coach's alleged negligence in letting the young assistant coach drive his car was for the jury to decide.

Allowing young people to drive motor vehicles is risky and should be avoided whenever possible. This case illustrates the risks of allowing young students to drive.

Schnarrs v. Girard Bd. of Edn.

In *Schnarrs v. Girard Bd. of Edn.*, 168 Ohio App. 3d 188, 858 N.E.2d 1258 (2006), a high school basketball player filed a lawsuit against the school board and others for injuries she sustained at basketball practice. To improve the girls' basketball skills, the coach asked males who had recently graduated from the high school to practice with the girls. In the course of practicing a rebound drill, one of the guys who were helping out hit the ball out of the plaintiff's hand, causing her arm to fracture. The court determined that the school board was statutorily immune from suit because utilizing the boys for practice was within the discretion of the coach.

In this case, the incident possibly could have been prevented if the basketball coach cautioned the boys to not engage in rough play and if the coach or other adults supervised the drills closely. If the case was not dismissed, it might have become clearer from the facts whether the coach was negligent by allowing the older boys to play with the girls.

Yatsko v. Berezwick

In *Yatsko v. Berezwick*, Slip Copy, WL 4276555 (M.D. Pa. 2007), the plaintiff sued her high school basketball coaches and the school district for damages arising from a severe head injury she sustained in a basketball game. The plaintiff's head collided with another player's after she jumped for a rebound. After she hurt her head, the plaintiff did not return to the game. The plaintiff's mother checked on her throughout the night, and the plaintiff told her friends she had a concussion. Despite this and continuing symptoms, she attended the next game. The plaintiff's coaches were aware that the plaintiff was not feeling well but allowed her to play anyway. She collapsed after the game, and rather than call an ambulance, the coaches helped her board a bus after the opposing team's trainer gave her a chocolate bar. The plaintiff was taken to her mother, who was told by the head coach to take her to a hospital. The plaintiff had sustained a serious brain injury, which caused her to miss months of high school, drop out of college, and cease her participation in sports. The court dismissed the various claims the plaintiff brought against the defendants because the facts as alleged, even if proven at trial, would not entitle her to relief under the law.

This case illustrates the need for coaches, trainers, athletes, and their parents to exercise extreme caution when an athlete sustains a head injury. Whether an athlete can return to play after a concussion should be left to the athlete's treating physician to determine rather than to the discretion of the coach. In this case, it does not appear that the plaintiff was released to play basketball by her doctor.

Violations

Seibert v. Amateur Athletic Union of U.S., Inc. In *Seibert v. Amateur Athletic Union of U.S., Inc.*, 422 F. Supp. 2d 1033 (D. Minn. 2006), the plaintiffs were refused an American Sign Language interpreter by the AAU for use while playing basketball on an AAU team. The lawsuit was brought pursuant to the Americans with Disabilities Act (ADA). One of the primary issues was whether the plaintiffs were subject to the arbitration provision that is a component of the AAU contract. The AAU membership is entered on the Internet. The coach submitted the memberships for the plaintiffs, clicking to consent to the contract that included an arbitration clause. The plaintiffs received membership cards, which stated they were bound by the AAU code and procedures and policies, which include arbitration. Consequently, the court held that the plaintiffs were required to have the action decided in arbitration rather than court. Essentially, the coach consented on their behalf when he clicked approval when filling out the Internet AAU application form.

In this case, the court validated consent performed by clicking approval on a form on the Internet. This case could be used in support of the position that when an athlete or anyone else consents to something on the Internet, such consent is binding.

BASKETBALL SAFETY CONSIDERATIONS

These reported appellate cases span a wide area of risk management and safety concerns as they relate to basketball, but they could occur in other sports as well. Understanding the potential for injury allows safeguards to be taken to prevent problems in the future. To facilitate your organization's safety standards in basketball, please use all the forms on pages 178 to 181.

SUMMARY

Because basketball is a fast-moving and aggressive sport, players are accustomed to sustaining some musculoskeletal injuries. Serious injuries can hopefully be prevented by paying close attention to the safety issues addressed in this chapter. The reported appellate court decisions about injuries that have occurred from basketball are also helpful in considering how to address risk management concerns.

INSPECTION OF THE BASKETBALL COURT

Before using a basketball court, it is prudent to inspect it to ascertain whether there are any defects that can be corrected or should at least be avoided during the course of play. It may be prudent to consider another location if defects are particularly hazardous. The following questions should be addressed for indoor basketball courts and before allowing play on outdoor basketball courts.

Considerations	Yes or No (check one)	Notes for follow-up
INDOOR BASKETBALL COURTS		
Are the basketball goals (backboards, nets, hoops, and posts) in good condition?	❑ Yes ❑ No	
Is backboard padding used?	❑ Yes ❑ No	
Is the floor in good condition, without holes, defects, and uneven or slippery surfaces?	❑ Yes ❑ No	
Was the floor constructed so it has proper shock absorption, such as a wooden spring-loaded floor?	❑ Yes ❑ No	
Does the floor meet the proper industry standards for a gymnasium floor?	❑ Yes ❑ No	
Is the floor clean and free of dust, dirt, and moisture?	❑ Yes ❑ No	
If an older floor has been refinished, are there slippery or uneven surfaces?	❑ Yes ❑ No	
Are any floor plates in the gymnasium flush with the floor so that tripping will not occur?	❑ Yes ❑ No	
Does the gymnasium have sufficient room around the court so that athletes will not run into walls?	❑ Yes ❑ No	
Do walls and other objects around the court have sufficient protective padding?	❑ Yes ❑ No	
Are the walls behind the basketball goals padded, with padding placed high enough to protect players from hitting their heads?	❑ Yes ❑ No	
If there are adjacent basketball courts in the gymnasium, is there sufficient space separating the courts?	❑ Yes ❑ No	
If there are glass doors or windows in the gymnasium, are they protected or made of safety glass?	❑ Yes ❑ No	

(continued)

From Katharine M. Nohr, 2009, *Managing Risk in Sport and Recreation: The Essential Guide for Loss Prevention* (Champaign, IL: Human Kinetics).

Inspection of the Basketball Court *(continued)*

Considerations	Yes or No (check one)	Notes for follow-up
INDOOR BASKETBALL COURTS *(continued)*		
Are all electrical control panels, light switches, and other protruding objects protected with sufficient padding or recessed in the wall?	❑ Yes ❑ No	
Do electrical control panels and light switches have locking mechanisms?	❑ Yes ❑ No	
Are scoring and press tables and equipment padded and located a reasonable distance from the court?	❑ Yes ❑ No	
Is the gymnasium's ventilation system working, and does it provide sufficient ventilation to support basketball play with spectators?	❑ Yes ❑ No	
Does the gymnasium contain mildew or mold?	❑ Yes ❑ No	
Do the rims that are used break away or snap back?	❑ Yes ❑ No	
Are the backboards made out of shatterproof material?	❑ Yes ❑ No	
Are there any defects, cracks, or slivers in the rims?	❑ Yes ❑ No	
Are there any loose, missing, or defective screws, nuts, or bolts on the backboards or rims?	❑ Yes ❑ No	
Has the area surrounding the court been inspected for any defects that might cause injury to players or spectators?	❑ Yes ❑ No	
Have gym dividers been inspected to determine if they are working properly and have sufficient padding if they pose a hazard to players?	❑ Yes ❑ No	
Is the gymnasium sufficiently illuminated?	❑ Yes ❑ No	
Are there other considerations for inspection of indoor basketball courts?	❑ Yes ❑ No	
OUTDOOR BASKETBALL COURTS		
Is the court adjacent to other courts or play areas?	❑ Yes ❑ No	
Is there at least 3 feet (.9 m) between adjacent courts?	❑ Yes ❑ No	
Are there sufficient barriers between the court and vehicular traffic?	❑ Yes ❑ No	

(continued)

From Katharine M. Nohr, 2009, *Managing Risk in Sport and Recreation: The Essential Guide for Loss Prevention* (Champaign, IL: Human Kinetics).

Inspection of the Basketball Court *(continued)*

Considerations	Yes or No (check one)	Notes for follow-up
OUTDOOR BASKETBALL COURTS *(continued)*		
Have apparatuses used in other sports been left on the court or in the immediate vicinity?	❏ Yes ❏ No	
Are there any environmental concerns, such as proximity to pollutants or environmental hazards (e.g., industrial exhaust coming from a nearby building)?	❏ Yes ❏ No	
Is the court made of an uneven surface that pools with water or could cause athletes to trip?	❏ Yes ❏ No	
Are the basketball posts padded and in good condition?	❏ Yes ❏ No	
Are all poles on the court or adjacent to the court padded or painted bright colors in order to warn athletes?	❏ Yes ❏ No	
Are the backboards padded?	❏ Yes ❏ No	
Are fences that surround the court padded where athletes can run into them and a safe distance behind the court endlines?	❏ Yes ❏ No	
Do the rims that are used break away or snap back?	❏ Yes ❏ No	
Are the backboards made out of shatterproof material?	❏ Yes ❏ No	
Is the court sufficiently illuminated at night?	❏ Yes ❏ No	
Are there other considerations for inspection of outdoor basketball courts?	❏ Yes ❏ No	

From Katharine M. Nohr, 2009, *Managing Risk in Sport and Recreation: The Essential Guide for Loss Prevention* (Champaign, IL: Human Kinetics).

PREPARING THE BASKETBALL COURT OR GYMNASIUM FOR PLAY

After inspections have been performed and documented, defects and hazards should be repaired or removed before play begins. The following questions should be addressed in preparing the basketball court and gymnasium for play.

Considerations	Yes or No (check one)	Notes for follow-up
If a hazard cannot be corrected before play, has it been determined whether the court is safe for play or whether to cancel the practice or game?	❑ Yes ❑ No	
If the court is safe for play but a hazard exists in the gym or in the area surrounding the court, have clear and adequate warnings been provided to all players and other persons who will be utilizing the area of play (e.g., referees and coaches)?	❑ Yes ❑ No	
Are extra balls removed from the court during play?	❑ Yes ❑ No	
If defects, holes, tears, or other problems have been identified, have you blocked off those areas to spectators before beginning play if the defects are not able to be repaired beforehand?	❑ Yes ❑ No	
Are all protruding wall fixtures and switches padded or painted a bright color so as to warn players?	❑ Yes ❑ No	
If the area of play is inside and there is insufficient ventilation on a hot and humid day, have you relocated or canceled the game or practice in order to prevent heat-related illnesses?	❑ Yes ❑ No	
Are there other considerations for preparing the court or gymnasium for play?	❑ Yes ❑ No	

From Katharine M. Nohr, 2009, *Managing Risk in Sport and Recreation: The Essential Guide for Loss Prevention* (Champaign, IL: Human Kinetics).

Cycling

Get a bicycle. You will not regret it if you live.

—Mark Twain

Safety is a significant component of cycling on roadways, especially when bicyclists share the road with motor vehicles. Good cyclists use clothing, reflectors, hand signals, and lights to make sure automobile drivers and other cyclists see them and can anticipate their moves. Because of the significant risk of head injuries, it is important that anyone riding a bicycle wear a properly fitted helmet with a buckled chin strap. USA Cycling, the national governing body of the sport in the United States, has a policy that while preparing for and participating in all sanctioned events, cyclists are required to wear helmets that meet U.S. Department of Transportation standards or other equivalent standards. Another concern is that the ends of handlebars be solidly plugged so that a crash does not result in impalement.

CYCLING LAWSUITS AND SETTLEMENTS

Most cycling injuries that result in lawsuits or settlements arise out of accidents between motor vehicles and bicycles. The reality is that where there is coverage under an automobile insurance policy—when an accident arises out of the operation or use of a motor vehicle—litigation is more likely. Accidents between cyclists could result in an insurance claim under a homeowner's policy, but this is less likely to happen because of the relationships involved.

In motor vehicle versus bicycle accidents, the cyclist may be found to be partially or entirely at fault so that recovery is reduced or prohibited. However, when the motor vehicle driver is negligent, cyclists have settled cases for large sums to compensate them for serious injuries. Some examples follow:

- The plaintiff, a 40-year-old man who was riding a bicycle on a California bike path, was hit by a car driven by an elderly man. The plaintiff suffered a major head injury with a coma and brain damage. The case was settled for $3.5 million for the man and $1 million for loss of consortium for his wife.

- A 22-year-old San Francisco bike messenger suffered internal injuries and a fractured pelvis when he was hit by a truck that ran over him. The bike rider filed a lawsuit against the trucking company, settling the case for $400,000.

Most of the reported court decisions that involve bicycle racing address the issue of whether the release signed by the plaintiff participant was enforceable. Where the releases were not contrary to public policy, defendants were generally granted summary judgment rather than having to proceed to trial. In some instances the releases did not hold up, and the appellate court remanded the case to trial.

Facility

Umali v. Mount Snow, Ltd.   In *Umali v. Mount Snow, Ltd.*, 247 F. Supp. 2d 567 (D. Vt. 2003), releases signed by the plaintiff were determined to be void and contrary to public policy. The plaintiff was a beginner dual slalom bike racer. The race finish was a double jump, which was very difficult for beginners. On the plaintiff's third practice run, he was airborne from the first jump and landed headfirst into the second jump. The plaintiff was rendered paraplegic as a result of this accident. The court analyzed Vermont law, primarily as it relates to exculpatory releases for mountain sports such as skiing. The releases were found to be void and against public policy as they would reduce the incentive for the defendants to practice risk management. The court also looked at a sports injury statute that was applicable in this Vermont case. Since expert testimony presented by the plaintiff that the jump at the end of the race was not a necessary or obvious risk, the statute applied so that the case would go to the jury for a decision on its merits.

Participant

Estate of Peters by Peters v. U.S. Cycling Federation   In a Kentucky appellate court case, *Estate of Peters by Peters v. U.S. Cycling Federation*, 779 F. Supp. 853 (E.D. Ky. 1991), the deceased participated in a bicycle race that had a steep downhill portion. As the 51-year-old experienced racer attempted the sharp turn at the bottom of the hill, his bicycle went off the road, hitting a tree. He died from the injuries sustained, and his estate filed a lawsuit against the race organizer and the United States Cycling Federation. The deceased had signed two releases—one for USCF and the other for the race. The court noted that the release would be considered a valid contract but would not exempt persons from liability if their conduct was intentional or if they owed a duty to the public. The release would provide exemption from liability if the acts were negligent, but not if the acts were willful or wanton. In this case, there was no evidence that any actions of the defendants were intentional, willful, or wanton. The race course was inspected beforehand, a sign was posted to warn riders, a police officer was assigned to the hill, and participants were provided with a course map at registration of the event. The defendants prevailed on a motion for summary judgment. It appears that the race directors did everything they could to protect themselves and so it is not surprising that they prevailed in court.

Lloyd v. Sugarloaf Mountain Corp.

In *Lloyd v. Sugarloaf Mountain Corp.*, 833 A.2d 1 (Me. 2003), the plaintiff was injured when he collided with another participant in a required practice session preceding the Widowmaker Challenge mountain bike race held at Sugarloaf Ski Resort. The plaintiff signed several releases before the event. The court declined to follow previous decisions that found releases violated public policy. Since the event was called the Widowmaker Challenge, the court noted that participants clearly knew that the race was dangerous, participation was voluntary, and it was not held as a public service. The language of the releases was clear, and so the court

Make sure that releases contain specific language as to the potential dangers that are involved in participating in the event as well as in traveling to and from the event location.

determined the defendants were entitled to summary judgment. This case and the cases below are examples of the value of having participants sign releases before participating in an event or sport.

Nishi v. Mount Snow, Ltd.   In a Vermont case, *Nishi v. Mount Snow, Ltd.*, 935 F. Supp. 508 (D. Vt. 1996), the plaintiff participated in a mountain bike race held at Mount Snow, located in West Dover, Vermont. After the race, he had dinner and then started to ride his bike to his car, which was parked at a lower elevation. The plaintiff found his way back on the race trail and rode his bike into a rope, causing him to fall backward and sustain injury. The plaintiff had signed two releases preceding the accident, one for the National Off-Road Bicycle Association (NORBA) and the other in order to participate in the race. The NORBA release contained language that included releasing the defendants from liability for the plaintiff's travel to and from the event. Since the plaintiff was traveling from the event to his car at the time of the accident, the court found that the release was applicable and granted the defendant's motion for summary judgment.

Okura v. United States Cycling Federation   In a California appellate court case, *Okura v. United States Cycling Federation*, 186 Cal. App. 3d 1462, 231 Cal. Rptr. 429 (1986), the plaintiff was participating in the Hermosa Beach Grand Prix, a bicycle race put on by South Bay Wheelmen, Inc. The race took place in Hermosa Beach on public streets that were closed to traffic. The plaintiff was injured when he biked over loose debris while crossing some railroad tracks on the course. His body hit a guardrail after the debris caused him to slide. Before the race, the plaintiff signed a release that stated he understood the risk of injury from bicycle racing and he was waiving and releasing all claims against promoters, sponsors, officials, involved municipalities, and so on. The plaintiff filed a lawsuit against South Bay Wheelmen, the United States Cycling Federation, and the City of Hermosa Beach. The defendants prevailed on a motion for summary judgment because the release the plaintiff signed as part of his entry form was valid. His participation was voluntary, and the race did not have characteristics affecting the public interest that would render the release invalid.

Staff

Bennett v. United States Cycling Federation   In another California appellate court decision, *Bennett v. United States Cycling Federation*, 193 Cal. App. 3d 1485, 239 Cal. Rptr. 55 (1987), the plaintiff was injured when a motor vehicle collided with him while he was participating in a bicycle race. The plaintiff signed the standard entry and release form required by the local cycling federation before he participated in the race. The accident occurred when a race attendant allowed a vehicle to enter the course so the driver could return a camera to his workplace. The plaintiff did not know that automobiles would be on the course. He was cycling at high speed in the middle of the road when the vehicle that was allowed on the course hit him. In response to a motion for summary judgment brought by the defendants, the plaintiff argued that the release's type size was too small and that the car accident was an unexpected risk he did not contemplate. The court concluded that the size of the type in the release was legible and clear, and so it was not invalid because of print size. On the other hand, there was an issue of fact regarding whether the plaintiff could reasonably foresee that a car would enter the course, and so the appellate court concluded that this issue was for a jury to decide. Race directors should be careful to instruct race staff volunteers and police officers regarding any motor vehicle restrictions and road closures before the event in order to prevent motor vehicle vs. bicycle accidents.

CYCLING SAFETY CONSIDERATIONS

As you can see from review of these cases, it is a good idea for race directors to have athletes read and sign carefully drafted releases and waivers before participating in a race. This decision will certainly depend on the applicable state law, and you should consult an attorney licensed to practice law in the state where the race will be held. To facilitate your organization's safety standards in cycling, please use all the forms on pages 188 to 194.

SUMMARY

Cycling is one of the few sports that have utilitarian purpose—that of transportation—and is enjoyed as a sport. Another unique feature is that riding among automobiles increases the danger significantly. The reported appellate court decisions regarding bicycle race injuries generally focus on the validity of releases signed by participants. Generally, defendants have been successful in being dismissed where the participant has signed a release. Nevertheless, it is important for riders to use safe equipment and learn safe riding techniques, both for road cycling and mountain biking. People should enjoy cycling but adhere carefully to the safety tips described in this chapter and wear proper equipment at all times.

CYCLING EQUIPMENT SAFETY

Bicyclists risk serious injury when racing. Since cycling is an individual sport, athletes almost always own their own equipment, including a bicycle, helmet, shoes, clothing, and any other protective gear. An important part of safety in cycling involves inspection and maintenance of equipment and wearing highly visible clothing. Cyclists should inspect their equipment before and after each use. The following questions should be considered when assessing the safety and soundness of bicycles and equipment.

Considerations	Yes or No (check one)	Notes for follow-up
Does the helmet fit properly?	❑ Yes ❑ No	
Are there any cracks or defects in the helmet?	❑ Yes ❑ No	
Is the chin strap buckle working and adjusted so it is not too loose?	❑ Yes ❑ No	
Are the cleats on the bike shoes working properly?	❑ Yes ❑ No	
Are there end plugs in the handlebars?	❑ Yes ❑ No	
Are the handlebars securely in place?	❑ Yes ❑ No	
Are the tires in good condition?	❑ Yes ❑ No	
Are the tires properly inflated?	❑ Yes ❑ No	
Does the bike have spare tires, a pump, CO_2 cartridges, tire levers, and necessary items to fix a flat tire on the road?	❑ Yes ❑ No	
Is the cyclist wearing padded bike shorts?	❑ Yes ❑ No	
Is the cyclist wearing a protective bike jersey?	❑ Yes ❑ No	
Is the cyclist wearing a brightly colored bike jersey if riding on the road with cars?	❑ Yes ❑ No	
Does the cyclist have protective gloves?	❑ Yes ❑ No	

(continued)

Cycling Equipment Safety *(continued)*

Considerations	Yes or No (check one)	Notes for follow-up
Does the bike have a rear reflector and a headlight?	❑ Yes ❑ No	
Are all spokes in the wheels secured?	❑ Yes ❑ No	
Is the saddle securely on the bike?	❑ Yes ❑ No	
Are the derailleurs clean and working properly?	❑ Yes ❑ No	
Have all moving parts of the bike been oiled and maintained in working condition?	❑ Yes ❑ No	
Are the brakes working properly?	❑ Yes ❑ No	
Are all gears working properly?	❑ Yes ❑ No	
Are the chain rings and chain working properly?	❑ Yes ❑ No	
Are there other considerations for cycling equipment safety?	❑ Yes ❑ No	

From Katharine M. Nohr, 2009, *Managing Risk in Sport and Recreation: The Essential Guide for Loss Prevention* (Champaign, IL: Human Kinetics).

CYCLING HELMET SAFETY STANDARDS

Cycling helmets should meet any one of the following helmet safety standards.

Standard	Notes for follow-up
❏ US DOT helmet standards	
❏ American Society for Testing and Materials (ASTM) standard F-1447	
❏ Snell Memorial Foundation standard B or N series	
❏ American National Standards Institute (ANSI) standard Z90.4	
❏ U.S. Consumer Product Safety Commission (CPSC) standard for bicycle helmets	
❏ Canadian Standards Association (CSA) standard CAN/CSA D113.2-M	
❏ European Committee for Standardization (CEN) standard for bicycle helmets	

From Katharine M. Nohr, 2009, *Managing Risk in Sport and Recreation: The Essential Guide for Loss Prevention* (Champaign, IL: Human Kinetics).

ROAD CYCLING SAFETY

The biggest concern with cycling on the road is avoiding being hit by cars. There are a number of common scenarios in which cyclists can be hit. If cyclists are trained in safe riding, they should be able to avoid most accidents.

Considerations	Yes or No (check one)	Notes for follow-up
DO YOU AVOID BEING HIT BY A CAR THAT IS PULLING OUT OF A SIDE STREET BY DOING THE FOLLOWING:		
Making yourself visible with a headlight if at night or catching the driver's attention by waving or signaling	❑ Yes ❑ No	
Making yourself heard by using a horn or bell	❑ Yes ❑ No	
Slowing down or stopping	❑ Yes ❑ No	
Moving over to the left so that you are more visible	❑ Yes ❑ No	
DO YOU AVOID BEING HIT BY A DOOR OF A CAR PARKED ON THE SIDE OF THE ROAD THAT OPENS INTO THE BIKE PATH BY DOING THE FOLLOWING:		
Riding far enough to the left so that the door cannot open into you	❑ Yes ❑ No	
Making yourself heard using a horn or bell	❑ Yes ❑ No	
DO YOU AVOID BEING HIT BY A CAR THAT TURNS RIGHT IN FRONT OF YOU BY DOING THE FOLLOWING:		
Not stopping in the blind spot of a car	❑ Yes ❑ No	
Positioning yourself so that cars can see you	❑ Yes ❑ No	
Waiting for a motorist to turn before proceeding forward	❑ Yes ❑ No	
Making yourself visible with lights and reflectors and brightly colored and reflective clothing	❑ Yes ❑ No	
Not riding on the sidewalk	❑ Yes ❑ No	
Looking over your left shoulder for cars or into a rearview mirror before you enter an intersection	❑ Yes ❑ No	
Riding farther to the left	❑ Yes ❑ No	

(continued)

From Katharine M. Nohr, 2009, *Managing Risk in Sport and Recreation: The Essential Guide for Loss Prevention* (Champaign, IL: Human Kinetics).

Road Cycling Safety *(continued)*

Considerations	Yes or No (check one)	Notes for follow-up
DO YOU AVOID BEING HIT BY A CAR THAT MAKES A LEFT TURN INTO YOU BY DOING THE FOLLOWING:		
Wearing brightly colored clothing and helmet	❑ Yes ❑ No	
Making eye contact with drivers	❑ Yes ❑ No	
Getting the driver's attention by waving	❑ Yes ❑ No	
Not riding on the sidewalk	❑ Yes ❑ No	
Using a headlight	❑ Yes ❑ No	
Slowing down or stopping	❑ Yes ❑ No	
DO YOU AVOID BEING HIT FROM THE REAR BY CARS BY DOING THE FOLLOWING:		
Wearing bright, reflective clothing and helmet	❑ Yes ❑ No	
Using a reflector or a flashing rear light	❑ Yes ❑ No	
Not making maneuvers that drivers will not see or expect	❑ Yes ❑ No	
Not moving left without looking first	❑ Yes ❑ No	
Using a rearview mirror	❑ Yes ❑ No	
Riding on wider and less busy streets	❑ Yes ❑ No	
DO YOU USE OTHER TIPS TO AVOID COLLISIONS WITH CARS, SUCH AS THE FOLLOWING:		
Assuming that others cannot see you	❑ Yes ❑ No	
Using turn signals and signaling stops using your arm	❑ Yes ❑ No	
Riding with traffic	❑ Yes ❑ No	
Following all traffic laws	❑ Yes ❑ No	
Not riding on the side of the street opposite to how traffic is moving	❑ Yes ❑ No	

(continued)

From Katharine M. Nohr, 2009, *Managing Risk in Sport and Recreation: The Essential Guide for Loss Prevention* (Champaign, IL: Human Kinetics).

Road Cycling Safety *(continued)*

Considerations	Yes or No (check one)	Notes for follow-up
DO YOU USE OTHER TIPS TO AVOID COLLISIONS WITH CARS, SUCH AS THE FOLLOWING: *(continued)*		
Taking all of the lane, if appropriate	❑ Yes ❑ No	
Riding on the safest streets possible—less traffic, wider roads	❑ Yes ❑ No	
Riding on bike paths and in bike lanes	❑ Yes ❑ No	
Using lights, reflectors, and blinking lights	❑ Yes ❑ No	
Wearing brightly colored clothing and helmet	❑ Yes ❑ No	
Establishing eye contact by waving at drivers when appropriate	❑ Yes ❑ No	
Not drinking alcohol before riding a bike	❑ Yes ❑ No	
Not wearing headphones or listening to music while riding	❑ Yes ❑ No	
Not talking on a cell phone while riding	❑ Yes ❑ No	
Not answering a cell phone while riding	❑ Yes ❑ No	
Staying alert and giving complete attention to the road	❑ Yes ❑ No	
Not carrying anything that could get caught in your wheel	❑ Yes ❑ No	
Keeping your load light	❑ Yes ❑ No	
Are there other considerations for road cycling safety?	❑ Yes ❑ No	

From Katharine M. Nohr, 2009, *Managing Risk in Sport and Recreation: The Essential Guide for Loss Prevention* (Champaign, IL: Human Kinetics).

MOUNTAIN BIKING SAFETY

The dangers in mountain biking are what make it exciting and fun for participants. A challenging course that requires skill to maneuver brings great satisfaction to the experienced but can cause significant injuries to those who are less prepared. If the following safety tips are followed consistently when mountain biking, the chance of injuries occurring will be significantly reduced and severity of injuries should be lessened.

Considerations	Yes or No (check one)	Notes for follow-up
Do you pay close attention to your speed so you can maneuver around obstacles and adjust to changes in the trail conditions?	❑ Yes ❑ No	
Do you slow down when you approach a blind corner?	❑ Yes ❑ No	
Do you make sure you are familiar with the trail?	❑ Yes ❑ No	
Do you become familiar with a trail by riding at slower speeds at first?	❑ Yes ❑ No	
Do you always stop and analyze potentially challenging parts of a trail before riding forward?	❑ Yes ❑ No	
Do you anticipate what might happen if you crash while riding a particular section of trail or while doing a stunt? If the consequences are too serious, do you trust your instincts and reconsider?	❑ Yes ❑ No	
Do you practice doing moves and stunts in safer environments and at low speeds before attempting them on the trail?	❑ Yes ❑ No	
Do you concentrate on being safe so you can enjoy mountain biking another day?	❑ Yes ❑ No	
Are there other considerations for mountain biking safety?	❑ Yes ❑ No	

From Katharine M. Nohr, 2009, *Managing Risk in Sport and Recreation: The Essential Guide for Loss Prevention* (Champaign, IL: Human Kinetics).

13

Golf

The reason the pro tells you to keep your head down is so you can't see him laughing.

—Phyllis Diller

Golfers might be surprised at the frequency and severity of injuries that arise from hazards that are fundamental to the game of golf. This makes sense since the sport uses expansive areas of land made up of various types of potentially slippery grass surfaces, water hazards, and sand traps. Add to this the use of golf carts driven by potentially intoxicated players on uneven, hilly, and curvy land. Then factor in that players can hit others with balls and clubs and that those steel clubs can serve as lightning rods. It is no wonder that lawsuits and insurance claims are not uncommon, especially when injuries are severe.

GOLF LAWSUITS

The following court and arbitration awards have been made as a result of injuries that have occurred on golf courses and driving ranges:

- The plaintiff sustained herniated discs in his neck requiring surgery as a result of his golf cart being rear-ended by another golf cart. An arbitrator awarded the injured plaintiff $300,000, which was the maximum amount that could be awarded in the binding arbitration.

- In another golf cart incident, a golfer was awarded a jury verdict of $1.4

million for a spinal fracture injury. The golfer was injured when the brakes of the golf cart he was using failed.

- A golfer was awarded $7.5 million for injuries sustained when he was struck in the neck by a golf ball hit from a driving range.

- In Michigan, the estate of a golfer who died when he tripped on timber used to landscape a golf course was awarded a jury verdict of $1.37 million.

- A teenager whose face was injured when she was struck by a golfer's backswing at a driving range was awarded $90,000 because Windmill Driving Range was found to be negligent for failure to warn pedestrians of a known unsafe condition and for not providing a safe means of walking through the area. *Travanti v. Windmill Driving Range* (Pa. Common Pleas Ct., 95017231).

The following reported appellate court decisions address a number of safety hazards in golf.

Equipment

MacDonald v. B.M.D. Golf Associates, Inc.
In *MacDonald v. B.M.D. Golf Associates, Inc.*, 148 N.H. 582, 813 A.2d 488 (2002), the parties went to trial in relation to a golf cart accident. The plaintiff was injured when a golf cart he was riding in at the defendant's Indian Mound Golf Club overturned, injuring the plaintiff's ankle. The golf cart driver, an adolescent boy, mistakenly turned right at a fork in the road. When he tried to correct the mistake, he caused the cart to overturn. The boy admitted at the scene that he was not supposed to be driving the cart. The golf course prevailed at trial. The plaintiff appealed the verdict and won on appeal, so the case was reversed and remanded to the trial court for a new trial.

It is reasonable for golf courses to establish rules prohibiting young golfers from driving golf carts.

Pine v. Arruda
In *Pine v. Arruda*, 448 F. Supp. 2d 282 (D. Mass. 2006), Beverly Pine and Jean Arruda were golfing in a tournament at the Hawthorne Country Club when a lightning storm began and a siren signaled the players to get off the course. Pine and Arruda followed the instructions but had left Pine's golf clubs on the seat of their golf cart. They decided to move the cart to protect the clubs. In the process of doing this, the golf clubs fell on the floor of the car, depressing the accelerator. Pine was knocked to the ground and the cart ran over her, causing injury. Pine filed a lawsuit against Arruda and the Hawthorne Country Club.

The plaintiff claimed that Hawthorne was negligent for failing to stop the tournament earlier and failing to exercise due care by not having covered storage for its golf carts. The court determined that Hawthorne owed a duty to the plaintiff and so was required to maintain the course in a reasonably safe condition. However, the court found that no reasonable jury would find Hawthorne negligent because it could not have anticipated that the lack of covered parking for golf carts would cause a golf cart to run over a guest. The incident in question was not reasonably foreseeable.

The facts of this case are unusual and likely not to have been anticipated by the golf course.

Facility

Barbato v. Hollow Hills Country Club   One of the realities of golf is that watering the grass with sprinkler systems means the grass may become slippery for golfers who walk between holes. In the New York Supreme Court case of *Barbato v. Hollow Hills Country Club*, 14 A.D.3d 522, 789 N.Y.S.2d 199 (2005), a golfer slipped and fell on a golf course made wet by a sprinkler system. The plaintiff was an experienced golfer and had played the Hollow Hills Country Club course a number of times before he was injured. He also noticed that next to the green, a manually operated sprinkler was watering the course. The plaintiff was injured when he slipped and fell when walking down the side of the green. The court determined that the plaintiff assumed the risk of injury when playing golf on the wet golf course. There was no evidence presented to support that the golf club acted negligently in watering the course. The plaintiff did not present an expert's affidavit with the industry standard supporting negligence on the part of Hollow Hills Country Club.

This decision seems reasonable in light of the inherent nature of golf courses. If a golfer is concerned about slipping, playing later in the day after the course has had a chance to dry out would be a safer option.

Finkler v. Minisceongo Golf Club   A good example of a lawsuit that arose out of a failure to inspect a golf course is the case of *Finkler v. Minisceongo Golf Club*, 16 Misc. 3d 1007, 841 N.Y.S.2d 424 (2007). Marilyn Finkler, who had been a member of the Minisceongo Golf Club for 11 years, playing three to five times per week, slipped and fell on approximately 30 golf balls that were obscured by a pile of leaves and clippings next to the 12th hole green. The golf club claimed that tripping on a golf ball is a reasonable foreseeable hazard in the game of golf and that the plaintiff assumed the risk. The plaintiff argued that the circumstances that caused her to slip and fall, an accumulation of 30 golf balls hidden by leaves and grass clippings, was not a hazard that could have been anticipated and is not an ordinary risk associated with golf. The golf club was not entitled to summary judgment because it failed to show that the 30 hidden golf balls were an inherent risk of golf and not a dangerous condition outside the usual dangers of the sport.

If a golf course has 30 hidden golf balls in one spot, one must wonder what other hidden and obvious dangers exist that could cause injury. Regular inspections and maintenance are essential.

Freiberger v. Four Seasons Golf Center

A case involving problems with a safety net at a driving range is *Freiberger v. Four Seasons Golf Center*, LLC, Slip Copy, WL 1674020 (Ohio App. 10 Dist. 2007). Plaintiff Charles Freiburger was hitting balls on the upper floor of Four Seasons driving range when one of his friends came to join him. In the process of greeting his friend, the plaintiff stepped back and fell off the ledge of the upper level and was not caught by the safety net. The plaintiff sued Four Seasons for negligence, claiming that it breached its duty of care by failing to warn him that the safety net would not catch him if he fell and for failing to maintain the safety net in a safe condition. Since there was a safety net in place, the court asked whether there continued to be an open and obvious danger, as there would be if no safety net existed. The court concluded that the case would have to proceed to trial in order to decide whether the defendant was negligent.

Jones v. Kite/Cupp Legends Golf Development

In *Jones v. Kite/Cupp Legends Golf Development*, Slip Copy, WL 2751784 (Tenn. Ct. App. 2007), Charles Jones was playing golf at the Legends golf course in Franklin, Tennessee, when he came upon a bench located by the 13th tee that was made of wood, had four legs made of timber, and was situated on a concrete slab. As the plaintiff attempted to step on the bench to get a better view of the fairway, the unsecured bench flipped forward, causing the plaintiff to fall on the concrete slab. The plaintiff fractured his nose and both wrists and experienced substantial facial bleeding. The defendant claimed that the plaintiff's misuse of the bench should establish his own negligence, and so the golf course should not be found liable. However, the plaintiff submitted affidavits to support the fact that golfers on occasion stand on benches in order to view the course. It was the plaintiff's position that the misuse of the bench was foreseeable, and so the golf course had a duty of care. The golf course lost its motion for summary judgment. The court stated that the plaintiff's own negligence could partly depend on whether it was reasonable for him to assume that the bench was anchored when he attempted to stand on it.

Benches and other fixtures on a golf course should be inspected and repaired if found to be unsafe.

Little v. Jonesboro Country Club

A relevant legal case addressing the issue of inspection is *Little v. Jonesboro Country Club*, 92 Ark. App. 214, 212 S.W.3d 57 (2005). Plaintiff Loretta Little was playing in a golf tournament at Jonesboro Country Club when she fell near the 16th hole in an uncovered irrigation system valve hole that was covered by thick grass so that it was not visible. The defendant golf course provided affidavits to support the fact that the superintendent of the course had no information about a problem with a valve cover anywhere on the course and that he inspected the entire golf course at least twice per week and had performed an inspection of most of the course on the morning of the incident. Other testimony of golfers provided information that they had never observed a broken valve cover on the golf course. To determine if the defendant was negligent, the court would have to answer the question of whether the hole the plaintiff fell in was so apparent that, through the use of ordinary care, the golf course should have discovered it and repaired it. Since a material issue of fact regarding this matter existed, the golf course was not successful in bringing a motion for summary judgment. The case would have to proceed to trial, unless the parties were able to enter into a settlement agreement beforehand.

Testimony of the regular inspections of the golf course will assist the defendant in its defense in this case.

Lombardo v. Cedar Brook Golf & Tennis Club   In *Lombardo v. Cedar Brook Golf & Tennis Club*, 39 A.D.3d 818, 834 N.Y.S.2d 326 (2007), plaintiff Joseph Lombardo was injured when he was walking from the 17th tee and slipped on wet grass. The plaintiff was an experienced golfer and had knowledge

Regularly inspect golf courses so you can correct any repairs or issues before they cause injury to participants.

that torrential rains had required the course to close the day before. The defendant golf course prevailed on a motion for summary judgment on the grounds that the plaintiff assumed the risk of injury by playing golf on the wet grass.

Torrential rains, in this case, caused the course to close, which seems reasonable. The court did not impose upon the golf course the duty to close the course on subsequent days, even though the grass was still wet.

Manias v. Golden Bear Golf Center

In *Manias v. Golden Bear Golf Center*, 348 N.Y.S.2d 491 (2007), plaintiff Giles Manias was injured when he fell from the upper level of the Golden Bear Golf Center's indoor golf facility. The plaintiff alleged that the safety net was negligently constructed and designed, because when he lost his balance on the upper level, the net did not support him and he fell off the edge of a platform. The court concluded that the plaintiff did not assume the risk because the safety net providing protection to golfers at the defendant's driving range was not an inherent risk of the sport of golf. The plaintiff submitted an affidavit from an engineer that provided his opinion that the nylon twist ties that were used to secure the safety net were ineffective for that purpose. The court found that this created an issue for trial, and the case would proceed forward.

Parsons v. Arrowhead Golf, Inc.

In *Parsons v. Arrowhead Golf, Inc.*, 874 N.E.2d 993 (Ind. App. 2007), Victor Parsons and his wife were playing golf at Arrowhead Golf Course. Parsons drove his golf cart on the cart path and parked near the 16th hole green. There was a drop-off on the asphalt path, which Parsons believed caused him to step down in a manner that caused him back pain. The owner of the course attested that he routinely inspected the course for hazards, and he routinely altered the cart paths by moving signs and ropes to protect the paths from being too worn down in any particular spot. Parsons alleged negligent golf course design, negligent maintenance, and failure to warn. There had been no previous complaints or injuries in the particular area where Parsons' injury occurred. Because golf is an outdoor sport that is played on uneven, grassy surfaces, the court concluded that stepping on such surfaces is an inherent risk of the game. Consequently, Arrowhead did not owe a duty to Parsons to prevent injury arising out of the inherent risk of walking on the golf course.

The court also applied a premises liability analysis, which means that a landowner is liable if he knows of a condition on the land, or through reasonable care could discover that condition, that he realizes is an unreasonable risk of harm to people he invites to use the property. It must also be shown that persons using the golf course would not discover the condition or recognize its danger and so would not protect themselves against it. The landowner must also act reasonably to protect the persons on his property against the dangerous condition.

Applying the premises liability analysis, the court did not find liability against Arrowhead. The court reasoned that since the ground of a golf course is uneven, a golfer must adapt and be alert to changes in elevation of the course and adapt to such changes.

The condition of uneven ground is similar to the cases in this chapter involving wet golf courses. Golfers assume the risk of the inherent nature of the sport.

Summy v. City of Des Moines, Iowa　Golf course owners should be concerned about how the design of the course affects the potential safety of golfers and others who may be on or near playing areas. In *Summy v. City of Des Moines, Iowa*, 708 N.W.2d 333 (Iowa 2006), a city-owned golf course had to defend against a lawsuit brought by a golfer standing on the 18th fairway who was hit in the eye by a golf ball hit from the tee of the 1st hole. Originally, the golf course had been designed to have 60 to 80 large trees between the 1st and 18th fairways, but with time, the trees had died and been replaced by fewer small trees. A jury found the city 75 percent at fault and the plaintiff 25 percent at fault, apparently for not paying attention to the golfers hitting from the first tee. On appeal, the court determined that the jury's decision was correct, as the city did not exercise reasonable care in protecting golfers from the foreseeable risk of balls hit between the 1st and 18th fairways. Note that the city was not immune from the lawsuit in this case pursuant to an applicable state statute because it did not protect the injured golfer from the foreseeable hazard of balls hit between the two fairways.

When the trees that provided protection died, the golf course could have reviewed the situation and considered how the golf course design could be modified in light of the lack of protection.

Tiger Point Golf and Country Club v. Hipple　Although inspection is important, repairing unsafe conditions in a timely fashion is necessary to prevent injuries. In *Tiger Point Golf and Country Club v. Hipple*, 977 So. 2d 608 (Fla. App. 1 Dist. 2007), the manager of Tiger Point Golf and Country Club had been told that a handrail on the property was in very bad condition and in need of immediate repair. Several weeks passed and several people, including the plaintiff, attempted to remove the deteriorating handrail. Unfortunately, it fell on the plaintiff's foot, fracturing his toe. A jury found the people who removed the handrail each 25 percent liable, and Tiger Point was also fount 25 percent responsible. Surprisingly, the jury found Tiger Point responsible for $85,000 in punitive damages. Fortunately for the golf course, the appellate court found that the trial court was in error, because Tiger Point's conduct did not have the element of outrage that normally would be present when a crime is committed. Failing to repair the handrail did not justify the excessive monetary punishment in addition to payment of 25 percent of the plaintiff's damages for his injury.

When a problem of maintenance is reported to any employee or management, something should be done immediately. If there will be a delay in repair of the problem, warning should be given or the area blocked off. A defective handrail could make the stairs dangerous, and so repair should be a high priority, unless there is an alternative route and the stairs can be effectively closed off from use.

Unzen v. City of Duluth   In *Unzen v. City of Duluth*, 683 N.W.2d 875 (Minn. App. 2004), the plaintiff fell down the stairs at the clubhouse of a municipal golf course. There had been previous falls on those stairs because of a metal nosing that protruded above a rubber tread. The lawsuit was filed against the City of Duluth, the owner of the golf course, and against Steven Dornfeld, Inc., the company that had contracted with the city to operate the concessions at the golf course's clubhouse. Dornfeld argued that it fell under the recreational-use statute, so it would be immune from the lawsuit. Because the dangerous conditions of the stairway were not visible, Dornfeld was not immune from the lawsuit. The other defendant, the City of Duluth, attempted to invoke governmental immunity but failed because it could have warned patrons of the condition of the dangerous stairs but did not.

Stairs are safety hazards and should be inspected regularly and well maintained in accordance with building codes and government regulations.

Williams v. Linkscorp Tennessee Six, LLC   The Court of Appeals of Tennessee addressed the issue of whether a golf course was negligent for injuries sustained by a golfer who fell on stairs. In *Williams v. Linkscorp Tennessee Six, LLC*, 212 S.W.3d 293 (Tenn. Ct. App. 2006), the court considered the complaint of Williams, who was playing golf at Nashboro Golf Club. He was descending the railroad cross-tie stairs near the 8th green when he fell on the slippery stairs, injuring his right shoulder and knee. The plaintiff provided affidavits supporting his position that there was water and a substance similar to algae on the steps, causing them to be slippery. The defendant golf course provided evidence that the stairs were repaired when damaged, but they had never been cleaned. There had been only one other incident involving railroad cross-tie stairs, but that was in another area, and so the golf course claimed not to have notice of the slippery stairs. The golf course had a duty to maintain the premises in a reasonably safe condition and where required to remove or repair dangerous conditions or to warn players of any dangerous conditions. The court ruled in favor of the plaintiff, concluding that the defendant golf course should have known about the slippery substance on the steps and the hazards that would arise out of that condition when the stairs were wet.

Slippery steps are especially dangerous and should be repaired using nonslip materials or other measures.

Yoneda v. Tom   In *Yoneda v. Tom*, 110 Hawaii 367, 133 P.3d 796 (2006), Yoneda was a passenger in a golf cart riding on a designated path at the

Mililani Golf Course. The cart path looped behind a restroom building on the course. When the cart came from behind the building, a ball that had been hit by the defendant hit Yoneda in the left eye. Tom did not yell, "Fore!" because he did not see the cart when he hit the ball, as the cart path was behind the building.

Regarding Yoneda's claims against Tom, the court decided that Yoneda assumed the risk, and so that action was barred. Regarding Yoneda's claims against the owners of the course, Sports Shinto, Co., there was an issue of fact for the jury to decide as to whether the golf course design, with the golf path running behind the restroom, increased the risk of people being struck by errant balls.

In this case, a player sued another player and the court barred such action, as is often the case, unless there is a showing of willful and wanton behavior. The golf course, which was left in the action, would likely attempt to settle out of court before trial rather than face an uncertain jury verdict.

Hazards

Bowman v. McNary   In *Bowman v. McNary*, 852 N.E.2d 984 (Ind. App. 2006), the plaintiff Bowman and the defendant McNary, high school golf team members, were directed by their coach to warm up at the driving range. While doing so, McNary did not step far enough away from Bowman when swinging her golf club, and she hit Bowman in the head with her club. As a result, Bowman was rendered blind in one eye. The plaintiff sued McNary and the Tippecanoe School Corporation and its board of trustees. The appellate court addressed the issue of whether McNary owed her golf team teammate a duty of reasonable care. In addressing that issue, the court looked at the relationship between the parties, whether the conduct was foreseeable, and the impact on public policy. Since the girls were coparticipants and they knew the risk of participating in sports, it was determined that the relationship between them did not establish a duty. The issue of foreseeability was addressed by the court, which determined that negligent behavior during golf, such as swinging a golf club and accidentally hitting someone, was a risk that is inherent in the sport. As for public policy, it was concluded that it would be poor public policy to allow participants to sue participants for injuries that arise out of an inherent risk of the sport. Consequently, the Indiana Court of Appeals concluded that a golf team participant did not owe a duty to another participant, and so the plaintiff's claim against the defendant for negligence failed.

Likewise, the plaintiff's claim that McNary acted recklessly failed. McNary made an error of judgment by not looking around to make sure she would not strike anyone when she swung her golf club. For this behavior to be deemed reckless, there would have to be an intentional component. For example, recklessness in golf might occur when a player flings a club in anger or swings wildly in frustration, knowing that doing so might injure another person. It was noted by the court that recklessness by a pro, such as Tiger Woods, might be different from that of an amateur. Tiger Woods would have more knowledge of his ability to hit a ball a certain distance, whereas an amateur might accidentally hit a ball farther than intended. Hence, a pro's behavior would more readily be determined to be reckless.

The plaintiff's lawsuit against the school was also dismissed. The plaintiff had signed a release form in which she accepted the responsibility of her own safety and understood the risks of the sport. Since the plaintiff voluntarily accepted the risk of being a member of the school golf team, the school, as a matter of law, was entitled to summary judgment and so was dismissed from the lawsuit.

MEC Leasing, LLC, v. Jarrett

In an Oregon appellate court case, *MEC Leasing, LLC, v. Jarrett*, 214 Or. App. 294, 164 P.3d 344 (2007), four vehicles that were parked next to the Mountain View Golf Club were struck by golf balls and damaged. The owner of the cars sued the golf course, alleging that the 15th hole was hazardous and dangerous, causing balls to be hit out of the limits of the golf course, threatening property damage and bodily injury. The court determined that there was a question for the jury as to whether there was a reasonably foreseeable risk of harm. The jury would also address the issue of whether the golf course was informed of the risk and whether reasonable measures were taken to prevent injury and damages.

If you park your car next to a golf course, it stands to reason that your car could be hit by a golf ball.

Sall v. T's, Inc.

Since golf is played outdoors, it is constantly subjected to weather conditions. One of the most dangerous conditions is lightning. In *Sall v. T's, Inc.*, 136 P.3d 471 (Kan. 2006), the plaintiff filed a lawsuit against T's, Inc., doing business as Smiley's Golf Course, as a result of injuries he sustained when struck by lightning while golfing at the defendant's course. At noon on the day of the incident, the manager of the golf course saw the television weather forecast, predicting storms. The manager continued to check the weather by walking outside every 10 to 15 minutes in accordance with the golf course policy. At one point, he observed dark clouds, and so he closed the complex. In the afternoon, the next manager came on duty, noticing that the skies were clearing. Computer radar images also confirmed that storms were moving out of the area. When the sun came out, the golf course was reopened. The plaintiff decided to golf, believing the golf course would not be open if it was not safe. As the plaintiff and his friend were golfing, it started to rain. They anticipated that the golf course would blow an air horn if dangerous weather was moving in. They saw a lightning bolt in the distance while putting on the second green. The twosome decided to finish the second hole and then begin walking back to the clubhouse. Meanwhile, the golf course manager blew the air horn. As the plaintiff was walking back, he saw a flash, heard a loud boom, and was knocked unconscious.

In the course of the lawsuit, the court addressed whether Smiley's has a duty to protect golfers from harm caused by lightning strikes on its golf course. The evidence established that the defendant did the following to protect its patrons from inclement weather: (1) monitoring weather through broadcasts on television, radio, and Internet reports; (2) going outside and visually inspecting the weather; (3) warning golfers by use of an air horn to come off the golf course in poor weather conditions; and (4) informing golfers with signage about what they should do in case of inclement weather.

The court concluded that the golf course had adopted a safety system for inclement weather and had a duty of reasonable care to use it correctly. In this case, the golf course did not have a play-at-your-own-risk policy that was communicated to the golfers. The plaintiff was aware that the golf course was monitoring the weather and would issue warnings, and so he relied on the fact that the golf course would be doing this properly. The appellate court determined that there were issues of fact as to whether the golf course was negligent in its warning of the plaintiff, and so the case was directed to proceed to trial.

If the golf course had a play-at-your-own-risk policy, perhaps the court would have ruled in its favor.

Golf courses should have clear procedures in place for handling weather-related events.

Thomas v. Wheat   In *Thomas v. Wheat*, 143 P.3d 767 (Okla. Civ. App. Div. 2006), plaintiff Lonnie Thomas was painting a house located next to a golf course. Thomas knew there was a danger of golf balls being hit into the yard. Shortly before he was hit by a golf ball, he was behind the house, cleaning paint brushes. He then walked over to a large tree so he could see whether there were golfers nearby. Before he could make that determination, defendant Diane Wheat teed off, hooking the ball in the direction of Thomas. She yelled, "Fore!" in order to warn the plaintiff, but he did not hear her and was hit in the mouth by the ball, causing injury. The court concluded that liability against a golfer hitting an errant shot depends on whether the person who is hit by the ball is inside the "zone of risk" and whether sufficient warning is given by the golfer hitting the ball. If a person is within the bounds of the golf course, it is presumed that the person assumed the risk, but if the person is outside the golf course, then such presumption does not apply. It was determined in this case that the matter was not appropriate for summary judgment, as there were material facts a jury had to decide.

Anyone who chooses to live or work adjacent to a golf course runs the risk of being hit by an errant ball.

Participant

Hemady v. Long Beach Unified School District, et al.   A California appellate court case, *Hemady v. Long Beach Unified School District, et al.*, 49 Cal. Rptr. 3d 464, 143 Cal. App. 4th 566, involving school children learning how to swing golf clubs, is applicable not only to golf classes but also to the activities of a driving range. Jane Hemady, a 12-year-old student, filed a lawsuit against the Long Beach Unified School District after she was hit in the face with a golf club that was swung by another student during a golf class for seventh-grade physical education. According to the teacher of the class, Mr. Feely, he devised a system for the 54 students to hit Wiffle balls with golf clubs. The children were broken up into 11 groups and would hit the balls on whistle commands, while other students would wait in a designated area that was 10 feet (3 m) behind the students who were hitting the balls. The plaintiff took the position that the class was unorganized and students were making their own decisions as to when to hit the balls. The plaintiff was injured when she stepped forward when a student appeared to be finished, but instead the other student swung the club back, striking the plaintiff in the mouth. The court addressed the issue of whether the defendant school had a limited duty of care or was governed by the prudent standard of care. The court concluded that the prudent standard of care was applicable, because being hit by another person swinging a golf club is not an inherent risk of golf. Applying a prudent standard of care to the coach does not lessen his ability to teach his students or discourage vigorous participation or competition between the players. Golfers should be charged with a prudent person duty to make sure the area around them is clear before swinging the club, and a coach or teacher must make sure the distance between golfers is sufficient to allow them to swing without hitting each other. Imposing these duties does not have anything to do with the mechanics of swinging a golf club and does not affect the fundamental nature of golf.

Beginning golfers, novices, spectators, and even seasoned players who might not be paying attention are susceptible to being hit by golf clubs. Written and verbal warnings and reminders can help prevent injuries.

Mavrovich v. Vanderpool

In *Mavrovich v. Vanderpool*, 427 F. Supp. 2d 1084 (D. Kan. 2006), plaintiff Andrew Mavrovich filed a lawsuit against various individuals who he claimed were trespassing on his property when they retrieved their golf balls, which had landed in the plaintiff's yard. The property owner was not able to obtain a temporary restraining order against the defendants in this particular case.

Note that this case did not involve a golf course as a defendant. It would be reasonable for a golfer to ask permission of the owner of the property before retrieving balls in someone's yard.

Shin v. Ahn

One of the inherent risks of teeing off, or even hitting the golf ball on any part of the course, is the possibility of hitting another person. This occurred in the case of *Shin v. Ahn*, 141 Cal. App. 4th 726 (2006). Ahn and Shin were golfing in the same threesome. Ahn was preparing to tee off on the 13th hole when Shin was putting on the 12th hole green. Shin then walked up an embankment approximately 7 yards (7 m) behind Ahn, whom he had seen headed toward the 13th hole tee box. Shin stopped on the cart path, checked his cell phone messages, retrieved a bottle of water from his bag, and claimed he made eye contact with Ahn as he was standing to the front and left of him. Ahn took a practice swing, not seeing anyone on the fairway. He then swung at the ball, causing the ball to hit Shin in the head. Shin filed a lawsuit against Ahn, alleging negligence. Ahn responded by stating that Shin assumed the risk. The appellate court addressed the issue of whether Shin assumed the risk of being injured by a ball hit by a member of his group who did not check to see where the others in his group were standing before teeing off. The court determined that Shin did not assume this risk and that Ahn owed a duty of care to look to see where Shin and the other member of their threesome were standing before teeing off. The court found that Ahn breached his duty of care and directed that the trial address the issue of any comparative negligence on the part of Shin.

This case is unusual because it is a player-versus-player case, and the court did not find assumption of risk.

Staff

Mallin v. Paesani   In *Mallin v. Paesani*, 49 Conn. Supp. 457, 892 A.2d 1043 (2005), both Mallin and Paesani were competitors in a PGA tournament. Mallin alleged that Paesani drove a golf ball, striking the plaintiff in the head and causing injury. The plaintiff brought an apportionment action against Tashua Knolls Golf Course and the town of Trumbull, claiming their negligence in possession and control of the golf tournament was a proximate cause of the plaintiff's injuries. The issue in this case was whether the sports-exception doctrine was applicable. The sports-exception doctrine states that mere negligence is not enough to establish liability; there has to be an allegation of intentional conduct or recklessness. The court discussed whether the sports-exception doctrine applies only to contact team sports or whether it is applicable to individual and noncontact sports. Citing a case involving skiing, the court concluded that the sports-exception doctrine was not applicable to golf, and so the plaintiff could maintain its action against defendants Tashua Knolls Golf Course and the town of Trumbull on a negligence theory.

Wu v. Sorenson   In *Wu v. Sorenson*, 440 F. Supp. 2d 1054 (D. Minn. 2006), an 11-year-old student of Shattuck-St. Mary's School (SSMS), Lucas Sorenson, was hitting golf balls from stations on the west side of a netted structure into the east side of the structure. The students were taught by a member of the PGA, Greg Paine. The students were instructed not to hit golf balls if anyone was retrieving balls on the east side of the structure. During a lesson, Sorenson was being given one-on-one instruction by Paine. Paine was making adjustments to Sorenson's backswing by having him stop his swing so Paine could put his hands on Sorenson's shoulders. Paine would then step back and instruct Sorenson to swing. On one of these occasions, Sorenson's ball sliced to the south of the structure, striking the 14-year-old plaintiff, who was retrieving balls on the east side of the structure. The ball hit Wu in the temple, causing a brain injury. Sorenson was successful in prevailing by motion for summary judgment. Golf experts on behalf of the plaintiff attested that Paine did not enforce the rules regarding hitting balls while others retrieved balls; did not make sure it was safe before instructing Sorenson to hit the ball; and created confusion about the procedures for retrieving balls. Further, Paine had a responsibility to make sure it was safe before he instructed Sorenson to strike the ball. The defendants Paine and SSMS were unsuccessful in bringing a motion for summary judgment. After that, they settled the lawsuit by paying the plaintiff $10 million.

Violations

Celano v. Marriott International, Inc.   In 2008, the United States District Court in California, in *Celano v. Marriott International, Inc.*, 2008 WL

239306 (N.D. Cal.), considered the issue of whether Marriott International, Inc., was required to provide mobility-impaired golfers use of single-rider golf carts at its golf courses. The single-rider golf carts in question have swivel seats, allowing disabled golfers to hit a golf ball while seated in the cart. They also contain hand brakes and hand accelerators. The three plaintiffs who filed the lawsuit had been injured and were not able to golf without use of such a special cart. They had each requested use of single-rider carts in order to play some of the 27 golf courses that Marriott owns and operates. Marriott did not provide these carts but invited the plaintiffs to bring their own if they wanted to play. The plaintiffs claimed that bringing their own carts would be too difficult.

The plaintiffs filed a lawsuit under Title III of the Americans with Disabilities Act (ADA), which prohibits against discrimination of disabled individuals in public places. The plaintiffs, in order to prove discrimination, had to show that (1) they were disabled; (2) Marriott is a private entity that "owns, leases, or operates a place of public accommodation"; (3) Marriott employed a discriminatory policy or practice; and (4) Marriott discriminated against them based on their disabilities by not providing the single-rider carts as requested or otherwise making necessary accommodations.

The court concluded that the plaintiffs were successful in proving they were discriminated by Marriott under Title III of the ADA, based on Marriott's not making reasonable accommodations of providing the special golf carts. The required elements were proven by the plaintiffs, and it was determined that the golf carts were reasonable and necessary in providing accommodation to the plaintiffs' disabilities. The cost of the carts was not burdensome, use of the carts would allow the plaintiffs to golf on Marriott's courses, and Marriott did not establish that the carts were dangerous to others.

Morgan v. Fuji Country USA, Inc.

In *Morgan v. Fuji Country USA, Inc.*, 34 Cal. App. 4th 127, 40 Cal. Rptr. 2d 249 (1995), the court concluded that the defendant golf course owed Morgan a duty of care to provide a reasonably safe golf course, minimizing the risks without affecting the nature of the game.

Morgan was a member of the Castle Creek Country Club, a golf course owned by the defendant, Fiji Country USA, Inc. Morgan had seen golf balls hit from the fourth tee land on the fifth tee or green. The trees that separated the fourth and fifth holes were diseased and removed by the defendant. Morgan alleged that the defendant was negligent and asserted premises and landowner liability while the defendant argued that Morgan assumed the risk.

The court noted that the golf course owner may have a duty to protect players from being hit by golf balls where it was reasonably expected that golfers would be hit and where the greatest danger of being hit existed. The plaintiff presented evidence to establish that the area of the fifth tee, where he was hit, was particularly dangerous because of the golf course design and tree removal. Since this evidence could support a finding of the defendant's breach of care, the case was to proceed to trial.

GOLF SAFETY CONSIDERATIONS

These cases illustrate various factual scenarios that have led to lawsuits and reported appellate court decisions. By examining the facts in each decision, it is apparent that there are many safety precautions that course owners and operators, golfers, and people in the vicinity of golf courses should consider. To facilitate your organization's safety standards in golf, please use all the forms on pages 211 to 224.

SUMMARY

Numerous safety concerns and issues have been addressed by courts and should be addressed by golf course management, including golf course inspection, maintenance and repairs, slippery wet grass, golf course design, errant golf balls, benches and fixed objects, rules of golf, property adjacent to golf courses, golf carts, lightning, driving ranges, clubhouses and pro shops, the Americans with Disabilities Act (ADA), warning signage, and alcohol use. Because of the complexity of the safety issues related to golf, it is particularly important that safety guidelines and procedures be established and followed. Rules should be communicated and enforced, and warnings of hazards should be clearly communicated with signage and by other reasonable means.

GOLF COURSE DESIGN AND SAFETY

Golf course design may create a beautifully landscaped environment and a difficult and fun course to play. However, such design might create hazardous situations, with people crossing the path of play or errant balls; precarious golf cart paths; or dangerous water hazards. The following questions are ones to consider related to golf course design.

Considerations	Yes or No (check one)	Notes for follow-up
Are fairways spaced properly so that errant golf balls will not pose a danger to golfers and others?	❏ Yes ❏ No	
If fairways are narrow and close to one another, are golfers given proper warning?	❏ Yes ❏ No	
Is supervision provided so that people do not cross fairways while golfers are hitting balls?	❏ Yes ❏ No	
Are injuries likely to arise because of the course design?	❏ Yes ❏ No	
Is there a history of accidents and injuries that have occurred on or adjacent to the golf course?	❏ Yes ❏ No	
Is there proper lighting in areas where people will be walking or golfing when it becomes dusk or dark?	❏ Yes ❏ No	
Are there other considerations for golf course design and safety?	❏ Yes ❏ No	

From Katharine M. Nohr, 2009, *Managing Risk in Sport and Recreation: The Essential Guide for Loss Prevention* (Champaign, IL: Human Kinetics).

INSPECTION OF THE GOLF COURSE

Inspecting a golf course for defects requires evaluation and examination of teeing grounds, fairways, putting greens, water hazards, bunkers, roughs, fencing, grass, lighting, drainage systems, and sprinkler systems. Defects in these have been known to cause injury. The following questions should be addressed.

Considerations	Yes or No (check one)	Notes for follow-up
Has the golf course been inspected by walking across it to look for balls, clubs, garbage, glass, rakes, shovels, or any other objects that should be picked up and cleared away before play begins?	❑ Yes ❑ No	
Have objects been cleared from the golf course before play begins?	❑ Yes ❑ No	
Has the grass been mowed so it is well groomed, with the proper height of grass on the teeing grounds, fairways, and putting greens?	❑ Yes ❑ No	
Have sprinkler heads, irrigation stand pipes, and drainage hole covers been inspected to make sure they will not pose a hazard to golfers?	❑ Yes ❑ No	
Have rocks and clumped mud been removed from the course to eliminate tripping hazards?	❑ Yes ❑ No	
Have all tripping hazards been eliminated before play begins?	❑ Yes ❑ No	
Are public restrooms and other facilities inspected for slippery surfaces or other defects or hazards?	❑ Yes ❑ No	
Are the teeing grounds, fairways, and putting greens in good condition?	❑ Yes ❑ No	
Are all benches placed at teeing areas sturdy and well anchored?	❑ Yes ❑ No	
Are there holes in the ground or protruding objects that are obvious or concealed by grass?	❑ Yes ❑ No	
Does the course have an adequate drainage and sprinkler system?	❑ Yes ❑ No	
Will sprinkler heads on the course pose a hazard?	❑ Yes ❑ No	
Are there trees in place that might prevent players from being hit by golf balls in areas located close to tee grounds?	❑ Yes ❑ No	
Where golfers might be hit by flying golf balls, are there any nets or screens that could serve as a temporary safety measure until the circumstance can be more permanently remedied by planting trees or redesign?	❑ Yes ❑ No	
Are there other considerations for golf course inspection?	❑ Yes ❑ No	

From Katharine M. Nohr, 2009, *Managing Risk in Sport and Recreation: The Essential Guide for Loss Prevention* (Champaign, IL: Human Kinetics).

GOLF COURSE SIGNAGE AND WARNINGS

Golf course employees and superintendents may become aware of dangerous conditions that exist on a golf course. If these conditions are known, the golf course has a duty to warn the public. Careful attention should be paid to complaints by patrons of hazardous conditions and injuries that occur. Inspections might also provide knowledge as to hazards that require warning signs. Warnings should be readily visible and understood. Because conditions change with time, warning signs should be regularly reviewed and updated. The following questions should be asked concerning warnings and signage.

Considerations	Yes or No (check one)	Notes for follow-up
Is signage placed in appropriate places on the golf course to communicate warnings of danger?	❑ Yes ❑ No	
Are golf course rules and regulations posted conspicuously?	❑ Yes ❑ No	
Are golfers warned that certain areas are very slippery or muddy?	❑ Yes ❑ No	
Are golfers warned that they need to keep their distance from other golfers to avoid being hit by swinging golf clubs?	❑ Yes ❑ No	
Are golf course crossing signs located at appropriate places?	❑ Yes ❑ No	
Are "golfers only beyond this point" signs located at appropriate places where people might walk onto the course?	❑ Yes ❑ No	
Are warning signs erected in response to knowledge regarding hazards?	❑ Yes ❑ No	
Are warning signs visible and easily understood?	❑ Yes ❑ No	
Are warning signs regularly reviewed and updated in response to changing conditions?	❑ Yes ❑ No	
Are there other considerations for golf course signage and warnings?	❑ Yes ❑ No	

From Katharine M. Nohr, 2009, *Managing Risk in Sport and Recreation: The Essential Guide for Loss Prevention* (Champaign, IL: Human Kinetics).

TEE AREAS

Tee areas should be regularly inspected and made safe for play. The following questions may be addressed in this regard.

Considerations	Yes or No (check one)	Notes for follow-up
Are tee areas regularly inspected for debris, holes in the ground, sprinkler heads, golf balls, bottles, and other tripping hazards?	❏ Yes ❏ No	
Are all benches located in tee areas situated far enough away from the tee?	❏ Yes ❏ No	
Are all benches anchored properly and free of defects so they will not cause injury?	❏ Yes ❏ No	
Are there other considerations for tee areas?	❏ Yes ❏ No	

From Katharine M. Nohr, 2009, *Managing Risk in Sport and Recreation: The Essential Guide for Loss Prevention* (Champaign, IL: Human Kinetics).

WATER HAZARDS ON THE GOLF COURSE

Wherever there is water, there are dangers associated with drowning. Even though this seems unlikely on a golf course, it has been known to happen when golf carts are inadvertently driven into water, when golfers are retrieving balls, or in other accidental circumstances when children or adults enter the water. Because of this, the following questions should be asked.

Considerations	Yes or No (check one)	Notes for follow-up
Are lakes, ditches, and other water hazards off-limits to golfers?	❏ Yes ❏ No	
Are there chains or ropes around water hazards to prohibit golfers from entering such areas?	❏ Yes ❏ No	
Are there signs warning golfers of the danger of water hazards?	❏ Yes ❏ No	
Are there other considerations for water hazards?	❏ Yes ❏ No	

From Katharine M. Nohr, 2009, *Managing Risk in Sport and Recreation: The Essential Guide for Loss Prevention* (Champaign, IL: Human Kinetics).

PROPERTY ADJACENT TO GOLF COURSES AND NONGOLFERS

Commonly, people residing on property located on or near golf courses complain about golfers and stray golf balls entering their property. Another problem that arises with property adjacent to golf courses involves the risk of someone being hit by a golf ball. The following questions address this issue.

Considerations	Yes or No (check one)	Notes for follow-up
Are neighbor residents and businesses protected from errant golf balls?	❏ Yes ❏ No	
Are passing motor vehicles protected from errant golf balls?	❏ Yes ❏ No	
Are people who are not golfing prohibited from entering the golf course?	❏ Yes ❏ No	
Are people who are walking near the golf course protected or warned of errant balls?	❏ Yes ❏ No	
Are walkers, joggers, spouses, parents, kids, bicyclists, and others who are not accustomed to golf warned about possibly being hit by balls or golf clubs if they get too close to a golfer's swing?	❏ Yes ❏ No	
Are there other considerations for adjacent property and nongolfers?	❏ Yes ❏ No	

From Katharine M. Nohr, 2009, *Managing Risk in Sport and Recreation: The Essential Guide for Loss Prevention* (Champaign, IL: Human Kinetics).

GOLF CART PATHS

The path a golf cart takes through the course has been the alleged reason for injury in several court cases. The following questions address the safety concerns related to golf cart paths.

Considerations	Yes or No (check one)	Notes for follow-up
Does the golf cart path have any dangerous conditions such as steep hills, sharp curves, blind areas, or drop-offs?	❑ Yes ❑ No	
Are there any conditions of the golf cart path that could lead to golf cart collisions or rollovers?	❑ Yes ❑ No	
Are golf cart paths swept for debris that could interfere with the operation of golf carts?	❑ Yes ❑ No	
Are golf cart paths cleaned of any accumulated oil that might cause slippery conditions?	❑ Yes ❑ No	
Are golf cart paths clearly marked?	❑ Yes ❑ No	
Are signs posted to warn golf cart drivers of potentially hazardous conditions?	❑ Yes ❑ No	
Are there other considerations for golf cart paths?	❑ Yes ❑ No	

From Katharine M. Nohr, 2009, *Managing Risk in Sport and Recreation: The Essential Guide for Loss Prevention* (Champaign, IL: Human Kinetics).

GOLF CARTS

Just like any motorized vehicles, golf carts can be dangerous and cause injury if they are driven negligently. It is important that golf courses impose rules for the use of golf carts and that such rules be enforced. It is equally important that drivers of golf carts exercise reasonable care in their use. Rules associated with golf cart use are usually provided or available at golf courses, and golf cart users should make themselves familiar with such requirements. The following questions should be addressed in relation to golf cart use.

Considerations	Yes or No (check one)	Notes for follow-up
Does your club have a minimum age requirement for golf cart drivers?	❑ Yes ❑ No	
Are conspicuous signs posted that prohibit children under the age of 16 or minors from driving golf carts?	❑ Yes ❑ No	
Are golf cart operators prohibited from drinking alcohol before or during the operation of the golf cart?	❑ Yes ❑ No	
Are users warned to keep their entire body in the golf cart while it is being operated?	❑ Yes ❑ No	
Is a speed limit established for use of golf carts?	❑ Yes ❑ No	
Are golf cart paths regularly inspected and maintained?	❑ Yes ❑ No	
Are golf carts inspected before and after each use for any mechanical problems?	❑ Yes ❑ No	
Are golf carts given periodic maintenance in accordance with the recommendations of the manufacturer?	❑ Yes ❑ No	
Are golf carts stored so that children and others cannot operate them without permission?	❑ Yes ❑ No	
Is golf cart use limited to the golf course property?	❑ Yes ❑ No	
Are there other considerations for golf carts?	❑ Yes ❑ No	

From Katharine M. Nohr, 2009, *Managing Risk in Sport and Recreation: The Essential Guide for Loss Prevention* (Champaign, IL: Human Kinetics).

DRIVING RANGE

One of the primary safety issues with driving ranges, as made evident if you reviewed the court decisions regarding this topic, is that people can be struck and injured by swinging golf clubs. The following questions should be addressed on this topic.

Considerations	Yes or No (check one)	Notes for follow-up
Is there a pedestrian passageway that allows people to walk safely behind those who are swinging golf clubs?	❑ Yes ❑ No	
Is there conspicuous signage warning people to stay a safe distance from those who are swinging golf clubs?	❑ Yes ❑ No	
Have safety railings and other necessary precautions been provided for multiple-level driving ranges?	❑ Yes ❑ No	
Are there other considerations for the driving range?	❑ Yes ❑ No	

From Katharine M. Nohr, 2009, *Managing Risk in Sport and Recreation: The Essential Guide for Loss Prevention* (Champaign, IL: Human Kinetics).

GOLF SCORECARDS

Scorecards should provide information on the layout of the golf course and are also a means of communicating rules, safety information, and warnings to golfers. The following questions may be asked with regard to scorecards.

Considerations	Yes or No (check one)	Notes for follow-up
Are yardage markings on scorecards and signs accurate?	❑ Yes ❑ No	
If yardage markings have changed, have scorecards and signage changed accordingly?	❑ Yes ❑ No	
Are general safety warnings placed on scorecards so they are easy to read and legible?	❑ Yes ❑ No	
Are there other considerations for scorecards?	❑ Yes ❑ No	

GOLFING EQUIPMENT AND FOOTWEAR

Golf clubs are the primary equipment used by golfers and can potentially lead to injury if a portion of a club should become loose or a golfer loses his or her grip because of sweaty or wet hands. Proper footwear should be required on golf courses to prevent slips and falls. The following questions may be asked in relation to equipment and footwear.

Considerations	Yes or No (check one)	Notes for follow-up
Have all rented or loaned golf clubs been inspected for cracks, loose grips or heads, and any other defects?	❏ Yes ❏ No	
Have golfers inspected their own clubs for cracks, loose grips or heads, and any other defects?	❏ Yes ❏ No	
Is a glove worn while golfing so as to establish a firm grip on the club and prevent it from slipping and hitting another person?	❏ Yes ❏ No	
Are players required to wear cleats on the golf course? If Yes, please note how it is communicated to golfers in the Notes column.	❏ Yes ❏ No	
Are footwear rules enforced?	❏ Yes ❏ No	
Are there other considerations for equipment and footwear?	❏ Yes ❏ No	

From Katharine M. Nohr, 2009, *Managing Risk in Sport and Recreation: The Essential Guide for Loss Prevention* (Champaign, IL: Human Kinetics).

ALCOHOL USE ON THE GOLF COURSE

An important part of the golf experience is the 19th hole, where alcohol is likely served. Golfers may like to get an early start and carry beer or other alcoholic beverages on the golf course. Mixing intoxication with golf cart driving and hitting golf balls could lead to injury and dangerous behavior. Another concern is the possibility that patrons who are served alcohol at a golf course clubhouse will drive their vehicles in a negligent manner, resulting in a lawsuit against the golf course. The following questions should be addressed in relation to alcohol.

Considerations	Yes or No (check one)	Notes for follow-up
Is a no-alcohol rule in force for golfers during play?	❑ Yes ❑ No	
Are coolers with alcoholic beverages banned from golf carts to prevent golfers from drinking alcohol while playing?	❑ Yes ❑ No	
Is alcohol sold on the premises?	❑ Yes ❑ No	
Are golfers able to purchase and consume alcohol before or during play?	❑ Yes ❑ No	
Are persons who consume alcohol on the premises supervised so they do not drive golf carts, walk onto the fairways, play golf, or interfere with others?	❑ Yes ❑ No	
Are patrons of golf course restaurants and bars refused service of alcohol if they are visibly intoxicated?	❑ Yes ❑ No	
Are measures taken to help prevent inebriated persons from driving motor vehicles after they have been served alcohol at your golf course bar or restaurant?	❑ Yes ❑ No	
Are there other considerations for alcohol use?	❑ Yes ❑ No	

From Katharine M. Nohr, 2009, *Managing Risk in Sport and Recreation: The Essential Guide for Loss Prevention* (Champaign, IL: Human Kinetics).

SEVERE WEATHER CONDITIONS AND GOLF

Lightning is an important risk associated with golfing. Golf course owners, golf course operators, and golfers should pay careful attention to impending storms and make sure evacuation takes place when lightning is imminent. The United States Golf Association has printed its lightning safety guidelines on handy posters that can be posted in areas visible to golfers and staff. Procedures should be established and consistently followed in relation to lightning and other serious weather conditions, such as tornadoes, hurricanes, hail, and heavy rains that might cause flooding. The following questions should be asked when addressing weather concerns.

Considerations	Yes or No (check one)	Notes for follow-up
Do golf course personnel monitor weather conditions?	❏ Yes ❏ No	
Are potential severe weather conditions communicated to golfers?	❏ Yes ❏ No	
Are golfers pulled from the course in severe weather conditions?	❏ Yes ❏ No	
Is there a system for determining if the golf course is in imminent danger of being struck by lightning?	❏ Yes ❏ No	
When lightning is imminent, is there a communication system for notifying golfers?	❏ Yes ❏ No	
Are golfers told to evacuate when lightning is imminent?	❏ Yes ❏ No	
Are scorecards used to communicate information regarding lightning emergency information and warnings?	❏ Yes ❏ No	
Are there other considerations for severe weather conditions?	❏ Yes ❏ No	

From Katharine M. Nohr, 2009, *Managing Risk in Sport and Recreation: The Essential Guide for Loss Prevention* (Champaign, IL: Human Kinetics).

GENERAL GOLF COURSE SAFETY

Golf course management and personnel should place a high priority on safety. To this end, the following questions should be addressed.

Considerations	Yes or No (check one)	Notes for follow-up
Does your golf course offer junior golf safety training?	❑ Yes ❑ No	
Is safety information posted on the Web site and bulletin boards?	❑ Yes ❑ No	
Does your golf course have a system for investigating and correcting all reported potentially unsafe conditions on the golf course or facilities?	❑ Yes ❑ No	
Are there other considerations for general golf course safety?	❑ Yes ❑ No	

From Katharine M. Nohr, 2009, *Managing Risk in Sport and Recreation: The Essential Guide for Loss Prevention* (Champaign, IL: Human Kinetics).

14

Gymnastics

It's hard to be humble when you can jump, stunt, and tumble!

—Author Unknown

Gymnastics, if not done safely, can be a dangerous sport in which catastrophic injuries can occur, resulting in insurance claims and lawsuits. USA Gymnastics, the sport's national governing body in the United States, requires certification in safety and risk management for members of the organization. It is important that teachers, coaches, meet directors, club owners, athletes, and judges receive safety education and use the information learned in order to prevent serious injuries.

GYMNASTICS LAWSUITS

Some lawsuits that have arisen out of gymnastics injuries have made it to appellate courts, resulting in reported decisions. The bulk of these cases have addressed negligence issues in relation to trampoline injuries. The following appellate court decisions address injuries that occurred when athletes were using apparatus, such as high bar, uneven parallel bars, pommel horse, and balance beam. Although there were issues presented in relation to supervision, equipment safety, instruction, and safety procedures, all of the cases addressed the applicability of governmental immunity statutes to the defendants.

Equipment

Benbenek v. Chicago Park Dist.

In *Benbenek v. Chicago Park Dist.*, 279 Ill. App. 3d 930, 665 N.E.2d 500 (1996), the plaintiff filed a lawsuit against the Chicago Park District and its employee on behalf of her minor daughter who was injured when she fell off a balance beam during a gym show sponsored by the defendant. The plaintiff asserted that the defendant did not provide properly trained instructors and spotters; the balance beam was not adjusted to an appropriate height; and there was inadequate padding on the gym floor. The court determined that the applicable governmental employee's tort immunity act served to protect the defendants from the claims set forth in the lawsuit, and so it was dismissed.

It is important to make sure that gymnastics equipment is properly adjusted and that all safety measures are in place.

Carmack v. Macomb County Community College

A Michigan appellate court addressed the applicability of government immunity to the defendant. In *Carmack v. Macomb County Community College*, 199 Mich. App. 544, 502 N.W.2d 746 (1993), the plaintiff filed a lawsuit against the defendant arising out of an injury she sustained while performing an exercise on the uneven parallel bars. A bolt on the apparatus fractured, causing the equipment to fail. The public building exception to the applicable governmental immunity statute was not met because the uneven parallel bars were not determined to be a fixture, because they were a portable object. The apparatus was movable and was moved almost daily. Consequently, the college was granted governmental immunity and was dismissed from the lawsuit.

Staff

Acosta v. Los Angeles Unified School Dist.   In a California appellate case, *Acosta v. Los Angeles Unified School Dist.*, 31 Cal. App. 4th 471, 37 Cal. Rptr. 2d 171 (1995), the plaintiff was rendered quadriplegic when he was practicing a new trick on the high bar. He did not catch the bar as he came down after performing a somersault, falling and landing on his neck. At trial, the court found that the coach was negligent in supervising the plaintiff's practice, which substantially caused his injury. However, such negligence did not constitute gross negligence, and so judgment was rendered in favor of the defendant school district. A new trial was granted to determine whether the activity engaged in was recreational or school directed. Appeals were filed. It was noted that the accident occurred when the plaintiff was practicing in the high school gym, on their equipment, and supervised by the high school gymnastics coach, who suggested that he try the new high bar trick. Consequently, it was concluded that the plaintiff was engaged in school-supervised and school-sponsored activities at the time he was injured. The immunity statute did not apply, and so the plaintiff essentially prevailed. A new trial was granted on the issue of the plaintiff's comparative negligence, liability apportionment, and damages.

Hayes Through Hayes v. Walters   In *Hayes Through Hayes v. Walters*, 628 So. 2d 558 (Ala. 1993), the plaintiff was injured from a fall off a pommel horse during a middle school gymnastics class. She claimed that the principal of the school was wanton and negligent because he failed to develop proper safety procedures for use of the pommel horse. The question considered by the court was whether the supervisory responsibilities fell within the doctrine of discretionary function immunity or whether they were ministerial. After some analysis, the appellate court concluded that the principal's supervisory responsibilities would be classified as protected discretionary function, and so the lower court's granting of summary judgment in favor of the defendant was proper.

GYMNASTICS SAFETY CONSIDERATIONS

These reported appellate cases consider various risk management and safety concerns as they relate to gymnastics, but they could occur in other sports as well. Understanding the potential for injury allows safeguards to be taken in order to prevent problems in the future. To facilitate your organization's safety standards in gymnastics, please use all the forms on pages 229 to 236.

SUMMARY

USA Gymnastics requires certification in safety and risk management for members. This is important because stringent safety guidelines must be adhered to in order to prevent serious injury or death with each skill performed. Many of the reported appellate court decisions in gymnastics address the issue of governmental immunity in determining whether a defendant could be dismissed from the lawsuit. Even so, issues related to supervision, equipment safety, instruction, and safety procedures were before the courts. Selection of appropriate equipment, professional installation, inspection, regular maintenance, upgrading of equipment, and repair are essential for the safety of athletes. Care should also be given to make sure a facility is prepared to respond to injuries and emergencies should they arise.

GYMNASTICS EQUIPMENT SAFETY

Selection of appropriate equipment, professional installation, inspection, regular maintenance, upgrading of equipment, and repair are essential for the safety of athletes engaged in all levels of gymnastics. The following questions should be addressed in considering the safety of gymnastics equipment.

All inspections, maintenance, and repairs of equipment should be documented. These documents should be kept and reviewed periodically by your risk management team or consultant.

Considerations	Yes or No (check one)	Notes for follow-up
Are mats placed in designated landing areas so they are not overlapping?	❑ Yes ❑ No	
Are mats of appropriate thickness and material to absorb landings from the apparatus?	❑ Yes ❑ No	
Are mats clean and free of debris?	❑ Yes ❑ No	
Are mats reasonably free of chalk dust?	❑ Yes ❑ No	
Have mats been checked for wear and tear and been replaced where necessary?	❑ Yes ❑ No	
Do mats have the appropriate compaction rating for the apparatus and skills?	❑ Yes ❑ No	
Have all locking mechanisms been checked before use?	❑ Yes ❑ No	
Is equipment properly locked and stored when no supervisors are present?	❑ Yes ❑ No	
Have springboards and takeoff boards been inspected for defects, for loose or missing bolts or screws, and for workability?	❑ Yes ❑ No	
Are springboards and takeoff boards locked and stored properly when not in use?	❑ Yes ❑ No	
Has the balance beam been inspected for defects, wear and tear, missing or loose parts, moisture, excessive chalk buildup, or any other problems?	❑ Yes ❑ No	
Have the uneven parallel bars been inspected for defects, wear and tear, missing or loose parts, moisture, excessive chalk buildup, or any other problems?	❑ Yes ❑ No	
Has the vault been inspected for defects, wear and tear, missing or loose parts, moisture, excessive chalk buildup, or any other problems?	❑ Yes ❑ No	

(continued)

From Katharine M. Nohr, 2009, *Managing Risk in Sport and Recreation: The Essential Guide for Loss Prevention* (Champaign, IL: Human Kinetics).

Gymnastics Equipment Safety *(continued)*

Considerations	Yes or No (check one)	Notes for follow-up
Have the parallel bars been inspected for defects, wear and tear, missing or loose parts, moisture, excessive chalk buildup, or any other problems?	❑ Yes ❑ No	
Have the rings been inspected for defects, wear and tear, missing or loose parts, moisture, excessive chalk buildup, or any other problems?	❑ Yes ❑ No	
Has the pommel horse been inspected for defects, wear and tear, missing or loose parts, moisture, excessive chalk buildup, or any other problems?	❑ Yes ❑ No	
Has the high bar been inspected for defects, wear and tear, missing or loose parts, moisture, excessive chalk buildup, or any other problems?	❑ Yes ❑ No	
Have all trampolines been inspected for defects, wear and tear, missing or loose parts, moisture, excessive chalk buildup, or any other problems?	❑ Yes ❑ No	
Are walls around equipment padded and free of electrical boxes, switches, windows, and other hazards?	❑ Yes ❑ No	
Are all apparatuses securely attached to the floor?	❑ Yes ❑ No	
Have floor plates been checked for possible loosening?	❑ Yes ❑ No	
Is there enough space between apparatuses so they can be used by athletes at the same time without risk of athletes crashing into each other or other equipment?	❑ Yes ❑ No	
Are there any protrusions from the floor or equipment?	❑ Yes ❑ No	
Is the gymnasium closed to children and adults who are not authorized?	❑ Yes ❑ No	
Is there sufficient room to allow proper use of equipment?	❑ Yes ❑ No	
Is the room sufficiently illuminated but without problems of glare of lights in athletes' eyes?	❑ Yes ❑ No	
Are all potential landing surfaces padded?	❑ Yes ❑ No	
Are there other considerations for equipment safety?	❑ Yes ❑ No	

From Katharine M. Nohr, 2009, *Managing Risk in Sport and Recreation: The Essential Guide for Loss Prevention* (Champaign, IL: Human Kinetics).

GYMNASTICS EQUIPMENT

The following questions should be considered in order to avoid injury.

Considerations	Yes or No (check one)	Notes for follow-up
Is all equipment properly maintained?	❑ Yes ❑ No	
Has equipment been arranged so that gymnasts do not collide with each other during workouts?	❑ Yes ❑ No	
Is all equipment stored so that it cannot be used by children or others without supervision?	❑ Yes ❑ No	
Is all equipment that cannot be properly stored locked?	❑ Yes ❑ No	
Have springboards been placed away from low ceilings or doorways?	❑ Yes ❑ No	
Is equipment of high quality, and does it meet strict safety standards?	❑ Yes ❑ No	
Is equipment replaced with the latest, safest models when reasonable?	❑ Yes ❑ No	
Is equipment regularly inspected by a qualified inspector?	❑ Yes ❑ No	
Is equipment fitted, adjusted, and maintained by trained personnel only?	❑ Yes ❑ No	
Is equipment moved only with supervision and sufficient strength and ability to do so?	❑ Yes ❑ No	
Are there other considerations for equipment?	❑ Yes ❑ No	

From Katharine M. Nohr, 2009, *Managing Risk in Sport and Recreation: The Essential Guide for Loss Prevention* (Champaign, IL: Human Kinetics).

GYMNASTICS MATTING

Insufficient matting around and under gymnastics apparatuses has also led to injuries. The following questions are related to safety tips concerning matting.

Considerations	Yes or No (check one)	Notes for follow-up
Is floor padding appropriate to help reduce the force of landing?	❑ Yes ❑ No	
Are mats placed under and around equipment?	❑ Yes ❑ No	
Are mats secured properly?	❑ Yes ❑ No	
Is matting of sufficient thickness and compression for its use?	❑ Yes ❑ No	
Are there other considerations for matting?	❑ Yes ❑ No	

From Katharine M. Nohr, 2009, *Managing Risk in Sport and Recreation: The Essential Guide for Loss Prevention* (Champaign, IL: Human Kinetics).

GYMNASTICS FACILITY ENVIRONMENT

Care should be taken to make sure that ventilation and environmental factors do not contribute to injuries. The following questions relate to environmental considerations.

Considerations	Yes or No (check one)	Notes for follow-up
Does the gymnasium have proper ventilation?	❑ Yes ❑ No	
Is chalk dust removed so it does not accumulate and interfere with athletes' vision?	❑ Yes ❑ No	
Is the gymnasium environment monitored so as not to be excessively humid or filled with chalk (which makes equipment slippery)?	❑ Yes ❑ No	
Are there other considerations for facility environment?	❑ Yes ❑ No	

From Katharine M. Nohr, 2009, *Managing Risk in Sport and Recreation: The Essential Guide for Loss Prevention* (Champaign, IL: Human Kinetics).

SUPERVISION FOR GYMNASTS

Negligent supervision is a common allegation by plaintiffs in gymnastics injury lawsuits. Because of this, supervision and spotting should be integral parts of any safety program. The following questions relate to safety tips on this topic.

Considerations	Yes or No (check one)	Notes for follow-up
Is proper spotting done by coaches and other trained personnel whenever complex or challenging moves or routines are performed?	❑ Yes ❑ No	
Do coaches and athletes communicate so that proper spotting can be accomplished?	❑ Yes ❑ No	
Are all persons using equipment supervised at all times?	❑ Yes ❑ No	
Is the use of trampolines supervised at all times by trained personnel?	❑ Yes ❑ No	
Are all coaches and supervisors properly trained for the age and level of gymnastics involved?	❑ Yes ❑ No	
Do coaches provide adequate instruction for each skill performed?	❑ Yes ❑ No	
Do coaches teach all lead-up skills and make sure they are performed adequately before teaching more advanced skills?	❑ Yes ❑ No	
Do coaches require that safety belts or other protective gear be worn whenever appropriate?	❑ Yes ❑ No	
Are supervisors and spotters old enough and large enough to perform their duties?	❑ Yes ❑ No	
Are there other considerations for supervision?	❑ Yes ❑ No	

From Katharine M. Nohr, 2009, *Managing Risk in Sport and Recreation: The Essential Guide for Loss Prevention* (Champaign, IL: Human Kinetics).

RESPONDING TO ORTHOPEDIC
AND OTHER INJURIES IN GYMNASTICS

As with any sport, steps should be taken so that athletes' injuries can be responded to quickly. The following questions should be considered when evaluating preparedness.

Considerations	Yes or No (check one)	Notes for follow-up
Is a first aid kit available?	❑ Yes ❑ No	
Are coaches and other personnel trained in how to administer basic first aid for minor cuts, bruises, abrasions, strains, and sprains?	❑ Yes ❑ No	
Are telephones available for 911 calls?	❑ Yes ❑ No	
Are incident reports filled out in response to reported injuries?	❑ Yes ❑ No	
Is there an emergency plan in place to respond to serious injuries such as concussions, dislocations, fractures, and other injuries?	❑ Yes ❑ No	
Are there other considerations for responding to orthopedic and other injuries?	❑ Yes ❑ No	

From Katharine M. Nohr, 2009, *Managing Risk in Sport and Recreation: The Essential Guide for Loss Prevention* (Champaign, IL: Human Kinetics).

MINIMIZING AND PREVENTING INJURIES IN GYMNASTICS

In order to avoid injury, gymnasts should be coached to warm up before performing skills. Rules should be established and enforced in each gym in order to minimize and prevent injuries. Athletes should not be permitted to do skills until they have been properly taught and are ready to do so.

Considerations	Yes or No (check one)	Notes for follow-up
Do athletes warm up and stretch first?	❑ Yes ❑ No	
Is muscle conditioning a primary focus so that athletes have sufficient muscular support to do gymnastics skills?	❑ Yes ❑ No	
Do athletes always understand the basic mechanics of the skill before they attempt a trick they are unfamiliar with?	❑ Yes ❑ No	
Before athletes perform a trick, are they instructed on what to do if something goes wrong so that they can safely bail out?	❑ Yes ❑ No	
Do athletes have an understanding of how their bodies are oriented in a skill such as twisting or flipping so that if something goes wrong, they can land safely?	❑ Yes ❑ No	
Is there sufficient communication between gymnasts so that athletes can avoid collisions?	❑ Yes ❑ No	
Is horseplay prohibited, and is this rule promptly and consistently enforced?	❑ Yes ❑ No	
Is proper attire worn so that clothing and jewelry are not caught in apparatuses?	❑ Yes ❑ No	
Is long hair tied back so it does not interfere with visibility and is not caught in equipment?	❑ Yes ❑ No	
Are chewing gum and eating prohibited in the gym?	❑ Yes ❑ No	
Are athletes reminded to concentrate at all times when performing skills?	❑ Yes ❑ No	
Are athletes reminded not to distract other gymnasts during practice?	❑ Yes ❑ No	
Are there other considerations for minimizing and preventing injury?	❑ Yes ❑ No	

From Katharine M. Nohr, 2009, *Managing Risk in Sport and Recreation: The Essential Guide for Loss Prevention* (Champaign, IL: Human Kinetics).

15

Ice Hockey

Ice hockey is a form of disorderly conduct in which the score is kept.

—Doug Larson

Fights, collisions, and rough play have become an expected element in hockey, making it a challenge for organizers to control risks and prevent injuries. The sport's national governing body in the United States is USA Hockey, which provides safety and risk management training and guidelines for members as well as insurance. USA Hockey is concerned about prevention of injuries, including serious neck lacerations and concussions.

ICE HOCKEY LAWSUITS AND SETTLEMENTS

A number of large jury awards and out-of-court settlements have resulted from injuries sustained at hockey games.

- A jury awarded $2.5 million to goalie Steve McKichan, who was knocked unconscious and had his career ended by player Tony Twist. *McKichan v. St. Louis Hockey Club*, 967 S.W.2d 209 (Mo. Ct. App. 1998).
- A 7-year-old boy was awarded $1,375 after it was proven that a school failed to provide eye protection for players of a supervised hockey game.
- A high school cheerleader, seated in the stands at a hockey game, was struck by a puck that ricocheted into the stands. The facility had removed

the Plexiglas that protected spectators in order to install locker rooms. The plaintiff sustained a brain injury and settled the case for $600,000 before trial.

The following reported appellate court cases address injuries sustained by hockey players from a hockey rink door, flying pucks injuring players and spectators, and a player being illegally checked from behind.

Facility

Brisbin v. Washington Sports and Entertainment, Ltd.   In *Brisbin v. Washington Sports and Entertainment, Ltd.*, 422 F. Supp. 2d 9 (D.D.C. 2006), the plaintiff sued the owner of the stadium where she was injured while watching a hockey game. Above the plaintiff in the highest tier of seats in the stadium, another spectator was bumped, causing him to tumble down the seats and land on her. The plaintiff sustained injury and claimed in her lawsuit that Washington Sports was negligent. The plaintiff failed to prove that the defendant could have done anything differently that would have prevented the accident, and so it was determined that Washington Sports did not breach its duty of reasonable care. Summary judgment was granted in favor of the defendant.

Incidents like this could happen in any stadium. Limiting alcohol consumption by patrons can assist in preventing such injuries. Providing adequate lighting and making sure the stadium is designed so there is sufficient room between rows of seats is another means of prevention. It is always important to have personnel stationed throughout the stadium and emergency action plans in place so that injured spectators can be attended to immediately.

Gernat v. State   In *Gernat v. State*, 23 A.D.3d 1015, 803 N.Y.S.2d 845 (2005), the plaintiff, a Buffalo State College varsity hockey player, was injured when his body collided with a hockey rink door that swung open. The hockey player filed suit against the State of New York. The state prevailed because the plaintiff's expert did not have sufficient expertise regarding the hockey rink door design, and there was no evidence that the defendant had notice of any problem with the door latch, which opened when hit by another hockey player.

Regular inspections of facilities should be done and repairs made. Unfortunately, in this case, the problem with the door was not evident until an injury occurred.

Guenther v. West Seneca Cent. School Dist.   In *Guenther v. West Seneca Cent. School Dist.*, 19 A.D.3d 1171, 796 N.Y.S.2d 465 (2005), the plaintiff, a high school student, was watching from the bleachers when hit in the nose by a puck that was deflected off the ice during a hockey game. The plaintiff filed a lawsuit against the owner of the ice rink and the school district. The

company that owned the ice rink was not successful in its attempt to have the case dismissed because it failed to prove that the rink's protective screening was sufficient to satisfy the duty it owed to the plaintiff.

Hockey pucks can be dangerous to spectators who are not paying careful attention. Protective screening should be installed and maintained in order to prevent injuries to hockey fans.

Sciarrotta v. Global Spectrum In *Sciarrotta v. Global Spectrum*, 392 N.J. Super. 403, 920 A.2d 777 (2007), the plaintiff was attending a hockey game for the purpose of watching her daughter perform the national anthem. She was sitting in the general admission area, in an area above Plexiglas protection, during the warm-up session. Players were practicing with about 25 pucks when one of the pucks deflected off a goalpost, flew into the stands, and hit the

Protective screening is imperative in a sport such as hockey, where pucks can leave the area of play at high speeds.

plaintiff on the head. The court discussed the limited duty rule established in a previous New Jersey Supreme Court case concerning baseball, requiring owners and operators of sporting events to provide protected seating for desirous attendees and for the most dangerous areas of the stands. The limited duty had also been applied to hockey rinks in a previous New Jersey case, requiring rink operators to screen high-risk areas and provide protected areas for spectators who do not want to be exposed to the risk of flying pucks. It was noted that other jurisdictions apply the same duty of care to owners of ice hockey rinks that is applied to owners of baseball parks. The court distinguished the facts in this case involving a warm-up with multiple pucks from a hockey game or a baseball game, where there is only one puck or ball for a spectator to keep track of. The defendant's motion for summary judgment was denied so it could be determined whether appropriate actions were taken to protect or warn the plaintiff about the risks associated with the warm-up and whether the plaintiff acted reasonably in protection of her own safety while viewing the warm-up session.

The court applied the baseball laws related to protective screening to ice hockey. In light of the frequent comparison by various courts, in defending errant puck injury cases, use of these cases is advisable. Again, this does not excuse a facility from exercising reasonable care in protecting its patrons.

Hazards

Hurst v. East Coast Hockey League, Inc. In *Hurst v. East Coast Hockey League, Inc.*, 371 S.C. 33, 637 S.E.2d 560 (2006), the plaintiff was hit by a hockey puck while she walked through a concourse entrance that was curtained but situated behind a goal. Dasher boards and a Plexiglas wall surrounding the rink served as protection for patrons. The court compared flying pucks at hockey games with foul balls at baseball games, considering whether defendants owed a duty to spectators, such as the plaintiff, to eliminate the inherent risks of flying pucks at a hockey game. The defendants prevailed in this case because the plaintiff assumed the risk of injury.

Although this case should be helpful in the defense of errant puck injury lawsuits, it is important to erect and maintain barriers so that passing spectators are protected.

Violations

Karas v. Strevell In *Karas v. Strevell*, 369 Ill. App. 3d 884, 860 N.E.2d 1163 (2006), the plaintiff was seriously injured in a junior varsity hockey game when two other players checked him from behind, which was prohibited by the rules of the local hockey associations. Each player's jersey has a "STOP" warning on the back to remind players not to check from behind. The evidence established that the local hockey associations were responsible for coaching as well as teaching the applicable rules and failed to instruct the players that checking from behind was dangerous and against the rules. The evidence also established that the associations were not penalizing players who were known to violate the rule.

Safety rules are effective only if they are consistently enforced. Penalizing players who endanger other players' health and safety should be a risk management priority.

HOCKEY SAFETY CONSIDERATIONS

These reported appellate cases address risk management and safety concerns as they relate to ice hockey, but they could occur in other sports as well. Understanding the potential for injury allows safeguards to be taken in order to prevent problems in the future.

Keeping hockey players safe and injury free should be an important priority that starts with inspection of the ice rink and facilities. Although most hockey injuries are caused by contact with other players and with pucks, skates, sticks, and ice, the safety of the rink and facility should not be overlooked. To facilitate your organization's safety standards in ice hockey, please use all the forms on pages 242 to 246.

SUMMARY

Ice hockey is known to be a dangerous sport to players, resulting in significant injuries that might sideline players temporarily or prevent players from ever playing again. The violent nature of the game is part of what makes it exciting, and the sport would certainly not be the same if physical contact between players was eliminated. Despite the potential for injury, with sufficient care in maintaining the facility and equipment and monitoring safe play and behavior, fewer injuries are possible and lawsuits can be prevented.

INSPECTION OF THE ICE HOCKEY RINK, FACILITIES, AND SURROUNDING AREAS

When inspecting the ice rink and facilities, keep in mind that the players will be skating up to 30 miles per hour (48 km/h), that the puck sometimes travels at more than 100 miles per hour (160 km/h), and that fights and violence are common. With these realities in mind, you should answer the following questions.

Considerations	Yes or no (check one)	Notes for follow-up
Are the goals in good condition, with no protrusions?	☐ Yes ☐ No	
Are the goal cages and nettings designed to break away if a skater crashes into them?	☐ Yes ☐ No	
Are ice surfaces smooth and free of debris?	☐ Yes ☐ No	
Is the ice kept at the proper temperature to allow for the best skating conditions?	☐ Yes ☐ No	
Are the nets, boards, glass, and other surfaces free of protrusions?	☐ Yes ☐ No	
Are all rink and dasher boards in good condition, not damaged or loosened?	☐ Yes ☐ No	
Is the arena sufficiently ventilated, with good air quality?	☐ Yes ☐ No	
Is there adequate illumination of the rink?	☐ Yes ☐ No	
Does the ice-resurfacing equipment work properly?	☐ Yes ☐ No	
Is the ice-resurfacing equipment regularly maintained?	☐ Yes ☐ No	
When goals are removed from moorings, are there any pegs protruding from the ice?	☐ Yes ☐ No	
Are all supporting posts and struts padded?	☐ Yes ☐ No	
Is there sufficient room between the goal cage and boards?	☐ Yes ☐ No	
Have players' benches and penalty boxes been examined for debris that can become stuck to players' skates?	☐ Yes ☐ No	

(continued)

From Katharine M. Nohr, 2009, *Managing Risk in Sport and Recreation: The Essential Guide for Loss Prevention* (Champaign, IL: Human Kinetics).

Inspection of the Ice Hockey Rink, Facilities, and Surrounding Areas *(continued)*

Considerations	Yes or no (check one)	Notes for follow-up
Was the ice resurfaced before the event?	❏ Yes ❏ No	
Is the ice resurfaced during the event at certain intervals?	❏ Yes ❏ No	
Do penalty boxes and players' benches have doors that swing in rather than out?	❏ Yes ❏ No	
Are there other considerations for inspection of the ice rink, facilities, and surrounding areas?	❏ Yes ❏ No	

From Katharine M. Nohr, 2009, *Managing Risk in Sport and Recreation: The Essential Guide for Loss Prevention* (Champaign, IL: Human Kinetics).

ICE HOCKEY PROTECTIVE EQUIPMENT AND PROCEDURE

Hockey players have to protect themselves from injuries that might be sustained from impacts with sticks, pucks, players, skate blades, and the ice. Because of the potentially violent nature of the game, it is important that each player be fully equipped with well-fitted protective equipment that is free from defects. The following questions should be asked related to equipment.

Considerations	Yes or no (check one)	Notes for follow-up
Are there helmets, shoulder pads, elbow pads, hockey gloves, hockey pants, shin guards, mouth guards, and athletic supporters available to fit each player?	❏ Yes ❏ No	
Are goaltenders equipped with goalie mask, chest and arm protector, blocker, catching glove, athletic supporter, goal pants, and goal pads that fit properly?	❏ Yes ❏ No	
Are skates kept sharp?	❏ Yes ❏ No	
Do skates have a well-constructed heel and ankle support?	❏ Yes ❏ No	
Are pucks used in accordance with any applicable regulations?	❏ Yes ❏ No	
Are mouth guards specially molded for each player?	❏ Yes ❏ No	
Are hockey sticks fitted for each player?	❏ Yes ❏ No	
Has the equipment been adjusted so it fits each player properly and will not slide away from the body and expose it to an oncoming puck?	❏ Yes ❏ No	
Is the person who is adjusting the equipment sufficiently trained in doing so?	❏ Yes ❏ No	
Are players prohibited from wearing jewelry or anything else that might cause injury?	❏ Yes ❏ No	
Are there other considerations for protective equipment and procedure?	❏ Yes ❏ No	

From Katharine M. Nohr, 2009, *Managing Risk in Sport and Recreation: The Essential Guide for Loss Prevention* (Champaign, IL: Human Kinetics).

ICE HOCKEY SAFETY TIPS

The following questions pertain to safety tips that should be followed to prevent injuries in hockey.

Considerations	Yes or no (check one)	Notes for follow-up
Are rink gates closed during play?	❑ Yes ❑ No	
Have players received proper instruction as to how to play hockey, and have they demonstrated the skills necessary to play at the level being played?	❑ Yes ❑ No	
Are all skates properly tied?	❑ Yes ❑ No	
Are players matched by size, strength, age, and ability? Unevenly matched teams can cause injury.	❑ Yes ❑ No	
Are players always properly supervised?	❑ Yes ❑ No	
Is the ice clear of skaters when the ice-resurfacing machine is on the ice?	❑ Yes ❑ No	
Is an announcement made over the loud speaker so that skaters can safely clear the ice before resurfacing?	❑ Yes ❑ No	
Have the drivers of the ice-resurfacing machine been properly trained and qualified?	❑ Yes ❑ No	
Are players sufficiently hydrated?	❑ Yes ❑ No	
Is dangerous play on the ice prohibited?	❑ Yes ❑ No	
Are players aware that horseplay will not be tolerated on or off the ice?	❑ Yes ❑ No	
Is alcohol consumption allowed before or during the game or practice?	❑ Yes ❑ No	
Do all players wear protective gear and face masks for all games and practices?	❑ Yes ❑ No	
Are only hockey helmets with face guards used? Other sports helmets should not be allowed.	❑ Yes ❑ No	
Is proper stretching and warm-up done before games and practices?	❑ Yes ❑ No	

(continued)

From Katharine M. Nohr, 2009, *Managing Risk in Sport and Recreation: The Essential Guide for Loss Prevention* (Champaign, IL: Human Kinetics).

Ice Hockey Safety Tips   *(continued)*

Considerations	Yes or no (check one)	Notes for follow-up
Are all drills safe so as not to subject players to potential harm or injury?	❑ Yes ❑ No	
When renting an ice rink, is the rink well maintained and safe for use?	❑ Yes ❑ No	
Are hockey players given a written warning of all possible physical injuries that might be caused by the sport?	❑ Yes ❑ No	
Do referees discourage aggressive behavior by calling checks consistently, often, and early?	❑ Yes ❑ No	
Are players warned when other players are known to engage in unreasonably dangerous and aggressive behavior?	❑ Yes ❑ No	
Are spectators aware that violence will not be tolerated by the management, making appropriate announcements and ejecting fans who become unruly?	❑ Yes ❑ No	
Are there other considerations for hockey safety tips?	❑ Yes ❑ No	

From Katharine M. Nohr, 2009, *Managing Risk in Sport and Recreation: The Essential Guide for Loss Prevention* (Champaign, IL: Human Kinetics).

16

Soccer

Why is there only one ball for 22 players? If you gave a ball to each of them, they'd stop fighting for it.

—Author Unknown

Soccer, known as *football* in most countries outside the United States and Canada, is wildly popular around the world. This popularity is bound to translate to increased lawsuits, especially if spectator and player violence finds its way to the United States as it has in other countries.

Reported appellate court decisions in soccer have arisen out of injuries caused by a number of safety and risk management issues. As for preventable safety concerns, hazards that are on the field and unsecured goalposts should consistently be addressed. Player and spectator violence are issues that have been reported in the news media but have not resulted in reported appellate court decisions. Players are also often hurt during the course of the game from body contact and falls, but those injuries are more clearly inherent in the sport and do not usually result in litigation.

SOCCER LAWSUITS AND SETTLEMENTS

There have been a few reported soccer cases in which the plaintiffs received significant settlements for injuries suffered on the soccer field.

- Mark Miller settled a lawsuit against local soccer organizations for insurance policy limits of $2 million. The 11-year-old was paralyzed when the top bar of a goalpost fell over, striking him on the head and shoulders. The accident occurred when Miller's teammates were pushing the soccer goal from behind, attempting to move it to another location.

- The family of 6-year-old Zachary Tran settled a lawsuit with Greater Libertyville Soccer Association for an undisclosed amount. Zachary was killed when a 200-pound (90 kg) poorly anchored soccer goal fell on him while he was practicing with his soccer team. Normally the goal is anchored with metal stakes, but not on the day it fell on Zachary.

A number of reported appellate court decisions address various causes of injuries in soccer. The following soccer cases address being injured by another player, playing soccer without a medical release, being hit by an errant soccer ball, defects on the field, tripping hazards in a concession area, alleged inadequate supervision, playing soccer as part of a college class, disparity of treatment of girls under Title IX, and sexual harassment.

Facility

Manoly v. City of New York
In *Manoly v. City of New York*, 29 A.D.3d 649 (2006), the plaintiff Manoly noticed a raised manhole cover and a fence in disrepair before he elected to play soccer on a field at the Parade Grounds in Brooklyn. While playing soccer, he tripped on the manhole cover, causing his face to hit the fence. The plaintiff filed a personal injury lawsuit against the City of New York and the New York City Parks Department. The court determined that the plaintiff assumed the risk of injury. The defendants were required to protect the plaintiff from unassumed, unreasonably increased, or concealed risks only.

It seems that a manhole cover on or around a soccer field would pose a danger. Perhaps it could have been painted a bright color to make it more visible?

Morales v. Town of Johnston
If a known hazard is present in or around the facilities, warnings of the presence of that hazard should be made. In *Morales v. Town of Johnston*, 895 A.2d 721 (2006), the plaintiff Morales played in a soccer game at Johnston High School. Before the game, the coaches discussed a partially grass covered water drain that was adjacent to the soccer field. According to the coaches, they warned their teams about the potential hazard before the game. The plaintiff did not hear any warning and severely injured her knee as she chased after a soccer ball near the drain. A jury awarded the plaintiff $400,000, which was reduced to $212,000 because of a finding of comparative negligence. On appeal of the jury award, the court concluded that the town of Johnston owed a special duty to students playing soccer on a field they owned and operated. The school district was immune from the lawsuit pursuant to an applicable

statute, and there was no showing of negligence by the landscaping service that maintained the field.

There will always be some people who do not pay attention to a verbal warning. In the case of a partially grass-covered water drain, players in a fast-paced soccer game will likely not be able to slow down enough to identify it and avoid it. A warning probably was not sufficient in this case.

Range v. Abbott Sports Complex   A good example of a lawsuit related to the inspection of a soccer field is *Range v. Abbott Sports Complex*, 269 Neb. 281, 691 N.W.2d 525 (2005). In this case, plaintiff Christopher Range sustained a serious knee injury, requiring six surgeries, when he fell in a hole on a soccer field that appeared to him to have been created by a burrowing animal. Before the soccer game, the referees had done their usual inspection of the soccer field and, not finding anything wrong, determined that the field was safe for play. For the defendants to be found negligent, it would have to be shown that they had constructive knowledge of the hole. Because there was an inference from the facts that the hole did not arise during the soccer game, the court determined that there was a material issue of fact as to whether the defendant owner and sponsors had knowledge of the hole in question, and the case would proceed to trial by jury.

Even with thorough inspections, holes and other hazards could arise, causing injury. Evidence presented of thorough inspections before play will assist the defense in prevailing in these types of cases.

Hazards

Sutton v. Eastern New York Youth Soccer Ass'n, Inc.   In *Sutton v. Eastern New York Youth Soccer Ass'n, Inc.*, 8 A.D.3d 855 (2004), the plaintiff was attending a soccer tournament in which his son was playing. Between games, the plaintiff walked past a group of players who were kicking a soccer ball, warming up for another game. As the plaintiff reached into a cooler that was under a tent approximately 30 to 50 yards (27 to 45 m) away from the goal, he was hit in the

Spectators need to be reminded to keep themselves safely away from the area of play so they don't get hit by wayward balls or players chasing after them.

chest by a soccer ball, knocked down, and injured. The plaintiff had been a spectator at soccer games for the past 14 years and so was well familiar with the risks of being hit by a ball. The court found that he assumed the risk of being hit by a ball when he went to a tent located beyond the goal line, and the defendants were found not liable. The court reasoned that the plaintiff should have understood the risk when he went to the tent. There was no evidence that the person who hit the ball that hurt the plaintiff was acting recklessly.

Parents attending their children's games have a knack for getting in the way of balls and otherwise being injured. Organizers could prevent injuries by reminding parents to pay attention and watch out for errant balls and other dangers. This could be done at meetings and by e-mail, fliers, or letters.

Participant

Fabricius v. County of Broome
In *Fabricius v. County of Broome*, 24 A.D.3d 853, 804 N.Y.S.2d 510 (2005), a teacher at Broome Community College used soccer as an illustration in a lesson he taught. Students were asked (or possibly compelled) to participate in a class soccer game. The 45-year-old plaintiff was injured when she kicked the ball. The court determined there was a question for the jury as to whether she was required to participate in the game. If she was not compelled, then assumption of risk could have been considered to be a possible defense.

Adults who participate in athletics run a high risk of injury. Make sure that waivers and releases are signed by each adult before such participation begins.

Jaworski v. Kiernan
In *Jaworski v. Kiernan*, 241 Conn. 399, 696 A.2d 332 (1997), a female soccer player filed a lawsuit against a male soccer player, claiming he was negligent and careless when he hit and tripped her from behind in violation of league rules. The plaintiff claimed she was injured from the defendant's conduct. The court concluded that the defendant owed the plaintiff a "duty of care to refrain from reckless or intentional conduct." The defendant's conduct was found to be negligent only and not reckless and intentional, and so the plaintiff did not prevail.

Player-versus-player lawsuits are generally dismissed unless there is evidence that the behavior was reckless or intentional. Players are not usually subject to waiver and release forms, as it would be unreasonable to imagine each athlete asking the other players (their own teammates and other teams) to sign release forms before a game or practice. Courts serve to protect athletes from lawsuits by other participants in order to promote sport and recreation.

Spectators

Roberts v. Timber Birch-Broadmore Athletic Ass'n   Injuries can occur at or around concession areas. In *Roberts v. Timber Birch-Broadmore Athletic Ass'n*, 371 N.J. Super. 189, 852 A.2d 271 (2004), Timber Birch-Broadmore Athletic Association (TBAA), a nonprofit organization, held a soccer tournament at which the plaintiff's two children were playing and her husband was a coach. During the tournament, the plaintiff tripped and fell over a cooler at a vendor stand and sustained injury. The question before the court was whether TBAA was immune from the lawsuit the plaintiff filed. According to the applicable law, TBAA would be immune if the plaintiff was a beneficiary of the organization and was attending the tournament to watch her children play, who were beneficiaries. TBAA would not be immune from the lawsuit under the applicable charity immunity statute if the plaintiff was serving as a bona fide volunteer. The plaintiff claimed she was there as a volunteer. The defendant argued she would not have been there if it wasn't for her children playing in the tournament and that she spent most of her time watching the tournament. The court concluded that this was an issue for a jury to decide.

Coaches and other personnel should pay attention to tripping hazards. With conscious attention, injuries can be reduced.

Staff

Stephenson v. Commercial Travelers Mutual Insurance Company, et al.   In *Stephenson v. Commercial Travelers Mutual Insurance Company, et al.*, 893 So. 2d 180 (La. App. 3 Cir. 2005), plaintiff Stephenson was a starting defender for the Opelousas Catholic School's soccer team. The plaintiff had a past sprain of her right ankle, so she wore an ankle brace and tape when she played. She hurt her left ankle, which caused the coach to remove her from the game. Thereafter, the plaintiff would dress for games but would not play. Ultimately, without being medically released to play, the coach put her in a game during which an opposing player kicked her in the right leg, causing multiple fractures. The plaintiff's mother filed a lawsuit on her behalf against the school, athletic director, principal, coach, and school board. The court concluded the plaintiff did not prove that the school's duty to keep her from playing in a soccer game was the legal cause of her injuries.

This case, even though decided in favor of the school, is yet another illustration of the importance of having injured athletes medically released before resuming play.

White v. Mount Saint Michael High School   In *White v. Mount Saint Michael High School*, 41 A.D.3d 220, 837 N.Y.S.2d 873 (2007), a child who was injured playing soccer during gym class sued the school. The court determined that inadequate supervision did not cause the injury. The injury was due to an unforeseeable and spontaneous act, and so the school prevailed.

Allegations of inadequate supervision are standard in lawsuits involving children. Schools should make sure that a sufficient number of adults supervise and that proper attention and direction are given to the children in accordance with their age and the activity.

Violations

Henderson v. Walled Lake Consol. Schools   In *Henderson v. Walled Lake Consol. Schools*, 469 F.3d

Make sure children or students playing soccer are sufficiently supervised.

479 (Mich. 2006), a soccer coach was blamed for sexually harassing and threatening harm to a student, who was a soccer team member who interfered with the coach's inappropriate relationship with another female soccer player. Henderson filed a lawsuit against the coach as well as the high school, school district, principal, assistant principal, athletic director, and school district superintendent, claiming sexual harassment and violation of Title IX as well as alleging various tort claims.

The school was informed of problems with the soccer coach by parents of one of the players. The school administration held a meeting with the coach, resulting in a memorandum that

- prohibited the coach from communicating with his team members after 9:30 p.m. and before 7:00. a.m.;
- required that he copy e-mails to his team members to the principal;
- required that he refrain from providing counseling on personal problems to team members;

- required that a parent be present at all off-campus activities; and
- prohibited him from engaging in relationships with team members that could be construed as inappropriate.

The principal also monitored the situation by frequently asking team members how things were going, attending some practices, and regularly attending the games. Despite this, the coach threatened the plaintiff with physical harm for interfering with his relationship with another team member. All the counts against the school defendants were dismissed because of lack of notice of the coach's misconduct against the plaintiff. The court concluded that the record showed the school acted reasonably in response to the notice it had received about the coach's alleged misbehavior.

This case illustrates how a school administration reasonably acted in response to sexual harassment claims. These actions did not prevent a lawsuit, but they ultimately earned the school dismissal from the lawsuit.

Jennings v. University of North Carolina

In a high-profile case, *Jennings v. University of North Carolina*, 482 F.3d 686 (N.C. 2007), former University of North Carolina soccer player Melissa Jennings filed a lawsuit against the university; coach Anson Dorrance, assistant coaches, the athletic trainer, and the athletic director; and the university's chancellor, attorney, and others under Title IX, alleging hostile environment sexual harassment. The defendants prevailed in the lower court, as a summary judgment was entered in their favor. However, the appellate court overturned the decision, finding in favor of the plaintiff. The facts set forth in the published court decision explicitly describe sexual comments and behavior of coach Dorrance, alleged to be sexual harassment. The plaintiff had complained of the behavior to legal counsel for the university, who told her to work things out with the coach herself and did nothing to address the plaintiff's allegations. In response to the plaintiff's parent's complaints to the chancellor's office, the athletic director performed an administrative review pursuant to the university's policy on sexual harassment. A letter of apology was sent out, which the coach signed. The apology was only for the coach's participation in inappropriate sexual discussions with the team. The appellate court concluded that the alleged behavior, if proven at trial, would constitute sexual harassment and create a hostile or abusive environment and that the defendants had notice of such an environment, so there could be liability under Title IX. After this decision, the defendants settled with plaintiff Jennings for $385,000.

Sport and recreation facilities will benefit from establishing policies and procedures regarding allegations of sexual harassment as well as by providing education to prevent such behavior.

McCormick ex rel. McCormick v. School Dist. of Mamaroneck

In *McCormick ex rel. McCormick v. School Dist. of Mamaroneck*, 370 F.3d 275 (N.Y. 2004), the parents of two female soccer players attending high schools in different school districts filed a lawsuit under Title IX of the Education Amendments of 1972. The claim was that because the girls' soccer season was scheduled in the spring, the girls were denied the equal opportunity of competing in championship games held at the end of the fall season. The boys of those schools do not face the same challenges with college recruiters and potential lost scholarships because their soccer season is in the fall. The court held that there was a substantial disparity between the girls' and boys' athletic opportunities. This was found to be a violation of Title IX. The school districts could remedy the violation by rescheduling the girls' soccer programs to the fall or by alternating seasons of boys' and girls' soccer so there would not be a disparity.

Schools should periodically review their athletic programs for Title IX compliance and adjust schedules and activities so that legal requirements are being met. By doing this, lawsuits can be avoided.

SOCCER SAFETY CONSIDERATIONS

These reported appellate cases span a wide area of risk management and safety concerns as they relate to soccer, but they could occur in other sports as well. Understanding the potential for injury allows safeguards to be taken in order to prevent problems in the future. To facilitate your organization's safety standards in soccer, please use all the forms on pages 255 to 259.

SUMMARY

Because of the fast-moving and aggressive nature of the sport, soccer players are accustomed to sustaining some musculoskeletal injuries. Serious injuries can hopefully be prevented by paying close attention to the safety issues addressed in this chapter. The reported appellate court decisions concerning injuries that have arisen from soccer are also helpful in considering how to address risk management concerns. Because violence among players and spectators has been a well-publicized issue in soccer, it should be guarded against and should not be tolerated.

INSPECTION OF THE SOCCER FIELD

Inspection of the field for defects requires evaluation and examination of the ground, fencing, grass or turf, lines used to mark the field, lighting, drainage system, and sprinkler system. Defects in these areas have been known to cause injury. You need to address the following questions.

Considerations	Yes or No (check one)	Notes for follow-up
Are there holes in the ground or protruding objects that are obvious or concealed by grass or synthetic turf?	❏ Yes ❏ No	
If play will be at night, how bright are the lights illuminating the field?	❏ Yes ❏ No	
Does the field have an adequate drainage system?	❏ Yes ❏ No	
Will sprinkler heads on a grass field pose a hazard?	❏ Yes ❏ No	
Are the lines marking the field made out of any substance that could cause injury to a player's eyes or respiratory system?	❏ Yes ❏ No	
Has the soccer field been inspected before the practice or game by walking across the grass to look for balls, equipment, garbage, glass, rakes, shovels, or any other objects that should be picked up and cleared away before play begins?	❏ Yes ❏ No	
Have objects been cleared from the field before play begins?	❏ Yes ❏ No	
If the field is made of artificial turf, has it been checked for exposed and unmatched seams and any other irregularities in the turf?	❏ Yes ❏ No	
Has the grass been mowed before the event?	❏ Yes ❏ No	
Have sprinkler heads, irrigation stand pipes, and drainage hole covers been inspected to make sure they will not pose a hazard to players?	❏ Yes ❏ No	
Have rocks and clumped mud been removed from the field to eliminate tripping hazards?	❏ Yes ❏ No	
Have all tripping hazards been eliminated before play begins?	❏ Yes ❏ No	
Are there other considerations for inspection of the soccer field?	❏ Yes ❏ No	

From Katharine M. Nohr, 2009, *Managing Risk in Sport and Recreation: The Essential Guide for Loss Prevention* (Champaign, IL: Human Kinetics).

STRUCTURES ON THE SOCCER FIELD

Just as with any sport, it is important to make sure that no structures on the field will likely injure players. In soccer, the goals are the primary safety concern. The following questions address this concern.

Considerations	Yes or No (check one)	Notes for follow-up
Are corner flag posts made of flexible material so they do not pose a hazard to players?	❑ Yes ❑ No	
Have corner flags made out of wood or metal been replaced?	❑ Yes ❑ No	
Are goals sturdy and well anchored so they will not fall and injure players?	❑ Yes ❑ No	
Can goalposts be stored so they will not cause injury to children or others who might play on them or attempt to move them?	❑ Yes ❑ No	
Have goalposts been sufficiently padded to protect players?	❑ Yes ❑ No	
Are nets on goalposts attached using Velcro rather than nails or hooks?	❑ Yes ❑ No	
Are the goals in good condition?	❑ Yes ❑ No	
Can the goals be secured so they cannot be tampered with when not being used?	❑ Yes ❑ No	
Have the goalposts been examined for defects, such as deteriorated or broken welds, splinters, or loose nuts and bolts?	❑ Yes ❑ No	
Has the anchor of the goalposts been exposed so that it might cause players to trip?	❑ Yes ❑ No	
Have the goalposts been checked to make sure they are stable?	❑ Yes ❑ No	
Have the goalpost nets been examined for gaps between the net and frame, holes, exposed nails, or any other defect that might cause injury?	❑ Yes ❑ No	
Have the nails or hooks that attach the nets to the goalposts been inspected?	❑ Yes ❑ No	
Have all rusted, broken, or otherwise damaged hooks or nails been replaced?	❑ Yes ❑ No	
Are there other considerations for structures on the field?	❑ Yes ❑ No	

From Katharine M. Nohr, 2009, *Managing Risk in Sport and Recreation: The Essential Guide for Loss Prevention* (Champaign, IL: Human Kinetics).

PREPARING THE SOCCER FIELD
AND FACILITY FOR PLAY

After inspections have been performed and documented, defects and hazards should be repaired before play begins. The following questions should be asked when preparing the field for play.

Considerations	Yes or No (check one)	Notes for follow-up
Have lines on the field been marked with slaked lime that could cause serious eye damage to players?	❏ Yes ❏ No	
Have you made sure the substance (chalk or paint) used to paint lines on the field will not be hazardous to players?	❏ Yes ❏ No	
If a hazard cannot be corrected before play, has it been determined whether the field is safe for play or whether to cancel play?	❏ Yes ❏ No	
If the field is safe for play but a hazard exists on the field, have clear and adequate warnings been provided to all players and other persons who will be utilizing the area of play (e.g., coaches, referees, and other officials)?	❏ Yes ❏ No	
Are extra balls and other equipment removed from the field during play?	❏ Yes ❏ No	
If the weather is excessively hot and humid or if there is lightning or rain, has the game or practice been relocated or canceled to prevent injuries or illnesses?	❏ Yes ❏ No	
Are there other considerations for preparing the field and facility for play?	❏ Yes ❏ No	

From Katharine M. Nohr, 2009, *Managing Risk in Sport and Recreation: The Essential Guide for Loss Prevention* (Champaign, IL: Human Kinetics).

PLAYING ON FIELDS THAT ARE USED FOR OTHER PURPOSES BESIDES SOCCER

Sometimes injuries occur when a field is used for a sport it is not intended for. If the structure of the field or objects or infrastructure that is part of the field can cause injury when it is being used for soccer, you should consider moving your game or practice to a more appropriate field. The following questions should be addressed.

Considerations	Yes or No (check one)	Notes for follow-up
Is the field designed and intended for soccer? If No, list what other sports or activities the field is used for in the Notes column.	❑ Yes ❑ No	
Has the field been properly designed for dual purposes? If No, list what hazards might exist if you use the field for soccer.	❑ Yes ❑ No	
Have all dangerous items or equipment been removed or separated from the field?	❑ Yes ❑ No	
Are there other considerations for fields that are used for other purposes besides soccer?	❑ Yes ❑ No	

From Katharine M. Nohr, 2009, *Managing Risk in Sport and Recreation: The Essential Guide for Loss Prevention* (Champaign, IL: Human Kinetics).

SOCCER PROTECTIVE EQUIPMENT

The only mandatory equipment for soccer is a ball. However, if you want your players to be protected from injuries, they should probably wear some limited protective gear. The following questions should be asked when addressing soccer equipment issues.

Considerations	Yes or No (check one)	Notes for follow-up
Are shin guards required to be worn by forwards, halfbacks, and fullbacks?	❑ Yes ❑ No	
Are other players required to wear shin guards?	❑ Yes ❑ No	
Are male players required to wear protective athletic supporters?	❑ Yes ❑ No	
Are players instructed to remove jewelry and watches?	❑ Yes ❑ No	
Is the goalie required to wear a goalkeeper's shirt with long sleeves and padded elbows as well as protective gloves?	❑ Yes ❑ No	
Are goalies provided with helmets?	❑ Yes ❑ No	
Are players allowed to wear only rubber-soled cleats?	❑ Yes ❑ No	
Are there other considerations for protective equipment?	❑ Yes ❑ No	

From Katharine M. Nohr, 2009, *Managing Risk in Sport and Recreation: The Essential Guide for Loss Prevention* (Champaign, IL: Human Kinetics).

17

Swimming

It's a good idea to begin at the bottom in everything except in learning to swim.

—Author Unknown

Swimming is not only a sport but also an important lifesaving skill taught to most children when they are young. Unfortunately, drowning is the number one cause of death for children in the United States. Knowing how to swim is also a fundamental requirement for participating in many water sports, including diving, water polo, surfing, windsurfing, wakeboarding, water skiing, and synchronized swimming and is essential for boating.

When addressing risk management in relation to swimming, understand that people of all ages can drown for reasons other than lack of swimming ability. Good swimmers can drown from heart conditions, drain entrapment, breath holding, or extremely strong currents or high surf. Poor to average swimmers face the same concerns that good swimmers face in addition to their lack of skill in the water.

SWIMMING LAWSUITS AND SETTLEMENTS

Most swimming lawsuits arise out of death by drowning or severe traumatic injury from shallow diving. Consequently, jury verdicts and settlement figures can be high. Following are some examples of court awards or settlement amounts in these types of cases.

- A court awarded $24 million to a 3-year-old girl who had suffered brain damage from falling into the deep end of a swimming pool while lifeguards were lying on the pool deck rather than scanning the pool.

- A Philadelphia jury returned a $6.6 million verdict for the family of an 8-year-old boy who drowned at summer camp. The pool where the boy drowned had two lifeguards on duty. Unfortunately, one lifeguard was on break, and the other was in the bathroom at the time of the incident.

- A 15-year-old boy drowned in a college swimming pool after losing consciousness while practicing holding his breath. The case settled with the college, paying $1.55 million to the family of the deceased. The plaintiffs had alleged that the college was negligent because it did not provide an adequate lifeguard lookout or proper training for the lifeguards, who allegedly did not begin lifesaving efforts quickly enough to save the boy's life.

A large number of published appellate court decisions address various causes of injuries and drowning deaths that occur in swimming pools and other bodies of water. Many of these written court decisions are very lengthy and detailed. The following cases represent a small number of them, but they address some of the facts and legal issues related to drowning and to injuries that occur around swimming pools.

Equipment

Sturdivant v. Moore   In *Sturdivant v. Moore*, 282 Ga. App. 863, 640 S.E.2d 367 (2006), a 44-year-old male who was considered a good swimmer was found unconscious at the bottom of a pool during a visit to the defendant's residence for a party. The plaintiff, the drowning victim's wife, alleged in her lawsuit that the defendant was negligent for not turning on the interior swimming pool lights. The plaintiff alleged that the darkness of the pool delayed discovery of the victim's body. The court determined that the defendant's failure to turn on the swimming pool lights was not the proximate cause of the victim's death.

Clearly, turning on swimming pool lights is an important safety measure.

Facility

Gorbey v. Longwill   In *Gorbey v. Longwill*, Slip Copy, WL 118298 (2007), a 20-month-old baby went through an open sliding-glass door and fell into an indoor swimming pool. The baby drowned, which led to a lawsuit, alleging negligence on the part of whoever left the door open. Summary judgment was denied on the part of several of the defendants because there remained material issues of fact relating to the open door. The court concluded that whoever left the door open owed a legal duty of care to the baby to keep the door closed.

Swimming pools should have protective perimeters so that young children are not allowed access. This includes keeping doors to swimming pools closed and locked.

Pinckney v. Covington Athletic Club and Fitness Center

In *Pinckney v. Covington Athletic Club and Fitness Center*, 288 Ga. App. 891, 655 S.E.2d 650 (2007), the plaintiff fell as she was stepping out of the defendant's swimming pool, where she was taking a swimming lesson. She was not able to explain why she fell on the day of the incident, as she did not see a substance on the ground. There were inconsistencies between the plaintiff's first and later statements, in that on a later date, she claimed there was some green slime on the pool deck. An employee's inspection of the area after the fall revealed nothing more than water. Summary judgment was granted on behalf of the defendant.

Inspection and maintenance of pool decks should be performed regularly.

Staff

Padilla v. Rodas

In *Padilla v. Rodas*, 160 Cal. App. 4th 742, 73 Cal. Rptr. 3d 114 (2008), the owners of a backyard swimming pool did not use a self-latching closing mechanism on the gate of their pool entrance. A 2-year-old

Inspect pools and pool decks regularly to keep them clean and free of debris that could cause slipping or tripping.

boy drowned when he was left unattended for five minutes while his mother went into the house to get a glass of water and another adult took a telephone call. The boy was found facedown on the bottom of the swimming pool. Summary judgment was granted to the homeowners on the ground that they owed no duty of care to the child while he was under the supervision of his mother, and it was determined that the accident was not caused by the condition of the gate.

Leaving a child unattended for only a moment can result in drowning. No telephone call is that important. Lifeguards and parents supervising their children should understand this rule.

SWIMMING SAFETY CONSIDERATIONS

Important safety precautions should be taken whenever there is a body of water, whether a swimming pool, lake, or ocean. A comprehensive risk assessment of a swimming pool should include evaluation of rules and regulations, emergency plans, lifeguard training and procedures, and the physical facility. This is an ongoing process that should be performed on a regular basis. It is a good idea to hire an experienced expert in water safety to assist you with this task. You may want to read *The Complete Swimming Pool Reference* (Griffiths, 2003) for more complete information on swimming pool safety and management. To facilitate your organization's safety standards in swimming, please use all the forms on pages 265 to 288.

SUMMARY

Swimming pools and bodies of water can be dangerous to nonswimmers and even good swimmers in certain circumstances. It is essential that anyone operating a swimming pool, running a swimming event, or running any event or practice on or near water take every precaution to prevent drowning and other injuries. It is also imperative that facilities guard against children entering a pool area without supervision. Proper training of lifeguards as well as constant parental supervision goes a long way toward pool safety. Strictly enforced rules, such as no diving except from the diving board and no breath-holding contests, will also save lives.

INSPECTION OF THE SWIMMING POOL

Inspecting the swimming pool and facility for defects requires evaluation and examination of the pool, surrounding pool area, locker rooms, chemical storage area, children's pool, hot tub or spa, pool filtration system, and any adjoining facilities. Defects in these areas have been known to cause injury.

If you are operating a swimming pool, an inspection should be completed at least every morning. The following questions should be asked with each inspection, and the inspection should be documented in your pool's log book.

Considerations	Yes or No (check one)	Notes for follow-up
Is signage that warns swimmers of dangers in place and visible?	❑ Yes ❑ No	
Have pool handrails and ladders been checked to make sure they are secure, with no protrusions?	❑ Yes ❑ No	
Do swimming pool, spa, and hot tub drain covers conform to the mandatory federal requirements for entrapment avoidance, pursuant to the standards set forth in ASME/ANSI A112.19.8?	❑ Yes ❑ No	
Is the pool deck clean, clear, and in good condition?	❑ Yes ❑ No	
Have walkways been cleaned and cleared of any potential tripping or slipping hazards?	❑ Yes ❑ No	
Is the fence in good condition?	❑ Yes ❑ No	
Does the gate latch properly?	❑ Yes ❑ No	
Are chairs, tables, umbrellas, benches, and any other pool furniture in good condition?	❑ Yes ❑ No	
Are the nonslip floors in locker rooms clean and in good condition?	❑ Yes ❑ No	
Are electrical outlets and fixtures in good condition and protected by ground-fault circuit interrupters?	❑ Yes ❑ No	
Are shower temperatures set not to exceed 120 degrees Fahrenheit (49 degrees Celsius)?	❑ Yes ❑ No	
Are poolside telephones available in case of an emergency?	❑ Yes ❑ No	
Is lifesaving equipment in good condition and readily accessible in case of an emergency?	❑ Yes ❑ No	

(continued)

From Katharine M. Nohr, 2009, *Managing Risk in Sport and Recreation: The Essential Guide for Loss Prevention* (Champaign, IL: Human Kinetics).

Inspection of the Swimming Pool *(continued)*

Considerations	Yes or No (check one)	Notes for follow-up
Are depth markers visible so it is clear what the pool depth is in all areas?	❑ Yes ❑ No	
Is the deep end of the pool separated from the shallow end of the pool?	❑ Yes ❑ No	
Are chemicals locked up and not accessible to anyone except those authorized?	❑ Yes ❑ No	
Have drain covers been inspected in the children's wading pool and hot tub?	❑ Yes ❑ No	
Is the main drain at the bottom of the pool clearly visible?	❑ Yes ❑ No	
Are dressing rooms, shower facilities, and restrooms clean and well maintained?	❑ Yes ❑ No	
Are lifeguard staff scheduled for the day?	❑ Yes ❑ No	
Do lifeguards have up-to-date certification in CPR, lifesaving, and first aid?	❑ Yes ❑ No	
If lifeguards are not on duty, is someone on the premises certified in CPR and familiar with applicable emergency procedures?	❑ Yes ❑ No	
Has inspection been documented in the daily pool log?	❑ Yes ❑ No	
Are there other considerations for inspection of the swimming pool?	❑ Yes ❑ No	

From Katharine M. Nohr, 2009, *Managing Risk in Sport and Recreation: The Essential Guide for Loss Prevention* (Champaign, IL: Human Kinetics).

SWIMMING RULES AND REGULATIONS

Following rules and regulations at a swimming pool could mean the difference between life and death. For example, if lifeguards and pool management enforce rules prohibiting diving in the shallow end of the pool, requiring parental supervision even when a lifeguard is on duty, and prohibiting breath-holding competitions, lives can be saved. The following questions should be asked concerning rules and regulations.

Considerations	Yes or No (check one)	Notes for follow-up
Have rules and regulations for your pool and surrounding areas been defined?	❑ Yes ❑ No	
Are the rules and regulations reasonable?	❑ Yes ❑ No	
Are there rules and regulations that should be added to make the pool safer?	❑ Yes ❑ No	
Are rules and regulations communicated effectively to those using the pool, by signage and in other manners?	❑ Yes ❑ No	
Are rules and regulation signs written so that important warnings do not get lost in a list of rules?	❑ Yes ❑ No	
Are there other considerations for rules and regulations?	❑ Yes ❑ No	

From Katharine M. Nohr, 2009, *Managing Risk in Sport and Recreation: The Essential Guide for Loss Prevention* (Champaign, IL: Human Kinetics).

DIVING SAFETY

Diving safety rules are also crucial in preventing serious injury and fatal accidents. Consider the following questions.

Considerations	Yes or No (check one)	Notes for follow-up
Have diving safety rules been established?	❑ Yes ❑ No	
Are diving safety rules communicated to divers? If Yes, record the diving safety rules communicated in the Notes column.	❑ Yes ❑ No	
Is the diving board functioning properly?	❑ Yes ❑ No	
Are there any defects in the diving board?	❑ Yes ❑ No	
Is the ladder that leads up to the diving board dangerous so that someone could fall?	❑ Yes ❑ No	
If falls occur from the diving area, is there protective ground covering so that the diver will not fall on cement or another hard surface?	❑ Yes ❑ No	
Is the water in the diving area deep enough for the height of the diving board?	❑ Yes ❑ No	
Is diving prohibited in less than 9 feet (3 m) of water?	❑ Yes ❑ No	
Is diving restricted to diving boards?	❑ Yes ❑ No	
Is the diving area cleared of swimmers before someone dives off the board?	❑ Yes ❑ No	
Is the diving area sufficiently large so that divers will not hit the sides of the pool?	❑ Yes ❑ No	
Are there other considerations for diving safety?	❑ Yes ❑ No	

From Katharine M. Nohr, 2009, *Managing Risk in Sport and Recreation: The Essential Guide for Loss Prevention* (Champaign, IL: Human Kinetics).

DECK SLIDES AND SWIMMING POOLS

Slides can be fun but dangerous. The following questions should be considered in relation to any slides mounted on the deck of a swimming pool.

Considerations	Yes or No (check one)	Notes for follow-up
Have rules and regulations been developed for the slide?	❑ Yes ❑ No	
Have rules and regulations been communicated to users of the slide?	❑ Yes ❑ No	
Is there a lifeguard who monitors and enforces the use of the slide?	❑ Yes ❑ No	
Is there someone directing when people can slide so that two people are not using the slide at the same time?	❑ Yes ❑ No	
Is the bottom of the slide area cleared so that slide users will not fall on other people?	❑ Yes ❑ No	
Is the depth of the pool at the end of the slide deep enough so that a slider will not hit the bottom?	❑ Yes ❑ No	
Has the slide been checked and cleared of all protrusions and sharp objects?	❑ Yes ❑ No	
Is the slide smooth?	❑ Yes ❑ No	
Are the steps or ladder leading up to the slide safe and made of nonslip material?	❑ Yes ❑ No	
Is running prohibited up the steps to the slide?	❑ Yes ❑ No	
Are there other considerations for the deck slide?	❑ Yes ❑ No	

From Katharine M. Nohr, 2009, *Managing Risk in Sport and Recreation: The Essential Guide for Loss Prevention* (Champaign, IL: Human Kinetics).

SEVERE WEATHER OR LIGHTNING AND SWIMMING

Just as in golf and baseball, bad weather can make a swimming pool dangerous. Consider the following questions.

Considerations	Yes or No (check one)	Notes for follow-up
Is the pool closed and evacuated when thunderstorms or lightning is expected?	❑ Yes ❑ No	
Is the pool closed and evacuated for other severe weather such as heavy rain, hail, or fog?	❑ Yes ❑ No	
Are there other considerations for weather or lightning?	❑ Yes ❑ No	

From Katharine M. Nohr, 2009, *Managing Risk in Sport and Recreation: The Essential Guide for Loss Prevention* (Champaign, IL: Human Kinetics).

POOL WATER QUALITY

Illnesses can be caused by infectious disease in and around a swimming pool, wading pool, or hot tub. The following questions should be addressed in this regard.

Considerations	Yes or No (check one)	Notes for follow-up
Is water quality checked throughout the day?	❑ Yes ❑ No	
Are chemicals added as recommended by the manufacturers to keep the quality of the water excellent?	❑ Yes ❑ No	
Is the pool closed when the water does not meet a certain level of quality?	❑ Yes ❑ No	
Is the pool closed when there is a fecal incident?	❑ Yes ❑ No	
Have a plan and procedure for fecal incidents been established?	❑ Yes ❑ No	
Is the pool closed when the water is cloudy?	❑ Yes ❑ No	
Is the pool closed when the bottom of the pool is not visible?	❑ Yes ❑ No	
Are there other considerations for water quality?	❑ Yes ❑ No	

From Katharine M. Nohr, 2009, *Managing Risk in Sport and Recreation: The Essential Guide for Loss Prevention* (Champaign, IL: Human Kinetics).

SWIMMING SUPERVISION

Supervision is an important factor in preventing drowning and pool injuries. The following questions should be addressed on this topic.

Considerations	Yes or No (check one)	Notes for follow-up
Is there a sufficient number of certified lifeguards employed and available to staff the pool?	❑ Yes ❑ No	
How is lifeguard staffing handled?	❑ Yes ❑ No	
Do lifeguards receive proper training?	❑ Yes ❑ No	
Are all lifeguards up to date with certification?	❑ Yes ❑ No	
Are lifeguards provided with lifeguard stands that provide them with good visibility of the pool and ease of movement?	❑ Yes ❑ No	
Are lifeguards positioned where they can scan the water effectively?	❑ Yes ❑ No	
Are lifeguards scanning the pool as trained?	❑ Yes ❑ No	
Are lifeguards relieved at intervals so they can take breaks?	❑ Yes ❑ No	
How is lifeguard rotation handled?	❑ Yes ❑ No	
Do lifeguards understand their zones of coverage?	❑ Yes ❑ No	
Do lifeguards have well-defined duties, and are those duties communicated and understood?	❑ Yes ❑ No	
Are lifeguards given performance reviews?	❑ Yes ❑ No	
Are lifeguards enforcing pool rules consistently?	❑ Yes ❑ No	
Are lifeguards visible to pool patrons because of their distinctive uniforms?	❑ Yes ❑ No	
Are lifeguard certification cards and information kept in a central place for easy access?	❑ Yes ❑ No	
Are lifeguards supplied with all needed lifesaving equipment?	❑ Yes ❑ No	

(continued)

From Katharine M. Nohr, 2009, *Managing Risk in Sport and Recreation: The Essential Guide for Loss Prevention* (Champaign, IL: Human Kinetics).

Swimming Supervision *(continued)*

Considerations	Yes or No (check one)	Notes for follow-up
Are parents given notice that they must watch their children even though lifeguards are on duty?	❑ Yes ❑ No	
Even with parents watching, are lifeguards watching children carefully?	❑ Yes ❑ No	
Are adults within arm's reach of all children who cannot swim (even if they are using water wings or another inflatable device)?	❑ Yes ❑ No	
Are children taken away from the pool area if the adult is leaving, even if only for a minute or to answer a telephone?	❑ Yes ❑ No	
Are there other considerations for supervision?	❑ Yes ❑ No	

From Katharine M. Nohr, 2009, *Managing Risk in Sport and Recreation: The Essential Guide for Loss Prevention* (Champaign, IL: Human Kinetics).

EMERGENCY PLANS FOR SWIMMING POOLS

Emergency plans should be established and practiced as part of any swimming pool risk management plan. Consider the following questions.

Considerations	Yes or No (check one)	Notes for follow-up
Has an emergency plan been developed for all possible emergencies?	❑ Yes ❑ No	
Are there designated persons who are charged with enacting the emergency plan?	❑ Yes ❑ No	
Has a chain of command been established?	❑ Yes ❑ No	
Is there a telephone available at poolside so the appropriate emergency agency can be contacted immediately?	❑ Yes ❑ No	
Are phone numbers of emergency agencies, key personnel, patrons' emergency contact numbers, and others included as part of the emergency plan?	❑ Yes ❑ No	
When the emergency plan is activated, is the water evacuated of all people?	❑ Yes ❑ No	
Are people evacuated to a safe area upon activation of the emergency plan?	❑ Yes ❑ No	
Are there other considerations for an emergency plan?	❑ Yes ❑ No	

From Katharine M. Nohr, 2009, *Managing Risk in Sport and Recreation: The Essential Guide for Loss Prevention* (Champaign, IL: Human Kinetics).

PRACTICE DRILLS FOR SWIMMING POOLS

Emergency planning requires that practice drills be performed on a regular basis. During these practices, an organization can identify and correct weaknesses in their emergency plans. With practice, the kinks can be worked out, and when a real emergency occurs, personnel will be ready. Consider the following questions.

Considerations	Yes or No (check one)	Notes for follow-up
Are practice drills for emergencies regularly run so that personnel understand and can implement the emergency action plan?	❑ Yes ❑ No	
Are government agencies included in the practice drills?	❑ Yes ❑ No	
Are there other considerations for practice drills?	❑ Yes ❑ No	

From Katharine M. Nohr, 2009, *Managing Risk in Sport and Recreation: The Essential Guide for Loss Prevention* (Champaign, IL: Human Kinetics).

SWIMMING EMERGENCY COMMUNICATION AND EQUIPMENT

It is common for people to have cell phones handy, except when they are swimming in a pool or sitting in a hot tub. A cell phone in a person's locker will not do a lot of good in an emergency. Make sure a landline telephone is available, and consider the following questions about emergency equipment.

Considerations	Yes or No (check one)	Notes for follow-up
Is there a telephone located at poolside in order to contact emergency services?	❏ Yes ❏ No	
Are emergency telephone numbers mounted on the wall by the pool telephone or on the telephone?	❏ Yes ❏ No	
Is the address of the pool location mounted on the wall next to the pool telephone?	❏ Yes ❏ No	
Are approved flotation devices mounted near the pool?	❏ Yes ❏ No	
Is there an AED near the pool?	❏ Yes ❏ No	
Is there a shepherd's crook on a 12-foot (4 m) pole located near the pool?	❏ Yes ❏ No	
Is there a ring buoy located near the pool?	❏ Yes ❏ No	
Do lifeguards have rescue tubes?	❏ Yes ❏ No	
Is there a first aid kit and first aid equipment?	❏ Yes ❏ No	
Are CPR instructions mounted on a wall near the pool?	❏ Yes ❏ No	
Is there a blanket available?	❏ Yes ❏ No	
Is all rescue equipment mounted conspicuously around the pool?	❏ Yes ❏ No	
Are there other considerations for emergency communication and equipment?	❏ Yes ❏ No	

From Katharine M. Nohr, 2009, *Managing Risk in Sport and Recreation: The Essential Guide for Loss Prevention* (Champaign, IL: Human Kinetics).

SWIMMING POOL CHEMICAL STORAGE AND HANDLING

Chemical storage and handling could cause contamination or injury, so procedures should be established. The following questions should be addressed regarding pool chemicals.

Considerations	Yes or No (check one)	Notes for follow-up
Are chemicals kept in a dry place away from heat sources and other combustible items?	❑ Yes ❑ No	
Are chemicals stored in a locked room or closet that is not accessible to children?	❑ Yes ❑ No	
Are chemicals stored according to the manufacturer's recommendations?	❑ Yes ❑ No	
Are chemical containers clearly labeled, identifying their contents?	❑ Yes ❑ No	
Do chemical containers have clear warnings of any dangers associated with the chemicals?	❑ Yes ❑ No	
Are there other considerations for chemical storage and handling?	❑ Yes ❑ No	

From Katharine M. Nohr, 2009, *Managing Risk in Sport and Recreation: The Essential Guide for Loss Prevention* (Champaign, IL: Human Kinetics).

LIFEGUARD TRAINING

Training of lifeguards is a key part of a swimming pool risk management plan. Consider the following questions.

Considerations	Yes or No (check one)	Notes for follow-up
Are lifeguards and all personnel properly trained to perform all job functions?	❑ Yes ❑ No	
Are lifeguards and others trained in CPR for children and adults?	❑ Yes ❑ No	
Are lifeguards and others trained in first aid?	❑ Yes ❑ No	
Are there other considerations for lifeguard training?	❑ Yes ❑ No	

From Katharine M. Nohr, 2009, *Managing Risk in Sport and Recreation: The Essential Guide for Loss Prevention* (Champaign, IL: Human Kinetics).

SWIMMING POOL INCIDENT REPORTS AND LOGBOOKS

Incident reports and logbooks should reflect the details of injuries, accidents, and illnesses. This information should be kept for insurance underwriting purposes and in the event of a lawsuit. Analyzing incident reports and logbooks will also provide information for improvement. Consider the following questions.

Considerations	Yes or No (check one)	Notes for follow-up
Are incident reports filled out after every medical or other incident?	❑ Yes ❑ No	
Is a logbook kept recording illnesses and injuries reported?	❑ Yes ❑ No	
Are there other considerations for incident reports and logbooks?	❑ Yes ❑ No	

From Katharine M. Nohr, 2009, *Managing Risk in Sport and Recreation: The Essential Guide for Loss Prevention* (Champaign, IL: Human Kinetics).

SWIMMING POOL SIGNAGE

Conveying rules and regulations, hazards, and other important information is usually done, at least partly, by clear and visible signage. There is a danger of having too many signs—they can be ignored. If signage is created in a thoughtful manner, perhaps with expert guidance, it can assist an organization in defending a lawsuit and, hopefully, prevent injuries from occurring in the first place. Consider the following questions.

Considerations	Yes or No (check one)	Notes for follow-up
Is all signage clear, easy to read, and conveying the intended message?	❑ Yes ❑ No	
Is the most critical information set forth in signage that is the easiest to read and understand?	❑ Yes ❑ No	
Is signage about no diving or no diving into shallow water clear and easy to read?	❑ Yes ❑ No	
Is signage about no breath holding clear and easy to read?	❑ Yes ❑ No	
Is signage requiring parents to watch their kids clear and easy to read?	❑ Yes ❑ No	
Is signage depicting the depth markers of the pool clear and easy to read?	❑ Yes ❑ No	
Are pool rules conveyed, but with less emphasis than signage about diving, breath holding, and parents watching their children?	❑ Yes ❑ No	
Is signage done in unique and interesting ways so as to attract attention to it?	❑ Yes ❑ No	
Does signage blend into the background so it is not noticed?	❑ Yes ❑ No	
Is signage written in a language that is used by the patrons of the pool?	❑ Yes ❑ No	
Has signage become faded with time, damaged, or vandalized?	❑ Yes ❑ No	
Does signage make guarantees that could be used against your organization if the organization is sued (e.g., "Our lifeguards guarantee they will scan the pool every 10 seconds")?	❑ Yes ❑ No	
Are there other considerations for signage?	❑ Yes ❑ No	

From Katharine M. Nohr, 2009, *Managing Risk in Sport and Recreation: The Essential Guide for Loss Prevention* (Champaign, IL: Human Kinetics).

OUTSIDE GROUP USE OF SWIMMING POOLS

Large groups converging on a swimming pool can cause confusion about supervision and lifeguarding functions. Roles should be communicated in advance. Consider the following questions regarding this topic.

Considerations	Yes or No (check one)	Notes for follow-up
When outside groups use the pool, are the lifeguards' roles clarified with the lifeguards and the group?	❑ Yes ❑ No	
Who will be supervising the outside group?	❑ Yes ❑ No	
Has the outside group been notified of all pool rules?	❑ Yes ❑ No	
Has the outside group been provided with the organization's safety plan and agreed to follow it?	❑ Yes ❑ No	
Are there other considerations for outside group use?	❑ Yes ❑ No	

From Katharine M. Nohr, 2009, *Managing Risk in Sport and Recreation: The Essential Guide for Loss Prevention* (Champaign, IL: Human Kinetics).

HOT TUBS AND SPAS

Soaking in hot water is a pleasure that can also become dangerous when not done safely. The following questions are important for consideration.

Considerations	Yes or No (check one)	Notes for follow-up
Is water drained periodically?	❑ Yes ❑ No	
Is the maximum temperature 104 degrees Fahrenheit (40 degrees Celsius)?	❑ Yes ❑ No	
Is there a maximum time limit imposed on users?	❑ Yes ❑ No	
Is alcohol strictly prohibited while using the hot tub?	❑ Yes ❑ No	
Is the temperature monitored with an audible alarm system?	❑ Yes ❑ No	
Are drain covers checked daily for any loosening or disrepair?	❑ Yes ❑ No	
Do drain covers use an antivortex design?	❑ Yes ❑ No	
Are there other considerations for hot tubs and spas?	❑ Yes ❑ No	

From Katharine M. Nohr, 2009, *Managing Risk in Sport and Recreation: The Essential Guide for Loss Prevention* (Champaign, IL: Human Kinetics).

FENCES AND GATES
SURROUNDING THE SWIMMING POOL

Keeping small children out of swimming pools is important in order to prevent drowning. The following questions should be asked in relation to this concern.

Considerations	Yes or No (check one)	Notes for follow-up
Is there a fence surrounding the pool that is at least 5 feet 6 inches (1.7 m) high all the way around, without a gap on the bottom of the fence bigger than 4 inches (10 cm), or in accordance with applicable standards?	❑ Yes ❑ No	
Are openings in the fence less than 4 inches (10 cm) apart or in accordance with applicable standards?	❑ Yes ❑ No	
Is there anything that will allow a child to get a footing and be able to climb the fence?	❑ Yes ❑ No	
Are all items that a child might climb to gain access to a pool removed?	❑ Yes ❑ No	
Is the fence in a good state of repair, with no holes or defects?	❑ Yes ❑ No	
If a wall serves as part of the barrier to the pool, is that wall free from anything that can cause a child to gain access to the pool, such as windows or doors?	❑ Yes ❑ No	
If doors open to the pool, are they monitored by people or alarms so that a child will not enter a pool area with no supervision?	❑ Yes ❑ No	
Are all door and window locks adjacent to the pool out of reach of children?	❑ Yes ❑ No	
Are there gates that latch automatically and that can be locked?	❑ Yes ❑ No	
Is the gate locked when the pool is not being used?	❑ Yes ❑ No	
Is the gate release mechanism configured and located in such a way that it cannot be opened from the outside by a small child?	❑ Yes ❑ No	
Do gates leading to the pool swing outward away from the pool rather than inward?	❑ Yes ❑ No	
Are there other considerations for fences and gates surrounding the pool?	❑ Yes ❑ No	

From Katharine M. Nohr, 2009, *Managing Risk in Sport and Recreation: The Essential Guide for Loss Prevention* (Champaign, IL: Human Kinetics).

SWIMMING POOL ELECTRICAL EQUIPMENT

Wherever electrical equipment and water meet, there can be danger. Consider the following questions.

Considerations	Yes or No (check one)	Notes for follow-up
Is power equipment grounded?	❑ Yes ❑ No	
Is pool lighting protected by ground-fault circuit interrupters?	❑ Yes ❑ No	
Is the electrical turnoff switch for the pool and hot tub pumps clearly marked?	❑ Yes ❑ No	
Have you made sure that overhead electrical lines do not pass over pool?	❑ Yes ❑ No	
Have you made sure that no electrical fixtures, except specially designed lighting systems, are within 5 feet (1.5 m) of the pool or in accordance with applicable standards?	❑ Yes ❑ No	
Have you made sure that any electrical wiring within 20 feet (6 m) of the pool has protection from a ground-fault circuit interrupter?	❑ Yes ❑ No	
Are there other considerations for electrical equipment?	❑ Yes ❑ No	

From Katharine M. Nohr, 2009, *Managing Risk in Sport and Recreation: The Essential Guide for Loss Prevention* (Champaign, IL: Human Kinetics).

SWIMMING POOL COVERS AND DRAIN COVERS

Pool covers and drain covers have been known to cause serious injuries or drowning. People can be caught in them or unable to escape powerful suction. The following questions should be asked.

Considerations	Yes or No (check one)	Notes for follow-up
Is the pool cover completely removed from the pool when it is in use?	❑ Yes ❑ No	
Has standing water been removed from the pool cover?	❑ Yes ❑ No	
Are pool drain grids and covers in place?	❑ Yes ❑ No	
Are pool drain grids and covers in good condition and in conformance with the Virginia Graeme Baker Pool and Spa Safety Act, which was in effect as of December 19, 2008?	❑ Yes ❑ No	
Is long hair tied back or put in a swim cap to guard against drain entrapment?	❑ Yes ❑ No	
Are children taught to stay away from drains located in the pool and hot tub?	❑ Yes ❑ No	
If a drain cover is loose, broken, or missing, is the pool or hot tub closed until it is replaced or repaired?	❑ Yes ❑ No	
Are there other considerations for pool covers and drain covers?	❑ Yes ❑ No	

From Katharine M. Nohr, 2009, *Managing Risk in Sport and Recreation: The Essential Guide for Loss Prevention* (Champaign, IL: Human Kinetics).

DANGEROUS OBJECTS IN THE SWIMMING POOL AND POOL AREA

Objects can be the source of injury or drowning if they obstruct views or constitute tripping hazards. Consider the following questions.

Considerations	Yes or No (check one)	Notes for follow-up
Are inflatable rafts and toys prohibited from use in the pool?	❑ Yes ❑ No	
Have all debris, toys, and other objects been cleared from the pool areas and adjacent walkways?	❑ Yes ❑ No	
Is glass prohibited from the pool area?	❑ Yes ❑ No	
Are toys and other objects kept out of the pool area and away from the edge of the water?	❑ Yes ❑ No	
Are there other considerations for dangerous objects in the pool and pool area?	❑ Yes ❑ No	

From Katharine M. Nohr, 2009, *Managing Risk in Sport and Recreation: The Essential Guide for Loss Prevention* (Champaign, IL: Human Kinetics).

GENERAL SWIMMING SAFETY TIPS

If general safety tips are consistently heeded by all swimmers and guardians, fewer drownings are likely to occur. The following are some general safety tips that will go a long way in the prevention of swimming fatalities.

Considerations	Yes or No (check one)	Notes for follow-up
Is there a designated adult watching children at all times?	❑ Yes ❑ No	
Are visitors reminded to never swim alone?	❑ Yes ❑ No	
Do visitors use the buddy system?	❑ Yes ❑ No	
Is there signage reminding visitors that running, pushing, and dunking are not allowed?	❑ Yes ❑ No	
Have staff learned water rescue techniques?	❑ Yes ❑ No	
Are entrapment hazards, pumps, and drains inspected by professionals?	❑ Yes ❑ No	
Are children prohibited from being alone near the water?	❑ Yes ❑ No	
Is running around or near the pool prohibited?	❑ Yes ❑ No	
Are children taught to swim at an early age?	❑ Yes ❑ No	
Have adults learned CPR, child CPR, and basic first aid?	❑ Yes ❑ No	
Do visitors warm up and stretch before swimming?	❑ Yes ❑ No	
Do inexperienced swimmers wear life jackets in the water?	❑ Yes ❑ No	
Are visitors reminded not to swim if tired, cold, or overheated?	❑ Yes ❑ No	
Are visitors reminded not to swim in the pool if they cannot see the bottom of the pool at the deepest point?	❑ Yes ❑ No	
Are visitors reminded to check the depth of the water before diving?	❑ Yes ❑ No	
Is diving allowed only off the end of the diving board?	❑ Yes ❑ No	

(continued)

From Katharine M. Nohr, 2009, *Managing Risk in Sport and Recreation: The Essential Guide for Loss Prevention* (Champaign, IL: Human Kinetics).

General Swimming Safety Tips *(continued)*

Considerations	Yes or No (check one)	Notes for follow-up
Is the diving board used only for diving?	❑ Yes ❑ No	
When swimming in open water, are visitors reminded to check for undercurrents and avoid diving headfirst into waves?	❑ Yes ❑ No	
Are visitors reminded to check the conditions of open water before entering by examining the current patterns and talking to a lifeguard and others who are familiar with the conditions?	❑ Yes ❑ No	
Are visitors advised to avoid swimming in a body of water after a storm, particularly if it appears that the water level is rising or the current has increased?	❑ Yes ❑ No	
Are visitors advised to avoid swimming during storms and to check weather reports and avoid swimming if a storm is expected?	❑ Yes ❑ No	
Are visitors reminded to avoid consuming alcohol or drugs before or during a swim outing?	❑ Yes ❑ No	
Is there a plan in place for emergency situations, and are there clear instructions on how to contact emergency personnel if necessary?	❑ Yes ❑ No	
Are there other considerations for general safety tips?	❑ Yes ❑ No	

18

Tennis

[Tennis is] a perfect combination of violent action taking place in an atmosphere of total tranquility.

—Billie Jean King

Tennis is a relatively safe sport, with injuries arising occasionally when a tennis ball strikes someone in the eye or face, when someone is hit by a tennis racket, or from slips and falls on the tennis court or elsewhere on the premises. Because injuries may arise at country clubs, tennis is similar to golf in that the players may have higher incomes than in other sports. This could potentially lead to higher damage awards because loss of income might be higher. If sport organizations and recreational facilities pay special attention to keeping their premises safe from trip and slip hazards, this can go a long way toward preventing injuries.

TENNIS LAWSUITS

Because injuries arising out of tennis are not generally severe and are less frequent (aside from muscular and overuse injuries), there are relatively few reported lawsuit settlements and very few published appellate decisions.

Facility

Atcovitz v. Gulph Mills Tennis Club, Inc. The issue of whether a facility owed a duty to a participant to have an AED on its premises arose in the case of *Atcovitz v. Gulph Mills Tennis Club, Inc.*, 571 Pa. 580, 812 A.2d 1218 (2002).

In this case, the 64-year-old plaintiff with a history of heart problems had a heart attack while playing tennis at the defendant's tennis club. The tennis club did not have an AED. Several club members performed CPR, and an ambulance arrived in approximately 10 minutes. Despite this emergency care, the plaintiff suffered severe and permanent injuries, for which he claimed the tennis club was negligent because it did not own and maintain an AED. The court concluded that the defendant did not have a duty to the plaintiff to have an AED, and so it was not negligent.

As AEDs become the standard of care through widespread use, the courts might rule differently and find those facilities that do not have an AED to be negligent.

Augusta Country Club, Inc., v. Blake

In *Augusta Country Club, Inc., v. Blake*, 230 Ga. App. 650, 634 S.E.2d 812 (2006), the Augusta Country Club appealed a jury verdict, which awarded compensatory damages in the amount of $78,000 to plaintiff Linda Blake. The case arose out of an incident in which Blake was at Augusta for the purpose of participating in a tennis match. While she was walking toward the tennis courts, she walked down some steps where magnolia seedpods regularly fall. Blake stepped on a pod that was hidden from view and fell, sustaining serious injury. The facts at trial established that Augusta was aware of the problem it had with magnolia seedpods and so had a maintenance and inspection program to keep the walkways safe. This program was not followed on the morning of the incident, and so the court found Augusta negligent. On appeal, the court upheld the jury's award.

This case illustrates the importance of developing and following maintenance schedules. In light of the challenges of the magnolia seedpods, a warning sign might have been reasonable.

Guardino v. Kings Park School District

In a New York appellate case, *Guardino v. Kings Park School District*, 300 A.D. 355 (N.Y. App. 2002), the plaintiff, a 45-year-old experienced tennis player, broke her wrist when she tripped on a crack in an asphalt tennis court. The plaintiff sued the company that repaired the asphalt and the school where the court was located. The defendants claimed that the defect was "open and obvious" and that the plaintiff should have seen it and assumed the risk of playing on such a surface. Ultimately, the court concluded that a jury would have to decide whether detection of the crack was difficult or whether it was open and obvious.

Regular inspection and maintenance would probably have prevented the injury in this case.

Marshall v. City of New Rochelle

In *Marshall v. City of New Rochelle*, 15 A.D.3d, 790 N.Y.S.2d 504 (2005), a child slipped and fell on an outdoor tennis court that was wet because it had rained the night before. The plaintiff sued the city and the New York Junior Tennis League, which organized the program the plaintiff was participating in. The defendants both prevailed when filing motions for summary judgment on the grounds that the plaintiff assumed the risk of injury on the wet surface.

Wet grounds in sports do not favor plaintiffs, who generally are found to assume the risk by playing on them.

Sammut v. City of New York
In *Sammut v. City of New York*, 37 A.D.3d 811, 830 N.Y.S.2d 779 (2007), the plaintiff tripped on a crack in an outdoor tennis court. The court ruled that the plaintiff assumed the risk of injury because the crack was open and obvious.

Vecchione v. Middle Country Cent. School Dist.
In *Vecchione v. Middle Country Cent. School Dist.*, 300 A.D.2d 471, 752 N.Y.S.2d 82 (2002), the plaintiff, a 10th-grade girl on the varsity tennis team, slipped and fell during a jumping drill while practicing with her team. The plaintiff was found to have assumed the risk, and the wet court did not constitute an unreasonably increased risk. The school district prevailed and was not found negligent.

Staff

Livshitz v. U.S. Tennis Ass'n Nat. Tennis Center
Lawsuits have arisen when tennis players have been hit in the eye by a tennis ball. In *Livshitz v. U.S. Tennis Ass'n Nat. Tennis Center*, 196 Misc. 2d 460, 761 N.Y.S.2d 825 (2003), the 52-year-old plaintiff, Mila Livshitz, was taking paid tennis lessons organized by the USTA National Tennis Center at Flushing Meadow Park. During a drill in which the tennis instructor was hitting balls to 8 to 10 students, Livshitz was not prepared, and the instructor served a ball, hitting her in the eye.

The tennis facility attempted to be dismissed from the case by motion for summary judgment, claiming that primary assumption of risk was applicable as a complete defense. The court determined there were material issues of fact that a jury must decide because Livshitz had paid for the lesson, and this did not invite the tennis instructor to launch balls at high speeds when the plaintiff was not paying attention. The jury would have to address the potential negligence not only of the instructor but also of the student, who may have been negligent in not paying sufficient attention during the lesson.

Special care should be used when teaching novices how to play tennis. It is not unusual for people who are not skilled or familiar with a ball sport to be hit and injured.

Petretti v. Jefferson Valley Racquet Club, Inc.
A New York appellate court issued a published decision in *Petretti v. Jefferson Valley Racquet Club, Inc.*, 246 A.D.3d 583, 668 N.Y.S.2d 221 (1998). In this case, a tennis instructor was hitting balls in rapid succession to the students when the plaintiff

Staff and instructors need to take care of novice players, who may be unaccustomed to the high speeds of tennis balls or the dangers they need to watch out for when playing on or standing near a tennis court.

was struck in the eye with a tennis ball. The plaintiff sued the Jefferson Valley Racquet Club, alleging negligence. The defendant filed a motion for summary judgment, asserting that the plaintiff assumed the risk of injury and so the club was not liable. The lower court granted the motion, agreeing with the defendant. The plaintiff appealed the decision, and the appellate court concluded that the lower court was wrong in ruling the way it did. The case should have gone to trial rather than be dismissed because there were issues of fact as to whether the plaintiff assumed the risk. One of the court's concerns was that the plaintiff was a novice player and did what her instructor told her to do during the tennis lesson.

Tennis instructors should consider the ability of their students in relation to the drills used as well as the speed at which balls are hit.

TENNIS SAFETY CONSIDERATIONS

These reported appellate cases address issues related to safe play, AEDs, playing surfaces, and facilities as they relate to tennis, but they could occur in other sports as well. Understanding the potential for injury allows safe-guards to be taken in order to prevent problems in the future. To facilitate your organization's safety standards, please use all the forms on pages 294 to 298.

SUMMARY

Although tennis is generally a very safe sport, tennis balls and rackets can cause injury. Most tennis lawsuits have occurred because of slip and fall hazards on tennis courts or adjacent property. Court hazards, such as unpadded hard objects, can also cause injury.

It is important for tennis clubs to develop a system of inspection, maintenance, and repair so that such injuries can be avoided. Athlete injuries arising out of lack of supervision, poor muscle conditioning, dehydration, horseplay, and other causes can be prevented by following the tips listed in this chapter.

ELIMINATING SLIP AND FALL HAZARDS ON THE TENNIS COURT

Most of the lawsuits outlined in this chapter arose out of slips and falls. Slip and fall hazards can occur anywhere on a tennis club's property. It is important to have a system in place for inspection and removal or correction of any hazards on the premises.

Considerations	Yes or no (check one)	Notes for follow-up
Has the court been swept and cleaned?	❑ Yes ❑ No	
Are there any ruts, holes, hollows, cracks, wear, or other defects on the surface of the court?	❑ Yes ❑ No	
Have all tripping hazards been removed from the court?	❑ Yes ❑ No	
Is the surface of the court in good condition?	❑ Yes ❑ No	
Has the net been inspected for holes, sharp edges, or other defects?	❑ Yes ❑ No	
Is there any broken glass on the court?	❑ Yes ❑ No	
Are there any slippery portions of the court?	❑ Yes ❑ No	
Is the court dry, without puddles of water or drops of sweat?	❑ Yes ❑ No	
Are there any gym bags, balls, rackets, water bottles, or other objects on or around the court that are a tripping hazard?	❑ Yes ❑ No	
Are there other considerations for eliminating slip and fall hazards?	❑ Yes ❑ No	

From Katharine M. Nohr, 2009, *Managing Risk in Sport and Recreation: The Essential Guide for Loss Prevention* (Champaign, IL: Human Kinetics).

ELIMINATING TENNIS COURT HAZARDS

Tennis players run the risk of hitting objects when they run after balls. It is important that hard surfaces be in good repair, removed, or padded in order to prevent injuries. The following questions should be considered when addressing this concern.

Considerations	Yes or no (check one)	Notes for follow-up
Is the fence around the court in good repair?	❑ Yes ❑ No	
Is the gate closed during play?	❑ Yes ❑ No	
Are net posts padded?	❑ Yes ❑ No	
Are all other hard surfaces that could be collided with during play padded or removed?	❑ Yes ❑ No	
Are there other considerations for eliminating court hazards?	❑ Yes ❑ No	

From Katharine M. Nohr, 2009, *Managing Risk in Sport and Recreation: The Essential Guide for Loss Prevention* (Champaign, IL: Human Kinetics).

TENNIS EQUIPMENT

Although tennis is not a sport requiring much equipment, considerations of safety should be made. The following questions should be addressed in order to prevent injuries related to tennis equipment.

Considerations	Yes or no (check one)	Notes for follow-up
Are all equipment and playing areas properly maintained?	☐ Yes ☐ No	
Are rackets and balls stored away when not being used so they will not be trip hazards?	☐ Yes ☐ No	
Are children or others allowed to swing rackets so they can strike others?	☐ Yes ☐ No	
Are equipment and all elements of the court of high quality and in adherence to strict safety standards?	☐ Yes ☐ No	
Are ball machines used in accordance with the manufacturer's guidelines and instructions?	☐ Yes ☐ No	
Are equipment and elements of the court replaced with the latest and safest models when reasonable?	☐ Yes ☐ No	
Are there other considerations for equipment?	☐ Yes ☐ No	

From Katharine M. Nohr, 2009, *Managing Risk in Sport and Recreation: The Essential Guide for Loss Prevention* (Champaign, IL: Human Kinetics).

TENNIS SUPERVISION

Tennis has resulted in lawsuits in which injured players have alleged negligent supervision. Consider the following issues when addressing proper supervision of tennis players.

Considerations	Yes or no (check one)	Notes for follow-up
Are novices and children properly supervised while playing tennis?	❏ Yes ❏ No	
Do coaches or instructors communicate with athletes in order to prevent injuries?	❏ Yes ❏ No	
Do coaches and instructors provide adequate instruction to players?	❏ Yes ❏ No	
Do coaches and instructors teach proper form in order to prevent overuse injuries?	❏ Yes ❏ No	
Are there other considerations for supervision?	❏ Yes ❏ No	

From Katharine M. Nohr, 2009, *Managing Risk in Sport and Recreation: The Essential Guide for Loss Prevention* (Champaign, IL: Human Kinetics).

MINIMIZING AND PREVENTING TENNIS INJURIES

It is not uncommon for tennis players to develop overuse and other orthopedic injuries. These do not usually result in insurance claims or lawsuits. Other medical conditions may arise, such as dehydration. The following questions should assist athletes and clubs in avoiding such injuries.

Considerations	Yes or no (check one)	Notes for follow-up
Do athletes warm up and stretch first?	❑ Yes ❑ No	
Is muscle conditioning a primary focus so that athletes have sufficient muscular support to play tennis without overuse injury?	❑ Yes ❑ No	
Is communication between doubles players sufficient so that athletes can avoid collisions?	❑ Yes ❑ No	
Is horseplay prohibited, and is this rule promptly and consistently enforced?	❑ Yes ❑ No	
Is long hair tied back so it does not interfere with visibility?	❑ Yes ❑ No	
Are chewing gum and eating prohibited while playing?	❑ Yes ❑ No	
Are athletes aware that they should concentrate at all times when playing so they are not hit by balls or rackets?	❑ Yes ❑ No	
Do players stay properly hydrated, especially when playing in hot weather?	❑ Yes ❑ No	
Does the club provide drinking water so that players can stay hydrated?	❑ Yes ❑ No	
Does the club have an automated external defibrillator (AED) available near each court?	❑ Yes ❑ No	
Are there other considerations for minimizing and preventing tennis injuries?	❑ Yes ❑ No	

From Katharine M. Nohr, 2009, *Managing Risk in Sport and Recreation: The Essential Guide for Loss Prevention* (Champaign, IL: Human Kinetics).

Track and Field

Most people run a race to see who is fastest. I run a race to see who has the most guts.

—Steve Prefontaine

Track and field, which is also known as athletics, involves running, jumping, and throwing events. Running includes sprints, middle-distance and long-distance track events, hurdles, relays, road races, and racewalking. Field events consist of throwing and jumping events. Throwing events consist of the discus throw, hammer throw, javelin throw, and shot put. Jumping events consist of the high jump, pole vault, long jump, and triple jump.

The national governing body for track and field in the United States is USA Track and Field (USATF), which licenses and approves events in track and field, long-distance running, and racewalking. It provides sanctioning for such events, which includes the provision of liability insurance and medical insurance for athletes. USATF requires that all participants who take place in a sanctioned event sign liability waivers and that incident reports be submitted in relation to injuries sustained at the event. These actions demonstrate USATF's commitment to risk management in track and field.

TRACK AND FIELD LAWSUITS AND SETTLEMENTS

A number of large jury awards and out-of-court settlements have resulted from injuries sustained at track and field events. The following are some examples:

- A participant in the triple jump for the Cal Berkeley track team was practicing on a triple jump runway when a throw by a hammer thrower struck him in the head, causing permanent brain damage. The plaintiff alleged that the defendant track coach was negligent for allowing participants to use the track while athletes were throwing the hammer. The plaintiff settled with the defendant for $2.25 million.

- A volunteer coach was awarded $831,000 for injuries sustained from being struck in the eye with a javelin that was thrown at a college track and field meet.

- A high school student was awarded $207,000 when he landed incorrectly when executing a high jump and injured his knee. The judge determined that the coach did not provide the proper coaching and instruction so that the high jump could be executed safely.

A number of published appellate court decisions address various causes of injuries in track and field. The following cases address circumstances in which plaintiffs were injured by a shot put, discus, hammer, and javelin and from falls in steeplechase, high jump, and hurdles.

Equipment

Bennett v. City of New York
In *Bennett v. City of New York*, 303 A.D.2d 614, 756 N.Y.S.2d 633 (2003), a 13-year-old girl slipped on a horizontal ground-level support bar of a hurdle when she attempted to jump over it while participating in a Police Athletic League track and field program. A jury awarded the plaintiff damages in the amount of $250,000. The Police Athletic League was not successful in persuading the appellate court that the plaintiff could not recover because of assumption of risk. The court concluded that the lower court erred and directed a new trial. The plaintiff alleged that the Police Athletic League failed to properly instruct her on jumping the hurdles. This case demonstrates the importance of providing adequate instruction to young athletes.

Mason v. Bristol Local School Dist. Bd. of Edn.
In *Mason v. Bristol Local School Dist. Bd. of Edn.*, Slip Copy, 2006 WL 2796660 (2006), a 13-year-old plaintiff was hit in the nose and badly injured by a discus thrown by another teenage girl. The plaintiff was standing as instructed by her coach, but the girl who threw the discus had overspun so that the discus ricocheted off a pole, striking the plaintiff. Summary judgment was granted in favor of the defendants because they were immune from liability under the tort claims act.

Novice athletes participating in throwing events can be particularly dangerous because it takes some time to learn how to properly execute the skill.

Moose v. Massachusetts Institute of Technology

In *Moose v. Massachusetts Institute of Technology*, 43 Mass. App. Ct. 420, 683 N.E.2d 706 (1997), a jury awarded $650,000 to a pole-vaulter who fractured his skull when practicing pole vault. His heels hooked on the back edge of the pole-vault landing pit, causing him to fall backward and strike his head against a hard surface. On the day of the accident, the pads that were usually placed on the sides and back of the pit were not in place. The evidence at trial supported the plaintiff's position that the accident was reasonably foreseeable to the defendant. The plaintiff was found to be 15 percent liable, which reduced the total amount of damages awarded by that percentage.

Protective padding should be installed and should be sufficient to prevent an injury such as occurred in this pole-vault case.

Morales v. Beacon City School Dist.

In *Morales v. Beacon City School Dist.*, 44 A.D.3d 724, 843 N.Y.S.2d 646 (2007), the plaintiff, who had never run hurdles before, fell over a varsity-height hurdle placed on asphalt in a parking lot during track practice. The plaintiff claimed that he was not given instruction by his coach and that the hurdle was not properly set up, as the horizontal bar was uneven. The defendant's motion for summary judgment was denied because there was an issue of whether the risk of injury was unreasonably increased because of negligent supervision and training and the fact that the hurdle practice occurred on an asphalt surface.

Whenever there is a risk of falling, the surface on which a person could fall should be considered. In this case, the asphalt surface may have contributed to the plaintiff's increased injury. Hurdles and other equipment should also be set up properly in order to prevent injuries.

Morr v. County of Nassau

In *Morr v. County of Nassau*, 22 A.D.3d 728, 804 N.Y.S.2d 391 (2005), the 7-year-old plaintiff was injured at a track meet when she fell into a steeplechase pit that was uncovered. The court did not grant the defendant's motion for summary judgment because there was a question of fact as to whether it had breached its duty to maintain the premises in a reasonably safe condition by failing to place the wooden cover on the steeplechase pit. There was also a remaining question of fact as to whether the plaintiff was properly supervised at the time of the incident. The case would proceed to trial.

This case illustrates the importance of covering the pit when it is not in use.

Siau v. Rapides Parish School

In *Siau v. Rapides Parish School*, 264 So. 2d 372 (1972), the plaintiff was running in a grassy field next to the school's track. He was not wearing his eyeglasses and was not paying attention to the area in front of him when he was impaled by a javelin that had been left on the ground. The court determined that the plaintiff's own negligence caused the accident, so he was not entitled to recover against the defendant.

Since the grassy area was next to the school's track, school personnel might not have considered inspecting the area for wayward javelins. It may be reasonable to periodically inspect and maintain such areas. Participants should be instructed not to leave equipment in the field.

Hazards

Kreil v. County of Niagara

In *Kreil v. County of Niagara*, 8 A.D.3d 1001, 778 N.Y.S.2d 601 (2004), the plaintiff was attending the Scottish Highland Games as a spectator when she sustained injury from being struck by a hammer thrown by one of the competitors. The court concluded that as a spectator she assumed the risks inherent in the competition, and so she assumed the risk of being hit by a hammer. The defendants prevailed by motion for summary judgment.

Rankey v. Arlington Bd. of Edn.

In *Rankey v. Arlington Bd. of Edn.*, 78 Ohio App. 3d 112, 603 N.E.2d 1151 (1992), the plaintiff was attending a high school track meet in which her son was competing. As the plaintiff was walking through the shot-put landing area toward the stands, she was struck in the

Spectators and athletes must all be warned of the dangers of any track and field event where objects are thrown or hurled.

face by a shot put thrown by an athlete who was practicing. The defendants were successful on motion for summary judgment based on immunity under the applicable recreational use statute.

Again, parents and spectators are often injured and should be cautioned to pay careful attention to their surroundings while attending events.

Staff

Feagins v. Waddy   In *Feagins v. Waddy*, 978 So. 2d 712 (Ala. 2007), a middle school student was told by her coach that she would have to perform the high jump. She responded that she had never done the high jump before and did not know how to do it. The coach essentially ordered the plaintiff to perform the jump, and she tore her ACL, requiring surgery. The plaintiff filed a lawsuit against the coach and athletic director. The coach prevailed by motion for summary judgment because he was entitled to state-agent immunity.

Athletes should be given proper instruction before performing maneuvers such as the high jump. If an athlete is not ready to perform a dangerous skill, she should not be made to do so. Incremental instruction and performance of fundamental skills that will lead to the higher-level skill should be undertaken first.

Poelker v. Warrensburg Latham Community Unit School Dist. No. 11   In *Poelker v. Warrensburg Latham Community Unit School Dist. No. 11*, 251 Ill. App. 3d 270, 621 N.E.2d 940 (1993), the plaintiff was hit on the head by a discus thrown by another athlete who was preparing for the school track and field meet. There were no adults supervising the discus circle, but 12 adults were available at the meet. The court determined that the defendant school district did not willfully and wantonly breach its duty to supervise, and it was immune from any negligence of the teachers and employees under the applicable governmental immunity statute.

Supervision is particularly important in track and field. The use of dangerous throwing implements requires proper instruction and supervision.

TRACK AND FIELD SAFETY CONSIDERATIONS

These lawsuits could have been prevented if the defendants had taken more care in supervision and instruction and if the plaintiffs had paid closer attention when walking in the vicinity of throwing practices and competitions. Track and field injuries can be prevented by careful attention to safety rules and procedures.

Pairing throwing events with running and jumping events creates risk of injuries. It is important to separate throwing events from other events and to make sure care is used in the execution of each of these events in order to prevent injury to the participants, officials, and spectators. An important preliminary step is making sure the surface on which the particular event is run is free of debris and defects. To facilitate your organization's safety standards, please use all the forms on pages 305 to 317.

SUMMARY

Track and field is a complex sport when it comes to risk management planning. Safety issues must be considered for running, jumping, and throwing events as well as for putting them all together in one venue. Athletes are injured in these sports on a regular basis even when conditions are safe. Since dangerous implements are used in track and field events, such as the javelin, hammer, shot put, and discus, the stakes are high, and any mistake could mean a serious injury or even death. A risk management program should consider these concerns and implement procedures so that these disciplines can be practiced safely and athletes and spectators will be free from harm.

GENERAL SAFETY INSPECTION
FOR TRACK AND FIELD

As discussed in chapter 5, inspections are important in revealing problems that need to be addressed before an injury occurs. This is particularly important in track and field.

Considerations	Yes or no (check one)	Notes for follow-up
Is the track inspected before each practice and meet, looking for obstructions, exposed roots, garbage, glass, rakes, equipment, or any other objects that should be picked up and cleared away before use?	❑ Yes ❑ No	
Are sprinkler heads, irrigation stand pipes, and drainage hole covers inspected to make sure they will not pose a hazard to participants?	❑ Yes ❑ No	
Is dirt checked for rocks and clumped mud?	❑ Yes ❑ No	
Is dirt raked to loosen it and checked to eliminate tripping and falling hazards?	❑ Yes ❑ No	
Are the bleachers, areas where spectators will sit or congregate, and public areas inspected for slippery surfaces, holes in netting or fences, broken benches, or other hazards?	❑ Yes ❑ No	
Has the protective cage surrounding the hammer and discus throwing areas been inspected for any holes or defects?	❑ Yes ❑ No	
Has the track been inspected for slippery surfaces or other hazards?	❑ Yes ❑ No	
Are there other considerations for general safety inspection for track and field?	❑ Yes ❑ No	

From Katharine M. Nohr, 2009, *Managing Risk in Sport and Recreation: The Essential Guide for Loss Prevention* (Champaign, IL: Human Kinetics).

SHOT-PUT SAFETY

Shot puts have the potential for causing injury if safety rules are not followed and enforced. The following safety questions should be asked in order to ensure that shot puts are used safely.

Considerations	Yes or no (check one)	Notes for follow-up
Has the ring been inspected for any defects, unevenness, indentations, or protrusions?	❑ Yes ❑ No	
Has the ring been swept of any debris that could interfere with the traction of the athletes' shoes?	❑ Yes ❑ No	
Are throwing areas segregated by fencing, barricades, or barriers to prevent the equipment from injuring other participants, officials, and spectators?	❑ Yes ❑ No	
Has the yellow area been marked with flags so that those not competing will not enter?	❑ Yes ❑ No	
Is the landing area clear of debris, divots, rocks, or other objects that could cause the shot to bounce?	❑ Yes ❑ No	
Have all divots been filled to prevent a tripping hazard?	❑ Yes ❑ No	
Have athletes been taught the proper form for throwing the shot?	❑ Yes ❑ No	
Have athletes and others been taught safety rules and guidelines for throwing the shot?	❑ Yes ❑ No	
Are shots carried back to the throwing area rather than thrown back?	❑ Yes ❑ No	
Have athletes been warned that they should not proceed with warming up or throwing the shot until the coach is present?	❑ Yes ❑ No	
Are you using a system in which all shots are thrown and then retrieved all at once before throwing begins again?	❑ Yes ❑ No	
Are athletes prohibited from entering the red zone while shots are being thrown?	❑ Yes ❑ No	
Are athletes prohibited from throwing anywhere other than the landing zone?	❑ Yes ❑ No	
Are all shots put away when practice has concluded?	❑ Yes ❑ No	
Is practice scheduled for a specific time and location?	❑ Yes ❑ No	
Are all practices supervised by adults with proper experience and training?	❑ Yes ❑ No	
Are there other considerations for shot-put safety?	❑ Yes ❑ No	

From Katharine M. Nohr, 2009, *Managing Risk in Sport and Recreation: The Essential Guide for Loss Prevention* (Champaign, IL: Human Kinetics).

DISCUS SAFETY

Discuses used in track and field have the potential for causing injury if safety rules are not followed and enforced. The following questions should be asked in order to ensure safety during discus use.

Considerations	Yes or no (check one)	Notes for follow-up
Has the ring been inspected for any defects, unevenness, indentations, or protrusions?	❏ Yes ❏ No	
Has the ring been swept of any debris that could interfere with the traction of the athletes' shoes?	❏ Yes ❏ No	
Are throwing areas segregated by fencing, barricades, or barriers to prevent the equipment from injuring other participants, officials, and spectators?	❏ Yes ❏ No	
Has the yellow area been marked with flags so that those not competing will not enter?	❏ Yes ❏ No	
Is the circle surrounded with a 15-foot (4.5 m) high U-shaped protective cage?	❏ Yes ❏ No	
Are the cage and netting inspected regularly and whenever a discus comes in contact with it?	❏ Yes ❏ No	
Have the cage and netting been replaced in accordance with the manufacturer's recommendations?	❏ Yes ❏ No	
Are the cage and netting sufficiently slack so that the discus will not bounce off and cause injury?	❏ Yes ❏ No	
Is the landing area clear of debris, divots, rocks, or other objects that could cause the discus to bounce?	❏ Yes ❏ No	
Have all divots been filled to prevent a tripping hazard?	❏ Yes ❏ No	
Have athletes been taught the proper form for throwing the discus?	❏ Yes ❏ No	
Have athletes and others been taught safety rules and guidelines for throwing the discus?	❏ Yes ❏ No	
Have athletes been warned that they should not proceed with warming up or throwing the discus until the coach is present?	❏ Yes ❏ No	
Are you using a system in which all discuses are thrown and then retrieved all at once before throwing begins again?	❏ Yes ❏ No	

(continued)

From Katharine M. Nohr, 2009, *Managing Risk in Sport and Recreation: The Essential Guide for Loss Prevention* (Champaign, IL: Human Kinetics).

Discus Safety *(continued)*

Considerations	Yes or no (check one)	Notes for follow-up
Have athletes been instructed to stay out of the red zone and away from the cage for safety purposes?	❑ Yes ❑ No	
Are discuses inspected for damage if they come into contact with a hard surface?	❑ Yes ❑ No	
Are discuses carried back to the throwing area rather than thrown back?	❑ Yes ❑ No	
Are athletes prohibited from entering the red zone while discuses are being thrown?	❑ Yes ❑ No	
Are athletes prohibited from throwing anywhere other than the landing zone?	❑ Yes ❑ No	
Are all discuses put away when practice has concluded?	❑ Yes ❑ No	
Is practice scheduled for a specific time and location?	❑ Yes ❑ No	
Are all practices supervised by adults with proper experience and training?	❑ Yes ❑ No	
Are there other considerations for discus safety?	❑ Yes ❑ No	

HAMMER SAFETY

Hammers used in track and field have the potential for causing injury if safety rules are not followed and enforced. The following questions should be asked in order to ensure safe hammer use.

Considerations	Yes or no (check one)	Notes for follow-up
Has the ring been inspected for any defects, unevenness, indentations, or protrusions?	❑ Yes ❑ No	
Has the ring been swept of any debris that could interfere with the traction of the athletes' shoes?	❑ Yes ❑ No	
Are throwing areas segregated by fencing, barricades, or barriers to prevent the equipment from injuring other participants, officials, and spectators?	❑ Yes ❑ No	
Has the yellow area been marked with flags so that those not competing will not enter?	❑ Yes ❑ No	
Is the circle surrounded with a 15-foot (4.5 m) high U-shaped protective cage?	❑ Yes ❑ No	
Are the cage and netting inspected regularly and whenever a hammer comes in contact with it?	❑ Yes ❑ No	
Have the cage and netting been replaced in accordance with the manufacturer's recommendations?	❑ Yes ❑ No	
Are the cage and netting sufficiently slack so that the hammer will not bounce off and cause injury?	❑ Yes ❑ No	
Is the landing area clear of debris, divots, rocks, or other objects that could cause the hammer to bounce?	❑ Yes ❑ No	
Have all divots been filled to prevent a tripping hazard?	❑ Yes ❑ No	
Have athletes been taught the proper form for throwing the hammer?	❑ Yes ❑ No	
Have the ends of the wires of the hammers been taped so they will not catch on netting or clothing?	❑ Yes ❑ No	
Have the hammers been inspected for defects?	❑ Yes ❑ No	
Are hammers that are defective taken out of use?	❑ Yes ❑ No	

(continued)

From Katharine M. Nohr, 2009, *Managing Risk in Sport and Recreation: The Essential Guide for Loss Prevention* (Champaign, IL: Human Kinetics).

Hammer Safety *(continued)*

Considerations	Yes or no (check one)	Notes for follow-up
Have athletes and others been taught safety rules and guidelines for throwing the hammer?	❑ Yes ❑ No	
Have athletes been warned that they should not proceed with warming up or throwing the hammer until the coach is present?	❑ Yes ❑ No	
Are you using a system in which all hammers are thrown and then retrieved all at once before throwing begins again?	❑ Yes ❑ No	
Have athletes been instructed to stay out of the red zone and away from the cage for safety purposes?	❑ Yes ❑ No	
Are hammers inspected for damage if they come into contact with a hard surface?	❑ Yes ❑ No	
Are hammers carried back to the throwing area rather than thrown back?	❑ Yes ❑ No	
Are athletes prohibited from entering the red zone while hammers are being thrown?	❑ Yes ❑ No	
Are athletes prohibited from throwing anywhere other than the landing zone?	❑ Yes ❑ No	
Are all hammers put away when practice has concluded?	❑ Yes ❑ No	
Is practice scheduled for a specific time and location?	❑ Yes ❑ No	
Are all practices supervised by adults with proper experience and training?	❑ Yes ❑ No	
Are there other considerations for hammer safety?	❑ Yes ❑ No	

From Katharine M. Nohr, 2009, *Managing Risk in Sport and Recreation: The Essential Guide for Loss Prevention* (Champaign, IL: Human Kinetics).

JAVELIN SAFETY

Javelins are dangerous objects and should be used only under strict safety guidelines. The following questions should be asked in order to ensure safe javelin use.

Considerations	Yes or no (check one)	Notes for follow-up
Has the runway been inspected for any defects, unevenness, indentations, or protrusions?	❑ Yes ❑ No	
Has the runway been swept of any debris that could interfere with the traction of the athletes' shoes?	❑ Yes ❑ No	
Are throwing areas segregated by fencing, barricades, or barriers to prevent the equipment from injuring other participants, officials, and spectators?	❑ Yes ❑ No	
Has the yellow area been marked with flags so that those not competing will not enter?	❑ Yes ❑ No	
Is the landing area clear of debris, divots, rocks, or other objects that could cause the javelin to bounce?	❑ Yes ❑ No	
Have all divots been filled to prevent a tripping hazard?	❑ Yes ❑ No	
Have athletes been taught the proper form for throwing the javelin?	❑ Yes ❑ No	
Have the javelins been inspected for defects?	❑ Yes ❑ No	
Are javelins that are defective taken out of use?	❑ Yes ❑ No	
Is the metal head fastened securely to the javelin?	❑ Yes ❑ No	
Is the grip of the javelin frayed or worn?	❑ Yes ❑ No	
Are there any cracks in the javelin that could cause it to break?	❑ Yes ❑ No	
Have athletes and others been taught safety rules and guidelines for throwing the javelin?	❑ Yes ❑ No	
Have athletes been warned that they should not proceed with warming up or throwing the javelin until the coach is present?	❑ Yes ❑ No	

(continued)

From Katharine M. Nohr, 2009, *Managing Risk in Sport and Recreation: The Essential Guide for Loss Prevention* (Champaign, IL: Human Kinetics).

Javelin Safety *(continued)*

Considerations	Yes or no (check one)	Notes for follow-up
Are you using a system in which all javelins are thrown and then retrieved all at once before throwing begins again?	❑ Yes ❑ No	
Are javelins inspected for damage if they come into contact with a hard surface?	❑ Yes ❑ No	
Are athletes prohibited from entering the red zone while javelins are being thrown?	❑ Yes ❑ No	
Are athletes prohibited from throwing anywhere other than the landing zone?	❑ Yes ❑ No	
Are javelins carried back to the throwing area rather than thrown back?	❑ Yes ❑ No	
Are javelins carried in a container?	❑ Yes ❑ No	
If javelins are not carried in a container, are they carried with the point down so they are perpendicular to the ground?	❑ Yes ❑ No	
Are wind conditions checked before javelins are thrown?	❑ Yes ❑ No	
Are all javelins put away when practice has concluded?	❑ Yes ❑ No	
Is practice scheduled for a specific time and location?	❑ Yes ❑ No	
Are all practices supervised by adults with proper experience and training?	❑ Yes ❑ No	
Are there other considerations for javelin safety?	❑ Yes ❑ No	

From Katharine M. Nohr, 2009, *Managing Risk in Sport and Recreation: The Essential Guide for Loss Prevention* (Champaign, IL: Human Kinetics).

LONG JUMP AND TRIPLE JUMP PITS

Athletes can be injured when engaging in the long jump and triple jump. The following questions should be asked when evaluating the safety of long jump and triple jump pits.

Considerations	Yes or no (check one)	Notes for follow-up
Are pits rototilled, raked, or otherwise prepared before each practice or competition to loosen sand so that athletes do not injure themselves?	❑ Yes ❑ No	
Are pits raked between each jump?	❑ Yes ❑ No	
Are athletes cautioned to be careful of tools such as rakes and shovels?	❑ Yes ❑ No	
Are there other considerations for long jump and triple jump pits?	❑ Yes ❑ No	

From Katharine M. Nohr, 2009, *Managing Risk in Sport and Recreation: The Essential Guide for Loss Prevention* (Champaign, IL: Human Kinetics).

LONG JUMP SAFETY

Athletes can avoid injury when performing the long jump if the following questions are addressed.

Considerations	Yes or no (check one)	Notes for follow-up
Is care taken to prevent people from crossing the long jump approach?	❑ Yes ❑ No	
Do athletes wait for a signal before starting their approach?	❑ Yes ❑ No	
Are closed long jump approaches marked (e.g., with construction cones) so athletes do not use them?	❑ Yes ❑ No	
Are there other considerations for long jump safety?	❑ Yes ❑ No	

From Katharine M. Nohr, 2009, *Managing Risk in Sport and Recreation: The Essential Guide for Loss Prevention* (Champaign, IL: Human Kinetics).

HIGH JUMP SAFETY

The high jump can be dangerous to athletes if sufficient safety measures are not in place. The following questions will aid an organization in making the high jump as safe as possible.

Considerations	Yes or no (check one)	Notes for follow-up
Has the high jump pit been properly assembled so that the sections are strapped together?	❑ Yes ❑ No	
Has the landing pad been properly attached to the high jump assembly?	❑ Yes ❑ No	
Is the landing pad of sufficient thickness and density for safe landing?	❑ Yes ❑ No	
Is the takeoff approach clean and clear, allowing for good footing?	❑ Yes ❑ No	
Is there spotting by coaches or other competent persons so that athletes land in the pit?	❑ Yes ❑ No	
Are there other considerations for high jump safety?	❑ Yes ❑ No	

From Katharine M. Nohr, 2009, *Managing Risk in Sport and Recreation: The Essential Guide for Loss Prevention* (Champaign, IL: Human Kinetics).

SAFETY CONSIDERATIONS
FOR TRACK AND FIELD MEETS

When running a track and field meet, certain safety considerations must be put in place. The following questions will assist in putting on a safe meet.

Considerations	Yes or no (check one)	Notes for follow-up
Have you identified the head official?	❏ Yes ❏ No	
Are officials and spectators warned with a horn or otherwise when a throw is being attempted?	❏ Yes ❏ No	
If you have seen a problem or safety concern, have you brought it to the attention of the head official?	❏ Yes ❏ No	
If there is a problem or safety concern that has not been addressed, have you continued to seek assistance and directed your athletes not to proceed until the concern is remedied?	❏ Yes ❏ No	
Have you documented the incident with a formal protest related to the hazard if you think it is appropriate?	❏ Yes ❏ No	
Are there other safety considerations for track and field meets?	❏ Yes ❏ No	

SAFETY CONSIDERATIONS
FOR CROSS COUNTRY EVENTS

Cross country events may be made safer if the following questions are addressed.

Considerations	Yes or no (check one)	Notes for follow-up
Has the course been inspected for any potential hazards?	❑ Yes ❑ No	
Are hazards clearly marked so they are visible to athletes running?	❑ Yes ❑ No	
Are support vehicles and checkpoints used to monitor athletes?	❑ Yes ❑ No	
Are water stations provided at frequencies that are consistent with the heat and humidity?	❑ Yes ❑ No	
Are there other safety considerations for cross country events?	❑ Yes ❑ No	

From Katharine M. Nohr, 2009, *Managing Risk in Sport and Recreation: The Essential Guide for Loss Prevention* (Champaign, IL: Human Kinetics).

20

Triathlon

*If God invented marathons to keep people from doing any-
thing more stupid, the triathlon must have taken him completely by surprise.*

—P.Z. Pcarce

The hazards associated with triathlons are significant when you consider that the sport combines the dangers of swimming, cycling, and running as well as the transitions in between these events when the athletes are trying to change as quickly as possible into the gear required for the next segment of the race. The governing body for triathlon is USA Triathlon (USAT), which has an excellent risk management program for USAT-sanctioned races. Insurance is provided as well as a waiver form and release that athletes must sign in order to participate. If a race director requests certification, a lengthy sanction application must be submitted, which includes safety plan information as well as confirmation that the race director has also obtained required insurance. USAT monitors the safety of each event and withholds sanctioning if there are concerns regarding the operation of a race. USAT also provides certification to race directors to improve the quality and safety of the sport.

There have been very few published legal decisions related to triathlons. In evaluating legal issues that could arise out of triathlons, it is best to review those that concern swimming, bicycles versus motor vehicles, pedestrians versus motor vehicles, and premises liability. Because of the complexity of this sport, the potential for litigation is tremendous. Triathlon is a relatively new sport, beginning as recently as 1974 and gaining in popularity over the years. Fortunately, USAT has responded to the popularity and has made tremendous strides in making it a much safer sport. Because of this, USAT sanctioning is the most important risk management tip that can be offered here. Sanctioning will not replace hard work on each race director's part to create safe events, but it will provide structure, guidelines, insurance, and risk management assistance.

The following sections address each segment of triathlon (swim, bike, and run), providing a summary of the few applicable published appellate legal cases.

THE SWIM

The triathlon swim ordinarily takes place in open water, a lake or an ocean. Sometimes, where open water is not available, the swim will take place in a swimming pool. The swim is first, probably for safety reasons. Athletes have less chance of cramping and potentially drowning when they perform the swim before biking and running. Some issues related to the triathlon swim are accountability of the swimmers, water quality, and water conditions. Swimmers have to be accounted for so that if it is noticed that a swimmer is missing, a search can be conducted before it is too late. Water should not be polluted so as to cause harm or illness to participants, and the wave conditions should not be too treacherous so as to become perilous to swimmers.

Hazards

Hiett v. Lake Barcroft Community Ass'n, Inc.   Triathlon swims can be held in the ocean, lakes, and swimming pools, and so a variety of conditions can exist. The only reported appellate case that has arisen out of a triathlon swim is *Hiett v. Lake Barcroft Community Ass'n, Inc.*, 244 Va. 191, 418 S.E.2d 894 (1992). In that case, the plaintiff was rendered quadriplegic in the Teflon Man Triathlon when he dove into the water at the start of the race. He had waded into the lake up to his thighs, and when he dove, he hit his head on the bottom of the lake or an object. The plaintiff had signed a release form that was part of the entry form, discharging his right to claim damages against the organizers and sponsors of the event. The court determined that the release form was void because it was against public policy. Novins, the defendant who had talked the plaintiff into doing the race, was dismissed because she did not own or control the lake and so did not have a duty to warn the plaintiff of the hazardous lake bottom.

The facts of this case illustrate that the same dangers that are present and need to be guarded against in swimming generally must be addressed in triathlons. Athletes have to be careful not to dive in locations where the depth could be shallow. Many triathletes and long-distance swimmers finish a swim race by doing the butterfly stroke. This can be dangerous if it causes them to make impact with objects or the bottom.

Accounting for Triathletes

To safeguard against drowning, it is crucial that each and every swimmer be accounted for. In the swim portion of the triathlon, athletes should wear brightly colored swim caps so they are visible to lifeguards, who should be monitoring the swim in the water and on land. The swim caps can correspond to the group or wave the athletes are starting the race with. Swimmers should not be allowed to start the race without wearing the assigned swim cap.

Athletes should also be monitored by using computer timing chips and checking to make sure that all bikes are picked up by swimmers after the swim portion of the race. Timing chips are usually strapped onto a swimmer's ankle. The computer records the time the swimmer enters and exits the water. If the swimmer fails to exit the water, the timer will notify the lifeguards, and a search can ensue. If a bike is left over in the transition area after the swim, the race director should order that the water be searched but should also determine whether the athlete actually started the race or might have exited the water at another location. It is not unusual for an athlete to abandon the race and leave the race site without telling the race director. Athletes should be informed that if they abandon the race at any point in the course, they should notify the race director, timer, or an official.

Lifeguards and Watercraft

The swim portions of races should be well staffed, with certified lifeguards and watercraft. The nature of the water course will dictate the type and number of watercraft used. Depending on the type of race, a race director may also ask for U.S. Coast Guard assistance. Watercraft should be spaced evenly throughout the course and may contain equipment such as extra life jackets, an emergency whistle, a first aid kit, and other useful items. Swimmers should be encouraged to seek assistance from watercraft volunteers without imposition of a penalty. As the swimmers complete the course, the watercraft can realign appropriately, with one watercraft following the last swimmer. Fatigued, injured, and ill swimmers should be pulled from the course. A cutoff time for the swim may be imposed, particularly if the conditions are rough or cold. Race directors should not hesitate to cancel the swim and turn the race into a duathlon (bike and run only) if the swim conditions are dangerous.

In addition to watercraft, there should be certified lifeguards and spotters located on the beach to monitor the swim. The spotters should notify the lifeguards if they see any swimmers in distress. Protocol should be established as to the response when swimmers are in distress. For example, whistles can be sounded and two watercraft can respond to assess the

One way to increase safety at an event is to make sure that certified lifeguards are on hand to monitor the swimmers at all times.

swimmer's condition and transport the swimmer, if necessary. It is important to return watercraft to their previous positions if no longer necessary so that the course can be continuously monitored.

Limiting Swimmers on Course

Safe and successful swim segments of triathlons usually involve wave starts with limited numbers of swimmers. The wave starts eliminate congestion when the athletes start the race so that swimmers are not bumping into each other. This also allows lifeguards to see individual swimmers and track their progress. Starting the athletes in waves also means less congestion at the start of the cycling leg of the race. With the advent of chip timing in triathlon, wave starts do not put any athletes at a disadvantage and allow for timing of each individual's performance whether starting at the front or the back of the pack.

BICYCLE COURSE

Ideally, a bicycle course will be closed to traffic on the day of a race. In many locales this is not realistic because of the needs of the local community. In planning the bike course, the day and time of the race should be considered. If the race is on a Sunday morning and will pass a church or businesses that are busy for Sunday brunch, you may have to reconsider the route. Rural areas with limited motor vehicle traffic make the best bicycle courses but may be difficult for athletes to travel to in the early morning of a race, and infrastructure may not be available to support the race. Some races are sponsored by resorts, beginning at the resort and using the resort and surrounding roads. This can work well, especially if the resort provides athletes hotel accommodations.

The bicycle course should be coned sufficiently, using signage so that athletes understand the prescribed course. Cones and signage should also be in place so that the bicycles and motor vehicle traffic are sufficiently separated. Police officers should be hired to direct traffic at major intersections. Volunteers should be placed at key locales to direct athletes so they do not deviate from the course.

It is important that the bicycle course consist of a smooth roadway and be free of debris, glass, and potholes. Narrow areas of the roadway might be designated as no-passing zones to eliminate potential bike-versus-bike accidents. It is important that the bike course and run course do not intersect at any point in order to prevent bike-versus-runner accidents. Athletes should be allowed to have a care bag at the halfway point on the bicycle in long races, which may contain nutrition, extra socks, or other items the athlete might need.

Hazards

Banfield v. Louis   There have been several reported appellate court decisions involving the bike portion of triathlons. In a Florida case, *Banfield v. Louis*, 589 So. 2d 441 (Fla. App. 4 Dist. 1991), the plaintiff was injured while riding his bicycle on the triathlon bike course when a motor vehicle hit him. The plaintiff had signed up for a triathlon series, of which the race was included. To participate in the series, the plaintiff had to sign a release, or waiver of negligence claims against race organizers, promoters, sponsors, and agents. Since the plaintiff's participation in the triathlon was voluntary, the court concluded that the release was not unconscionable. The defendants, including race organizers, sponsors, and promoters of the event, were dismissed because of the release signed by the plaintiff. The defendant driver of the motor vehicle that caused the collision remained in the case.

Many triathlons in the United States are sanctioned by USA Triathlon which requires athletes to sign a release. It is customary that athletes sign a release as part of their registration. This practice is a good one in light of cases such as the one just described.

Johnson v. Steffen   In an Indiana case, *Johnson v. Steffen*, 685 N.E.2d 1117 (Ind. App. 1997), a police officer was assigned to traffic control for a triathlon. He was attempting to direct a motor vehicle out of the coned-off area designated for bikes when a triathlete riding his bike crashed into him, causing injury. The police officer filed a lawsuit against race organizers, sponsors, and the bicyclist that hit him. One of the issues was whether the "fireman's rule" was applicable, which essentially provides that a landowner does not owe a duty to a firefighter who responds to an incident on his property. In this case, the location was the street used during the cycling leg of the triathlon. Since the streets are not owned by the defendants and they do not have control, a premises liability claim using the fireman's rule could not be made. Consequently, the defendants were not able to successfully use the fireman's rule in order to get out of the case by summary judgment.

The accident in this case probably could not have been prevented with any advance planning. However, it is important to notify motor vehicles of the race course in advance of the race. Proper signage and coning will also prevent vehicles from entering a closed course.

RUN COURSE

Once the triathletes have completed the bike course, they will get on wobbly legs and begin running. Usually, the athletes are fatigued and potentially dehydrated by the time they begin the run course. It is essential to provide sufficient aid stations for the participants so they can stay hydrated. Longer races will require more nutrition for athletes than water. Electrolyte fluid-replacement drinks and food should be provided for anything longer than an intermediate-distance race. Each aid station should have cell phones or radios so that medical assistance can be summoned if necessary. There should also be race vehicles on the course to monitor the run.

Medical personnel should be available on the run because some athletes suffer from dehydration and become ill. Athletes sometimes go into cardiac arrest or suffer aneurysms, requiring quick and adequate medical response. Many triathlons address these concerns by having a medical tent staffed with doctors or EMTs on site as well as mobile medical units and ambulances. Longer and bigger races are more likely to provide more extensive medical staffing. At the very least, an ambulance should be on site or close by to attend to medical emergencies.

TRIATHLON SAFETY CONSIDERATIONS

Since there are so many elements to a triathlon, it can be difficult to plan for a safe event and for everyone involved to execute that plan. To facilitate your organization's safety standards, please use all the forms on pages 326 to 335.

SUMMARY

Triathlon is a multisport event that includes essentially four segments: swimming, cycling, running, and transitions. With each segment there is potential for injury. Lifeguards must closely monitor the swim and aid swimmers in distress, and race management must implement a system so that all athletes are accounted for. The primary safety concern for the cycling segment of the race is the potential for accidents between bicycles and motor vehicles. Bikes can also collide with each other if cyclists are not riding safely. The run portion of the race has the potential for dehydration or other medical problems. Because of these concerns, a well thought out safety plan should be in place, and medical personnel should be at the scene.

ACCOUNTING FOR ATHLETES IN A TRIATHLON USING A COMPUTERIZED TIMING SYSTEM

Computerized timing systems have made it much easier for race directors to account for athletes on the race course. The following questions should be asked in relation to such systems.

Considerations	Yes or no (check one)	Notes for follow-up
Have athletes been assigned a timing chip to be worn on a strap, usually placed around the ankle?	❑ Yes ❑ No	
Have athletes been instructed that they must wear the chip at all times during the race and that it should be removed only after they have crossed the finish line?	❑ Yes ❑ No	
Are athletes aware that the chip must be scanned 6 times during the triathlon?	❑ Yes ❑ No	
Will accountability volunteers be available to keep track of athletes who have not completed segments using bib numbers and names?	❑ Yes ❑ No	
Are there other considerations when accounting for athletes using a computerized timing system?	❑ Yes ❑ No	

From Katharine M. Nohr, 2009, *Managing Risk in Sport and Recreation: The Essential Guide for Loss Prevention* (Champaign, IL: Human Kinetics).

TIMING-CHIP SCANNING FOR TRIATHLON EVENTS

Scanning timing chips allows race directors to obtain timing splits of each leg of a triathlon and account for athletes. The following questions should be asked in this regard.

Considerations	Yes or no (check one)	Notes for follow-up
Was the chip scanned at the start of the swim, before entering the water?	❑ Yes ❑ No	
Was the chip scanned at the end of the swim, confirming that the swimmer safely completed the swim?	❑ Yes ❑ No	
Was the chip scanned at the start of the bicycle course, confirming that the athlete started the cycling portion of the race?	❑ Yes ❑ No	
Was the chip scanned at the end of the bicycle course, confirming that the athlete finished this portion of the race?	❑ Yes ❑ No	
Was the chip scanned at the start of the run course, confirming that the athlete started the run?	❑ Yes ❑ No	
Was the chip scanned at the finish line, confirming that the athlete finished the entire course?	❑ Yes ❑ No	
Are there other considerations for timing-chip scanning?	❑ Yes ❑ No	

From Katharine M. Nohr, 2009, *Managing Risk in Sport and Recreation: The Essential Guide for Loss Prevention* (Champaign, IL: Human Kinetics).

LIFEGUARDS AND WATERCRAFT
AT TRIATHLON EVENTS

The swim portions of races should be well staffed with certified lifeguards and watercraft. The nature of the water course will dictate the type and number of watercraft used. The following questions provide such options.

Considerations	Yes or no (check one)	Notes for follow-up
Will you utilize one-person kayaks? If so, how many?	❑ Yes ❑ No	
Will you utilize motorized boats? If so, how many?	❑ Yes ❑ No	
Will you utilize jet skis? If so, how many?	❑ Yes ❑ No	
Will you utilize surfboards? If so, how many?	❑ Yes ❑ No	
Are there other considerations for lifeguards and watercraft?	❑ Yes ❑ No	

From Katharine M. Nohr, 2009, *Managing Risk in Sport and Recreation: The Essential Guide for Loss Prevention* (Champaign, IL: Human Kinetics).

TRIATHLON SWIM COURSE DESIGN

The design of the swim course will play an important role in its safety. The following questions should be asked when designing a swim course in open water.

Considerations	Yes or no (check one)	Notes for follow-up
Is the course a single loop so that swimmers will not hit each other?	❏ Yes ❏ No	
Is the course relatively close to shore?	❏ Yes ❏ No	
Is the current strong in the area of the swim?	❏ Yes ❏ No	
Will swimmers have to swim through shore break, waves, or undertow?	❏ Yes ❏ No	
Will the sun be shining brightly in swimmers' eyes at any point during the race?	❏ Yes ❏ No	
Is the course clearly marked with large fluorescent buoys?	❏ Yes ❏ No	
Is the swim exit clearly marked?	❏ Yes ❏ No	
Is the water murky?	❏ Yes ❏ No	
Is there coral or rocks that swimmers may come in contact with?	❏ Yes ❏ No	
Will swimmers exiting the water be able to run on a smooth or sandy surface?	❏ Yes ❏ No	
Can carpeting be put down over rocks to allow swimmers to run out of the water more comfortably?	❏ Yes ❏ No	
Are there other considerations for swim course design?	❏ Yes ❏ No	

From Katharine M. Nohr, 2009, *Managing Risk in Sport and Recreation: The Essential Guide for Loss Prevention* (Champaign, IL: Human Kinetics).

PREPARING FOR AN OPEN WATER SWIM COURSE IN ADVANCE OF THE TRIATHLON EVENT

Open water swim courses can be dangerous and careful preparation must occur in order to prevent drownings. Accordingly, the following safety questions should be asked.

Considerations	Yes or no (check one)	Notes for follow-up
Have athletes been warned of any particular dangers before the event?	❑ Yes ❑ No	
Is the area where athletes will be entering the water clean, clear, and in good condition?	❑ Yes ❑ No	
Have areas where athletes will be entering the water been cleared of any potential tripping or slipping hazards?	❑ Yes ❑ No	
Are short-wave radios and cellular telephones available in case of an emergency?	❑ Yes ❑ No	
Is lifesaving equipment in good condition and readily accessible in case of an emergency?	❑ Yes ❑ No	
Have lifeguard staff been scheduled for the event?	❑ Yes ❑ No	
Do lifeguards have up-to-date certification in CPR, lifesaving, and first aid?	❑ Yes ❑ No	
Are AEDs available at the event site?	❑ Yes ❑ No	
If AEDs are available, are there personnel with AED certification at the event site?	❑ Yes ❑ No	
Have buoys been placed throughout the course as communicated to the athletes?	❑ Yes ❑ No	
Have athletes been given safety instruction about the swim?	❑ Yes ❑ No	
Have weather reports been checked to make sure a storm is not expected?	❑ Yes ❑ No	
Have sufficient watercraft been scheduled for the event?	❑ Yes ❑ No	
Have timers been scheduled?	❑ Yes ❑ No	

(continued)

Preparing for an Open Water Swim Course in Advance of the Triathlon Event *(continued)*

Considerations	Yes or no (check one)	Notes for follow-up
Will computer chip timing be used?	❑ Yes ❑ No	
Have brightly colored swim caps been purchased and distributed to athletes for use during the swim?	❑ Yes ❑ No	
Have athletes been instructed that wearing the assigned swim cap is mandatory?	❑ Yes ❑ No	
Are watercraft equipped with lifesaving equipment?	❑ Yes ❑ No	
Has water quality been checked?	❑ Yes ❑ No	
Has water temperature been checked?	❑ Yes ❑ No	
Are there any hazards such as jellyfish that could injure participants?	❑ Yes ❑ No	
Will swimmers be making a water or land start?	❑ Yes ❑ No	
If swimmers are starting on the beach, has the area been cleared of any debris or obstacles?	❑ Yes ❑ No	
If swimmers are starting in the water, has the bottom been checked for any hazards?	❑ Yes ❑ No	
Has the swim exit area been cleared of any debris or obstacles?	❑ Yes ❑ No	
Has the swim exit been clearly marked and identified so that swimmers can see it while swimming?	❑ Yes ❑ No	
Are swimmers encouraged to warm up before the swim?	❑ Yes ❑ No	
Are lifeguards present during the warm-up time?	❑ Yes ❑ No	
Are wave starts timed and planned so that faster swimmers will not swim over those swimmers of less proficiency?	❑ Yes ❑ No	
Are swimmers encouraged to seed themselves at the swim start so that the fastest athletes go first?	❑ Yes ❑ No	
Are there other considerations when preparing for an open water swim course in advance of the event?	❑ Yes ❑ No	

From Katharine M. Nohr, 2009, *Managing Risk in Sport and Recreation: The Essential Guide for Loss Prevention* (Champaign, IL: Human Kinetics).

TRIATHLON BICYCLE COURSE PLANNING

The following questions should be asked when planning and developing your bicycle course.

Considerations	Yes or no (check one)	Notes for follow-up
Will the course be open to vehicular traffic? If Yes, record in the Notes column how the bikes and motor vehicles will be separated.	❑ Yes ❑ No	
Will the course be closed to vehicular traffic? If Yes, record in the Notes column how this will be communicated to motor vehicles.	❑ Yes ❑ No	
Will police officers be needed to control intersections?	❑ Yes ❑ No	How many will be needed?
Will cones be needed to establish the bike course?	❑ Yes ❑ No	Where will the cones be obtained? Who will place the cones for the race? When and how will the cones be placed?
Were the streets swept of debris the morning of the race?	❑ Yes ❑ No	
Have sufficient volunteers been placed on the bicycle course?	❑ Yes ❑ No	
Do the volunteers know their specific assignments?	❑ Yes ❑ No	
Is there sufficient signage so the athletes know which way to go?	❑ Yes ❑ No	
Have athletes and volunteers been given a race map so they will know the course?	❑ Yes ❑ No	
Have athletes been warned of any potential hazards?	❑ Yes ❑ No	
Are there warning signs of any potential hazards on the course?	❑ Yes ❑ No	
Have no-passing zones been designated?	❑ Yes ❑ No	
Have athletes been informed about any no-passing zones?	❑ Yes ❑ No	
Are there aid stations on the bike course?	❑ Yes ❑ No	
Has an emergency communication system been established for emergencies on the bike course?	❑ Yes ❑ No	

(continued)

From Katharine M. Nohr, 2009, *Managing Risk in Sport and Recreation: The Essential Guide for Loss Prevention* (Champaign, IL: Human Kinetics).

Triathlon Bicycle Course Planning *(continued)*

Considerations	Yes or no (check one)	Notes for follow-up
Have officials been retained to officiate the event?	❏ Yes ❏ No	
Have motorcyclists been hired for use by officials and race management on the bike course?	❏ Yes ❏ No	
Has a lead motorcyclist been designated?	❏ Yes ❏ No	
Has a motorcyclist been designated for the back of the field?	❏ Yes ❏ No	
Has a sag wagon been established to assist athletes?	❏ Yes ❏ No	
Have media been given passes to allow them on the bike course?	❏ Yes ❏ No	
Have race vehicles been identified so they can move freely throughout the course?	❏ Yes ❏ No	
Is there a mobile medical unit to assist injured cyclists?	❏ Yes ❏ No	
Have cyclists been instructed to ride to the right and pass on the left?	❏ Yes ❏ No	
Have cyclists been instructed that they will not be allowed on the course if their bicycles do not have bar end plugs?	❏ Yes ❏ No	
Have cyclists been instructed that they will not be allowed on the course without helmets with chin straps properly buckled?	❏ Yes ❏ No	
Have volunteers with brightly colored race T-shirts been assigned to each intersection?	❏ Yes ❏ No	
Have residents and businesses been notified of the date, time, and location of the triathlon?	❏ Yes ❏ No	
Have all city and county permits been obtained?	❏ Yes ❏ No	
Has a safety meeting been held for all athletes before the race?	❏ Yes ❏ No	
Have volunteers been instructed about their roles and safety?	❏ Yes ❏ No	
Have motorcycle drivers been instructed about their roles and safety?	❏ Yes ❏ No	
Are there other considerations for bicycle course planning?	❏ Yes ❏ No	

From Katharine M. Nohr, 2009, *Managing Risk in Sport and Recreation: The Essential Guide for Loss Prevention* (Champaign, IL: Human Kinetics).

TRIATHLON RUN COURSE PLANNING

The following questions should be asked when planning and developing your run course.

Considerations	Yes or no (check one)	Notes for follow-up
Will the course be open or closed to vehicular traffic?	❑ Yes ❑ No	
If the course is closed, how will this be communicated to motor vehicles?	❑ Yes ❑ No	
If the course is open to vehicles, how will the runners and motor vehicles be separated?	❑ Yes ❑ No	
Will police officers be needed to control intersections?	❑ Yes ❑ No	If so, how many will be needed?
Will cones be needed to establish the run course?	❑ Yes ❑ No	Where will the cones be obtained? Who will place the cones for the race? When and how will the cones be placed?
Has the run course been designed so that the bike course does not intersect with it?	❑ Yes ❑ No	
Have sufficient volunteers been placed on the run course?	❑ Yes ❑ No	
Do the volunteers know their specific assignments?	❑ Yes ❑ No	
Is there sufficient signage so the athletes know which way to go?	❑ Yes ❑ No	
Have athletes and volunteers been given a race map so they will know the course?	❑ Yes ❑ No	
Have athletes been warned of any potential hazards?	❑ Yes ❑ No	
Are there warning signs of any potential hazards on the course?	❑ Yes ❑ No	
Have trip hazards been removed from the course or appropriate signage placed to warn of such trip hazards?	❑ Yes ❑ No	
Have no-passing zones been designated?	❑ Yes ❑ No	
Have athletes been informed about any no-passing zones?	❑ Yes ❑ No	

(continued)

Triathlon Run Course Planning *(continued)*

Considerations	Yes or no (check one)	Notes for follow-up
Are there sufficient aid stations on the run course?	❑ Yes ❑ No	
Are aid stations supplied with enough water, cups, ice, and volunteers?	❑ Yes ❑ No	
If an aid station runs out of supplies, by what means will the aid station be resupplied?	❑ Yes ❑ No	
Does each aid station have electrolyte drinks and food, especially for longer races?	❑ Yes ❑ No	
Have runners been advised as to whether the men are permitted to go shirtless during the run portion of the triathlon?	❑ Yes ❑ No	
Have athletes been advised to wear sunscreen and hats, particularly during hot races?	❑ Yes ❑ No	
Is the temperature being monitored and athletes advised to stay hydrated?	❑ Yes ❑ No	
Has an emergency communication system been established for emergencies on the run course?	❑ Yes ❑ No	
Is there medical assistance for runners needing medical attention?	❑ Yes ❑ No	
Have volunteers with brightly colored race T-shirts been assigned to each intersection?	❑ Yes ❑ No	
Have residents and businesses been notified of the date, time, and location of the triathlon?	❑ Yes ❑ No	
Have all city and county permits been obtained?	❑ Yes ❑ No	
Was a safety meeting held for all athletes before the race?	❑ Yes ❑ No	
Have volunteers been instructed about their roles and safety?	❑ Yes ❑ No	
Are there other considerations for run course planning?	❑ Yes ❑ No	

21

Volleyball

Volleyball is one of the most interactive games going. It is a game of intuition, imagination, improvisation—but most of all, of reciprocity—of teamwork. There is no way to free-lance in volleyball.

—Marv Dunphy

Volleyball, whether played on the beach or in gymnasiums, is not a sport that leads to a lot of lawsuits and significant insurance claims. Injuries do occur, but few of them are severe enough that litigation ensues.

VOLLEYBALL LAWSUITS AND SETTLEMENTS

The following lawsuits arising out of volleyball games have resulted in significant out-of-court settlements:

- A premises liability action was filed against an apartment complex, alleging that the defendant was negligent for a sharp, uncapped volleyball net pole and loose gravel around a pool. The plaintiff settled with the defendant for $335,000 in damages caused by the loss of the plaintiff's right index finger.

- In a volleyball game involving alcohol consumption at a YMCA with no staff supervision, the plaintiff was injured by another player and so brought suit against the player and the YMCA. The other player settled with the plaintiff for $25,000. The YMCA was successfully dismissed from the action because the lack of supervision did not cause the plaintiff's injuries. *Hearl v. Waterbury YMCA*, 444 A.2d 211 (Conn. 1982).

There have been few reported appellate court decisions related to volleyball. The following such decisions relate to issues of supervision, a player tripping over a cord when chasing after a ball, and an injury sustained because of a hole in a grass court.

Facility

Eisenberg v. East Meadow Union Free School Dist.
In *Eisenberg v. East Meadow Union Free School Dist.*, 239 A.D.2d 384, 657 N.Y.S.2d 434 (1997), the plaintiff, a boys' varsity volleyball manager, sued her own school district for injuries she sustained when she chased after a volleyball under bleachers and tripped over a cord. Because the injury was sustained in the gym of an opposing team over which the defendant school district had no control, they were dismissed from the action.

Volleyball courts should be inspected and maintained to prevent injury, even in public places, such as parks.

Cords should be taped down in order to prevent people from tripping over them, even if they are run under bleachers where people don't usually walk.

Ryder v. Town of Lancaster
In *Ryder v. Town of Lancaster*, 289 A.D.2d 995, 735 N.Y.S.2d 312 (2001), the plaintiff filed a lawsuit against the town, claiming he sustained injuries while playing volleyball when he stepped in a large hole located on the grass court. The court denied the defendant's motion for summary judgment, determining it was an issue for the jury as to whether the city breached its duty to properly maintain the grass volleyball court.

Inspection and maintenance of the volleyball court probably would have prevented this injury.

Participant

Barretto v. City of New York   In *Barretto v. City of New York*, 229 A.D.2d 214, 655 N.Y.S.2d 484 (1997), the plaintiff, an 18-year-old high school student, sued the school board for injuries he sustained after diving over a volleyball net and landing on his head while the coach was out of the room. The coach had told the captains of the varsity volleyball team to set up the nets and not horse around. The jury awarded the plaintiff close to $19 million but found him to be 20 percent at fault, so that award would be reduced to almost $15 million. The appellate court reversed the jury's decision, concluding that the plaintiff created his own peril and assumed the risk of diving over the volleyball net. It wasn't unreasonable for the coach to leave 17- and 18-year-old athletes without supervision under the circumstances. There had been no previous problems with horseplay. Furthermore, the plaintiff had signed a waiver, releasing the board from liability.

Supervision of normally responsible 17- and 18-year-olds posed an issue in this case. On the one hand, they always behaved well and adhered to the warnings of the coach. Yet, in this case, the high school student engaged in dangerous behavior the moment the coach left the room.

The appellate court seemed to make the right decision, as the 18-year-old assumed the risk of his irresponsible behavior.

VOLLEYBALL SAFETY CONSIDERATIONS

These reported appellate cases address several areas of risk management and safety concerns as they relate to volleyball, but they could occur in other sports as well. Volleyball has resulted in very few reported appellate decisions in the United States and is generally considered a safe sport. Most volleyball injuries arise out of repetitive use, player collisions, and players diving for balls. It is relatively unusual that an injury results in actionable negligence. However, understanding the potential for injury allows safeguards to be taken in order to prevent problems in the future. To facilitate your organization's safety standards, please use all the forms on pages 340 to 343.

SUMMARY

Volleyball is a relatively low-risk sport. Inspection, maintenance, and repair of the court, net, and playing surface should go a long way in prevention of injuries. Supervision should be provided for minors. Outdoor volleyball requires protection from sun exposure, additional environmental concerns, and more careful attention to hydration.

INDOOR VOLLEYBALL COURTS (HARD SURFACE)

The volleyball court is usually contained in a larger gymnasium that may have bleachers for spectators. The court is often located in the same place that basketball or other sports are played. Before using a volleyball court, make the following determinations.

Considerations	Yes or no (check one)	Notes for follow-up
Are the net and posts holding the net in good condition?	❑ Yes ❑ No	
Are the posts capped?	❑ Yes ❑ No	
Do the posts have any sharp areas, protrusions, or anything else that might cause injury?	❑ Yes ❑ No	
Is the floor in good condition without holes, defects, or uneven or slippery surfaces?	❑ Yes ❑ No	
Was the floor constructed so it has proper shock absorption (e.g., a wooden spring-loaded floor)?	❑ Yes ❑ No	
Does the floor meet the proper industry standards for a gymnasium floor?	❑ Yes ❑ No	
Are any floor plates in the gymnasium flush with the floor so that tripping will not occur?	❑ Yes ❑ No	
Does the gymnasium have sufficient room around the court so that athletes will not run into walls?	❑ Yes ❑ No	
Do walls and other objects around the court have sufficient protective padding?	❑ Yes ❑ No	
If there are adjacent volleyball courts in the gymnasium, is there at least 3 feet (.9 m) separating the courts?	❑ Yes ❑ No	
If there are glass doors or windows in the gymnasium, are they protected or made of safety glass?	❑ Yes ❑ No	
Are all electrical control panels, light switches, and other protruding objects protected with sufficient padding or recessed in the wall?	❑ Yes ❑ No	
Do electrical control panels and light switches have locking mechanisms?	❑ Yes ❑ No	

(continued)

From Katharine M. Nohr, 2009, *Managing Risk in Sport and Recreation: The Essential Guide for Loss Prevention* (Champaign, IL: Human Kinetics).

Indoor Volleyball Courts (Hard Surface) *(continued)*

Considerations	Yes or no (check one)	Notes for follow-up
Are scoring and press tables and equipment padded and located at least 4 feet (1.2 m) from the court?	❏ Yes ❏ No	
Does the gymnasium's ventilation system provide sufficient ventilation to support volleyball play with spectators?	❏ Yes ❏ No	
Does the gymnasium contain mildew or mold?	❏ Yes ❏ No	
Is the gymnasium sufficiently illuminated?	❏ Yes ❏ No	
Does the volleyball court have sufficient overhead clearance?	❏ Yes ❏ No	
Have objects overhead such as basketball goals or lighting fixtures been cleared away from the space above the court?	❏ Yes ❏ No	
Have wires that may be supporting the volleyball net been covered with soft material?	❏ Yes ❏ No	
Are there other considerations for indoor volleyball courts (hard surface)?	❏ Yes ❏ No	

From Katharine M. Nohr, 2009, *Managing Risk in Sport and Recreation: The Essential Guide for Loss Prevention* (Champaign, IL: Human Kinetics).

BEACH VOLLEYBALL COURTS

Beach volleyball courts can be found in many parks and beach areas and in indoor facilities. Before using a beach volleyball court, make the following determinations.

Considerations	Yes or no (check one)	Notes for follow-up
Is the court adjacent to other courts or play areas from which there might be interference?	❑ Yes ❑ No	
Is there sufficient room between the adjacent courts or activities?	❑ Yes ❑ No	
Are there sufficient barriers between the court and vehicular traffic?	❑ Yes ❑ No	
Have apparatuses used in other sports been left on the court or in the immediate vicinity?	❑ Yes ❑ No	
Are there any environmental concerns, such as proximity to pollutants or environmental hazards (e.g., industrial exhaust coming from a nearby building)?	❑ Yes ❑ No	
Is the playing surface made of good-quality sand that is free of rocks, glass, and other objects?	❑ Yes ❑ No	
Is the playing surface relatively even so that athletes will not trip?	❑ Yes ❑ No	
Is the net in good condition, with capped posts?	❑ Yes ❑ No	
Is the court sufficiently illuminated at night?	❑ Yes ❑ No	
Are there shaded areas available so that players can rest while not playing?	❑ Yes ❑ No	
Have any overhead lighting or tree limbs that interfere with the space above the court been removed before play?	❑ Yes ❑ No	
Are there other considerations for beach volleyball courts?	❑ Yes ❑ No	

From Katharine M. Nohr, 2009, *Managing Risk in Sport and Recreation: The Essential Guide for Loss Prevention* (Champaign, IL: Human Kinetics).

VOLLEYBALL SAFETY TIPS

The following questions pertain to safety tips that should be followed to prevent injuries in volleyball.

Considerations	Yes or no (check one)	Notes for follow-up
Have players removed all jewelry, including piercings, before playing?	❑ Yes ❑ No	
Have players warmed up and stretched before playing?	❑ Yes ❑ No	
Have players been taught the proper body positions for setting the ball, serving, or spiking so these skills can be executed without causing injury?	❑ Yes ❑ No	
Have players been instructed to jump with both feet when executing spikes in order to prevent ankle and foot injuries?	❑ Yes ❑ No	
Has the outdoor court been checked for glass, rocks, or other objects before beginning play?	❑ Yes ❑ No	
Have players been reminded that physical contact should be avoided at all times?	❑ Yes ❑ No	
Are players aware of the location of other players at all times in order to avoid collisions?	❑ Yes ❑ No	
Are players aware that they are not allowed to grab the net or hang on the supports?	❑ Yes ❑ No	
Do players "call" the ball, communicating to others their intentions in order to avoid collisions?	❑ Yes ❑ No	
Do players stay hydrated?	❑ Yes ❑ No	
Is there a first aid kit available and someone present who is trained in basic first aid?	❑ Yes ❑ No	
Is there an emergency plan in place in the event of a serious injury?	❑ Yes ❑ No	
Is there sufficient room for performing drills indoors?	❑ Yes ❑ No	
Is proper supervision provided when minors are playing volleyball?	❑ Yes ❑ No	
Are players aware that alcohol is not to be consumed before or during play?	❑ Yes ❑ No	
Are there other considerations for volleyball safety tips?	❑ Yes ❑ No	

From Katharine M. Nohr, 2009, *Managing Risk in Sport and Recreation: The Essential Guide for Loss Prevention* (Champaign, IL: Human Kinetics).

22

Weightlifting and Weight Training

I was always interested in proportion and perfection. When I was fifteen, I took off my clothes and looked in the mirror. When I stared at myself naked, I realized that to be perfectly proportioned I would need twenty-inch arms to match the rest of me.

—Arnold Schwarzenegger

Weightlifting and weight training are often done as training for other sports or done independently in homes, schools, hotels, health clubs, or wherever there is a gym. Free weights and machines, if used improperly, can lead to injuries. Free weights can pose a tripping hazard when improperly stored. Weight machines can malfunction when not maintained properly, causing injury. Persons attempting to lift weights beyond their ability without vigilant spotters are at risk of being injured.

WEIGHTLIFTING AND WEIGHT TRAINING LAWSUITS AND SETTLEMENTS

The following are examples of significant out-of-court settlements and jury verdicts in weightlifting and weight training cases.

- A teacher stepped out of the gym, leaving teenage boys unsupervised with weight equipment. A 15-year-old attempted to lift heavy weights, which fell on his abdomen, injuring his spleen and pancreas. The case was settled for $850,000.

- The plaintiff seriously injured his neck, requiring a three-level cervical fusion, when the backrest of an incline bench press broke at 24 Hour Fitness. The plaintiff proved at trial that the defendant gym conducted only superficial inspections of the equipment, never analyzing the integrity of the bench during its use over 10 years. The jury awarded the plaintiff $1.88 million.

- The family of a man who died of a heart attack in a gym was awarded a jury verdict of $619,650 because the gym did not have an automatic external defibrillator (AED) when the incident occurred in 2003.

- A law student fractured his neck and sustained a severe injury to his spinal cord when a Smith machine apparently malfunctioned at Gold's Gym. The plaintiff settled his lawsuit against Gold's Gym for $7.5 million before the trial was concluded. The jury rendered a verdict in the amount of almost $3.3 million in special damages and $13 million in general damages, apportioning 90 percent to the defendant manufacturer of the machine and 10 percent to the plaintiff. *Bostwick v. Flex Equip. Co., Inc.*, 147 Cal. App. 4th 80, 54 Cal. Rptr. 3d 28 (2007).

A number of the appellate decisions hinge on whether the waiver and release signed by the gym member relieved the defendant of liability. In light of this, it is important to make sure that all persons using a fitness facility have signed a well-drafted waiver and release, in accordance with a licensed attorney's recommendations.

Equipment

Calarco v. YMCA of Greater Metropolitan Chicago　In an Illinois appellate case, *Calarco v. YMCA of Greater Metropolitan Chicago*, 149 Ill. App. 1037, 501 N.E.2d 268 (1986), the plaintiff was injured when assisting another member of the YMCA with a weight machine that was stuck. The plaintiff removed a pin from the machine, which caused five weights to fall on her hand, fracturing two fingers. The case hinged on the wording of the exculpatory clause the plaintiff signed when she joined the YMCA. Essentially, the YMCA was released from liability for injuries arising out of the plaintiff's participation in activities at the YMCA. It was not clear that such activities would include use of the weights and equipment in the gym. Because of the lack of specificity, the defendant was not successful with its motion for summary judgment, and so the case would proceed to trial to determine whether the YMCA was negligent in its inspection and maintenance of the weight equipment in question.

When drafting releases, it is important to include, with specificity, all potential hazards that are anticipated. It is a good idea to retain an experienced attorney to draft the releases used by your organization or event.

Hazards

American Powerlifting Ass'n v. Cotillo

In a Maryland appellate case, *American Powerlifting Ass'n v. Cotillo*, 401 Md. 658, 934 A.2d 27 (2007), a powerlifting contestant filed a lawsuit against the event organizer, the sanctioning powerlifting association, and the school board of the high school where the event was held, claiming injuries he received were caused by the defendant's negligence. The plaintiff elected to use spotters that were supplied by the high school, two young teenagers who allegedly were not instructed how to spot properly. The plaintiff failed to lift the 530 pounds (240 kg) he was attempting, and so the bar landed on his jaw, causing serious injury. The court determined it was the failed lift that caused the plaintiff's injury, and so he clearly assumed the risk. The plaintiff had 10 years of powerlifting experience and was aware that he risked injury when attempting to lift 530 pounds (240 kg). There was no evidence that the spotters acted intentionally or recklessly. The defendants prevailed on a motion for summary judgment in this action.

Even though it was determined that the spotters were not at fault, it is a good idea to use only experienced spotters for power lifting and other events.

Participant

Orlando v. FEI Hollywood, Inc.

In a Florida appellate case, *Orlando v. FEI Hollywood, Inc.*, 898 So. 2d 167 (Fla. App. 4 Dist. 2005), the plaintiff was startled and injured his back when a nearby gym patron dropped free weights onto the floor. The plaintiff's lawsuit against the gym was dismissed because there was no showing that the actions by the other gym patron were foreseeable. Dropping the weights was sudden and unexpected, and so the gym could not have foreseen such conduct and so had no duty to protect the plaintiff against it.

Most gyms have rules against dropping weights on the floor. However, such rules are generally in place in order to prevent the weights from being dropped on people, to minimize noise, and to prevent damage. This case illustrates another potential reason for the rule.

Staff

Evans v. Pikeway, Inc.

In a New York appellate court decision, *Evans v. Pikeway, Inc.*, 7 Misc. 3d 348, 793 N.Y.S.2d 861 (2004), the court found a waiver to be valid and enforceable. In this case, the plaintiff was injured while performing squats using a weight machine. This exercise was supervised by a certified personal trainer who was also the manager of the health club. The trainer was an independent contractor who had required the plaintiff to sign a separate release, which specifically released the trainer from any injuries arising out of the subject's exercise program.

This is another example of the value of having athletes and participants sign waivers before they participate in sport and recreation.

Holmes v. Health & Tennis Corp. of Am.

In *Holmes v. Health & Tennis Corp. of Am.*, 103 Ohio App. 3d 364, 659 N.E.2d 812 (1995), the plaintiff injured his back while lifting heavy weights that pinned him when an employee failed to spot him. He sued the health club, which relied on the waiver and release clause set forth in the plaintiff's membership contract. Essentially, the provision stated that he used the facilities at his own risk and that the health club was not liable for injury or damages during his use of the facilities. The court determined there remained a material issue of fact as to whether there was an intention of the parties to release the health club from its employee's negligent acts. The trial would proceed on that issue. If there was such intent, the health club would be entitled to judgment in its favor.

Spotters and trainers must be trained so they can properly help and advise someone wanting to lift weights. However, as a measure of protection, waivers should be signed by the participant, releasing the facility and the trainer or spotter from being liable for any injury sustained while weightlifting.

Just because a waiver has been signed does not mean that your organization will prevail in court. It is best to provide the safest environment possible for sport and recreation participants.

Lund v. Bally's Aerobic Plus, Inc.   In *Lund v. Bally's Aerobic Plus, Inc.*, 78 Cal. App. 4th 733, 93 Cal. Rptr. 2d 169 (2000), the plaintiff sued Bally's health club for neck injuries she sustained while receiving instruction from a personal trainer. The plaintiff informed the trainer that she had had previous neck surgery and was advised by her doctor not to lift weights over her head. The trainer gave her assurances that he could teach her how to use weight machines without causing injury to her neck. While the plaintiff was being shown how to use the incline bench press machine, lifting a 10-pound (5 kg) weight, she again seriously injured her neck, requiring surgery. The plaintiff had signed a comprehensive waiver and release agreement when she joined the health club, which included use of exercise equipment and negligent instruction by employees of Bally's. The court concluded that such a waiver and release barred the plaintiff's recovery of damages, and so Bally's was dismissed from the case.

Although Bally's prevailed because of the plaintiff's signed release, the trainer may have declined to work with this client. A physical therapist may have been a more appropriate person to work with the plaintiff.

Murphy v. Fairport Cent. School Dist.   In a 2008 New York appellate court case, *Murphy v. Fairport Cent. School Dist.* 48 A.D.3d 1037, 850 N.Y.S.2d 752 (N.Y.A.D.4 Dept. 2008), the plaintiff brought a lawsuit on behalf of her son, who was injured during a physical education class in which he was using a weight machine. The teacher was supervising the students by going back and forth between a room with students using free weights and another room where students were using weight machines. The court denied the school's summary judgment motion, stating there were material issues of fact as to whether there was adequate supervision, and if there was not, there was a question as to whether inadequate supervision led to the boy's injury. A jury would properly address those issues at trial.

The teacher supervising the students probably could have used assistance so that she would not have to leave students alone in a room when she assisted other students. Proper supervision requires a sufficient number of adults in proportion to the number of students.

WEIGHT TRAINING EQUIPMENT SAFETY

Care should be used in selecting the appropriate gym equipment. Equipment should be installed professionally and in accordance with the manufacturers' specifications. Weight training equipment should be regularly inspected, maintained, and repaired in accordance with the manufacturers' recommendations. Machines and free weights should also be upgraded when reasonable. People using such equipment will vary in ability and experience, so management needs to gear its safety plans to take into account those with the least amount of skill and experience. Supervision and spotters should be available when necessary. Gyms should not be accessible to the public or children when not open for business and when no supervision is available. To facilitate your organization's safety standards, please use all the forms on pages 352 to 362.

In addition to the issues covered in the forms, you should also consider the following:

- Gym cleanliness—It is important to keep locker rooms and gym equipment clean and disinfected to prevent methicillin-resistant Staphylococcus aureus (MRSA), a serious infection that is allegedly caused by unsanitary gym and locker room environments. Make sure that equipment is cleaned on a regular basis and that germs are not spread by shared towels.

- Parking lots at gyms—Patrons of gym facilities commonly leave their valuables in their cars when they work out. Thieves know this, watching to see if women carry their purses with them into the gym. If not, their cars are ripe for break-in. Means to deter such thefts include installing more lighting and increasing the brightness of existing lighting; installing security cameras and placing notices that the cameras are monitoring the area; using security personnel to monitor the parking lots; encouraging patrons to report unusual activity; and reminding patrons not to leave valuables in their cars and to keep them locked. You may wish to post signage warning your customers not to leave valuables in their cars and that the establishment is not responsible for thefts that occur in the parking lot.

SUMMARY

Weight training and weightlifting are important components in preparation for many sports and are popular features of most health clubs and fitness centers. Proper installation, inspection, maintenance, repair, and upgrades of equipment are important. Gym facilities should be kept well ventilated and be cleaned and sanitized to prevent spreading of germs. Proper supervision and spotters should be provided. Facilities should be equipped to handle medical emergencies as well as minor injuries by having telephones to call 911 as well as having basic supplies and personnel with CPR and basic first aid training. Facility patrons should be cleared by their doctors to engage in a weight training program if they have a serious medical condition. Patrons should use care in prevention of injury by properly warming up, gradually increasing their weight training, and using proper form. Security concerns in gym parking lots should be addressed, as they are a popular location for theft. The facility should also consider having patrons sign waivers and releases that comply with applicable state law. If these measures are taken, weight training and weightlifting safety can be maximized and potential injuries averted.

FITNESS CENTER SAFETY

Fitness centers can operate safely if care is given to floors, mats, equipment, and other potential safety hazards. The following questions should be asked.

Considerations	Yes or no (check one)	Notes for follow-up
Are there mats or carpeting covering the floor?	❑ Yes ❑ No	
Is the floor dry, clean, and free of debris?	❑ Yes ❑ No	
Are participants prohibited from bringing gym bags onto the floor that could pose a tripping hazard?	❑ Yes ❑ No	
Is the gym locked when no supervisors are present?	❑ Yes ❑ No	
Have machines, benches, cardio equipment, and other equipment been inspected for defects, for loose or missing bolts or screws, and for workability?	❑ Yes ❑ No	
Have all machines, benches, cardio equipment, and other equipment been inspected for any wear and tear, missing or loose parts, moisture, excessive dirt and grime buildup, and any other problems?	❑ Yes ❑ No	
Are walls around equipment from which someone could fall (e.g., treadmills) padded and free of electrical boxes, switches, windows, and other hazards?	❑ Yes ❑ No	
Are all machines and equipment securely attached to the floor?	❑ Yes ❑ No	
Have all floor plates or floor attachments been checked for possible loosening?	❑ Yes ❑ No	
Is there enough space between machines and equipment so they can be used by several people at the same time without risk of interference?	❑ Yes ❑ No	
Are there storage racks for free weights so they are not scattered on the floor?	❑ Yes ❑ No	
Are there any dangerous or sharp protrusions from the floor or equipment?	❑ Yes ❑ No	
Is the gym closed to children and adults who are not authorized to be there?	❑ Yes ❑ No	

(continued)

From Katharine M. Nohr, 2009, *Managing Risk in Sport and Recreation: The Essential Guide for Loss Prevention* (Champaign, IL: Human Kinetics).

Fitness Center Safety *(continued)*

Considerations	Yes or no (check one)	Notes for follow-up
Is there sufficient room to allow proper use of equipment?	❏ Yes ❏ No	
Is the room sufficiently illuminated?	❏ Yes ❏ No	
Are there emergency turnoff switches on all machines?	❏ Yes ❏ No	
Are there safety features on equipment?	❏ Yes ❏ No	
Are there other considerations for fitness center safety?	❏ Yes ❏ No	

From Katharine M. Nohr, 2009, *Managing Risk in Sport and Recreation: The Essential Guide for Loss Prevention* (Champaign, IL: Human Kinetics).

FITNESS CENTER EQUIPMENT SAFETY TIPS

As explained in chapter 5, all inspections, maintenance, and repairs of equipment should be documented. These documents should be kept and reviewed periodically by your risk management team or consultant.

Considerations	Yes or no (check one)	Notes for follow-up
Is all equipment properly maintained?	❑ Yes ❑ No	
Is equipment arranged so there is enough room to safely operate all equipment and to perform exercises?	❑ Yes ❑ No	
Has equipment been stored so it cannot be used by children or others without supervision?	❑ Yes ❑ No	
Is equipment of high quality, and does it meet strict safety standards?	❑ Yes ❑ No	
Has equipment been replaced with the latest and safest models when reasonable?	❑ Yes ❑ No	
Is equipment regularly inspected by a qualified inspector?	❑ Yes ❑ No	
Is equipment fitted, adjusted, and maintained by trained personnel only?	❑ Yes ❑ No	
Are trainers and gym personnel available to help patrons adjust equipment and move weights?	❑ Yes ❑ No	
Is fixed equipment moved only with supervision and sufficient strength and ability to do so?	❑ Yes ❑ No	
Are there other considerations for equipment safety?	❑ Yes ❑ No	

From Katharine M. Nohr, 2009, *Managing Risk in Sport and Recreation: The Essential Guide for Loss Prevention* (Champaign, IL: Human Kinetics).

GYM ATTIRE

A wide variety of workout clothing is worn and is permissible in gyms. The following are some specific considerations.

Considerations	Yes or no (check one)	Notes for follow-up
Are athletic shoes required, with no bare feet allowed?	❑ Yes ❑ No	
Are towels required to wipe up sweat so that equipment does not become slippery?	❑ Yes ❑ No	
Is jewelry kept to a minimum, and are clothing and accessories that might be hazardous prohibited?	❑ Yes ❑ No	
Are gloves worn to protect hands from calluses and to provide a more secure grip?	❑ Yes ❑ No	
Are there other considerations for gym attire?	❑ Yes ❑ No	

From Katharine M. Nohr, 2009, *Managing Risk in Sport and Recreation: The Essential Guide for Loss Prevention* (Champaign, IL: Human Kinetics).

WEIGHTLIFTING SUPERVISION TIPS

One issue that has arisen in litigation is whether proper supervision or the presence of spotters could have prevented an injury. The following questions concern supervision.

Considerations	Yes or no (check one)	Notes for follow-up
Is proper spotting done when patrons lift free weights of any significance?	❑ Yes ❑ No	
Are weight rooms supervised at all times?	❑ Yes ❑ No	
Is the use of trampolines supervised at all times by trained personnel?	❑ Yes ❑ No	
Are all trainers, personnel, and supervisors properly trained?	❑ Yes ❑ No	
Are all trainers, personnel, and supervisors trained to assist patrons with all available equipment?	❑ Yes ❑ No	
Are weight belts required whenever appropriate?	❑ Yes ❑ No	
Are there other considerations for supervision?	❑ Yes ❑ No	

From Katharine M. Nohr, 2009, *Managing Risk in Sport and Recreation: The Essential Guide for Loss Prevention* (Champaign, IL: Human Kinetics).

VENTILATION OF THE FITNESS CENTER FACILITY

Gyms with limited ventilation can become breeding grounds for germs, mold, and mildew. If air conditioning is insufficient, patrons could suffer from heat-related illnesses. In light of these concerns, the following questions are suggested.

Considerations	Yes or no (check one)	Notes for follow-up
Does the gym have proper ventilation?	❑ Yes ❑ No	
Does the gym have fans that can be moved in order to ventilate and provide cool air to patrons?	❑ Yes ❑ No	
Is the environment monitored for mold and mildew, and are steps taken to prevent its accumulation?	❑ Yes ❑ No	
Are there other considerations for ventilation of the facility?	❑ Yes ❑ No	

From Katharine M. Nohr, 2009, *Managing Risk in Sport and Recreation: The Essential Guide for Loss Prevention* (Champaign, IL: Human Kinetics).

RESPONDING TO WEIGHT TRAINING
MEDICAL EMERGENCIES AND INJURIES

No matter how careful a weight training facility is about safety, patrons will likely complain of minor to severe injuries or illnesses. The following questions can help in anticipation of these concerns.

Considerations	Yes or no (check one)	Notes for follow-up
Is a first aid kit available?	❑ Yes ❑ No	
Has an automatic external defibrillator (AED) been made available in a carefully selected accessible location? If so, has proper maintenance and training taken place as recommended by the manufacturer?	❑ Yes ❑ No	
Are trainers and other personnel knowledgeable about basic first aid and able to administer first aid to minor cuts, bruises, abrasions, strains, and sprains?	❑ Yes ❑ No	
Have selected personnel been trained in CPR, with regular recertification?	❑ Yes ❑ No	
Is an emergency plan in place to respond to serious injuries such as concussions, dislocations, and fractures?	❑ Yes ❑ No	
Are telephones available for 911 calls?	❑ Yes ❑ No	
Are incident reports filled out in response to reported injuries?	❑ Yes ❑ No	
Are there other considerations for responding to medical emergencies and injuries?	❑ Yes ❑ No	

From Katharine M. Nohr, 2009, *Managing Risk in Sport and Recreation: The Essential Guide for Loss Prevention* (Champaign, IL: Human Kinetics).

MEDICAL RISK FACTORS FOR WEIGHT TRAINING

Since many people who participate in weight training at local gyms might not have exercised for years or might have underlying health problems, it is advisable that they discuss with their physicians their desire to work out and obtain a medical release. Medical releases may be obtained and kept on file in appropriate circumstances, such as when a person joins a fitness club. If a patron appears to have a serious injury, illness, or health problem, it may be prudent to require a medical release before the person begins to use the facility. Some of the risk factors to be concerned about are listed here.

Medical Condition	Yes or no (check one)	Notes for follow-up
Cardiovascular disease or abnormal EKG	❏ Yes ❏ No	
History of coronary heart disease	❏ Yes ❏ No	
High cholesterol	❏ Yes ❏ No	
Smoking	❏ Yes ❏ No	
Obesity	❏ Yes ❏ No	
Pregnancy	❏ Yes ❏ No	
Arthritis	❏ Yes ❏ No	
Chronic muscle or joint injury	❏ Yes ❏ No	
Diabetes	❏ Yes ❏ No	
Asthma	❏ Yes ❏ No	
Recent surgery	❏ Yes ❏ No	
Other conditions	❏ Yes ❏ No	

From Katharine M. Nohr, 2009, *Managing Risk in Sport and Recreation: The Essential Guide for Loss Prevention* (Champaign, IL: Human Kinetics).

TIPS FOR MINIMIZING AND PREVENTING WEIGHT TRAINING INJURIES

It is extremely common for gym patrons to injure themselves using weight training equipment, especially when they have little experience with the activity or machine or are trying a new exercise. The following questions should assist in reducing the frequency and severity of weight training injuries.

Considerations	Yes or no (check one)	Notes for follow-up
Do patrons warm up and stretch first?	❏ Yes ❏ No	
Does each session begin with a short cardio warm-up of 5 to 7 minutes of walking on a treadmill or riding a stationary bike to increase blood flow to muscles?	❏ Yes ❏ No	
Does weight training start slowly and progress wisely? For example, a person should start lifting light weights comfortably for 8 to 15 repetitions and gradually progress to heavier weights. Deconditioned persons should start with lighter weights as well until they are able to rebuild their strength and endurance.	❏ Yes ❏ No	
Are weights lifted slowly?	❏ Yes ❏ No	
Are patrons encouraged to have at least several sessions with a certified personal trainer to learn how to use equipment properly?	❏ Yes ❏ No	
Are patrons experienced with weight training encouraged to have a certified personal trainer check their form?	❏ Yes ❏ No	
Do patrons use equipment only after proper instruction on its use?	❏ Yes ❏ No	
Do patrons understand which muscles should be working with each exercise and which muscles should be providing stabilization? This can often be shown in pictures attached to each machine along with instructions on how to use the equipment properly.	❏ Yes ❏ No	
Are patrons able to determine the correct range of motion for each exercise in order to avoid injury?	❏ Yes ❏ No	

From Katharine M. Nohr, 2009, *Managing Risk in Sport and Recreation: The Essential Guide for Loss Prevention* (Champaign, IL: Human Kinetics).

Tips for Minimizing and Preventing Weight Training Injuries *(continued)*

Considerations	Yes or no (check one)	Notes for follow-up
Is good posture used with each exercise in order to avoid injuring muscles not targeted in the particular exercise? For example, posture may be affected when patrons attempt to lift weights that are too heavy for their current level of fitness.	❑ Yes ❑ No	
Are mirrors provided so that patrons can check their posture and form while lifting weights and performing exercises?	❑ Yes ❑ No	
Is good technique always used and not abandoned in order to lift heavier weights?	❑ Yes ❑ No	
Do patrons only lift weights they are able to lift safely?	❑ Yes ❑ No	
Are full breaths taken with each repetition? Do patrons avoid holding their breath?	❑ Yes ❑ No	
Are patrons aware that, while light soreness may be expected, deep and severe soreness may signal an injury?	❑ Yes ❑ No	
Are opposing muscles trained in order to avoid imbalances that might lead to injury, such as training abdominal muscles and the lower back?	❑ Yes ❑ No	
Are machines and equipment adjusted so they line up properly with joints?	❑ Yes ❑ No	
After each workout, are stretches held for 30 to 60 seconds each?	❑ Yes ❑ No	
Do patrons rest between workout sessions to allow body parts adequate recovery time (48 hours is recommended)? For example, patrons can alternate body parts when exercising by focusing on the upper body one day and the lower body the next.	❑ Yes ❑ No	
Do patrons refrain from exercising any muscle group more than three times in one week?	❑ Yes ❑ No	
Is proper lifting technique used when moving weights?	❑ Yes ❑ No	
Is horseplay prohibited and this rule promptly and consistently enforced?	❑ Yes ❑ No	
Are appropriate clothing and footwear worn?	❑ Yes ❑ No	

(continued)

From Katharine M. Nohr, 2009, *Managing Risk in Sport and Recreation: The Essential Guide for Loss Prevention* (Champaign, IL: Human Kinetics).

Tips for Minimizing and Preventing Weight Training Injuries *(continued)*

Considerations	Yes or no (check one)	Notes for follow-up
Are chewing gum and eating prohibited in the gym?	❑ Yes ❑ No	
Are patrons who are not working out allowed in the gym?	❑ Yes ❑ No	
Are there other considerations for minimizing and preventing weight training injuries?	❑ Yes ❑ No	

From Katharine M. Nohr, 2009, *Managing Risk in Sport and Recreation: The Essential Guide for Loss Prevention* (Champaign, IL: Human Kinetics).

APPENDIX: GENERAL FORMS

 The following forms can be found on the pages that follow and also are available to print from the CD-ROM.

Incident Report
Vehicle Inspection Checklist
Equipment Safety Inspection Checklist
Maintenance and Repair Log
Cleaning Log

INCIDENT REPORT

Documentation Information

Date: _____ Time: _____ Report #: _____

Report taken by: _____

Position/Title: _____

Contact Information

Last name: _____ First name: _____ ID #: _____

Address: _____

Phone 1: _____ Phone 2: _____ E-mail: _____

Incident Information

Location: _____

Type: ❏ theft ❏ altercation ❏ trespass ❏ missing person
       ❏ vandalism ❏ natural disaster (specify) _____
       ❏ other (specify)_____

Additional information/notes: _____

Response Information

Action taken:_____

Assistance called:_____

Additional documentation attached:_____

Witness name:_____ Phone: _____

Witness name:_____ Phone: _____

Follow-Up Information

Date: _____ Time: _____ Method: _____

Name: _____

Position/Title: _____

Additional information/notes: _____

_____

_____

_____

_____

Resolution: _____

_____

_____

_____

_____

From Katharine M. Nohr, 2009, *Managing Risk in Sport and Recreation: The Essential Guide for Loss Prevention* (Champaign, IL: Human Kinetics).

VEHICLE INSPECTION CHECKLIST

	In good working order	Needs repair or fluid	Inspector	Date	Actions taken to correct issue	Date	Initials
Brakes							
Headlights							
Brake lights							
Turn signals							
Horn							
Windshield wipers							
Wiper fluid							
Tires							
Mirrors							
Steering							
Battery							
Gas							
Oil							
Antifreeze							

From Katharine M. Nohr, 2009, *Managing Risk in Sport and Recreation: The Essential Guide for Loss Prevention* (Champaign, IL: Human Kinetics).

EQUIPMENT SAFETY INSPECTION CHECKLIST

	Date	Time	Inspection actions	Outcome	Follow-up actions	Inspector's initials
Item						
Item						
Item						
Item						
Item						
Item						
Item						
Item						
Item						

From Katharine M. Nohr, 2009, *Managing Risk in Sport and Recreation: The Essential Guide for Loss Prevention* (Champaign, IL: Human Kinetics).

MAINTENANCE AND REPAIR LOG

Date: _____

Equipment item being repaired: _____

Task description: _____

_____

_____

_____

_____

Task accomplishments: _____

_____

_____

_____

_____

Location maintained/repair performed: _____

_____

_____

_____

Company performing task: _____

_____

Employee: _____

Title: _____

From Katharine M. Nohr, 2009, *Managing Risk in Sport and Recreation: The Essential Guide for Loss Prevention* (Champaign, IL: Human Kinetics).

CLEANING LOG

Item	Date	Time	Task	Equipment location	Person performing task

From Katharine M. Nohr, 2009, *Managing Risk in Sport and Recreation: The Essential Guide for Loss Prevention* (Champaign, IL: Human Kinetics).

REFERENCES AND RESOURCES

Acosta v. Los Angeles Unified School Dist., 31 Cal. App. 4th 471, 37 Cal. Rptr. 2d 171 (1995).

American Powerlifting Ass'n v. Cotillo, 401 Md. 658, 934 A.2d 27 (2007).

Americans with Disabilities Act of 1990, 42 U.S.C., section 12101 et seq.

Ammon, R., R.M. Southall, and D.A. Blair. (2004). *Sport Facility Management: Organizing Events and Mitigating Risks.* Morgantown, WV: Fitness Information Technology.

Anderson, P.M. (1999). *Sports Law: A Desktop Handbook.* Milwaukee, WI: National Sports Law Institute of Marquette University Law School.

Appenzeller, H. (2000). *Youth Sport and the Law: A Guide to Legal Issues.* Durham, NC: Carolina Academic Press.

Appenzeller, H. (2003). *Managing Sport and Risk Management Strategies* (2nd ed.). Durham, NC: Carolina Academic Press.

Appenzeller, H. (2005). *Risk Management in Sport Issues and Strategies.* Durham, NC: Carolina Academic Press.

Appenzeller, H. *From the Gym to the Jury*, Vol. 15, No. 2 (2004) to present.

Atcovitz v. Gulph Mills Tennis Club, Inc., 571 Pa. 580, 812 A.2d 1218 (2002).

Augusta Country Club, Inc., v. Blake, 230 Ga. App. 650, 634 S.E.2d 812 (2006)

Avila v. Citrus Community College District, 38 Cal. 4th 148, 131 P.3d 383 (2006).

Baggs ex rel. Baggs v. Little League Baseball, Inc., 17 Misc. 3d 212, 840 N.Y.S.2d 529 (2007).

Bahrenburg v. AT & T Broadband, LLC, 425 F. Supp. 2d 912 (N.D. Ill. 2006).

Banfield v. Louis, 589 So. 2d 441 (Fla. App. 4 Dist. 1991).

Baranoff, E.G., S.E. Harrington, and G.R. Niehaus. (2005). *Risk Assessment.* Malvern, PA: American Institute for Chartered Property Casualty Underwriters/Insurance Institute of America.

Barbato v. Hollow Hills Country Club, 14 A.D.3d 522, 789 N.Y.S.2d 199 (2005).

Barretto v. City of New York, 229 A.D.2d 214, 655 N.Y.S.2d 484 (1997).

Benbenek v. Chicago Park Dist., 279 Ill. App. 3d 930, 665 N.E.2d 500 (1996).

Bennet v. United States Cycling Federation, 193 Cal. App. 3d 1485, 239 Cal. Rptr. 55 (1987).

Bennett v. City of New York, 303 A.D.2d 614, 756 N.Y.S.2d 633 (2003).

Berthelsen, R. (2005). *Risk Control.* Malvern, PA: American Institute for Chartered Property Casualty Underwriters/Insurance Institute of America.

Bostwick v. Flex Equip. Co., Inc., 147 Cal. App. 4th 80, 54 Cal. Rptr. 3d 28 (2007).

Bourne v. Marty Gilman, Inc., 452 F.3d 632 (7th Cir. 2006).

Bowman v. McNary, 852 N.E.2d 984 (Ind. App. 2006).

Brisbin v. Washington Sports and Entertainment, Ltd., 422 F. Supp. 2d 9 (D.D.C. 2006).

Calarco v. YMCA of Greater Metropolitan Chicago, 149 Ill. App. 1037, 501 N.E.2d 268 (1986).

Carbonara v. Texas Stadium Corporation, 244 S.W.3d 651, 2008 WL 192345 (Tex. App. 2008).

Carmack v. Macomb County Community College, 199 Mich. App. 544, 502 N.W.2d 746 (1993).

Carpenter v. North Thurston School District (Wa. Super. Ct., 97-2-02984-5, Dec. 1999).

Casey v. Garden City Park–New Hyde Park School Dist., 40 A.D.3d 901, 837 N.Y.S.2d 186 (2007).

Celano v. Marriott International, Inc., WL 239306 (N.D. Cal. 2008).

Champion, W.T. (2000). *Sports Law in a Nutshell.* St. Paul, MN: West Group.

Chrismon v. Brown, 246 S.W.3d 102, WL 2790352 (Tex. App. 2007).

Cohen v. Sterling Mets, LP, 17 Misc. 3d 218, 840 N.Y.S.2d 527 (2007).

Cotten, D.J., and J.T. Wolohan. (2007). *Law for Recreation and Sport Managers* (4th ed.). Dubuque, IA: Kendall/Hunt.

DeRosa v. City of New York, 30 A.D.3d 323, 817 N.Y.S.2d 282 (2006).

Doe v. Fulton School Dist., 35 A.D.3d 1194, 826 N.Y.S.2d 543 (2006).

Dotzler v. Tuttle, 234 Neb. 176, 449 N.W.2d 774 (1990).

Dubinsky v. St. Louis Blues Hockey Club, 229 S.W.3d 126 (Mo. App. 2007).

Dwyer v. Diocese of Rockville Centre, 45 A.D.3d 527, 845 N.Y.S.2d 126 (2007).

Edwards v. Intergraph Services Co., Inc., __ So. 2d__, 2008 WL 162245 (Ala. Civ. App. 2008).

Eisenberg v. East Meadow Union Free School Dist., 239 A.D.2d 384, 657 N.Y.S.2d 434 (1997).

Elston v. Howland Local Schools, 113 Ohio St.3d 314, 865 N.E.2d 845 (2007).

Epstein, A. (2003). *Sports Law.* Clifton Park, NY: West Legal Studies.

Estate of Peters by Peters v. U.S. Cycling Federation, 779 F. Supp. 853 (E.D. Ky. 1991).

Evans v. Pikeway, Inc., 7 Misc. 3d 348, 793 N.Y.S.2d 861 (2004).

Fabricius v. County of Broome, 24 A.D.3d 853, 804 N.Y.S.2d 510 (2005).

Feagins v. Waddy, 978 So. 2d 712 (Ala. 2007).

Finkler v. Minisceongo Golf Club, 16 Misc. 3d 1007, 841 N.Y.S.2d 424 (2007).

Forester, J. (1994). *Effective Cycling* (6th ed.). Cambridge, MA: MIT Press.

Fortin, F. (2000). *Sports: The Complete Visual Reference.* Buffalo: Firefly Books.

Frazier v. City of New York, 47 A.D.3d 757, 850 N.Y.S.3d 552 (2008).

Freiberger v. Four Seasons Golf Center, LLC, Slip Copy, WL 1674020 (Ohio App. 10 Dist. 2007).

Fried, G. (1999). *Safe at First.* Ed. H. Appenzeller. Durham, NC: Carolina Academic Press.

Frosdick, S., and L. Walley. (1999). *Sport & Safety Management.* Woburn, MA: Butterworth-Heinemann.

Fugazy v. Corbetta, 34 A.D.3d 728, 325 N.Y.S.2d 120 (2006).

Gardner v. Town of Tonawonda, 48 A.D.3d 1083, 850 N.Y.S.2d 730 (2008).

Gernat v. State, 23 A.D.3d 1015, 803 N.Y.S.2d 845 (2005).

Goforth v. State, Slip Copy, WL 541820 (Tenn. Ct. App. 2007).

Gorbey v. Longwill, Slip Copy, WL 118298 (2007).

Grames v. King and Pontiac School District, 332 N.W.2d 615 (Mi. 1983).

Grappendorf v. Pleasant Grove City, 173 P.3d 166 (Utah 2007).

Griem v. Town of Walpole, 21 Mass.L.Rptr. 402, 2006 WL268488 (Mass.Super.2006).

Griffiths, T. 2003. *The Complete Swimming Pool Reference* (2nd ed.). Champaign, IL: Sagamore.

Guardino v. Kings Park School District, 300 A.D. 355 (N.Y. App. 2002).

Guenther v. West Seneca Cent. School Dist., 19 A.D.3d 1171, 796 N.Y.S.2d 465 (2005).

Harris v. Willie McCray, et al., 867 So. 2d 188 (Miss. 2003).

Harting v. Dayton Dragons Professional Baseball Club, LLC, 171 Ohio App. 3d 319, 870 N.E.2d 766 (2007).

Hawkins v. United States Sports Association, Inc., 633 S.E.2d 31 (W. Va. 2006).

Hayes Through Hayes v. Walters, 628 So. 2d 558 (Ala. 1993).

Haymon v. Pettit, 37 A.D.3d 1194, 829 N.Y.S.2d 766 (2007).

Hearl v. Waterbury YMCA, 444 A.2d 211 (Conn. 1982).

Heldman, K. (2005). *Project Manager's Spotlight on Risk Management.* Alameda, CA: Harbor Light Press.

Hemady v. Long Beach Unified School District, et al., 143 Cal. App. 4th 566, 49 Cal. Rptr. 3d 464 (2006).

Henderson v. Walled Lake Consol. Schools, 469 F.3d 479 (Mich. 2006).

Henry v. Roosevelt School District, 29 A.D.3d 954, 815 N.Y.S.2d 472 (2006).

Hiett v. Lake Barcroft Community Ass'n, Inc., 244 Va. 191, 418 S.E.2d 894 (1992).

Holmes v. Health & Tennis Corp. of Am., 103 Ohio App. 3d 364, 659 N.E.2d 812 (1995).

http://en.wikipedia.org/wiki/Anson_Dorrance

Hurst v. East Coast Hockey League, Inc., 371 S.C. 33, 637 S.E.2d 560 (2006).

Jaworski v. Kiernan, 241 Conn. 399, 696 A.2d 332 (1997).

Jennings v. University of North Carolina, 482 F.3d 686 (N.C. 2007).

Johnson v. Steffen, 685 N.E.2d 1117 (Ind. App. 1997).

Jones v. Kite/Cupp Legends Golf Development, Slip Copy, WL 2751784 (Tenn. Ct. App. 2007).

Karas v. Strevell, 369 Ill. App. 3d 884, 860 N.E.2d 1163 (2006).

Kindred v. Board of Education of Memphis City Schools, 946 S.W.2d 47 (Tenn. 1996).

Kobak, E.T. (2007). *The Sports Address Bible & Almanac* (19th ed.). Santa Monica, CA: Global Sports Productions.

Kreil v. County of Niagara, 8 A.D.3d 1001, 778 N.Y.S.2d 601 (2004).

Lewin v. Lutheran West High School, Slip Copy, WL 2269502 (Ohio App. 2007).

Little v. Jonesboro Country Club, 92 Ark. App. 214, 212 S.W.3d 57 (2005).

Livshitz v. U.S. Tennis Ass'n Nat. Tennis Center, 196 Misc. 2d 460, 761 N.Y.S.2d 825 (2003).

Lloyd v. Sugarloaf Mountain Corp., 833 A.2d 1 (Me. 2003).

Lombardo v. Cedar Brook Golf & Tennis Club, 39 A.D.3d 818, 834 N.Y.S.2d 326 (2007).

Longview Independent School District v. Vibra-Whirl, Ltd., 169 S.W.3d 511 (Tex. App. 2005).

Lund v. Bally's Aerobic Plus, Inc., 78 Cal. App. 4th 733, 93 Cal. Rptr. 2d 169 (2000).

MacDonald v. B.M.D. Golf Associates, Inc., 148 N.H. 582, 813 A.2d 488 (2002).

Maisonave v. Newark Bears Professional Baseball Club, Inc., 185 N.J. 70, 881 A.2d 700 (2005).

Mallin v. Paesani, 49 Conn. Supp. 457, 892 A.2d 1043 (2005).

Manias v. Golden Bear Golf Center, 348 N.Y.S.2d 491 (2007).

Manoly v. City of New York, 29 A.D.3d 649 (2006).

Marshall v. City of New Rochelle, 15 A.D.3d, 790 N.Y.S.2d 504 (2005).

Mason v. Bristol Local School Dist. Bd. of Edn., Slip Copy, 2006 WL 2796660 (2006).

Masteralexis, L.P., C.A. Barr, and M.A. Hums. (1998). *Principles and Practice of Sport Management*. Gaithersburg, MA: Aspen.

Mastropolo v. Goshen Cent. School Dist., 40 A.D.3d 1053, 837 S.2d 236 (2007).

Mavrovich v. Vanderpool, 427 F. Supp. 2d 1084 (D. Kan. 2006).

McCabe v. City of New York, 45 A.D.3d 541, 847 N.Y.S.2d 92 (2007).

McCollin v. Roman Catholic Archdiocese of New York, 54 A.D.3d 478, 846 N.Y.2d 158 (2007).

McCormick ex rel. McCormick v. School Dist. of Mamaroneck, 370 F.3d 275 (N.Y. 2004).

McGregor, I. (2000). *SportRisk: The Ultimate Risk Management Planning and Resource Manual*. San Rafael, CA: McGregor.

McGregor, I. *Risk Management for Campus Recreation*, March 2006-present.

McKichan v. St. Louis Hockey Club, 967 S.W.2d 209 (Mo. Ct. App. 1998).

MEC Leasing, LLC, v. Jarrett, 214 Or. App. 294, 164 P.3d 344 (2007).

Mei Kay Chan v. City of Yonkers, 34 A.D.3d, 824 N.Y.S.2d 380 (2006).

Moose v. Massachusetts Institute of Technology, 43 Mass. App. Ct. 420, 683 N.E.2d 706 (1997).

Morales v. Beacon City School Dist., 44 A.D.3d 724, 843 N.Y.S.2d 646 (2007).

Morales v. Town of Johnston, 895 A.2d 721 (2006).

Morgan v. Fuji Country USA, Inc., 34 Cal. App. 4th 127, 40 Cal. Rptr. 2d 249 (1995).

Morr v. County of Nassau, 22 A.D.3d 728, 804 N.Y.S.2d 391 (2005).

Murphy v. Fairport Cent. School Dist., 48 A.D.3d 1037, 850 N.Y.S.2d 752 (2008).

Murphy v. Polytechnic University, 18 Misc. 3d 623, 850 N.Y.S.2d 339 (2007).

Myhr, A.E. and J.J. Markham. (2004). *Insurance Operations, Regulation, and Statutory Accounting*. Malvern, PA: American Institute for Chartered Property Casualty Underwriters/Insurance Institute of America.

NIRSA. (2006). *NIRSA Recreational Sports Directory: The Essential Companion for Recreation Professionals*. Ed. M. Jacobson. Corvallis, OR: NIRSA.

Nishi v. Mount Snow, Ltd., 935 F. Supp. 508 (D. Vt. 1996).

Okura v. United States Cycling Federation, 186 Cal. App. 3d 1462, 231 Cal. Rptr. 429 (1986).

Ondras, pro ami v. Snohomish School District, No. 201 (Wa. Super. Ct., 97-2-08571-1, January 1998).

Orlando v. FEI Hollywood, Inc., 898 So. 2d 167 (Fla. App. 4 Dist. 2005).

Padilla v. Rodas, 160 Cal. App. 4th 742, 73 Cal. Rptr. 3d 114 (2008).

Parks, J.B., J. Quarterman, and L. Thibault. (Eds.). (2007). *Contemporary Sport Management* (3rd ed.). Champaign, IL: Human Kinetics.

Parsons v. Arrowhead Golf, Inc., 874 N.E.2d 993 (Ind. App. 2007).

Pekin Insurance Co. v. Main St. Construction, Inc., Slip Copy, WL 1597924 (S.D. Ind. 2007).

Petersen v. Joliet Park District, 483 N.E.2d 21 (Ill. 1985).

Petretti v. Jefferson Valley Racquet Club, Inc., 246 A.D.3d 583, 668 N.Y.S.2d 221 (1998).

Pinckney v. Covington Athletic Club and Fitness Center, 288 Ga. App. 891, 655 S.E.2d 650 (2007).

Pine v. Arruda, 448 F. Supp. 2d 282 (D. Mass. 2006).

Pittman, A.T., J.O. Spengler, and S.J. Young. (2008). *Case Studies in Sport Law*. Champaign, IL: Human Kinetics.

Poelker v. Warrensburg Latham Community Unit School Dist. No. 11, 251 Ill. App. 3d 270, 621 N.E.2d 940 (1993).

Pope v. Trotwood-Madison City School District Board of Education, 162 F. Supp. 2d 803 (S.D. Ohio 2000).

Popke, M. (2008). *Athletic Business*, Vol. 32, No. 1.

Poston v. Unified School District No. 387, 37 Kan. App. 2d 694, 156 P.3d 685 (2007).

Quirk, C.E. (Ed.). (1996). *Sports and the Law*. New York: Garland.

Range v. Abbott Sports Complex, 269 Neb. 281, 691 N.W.2d 525 (2005).

Rankey v. Arlington Bd. of Edn., 78 Ohio App. 3d 112, 603 N.E.2d 1151 (1992).

Regan v. Mutual of Omaha Ins. Co., 375 Ill. App. 3d 956, 874 N.E.2d 246 (2007).

Reyes v. City of New York, 15 Misc. 3d 690, 835 N.Y.S.2d 852 (2007).

Ribaudo v. La Salle Institute, 45 A.D.3d 556, 846 N.Y.S.2d 209 (2007).

Roberts v. Boys and Girls Republic, Inc., 850 N.Y.S.2d 38 (2008).

Roberts v. Timber Birch-Broadmore Athletic Ass'n, 371 N.J. Super. 189, 852 A.2d 271 (2004).

Robinson v. Downs, 39 A.D.3d 1250, 834 N.Y.S.2d 770 (2007).

Ryder v. Town of Lancaster, 289 A.D.2d 995, 735 N.Y.S.2d 312 (2001).

Sall v. T's, Inc., 136 P.3d 471 (Kan. 2006).

Sammut v. City of New York, 37 A.D.3d 811, 830 N.Y.S.2d 779 (2007).

Schnarrs v. Girard Bd. of Edn., 168 Ohio App. 3d 188, 858 N.E.2d 1258 (2006).

Sciarrotta v. Global Spectrum, 392 N.J. Super. 403, 920 A.2d 777 (2007).

Seibert v. Amateur Athletic Union of U.S., Inc., 422 F. Supp. 2d 1033 (D. Minn. 2006).

Shain v. Racine Raiders Football Club, Inc., 297 Wis. 2d 869, 726 N.W.2d 346 (2006).

Shin v. Ahn, 141 Cal. App. 4th 726 (2006).

Siau v. Rapides Parish School, 264 So. 2d 372 (1972).

Spaid v. Bucyrus City Schools, 144 Ohio App. 3d 360, 760 N.E.2d 67 (2001).

Spengler, J.O., D.P. Connaughton, and A.T. Pittman. (2006). *Risk Management in Sport and Recreation*. Champaign, IL: Human Kinetics.

Springer v. University of Dayton, Slip Copy, WL 1717906 (Ohio App. 2006).

Stephenson v. Commercial Travelers Mutual Insurance Company, et al., 893 So. 2d 180 (La. App. 3 Cir. 2005).

Stowers v. Clinton Central School Corp., 855 N.E.2d 739 (2006).

Sturdivant v. Moore, 282 Ga. App. 863, 640 S.E.2d 367 (2006).

Summy v. City of Des Moines, Iowa, 708 N.W.2d 333 (Iowa 2006).

Sutton v. Eastern New York Youth Soccer Ass'n, Inc., 8 A.D.3d 855 (N.Y. 2004).

Tarlow, P.E. (2002). *Wiley Events: Event Risk Management and Safety*. New York: Wiley.

Thomas v. St. Mary's Roman Catholic Church, 283 N.W.2d 254 (S.D. 1979).

Thomas v. Wheat, 143 P.3d 767 (Okla. Civ. App. Div. 2006).

Tiger Point Golf and Country Club v. Hipple, 977 So. 2d 608 (Fla. App. 1 Dist. 2007).

Travanti v. Windmill Driving Range (Pa. Common Pleas Ct., 95017231).

Trevett v. City of Little Falls, 6 N.Y.3d 884, 849 N.E.2d 961 (2006).

Umali v. Mount Snow, Ltd., 247 F. Supp. 2d 567 (D. Vt. 2003).

United States v. Comprehensive Drug Testing, Inc., 473 F.3d 915 (9th Cir. 2006).

Unzen v. City of Duluth, 683 N.W.2d 875 (Minn. App. 2004).

Vaughan, E.J. (1997). *Risk Management.* New York: Wiley.

Vecchione v. Middle Country Cent. School Dist., 300 A.D.2d 471, 752 N.Y.S.2d 82 (2002).

Verni v. Stevens, 387 N.J. Super. 160, 903 A.2d 475 (2006).

Weinert v. City of Great Falls, 97 P.3d 1079 (Mont. 2004).

Wiening, E.A. (2002). *Foundations of Risk Management and Insurance.* Malvern, PA: American Institute for Chartered Property Casualty Underwriters/Insurance Institute of America.

White v. Mount Saint Michael High School, 41 A.D.3d 220, 837 N.Y.S.2d 873 (2007).

Willett v. Chatham County Bd. of Educ., 176 N.C. App. 268, 625 S.E.2d 900 (2006).

Williams v. Linkscorp Tennessee Six, LLC, 212 S.W.3d 293 (Tenn. Ct. App. 2006).

Wolohan, J.T. Sports Law Report, *Athletic Business*, January, 2006-present.

Wong, G.M. (2002). *Essentials of Sports Law.* Westport, CA: Greenwood.

Wu v. Sorenson, 440 F. Supp. 2d 1054 (D. Minn. 2006).

www.mcnicholaslaw.com/d_home.asp

www.overlawyered.com/2004/04/update_nj_15m_high_school_bask.html

www.totalinjury.com/verdicts_gen.asp#verdict15

www.usacycling.org

www.usa-gymnastics.org

www.usahockey.com

www.usatf.org

www.usga.org/playing/rules/pdf/2008ROG.pdf

Yarber v. Oakland Unified School District, 6 Cal. Rptr. 2d. 437 (Cal. 1992).

Yatsko v. Berezwick, Slip Copy, WL 4276555 (M.D. Pa. 2007).

Yoneda v. Tom, 110 Hawaii 367, 133 P.3d 796 (2006).

INDEX

Note: The italicized *f* following page numbers refers to figures.

A

Acosta v. Los Angeles Unified School Dist. 227
ADA. *See* Americans with Disabilities Act of 1990
adjacent activities safety 50, 56
AEDs. *See* automated external defibrillators
airline industry 77
alcohol consumption
  by athletes 70
  concession areas safety and 51
  on golf course 222
  regulation of 131-132, 238
  supervision and 337-338
  violence and 53, 69
alternative dispute resolution 38-39
American football
  equipment 142
  facilities 126-127, 139, 143-144
  field considerations in 128-129, 134-139
  hazards 127-130
  lawsuits and settlements in 125-132
  lighting in 139
  personnel 130-131
  protective gear for 140-141
  safety 132-143
  spectators 130, 139, 143-144
  violations 131-132
American Powerlifting Ass'n v. Cotillo 347
Americans with Disabilities Act of 1990 (ADA) 16, 176, 209
appellate court decisions 121-124
appellate process 41
arbitration 38
assault and battery 25-26, 172-173
assumption of risk 21-22, 169
Atcovitz v. Gulph Mills Tennis Club, Inc. 289-290
athletes
  adequate instruction to 300, 303
  alcohol consumption by 70
  first aid for 54, 73
  in lawsuits and settlements 172-173, 184-186, 206-207, 250, 338, 347
  safety and health of 53-54, 70, 128-130, 148-149, 151-153, 175-176, 184-186, 235, 250, 298
  supervision of 53, 70, 130-131, 174-175, 234, 297, 339, 349

transportation of 115, 120
violence and 52, 67-68, 172, 241
Augusta Country Club, Inc., v. Blake 290
authority, lines of 106
automated external defibrillators (AEDs) 5-6, 19, 54, 73, 75, 289-290, 346
automobile liability loss exposures 46
Avila v. Citrus Community College District 149
avoidance 76

B

Baggs ex rel. Baggs v. Little League Baseball, Inc. 146
Bahrenburg v. AT&T Broadband, LLC 130
balance beam 226
Banfield v. Louis 323
Barbato v. Hollow Hills Country Club 197
baseball and softball
  equipment 146-147, 162-163
  facilities 147-149
  field considerations in 155-160, 166
  foul balls in 148-151
  hazards 149-151
  lawsuits and settlements in 145-153
  lighting in 159, 166
  personnel 151-153
  protective gear for 161
  safety 153-166
bases 147, 162
basketball
  courts 181
  equipment 168-169
  facilities 169-172, 178-181
  lawsuits and settlements in 167-176
  participants 172-173
  personnel 173-176
  safety 176-181
  violations 176
bats 146, 163
batting practice tips 165
beach volleyball courts 342
Benbenek v. Chicago Park Dist. 226
Bennett v. City of New York 300
Bennett v. United States Cycling Federation 186-187
bicycle course, in triathlons 322-324, 332-333. *See also* cycling
binding arbitration 38

bleacher safety 50, 60, 127, 172
bodily injury liability motor vehicle insurance 113-114
Bourne v. Marty Gilman, Inc. 126
Bowman v. McNary 203-204
breach of contract 14-15
breach of duty 17
breach of warranty 28
Brisbin v. Washington Sports and Entertainment, Ltd. 238
business continuity 102

C

Calarco v. YMCA of Greater Metropolitan Chicago 346-347
captive insurance plans 95-96
Carbonara v. Texas Stadium Corporation 126-127
Carmack v. Macomb County Community College 226
case law 122-123
Casey v. Garden City Park–New Hyde Park School Dist. 169-170
Celano v. Marriott International, Inc. 208-209
CGL. *See* commercial general liability
chemical storage and handling 277
chief risk management officer (CRMO) 96
children. *See* minors
Chrismon v. Brown 19
civil law 13-14
claims, insurance
    adjusters of 33-35, 38-39
    coverage questions in 35-36
    defense attorney for 36-38
    incident report and 32-33
    injury and 31, 153
    investigation of 33-35
    litigation process and 36-41
    reporting 33
cleaning, of facilities 80, 148, 350, 368
clothing safety 51-52, 65-66, 355
Cohen v. Sterling Mets, LP 147
collision coverage 114
commercial general liability (CGL) 35
communication
    emergency 276
    maintenance of 104-105
comparative negligence. *See* contributory negligence
compensatory damages 20
computerized timing systems 321, 326-327
concession areas safety 51, 63, 151
contact sports 84-85
contracts 14-15, 29, 44
contributory negligence 21
copyright 47
courts, playing
    basketball 181
    hazards of 294-295
    preparation of 80, 89, 181

tennis 294-295
    volleyball 340-342
criminal law 13-14
criminal loss exposures 47
CRMO. *See* chief risk management officer
cross country running 317
crowd management 80-81
current-loss funding 92
cyberstalking 27
cycling
    equipment 188-189
    facilities 184
    helmets 183, 188-190
    lawsuits and settlements in 183-187
    motor vehicle accidents in 183-184, 186, 191-193, 323-324
    mountain biking and 194
    participants 184-186
    personnel 186-187
    safety 183, 187-194
    in triathlons 322-324, 332-333

D

damages 18-20, 29
deck slides 269
defamation 25-27
defense attorney, insurance 36-38
defenses, in negligence torts 20-22, 29
deposition 37
DeRosa v. City of New York 147-148
disaster loss exposures 47-48
disasters. *See* emergency and disaster planning; natural disasters
discovery 36-37
discus 300, 303, 307-308
diversification 76
diving 268, 320
documentation
    of cleaning, repair, and maintenance 80
    of inspections 79, 88, 363
Doe v. Fulton School Dist. 130-131
Dotzler v. Tuttle 172
drain covers 285
driving range 198, 203, 219
drowning 261-264, 272, 283, 285-288
drugs 53, 70
Dubinsky v. St. Louis Blues Hockey Club 16
duplication 76
duties of care 17-20, 150-151

E

Edwards v. Intergraph Services Co., Inc. 170-171
Eisenberg v. East Meadow Union Free School Dist. 238
electrical equipment 284
Elston v. Howland Local Schools 151
e-mail, monitoring of 27
emergency and disaster planning
    content of 78-79

disaster effects and 99
emergency plan developed and prepared in 101-107, 274
equipment and 111-112, 118-119
personnel in 103-104, 106
practice drills for 275
risk analysis in 100-101
risk financing for natural disasters in 107-108
for swimming pools 274
transportation and 111-112, 118-119
emergency communication 276
emergency lights 105-106
enterprise risk management (ERM) 96-97
entryway safety 50, 61
environmental safety 48-52, 56
equipment. *See also* protective gear
American football 142
baseball and softball 146-147, 162-163
basketball 168-169
cycling 188-189
electrical 284
emergency 111-112, 118-119
golf 196-197, 209, 218, 221
gymnastics 226, 229-230
inspection 85, 349, 366
in lawsuits and settlements 146-147, 168-169, 196, 226, 262, 300-301, 346
maintenance 85, 350, 367
medical 105-106
repair 86, 350
safety 51-52, 65-66, 82, 85-86, 188-189, 229-230, 349-350, 354, 366
swimming 262, 276
tennis 296
track and field 300-302
transportation and 111-112, 118-119
weightlifting and weight training 346-347, 349-350, 354
ERM. *See* enterprise risk management
escalators 126-127
Estate of Peters by Peters v. U.S. Cycling Federation 184-185
evacuation 101, 105
Evans v. Pikeway, Inc. 347-348
exit safety 50, 61
expert witnesses 35, 37-38

F

Fabricius v. County of Broome 250
facilities
American football 126-127, 139, 143-144
baseball and softball 147-149
basketball 169-172, 178-181
cleaning of 80, 148, 350, 368
crowd management in 81
cycling 184
fitness center 352-354, 357
golf 197-203, 211-217, 219
gymnastics 233
ice hockey 238-240, 242-243
inspection of 79, 88, 143-144, 155-156, 169, 178-180, 197-199, 212, 214, 238, 242-243, 249, 255, 263, 265-266, 290, 302, 305, 338
in lawsuits and settlements 126-127, 147-148, 169-172, 184, 197-202, 238-239, 248-249, 262-263, 289-291, 338
maintenance of 80, 202, 290, 338
medical 49
protection of 102
repair of 80, 171, 198, 202, 238
safety of 48-52, 56-73
secured 106
soccer 248-249, 255-258
spectator 139, 143-144, 159
swimming 262-263, 265-266, 269, 274-275, 277, 280-286
tennis 289-291, 294-295
volleyball 238, 340-342
weightlifting and weight training 352-354, 357
false imprisonment 25-26
Feagins v. Waddy 303
Federal Tort Claims Act 22
fencing 151, 160, 283
fields
American football 128-129, 134-139
baseball and softball 155-160, 159, 166
inspection of 135, 255-256
lighting of 139, 159, 166
preparation of 80, 89, 137, 157, 256
purposes of 138, 158, 258
slippery 128-129
soccer 255-258
structures on 136, 256
Finkler v. Minisceongo Golf Club 197-198
fireman's rule 324
first aid 54, 73
fitness center facilities 352-354, 357
flooring 171-172
food, provision of 105
football. *See* American football; soccer
footwear 221
foul balls 148-151
Frazier v. City of New York 148
Freiberger v. Four Seasons Golf Center 198
fuel, provision of 105
Fugazy v. Corbetta 173

G

Gardner v. Town of Tonawanda 127-128
gates 283
generators 105-106
Gernat v. State 238
glass 170, 172
goalposts 126
goals
organizational 7-9
of risk financing 93-94
Goforth v. State 128

golf
  alcohol use and 222
  driving range and 198, 203, 219
  equipment 196-197, 209, 218, 221
  facilities 197-203, 211-217, 219
  hazards 203-206
  lawsuits and settlements in 195-210
  participants 206-207
  personnel 208
  safety 195, 210-224
  violations 208-210
  weather and 204-205, 223
Gorbey v. Longwill 262-263
governmental immunity. *See* sovereign
  immunity
Grames v. King and Pontiac School District 173-174
Grappendorf v. Pleasant Grove City 146-147
Griem v. Town of Walpole 127
Guardino v. Kings Park School District 290
Guenther v. West Seneca Cent. School Dist. 238-239
gymnasium
  cleanliness 350
  preparation of 80, 89, 181
gymnastics
  equipment 226, 229-230
  facilities 233
  lawsuits and settlements in 225-227
  personnel 227
  safety 225, 227-236

H
hammer 302, 309-310
harassment 27, 252-253
Harris v. Willie McCray, et al. 128-129
Harting v. Dayton Dragons Professional Baseball Club, LLC 149-150
Hawkins v. United States Sports Association, Inc. 148
Hayes Through Hayes v. Walters 227
Haymon v. Pettit 148-149
hazards
  American football 127-130
  baseball and softball 149-151
  definition of 76
  golf 203-206
  ice hockey 240
  in lawsuits and settlements 127-129, 149-151, 203-206, 240, 249, 302, 320-321, 323, 347
  slip and fall 294
  soccer 249-250
  tennis court 294-295
  track and field 302-303
  triathlon 320-321, 323-324
  water 215
  weightlifting and weight training 347
head injuries 149, 151-152

Health Insurance Portability and Accountability Act of 1996 (HIPAA) 37
Hearl v. Waterbury YMCA 338
heatstroke 128-130
helmets 82-83, 86, 140, 183, 188-190
Hemady v. Long Beach Unified School District, et al. 206-207
Henderson v. Walled Lake Consol. Schools 252-253
Henry v. Roosevelt School District 129
Hiett v. Lake Barcroft Community Ass'n, Inc. 320-321
high bar 227
high jump 300, 303, 315
HIPAA. *See* Health Insurance Portability and Accountability Act of 1996
hockey. *See* ice hockey
hold harmless agreement 15
Holmes v. Health & Tennis Corp. of Am. 348-349
hot tubs 282
Hurst v. East Coast Hockey League, Inc. 240

I
ice hockey
  facilities 238-240, 242-243
  hazards 240
  lawsuits and settlements in 237-240
  protective gear for 244
  pucks 238-240
  safety 237, 240-246
  spectators 238-240
  violations 240
incident reports 32-33, 279, 364
independent contractors 23-24
indoor volleyball courts 340-341
inspections
  documentation of 79, 88, 363
  equipment 85, 349, 366
  facility 79, 88, 143-144, 155-156, 169, 178-180, 197-199, 212, 214, 238, 242-243, 249, 255, 263, 265-266, 290, 302, 305, 338
  field 135, 255-256
  in risk control 79, 88
  vehicle 111, 117, 365
insurance
  captive plans 95-96
  fundamentals of 1-2
  loss exposure identification and 45
  motor vehicle 113-115
  premiums 6-7, 115
  risk financing and 94-96
  risk transfer to 91, 94-96
  self- 95
insurance claims
  adjusters of 33-35, 38-39
  coverage questions in 35-36
  defense attorney for 36-38
  incident report and 32-33
  injury and 31, 153

investigation of 33-35
litigation process and 36-41
reporting 33
intellectual property loss exposures 47
intentional torts 25-27, 29
Internet, defamation and 25-27
invasion of privacy 25-26

J
javelin 300-302, 311-312
Jaworski v. Kiernan 250
Jennings v. University of North Carolina 253
Johnson v. Steffen 323-324
joint and several liability 24
Jones v. Kite/Cupp Legends Golf Development 198
jump pits 313
jury selection 40
jury trials
appellate process and 41
in litigation process 39-40

K
Karas v. Strevell 240
Kindred v. Board of Education of Memphis City Schools 174
Kreil v. County of Niagara 302

L
lack of causation 22
lawsuits and settlements. *See also* litigation process
in American football 125-132
athletes in 172-173, 184-186, 206-207, 250, 338, 347
in baseball and softball 145-153
in basketball 167-176
in cycling 183-187
equipment in 146-147, 168-169, 196, 226, 262, 300-301, 346
facilities in 126-127, 147-148, 169-172, 184, 197-202, 238-239, 248-249, 262-263, 289-291, 338
in golf 195-210
in gymnastics 225-227
hazards in 127-129, 149-151, 203-206, 240, 249, 302, 320-321, 323, 347
history of 49
in ice hockey 237-240
importance of 121-124
participants in 172-173, 184-186, 206-207, 250, 338, 347
personnel in 130, 151-153, 173-175, 186, 201, 208, 227, 263, 291, 303, 348-349
risk retention and 6-7
in soccer 247-254
spectators in 130, 251
in swimming 261-264
in tennis 289-292
in track and field 299-303

in triathlons 320, 323-324
violations in 131, 176, 208-209, 240, 252-253
in volleyball 337-339
in weightlifting and weight training 345-349
legal counsel 4
legal liability
bodily injury liability motor vehicle insurance and 113-114
CGL 35
from contracts 14-15, 29, 44
joint and several 24
loss exposure from 44, 46-47, 169, 200
products 27-29
from statutes 15-16, 29
strict 27-29
from torts 16-29
vicarious 23
legal principles
civil law and 13-14
contracts in 14-15, 29
criminal law and 13-14
fundamentals of 1-2
statutes in 15-16, 29
torts in 16-29
Lewin v. Lutheran West High School 127
liability. *See* legal liability
liability loss exposure 44, 46-47, 169, 200
libel 26
lifeguards
training of 278
for triathlons 321-322, 328
lighting
in American football 139
in baseball and softball 159, 166
emergency 105-106
of fields 139, 159, 166
of parking lots 171
of swimming facilities 262
lightning
golf and 204-205, 223
risk control of 81-82, 90
swimming and 270
limited duty rule 150-151
litigation process
alternative dispute resolution and 38-39
appellate process and 41
discovery in 36-37
expert witnesses in 35, 37-38
insurance claims and 36-41
jury trials in 39-40
motions for summary judgment in 39
Little v. Jonesboro Country Club 198-199
Livshitz v. U.S. Tennis Ass'n Nat. Tennis Center 291
Lloyd v. Sugarloaf Mountain Corp. 185-186
locker room safety 50, 57-58, 130-131, 174, 350

Lombardo v. Cedar Brook Golf & Tennis Club 199-200
long jump 313-314
Longview Independent School District v. Vibra-Whirl, Ltd. 14-15
loss exposures
  analysis of 54
  automobile 46
  criminal 47
  disaster 47-48
  in ERM 96
  identification of 44-45, 55
  liability 44, 46-47, 169, 200
  management of 86
  net income 44, 48
  personnel 44, 48
  premises 46, 169, 200
  property 43-48, 169, 200
  in risk assessment 4-5, 8, 43-48, 54-55
  safety attitudes influencing 77
  from statutes 44
  from torts 44
  watercraft 46
  workers' compensation 46-47
loss history 49, 92-93, 93*f*
loss prevention and reduction 76. *See also* risk control
Lund v. Bally's Aerobic Plus, Inc. 349

M
MacDonald v. B.M.D. Golf Associates, Inc. 196
maintenance
  of communication 104-105
  documentation of 80
  equipment 85, 350, 367
  facility 80, 202, 290, 338
  vehicle 112-113
Maisonave v. Newark Bears Professional Baseball Club, Inc. 150-151
Mallin v. Paesani 208
Manias v. Golden Bear Golf Center 200
Manoly v. City of New York 248
Marshall v. City of New Rochelle 290-291
Mason v. Bristol Local School Dist. Bd. of Edn. 300-301
Mastropolo v. Goshen Cent. School Dist. 173
matting 232
Mavrovich v. Vanderpool 207
McCabe v. City of New York 147
McCollin v. Roman Catholic Archdiocese of New York 174-175
McCormick ex rel. McCormick v. School Dist. of Mamaroneck 253-254
McKichan v. St. Louis Hockey Club 237
MEC Leasing, LLC, v. Jarrett 204
mediation 38
medical emergencies 5-6, 358
medical equipment 105-106
medical facilities, proximity to 49

medical risk factors 359
medical treatment 31, 106, 152, 324
Mei Kay Chan v. City of Yonkers 168
minors
  adequate instruction to 300
  caring for and discharging 106
  injury to 53
  supervision of 53-54, 71-72, 252, 264
Moose v. Massachusetts Institute of Technology 301
Morales v. Beacon City School Dist. 301
Morales v. Town of Johnston 248-249
Morgan v. Fuji County USA, Inc. 209-210
Morr v. County of Nassau 301
motions for summary judgment 39, 122, 124
motions in limine 40
motor vehicles. *See* vehicles
mountain biking 194
mouth guards 83-84
Murphy v. Fairport Cent. School Dist. 349
Murphy v. Polytechnic University 152-153

N
natural disasters 100, 107-108. *See also* emergency and disaster planning
negligence per se 24
negligence torts
  alternative ways to prove 23-25, 29
  contributory negligence in 21
  damages from 18-20, 29
  defenses in 20-22, 29
  elements of 17-18, 20
negligent entrustment 23
net income loss exposures 44, 48
Nishi v. Mount Snow, Ltd. 186
no-fault motor vehicle insurance 113
noninsurance risk transfer 92

O
Okura v. United States Cycling Federation 186
open water swim course 330-331
organizational goals 7-9
Orlando v. FEI Hollywood, Inc. 347
orthopedic injuries 235, 298

P
padding 84-85, 168-169, 301
Padilla v. Rodas 263-264
parallel bars 226
parents 250
parking lot safety 51, 62, 127, 171, 350
Parsons v. Arrowhead Golf, Inc. 200-201
participants. *See also* athletes
  basketball 172-173
  cycling 184-186
  golf 206-207
  in lawsuits and settlements 172-173, 184-186, 206-207, 250, 339, 347
  soccer 250
  volleyball 339

weightlifting and weight training 347
patent 47
Patsy T. Mink Equal Opportunity in Education Act 16
Pedersen v. Joliet Park District 171
Pekin Insurance Co. v. Main St. Construction, Inc. 15
personnel
American football 130-131
baseball and softball 151-153
basketball 173-176
cycling 186-187
in emergency and disaster planning 103-104, 106
golf 208
gymnastics 227
in lawsuits and settlements 130, 151-153, 173-175, 186, 201, 208, 227, 263, 291, 303, 348-349
loss exposure 44, 48
safety-first attitudes of 78
soccer 251-252
swimming 263-264
tennis 291-292
track and field 303
transportation of 111
weightlifting and weight training 347-349
Petretti v. Jefferson Valley Racquet Club, Inc. 291-292
phone numbers 104-105
Pinckney v. Covington Athletic Club and Fitness Center 263
Pine v. Arruda 196-197
players. *See* athletes
Poelker v. Warrensburg Latham Community Unit School Dist. No. 11 303
pommel horse 227
Pope v. Trotwood-Madison City School District Board of Education 168
post-loss funding 92
Poston v. Unified School District No. 387 171
pre-loss funding 92
premises liability loss exposures 46, 169, 200
premiums, insurance 6-7, 115
press box safety 51, 64
products liability 27-29
property damage motor vehicle insurance 114
property loss exposures 43-48, 169, 200
protective gear
for American football 140-141
for baseball and softball 161
helmets 82-83, 86, 140, 183, 188-190
for ice hockey 244
in risk control 82
safety and 51-52, 65-66, 82-85
for soccer 259
Prouty approach chart 54
proximate cause 17-18

public areas safety 51, 64
public relations liaison 107
public restroom safety 50, 59
pucks, hockey 238-240
punitive damages 20

R

Range v. Abbott Sports Complex 249
Rankey v. Arlington Bd. of Edn. 302-303
recorded statements 34
Regan v. Mutual of Omaha Ins. Co. 153
releases 22, 130, 184-187, 204, 250, 320, 323, 346-347, 349
repair
documentation of 80
equipment 86, 350
facility 80, 171, 198, 202, 238
res ipsa loquitur 24-25
restroom safety 50, 59
Reyes v. City of New York 15
Ribaudo v. La Salle Institute 168-169
risk
identification 7-9
managers 3-4, 8
matrixes 54
retention 6-7, 92, 93f, 95
transfer 7, 91-92, 93f, 94-96
risk analysis
in emergency and disaster planning 100-101
risk assessment and 54-55
in risk management steps 7-10
risk assessment
of American football field 134
facility and environmental safety in 48-52, 56-73
loss exposures in 4-5, 8, 43-48, 54-55
players' safety and health in 53, 70
risk analysis and 54-55
supervision in 53-54, 70-72
swimming and 5
violence and unruly behavior in 52-53
risk control
crowd management in 80-81
facility cleaning, maintenance, and repair in 80
implementation of 75
inspection in 79, 88
introduction to 5-6, 7-8, 10-11
of lightning 81-82, 90
preparation of court, gymnasium, or field in 80, 89
protective gear in 82
risk management plan and 86-87
safety attitudes and 77-79
techniques 76, 86
weather and 81-82, 90
risk financing
ERM in 96-97
goals of 93-94
insurance and 94-96

risk financing *(continued)*
  introduction to 6-8
  for natural disasters 100, 107-108
  risk retention in 92, 93*f*, 95
  risk transfer in 91-92, 93*f*
  techniques for 92-93, 93*f*
risk management. *See also specific sports*
  definition of 3, 8
  enterprise 96-97
  ERM 96-97
  fundamentals of 1-2
  phases of 4-7
  plan 3-4, 7-8, 11, 86-87
  resources for 4
  scenario of 9-11
  steps of 7-11
  team 3-4
Roberts v. Boys and Girls Republic, Inc.
  151
*Roberts v. Timber Birch-Broadmore Ath-
  letic Ass'n* 251
Robinson v. Downs 175
rule(s)
  fireman's 324
  limited duty 150-151
  safety 78-79, 173, 240
  swimming 267-268
run course 324, 334-335
Ryder v. Town of Lancaster 238

S
safety
  adjacent activities 50, 56
  American football 132-143
  of athletes 53-54, 70, 128-130, 148-149,
    151-153, 175-176, 184-186, 235, 250, 298
  attitudes toward 77-79
  baseball and softball 153-166
  basketball 176-181
  bleacher 50, 60, 127, 172
  clothing 51-52, 65-66, 355
  concession areas 51, 63, 151
  cycling 183, 187-194
  entryway 50, 61
  environmental 48-52, 56
  equipment 51-52, 65-66, 82, 85-86, 188-
    189, 229-230, 349-350, 354, 366
  exit 50, 61
  facility 48-52, 56-73
  fitness center 352-354
  golf 195, 210-224
  gymnastics 225, 227-236
  ice hockey 237, 240-246
  locker room 50, 57-58, 130-131, 174, 350
  nets 198, 200
  parking lot 51, 62, 127, 171, 350
  plans 78-79
  press box 51, 64
  protective gear and 51-52, 65-66, 82-85
  public areas 51, 64
  restroom 50, 59

  rules 78-79, 173, 240
  soccer 247, 254-259
  spectator 50, 60, 147-151, 238-240,
    302-303
  stands 50, 60
  swimming 261, 264-287
  taking charge of 77-78
  tennis 289, 292-298
  ticket booths 51, 64
  track and field 299, 303-317
  traffic 50, 56
  transportation 120
  triathlon 319-320, 324-335
  viewing areas 50, 60
  volleyball 337, 339-343
  weightlifting and weight training 345,
    360-362
Sall v. T's, Inc. 204-205
Sammut v. City of New York 291
Schnarrs v. Girard Bd. of Edn. 175
Sciarrotta v. Global Spectrum 239-240
scorecards 220
*Seibert v. Amateur Athletic Union of U.S.,
  Inc.* 176
self-insurance plans 95
separation 76
settlement 38-40. *See also* lawsuits and
  settlements
sexual harassment 27, 252-253
*Shain v. Racine Raiders Football Club,
  Inc.* 129
shelter, provision of 105
Shin v. Ahn 207
shot put 302-303, 306
Siau v. Rapides Parish School 301-302
signage 213, 280
slander 26
slip and fall hazards 294
soccer
  facilities 248-249, 255-258
  fields 255-258
  hazards 249-250
  lawsuits and settlements in 247-254
  participants 250
  personnel 251-252
  protective gear for 259
  safety 247, 254-259
  spectators 251
  violations 252-254
softball. *See* baseball and softball
sovereign immunity 22, 168, 226-228
spas 282
spectators
  American football 130, 139, 143-144
  facilities for 139, 143-144, 159
  first aid for 54, 73
  foul balls and 148-151
  ice hockey 238-240
  injury to 130, 251
  in lawsuits and settlements 130, 251
  safety of 50, 60, 147-151, 238-240, 302-303

soccer 251
transportation of 110-111
violence 52-53, 69
sport risk management consultant 4
sports-exception doctrine 208
Springer v. University of Dayton 171
staff. *See* personnel
stairs 147-148
stands safety 50, 60
statute(s)
 liability from 15-16, 29
 of limitations 21
 loss exposure from 44
Stephenson v. Commercial Travelers Mutual Insurance Company, et al. 251
Stowers v. Clinton Central School Corp. 129-130
strict liability 27-29
Sturdivant v. Moore 262
subpoena 37
summary judgment, motions for 39, 122, 124
Summy v. City of Des Moines, Iowa 201
supervision
 alcohol consumption and 337-338
 of athletes 53, 70, 130-131, 174-175, 234, 297, 339, 349
 evaluation of need for 72
 of minors 53-54, 71-72, 252, 264
 in risk assessment 53-54, 70-72
 of swimming 264, 272-273, 281
 of tennis 297
 in track and field 303
 of weightlifting and weight training 349, 356
supervisory responsibility 22
Sutton v. Eastern New York Youth Soccer Ass'n, Inc. 249-250
swimming
 emergency and disaster planning for 274
 equipment 262, 276
 facilities 262-263, 265-266, 269, 274-275, 277, 280-286
 lawsuits and settlements in 261-264
 lighting for 262
 open water 330-331
 personnel 263-264
 risk assessment and 5
 rules and regulations 267-268
 safety 261, 264-287
 supervision of 264, 272-273, 281
 in triathlons 320-322, 329-331
 weather and 270

T

tailgating 52, 62, 143
tee areas 214
tennis
 equipment 296
 facilities 289-291, 294-295

hazards 294-295
 lawsuits in 289-292
 personnel 291-292
 safety 289, 292-298
 supervision of 297
Thomas v. St. Mary's Roman Catholic Church 172
Thomas v. Wheat 206
ticket booths safety 51, 64
Tiger Point Golf and Country Club v. Hipple 20, 201-202
timing chips 321, 326-327
Title IX of the Education Amendments of 1972 16, 252-254
tortfeasor 17
torts. *See also* negligence torts
 Federal Tort Claims Act and 22
 intentional 25-27, 29
 legal liability from 16-29
 loss exposure from 44
track and field
 cross country and 317
 equipment 300-302
 hazards 302-303
 lawsuits and settlements in 299-303
 meets 316
 personnel 303
 safety 299, 303-317
 supervision in 303
trademark 47
traffic safety 50, 56
transportation
 of athletes 115, 120
 emergency equipment in 111-112, 118-119
 of personnel 111
 riskiness of 109, 116
 safety tips for 120
 of spectators 110-111
 types of 110-111
 vehicle inspection in 111, 117, 365
 vehicle insurance in 113-115
 vehicle maintenance in 112-113
 vehicle operators and 110
trespassing 207
Trevett v. City of Little Falls 169
triathlon
 bicycle course of 322-324, 332-333
 hazards 320-321, 323-324
 lawsuits and settlements in 320, 323-324
 lifeguards for 321-322, 328
 run course of 324, 334-335
 safety 319-320, 324-335
 swimming in 320-322, 329-331
 watercraft in 321-322, 328
triple jump 300, 313

U

UIM. *See* underinsured motor vehicle coverage
UM. *See* uninsured motor vehicle coverage
Umali v. Mount Snow, Ltd. 184

underinsured motor vehicle coverage (UIM) 114
unforeseeable incidents 22
uninsured motor vehicle coverage (UM) 114
United States Cycling Federation (USCF) 184-187
United States v. Comprehensive Drug Testing, Inc. 14
unruly behavior 52-53, 67-68
Unzen v. City of Duluth 202
USA Cycling 183
USA Gymnastics 225
USA Hockey 237
USAT. *See* USA Triathlon
USA Track and Field (USATF) 299
USA Triathlon (USAT) 319-320
USCF. *See* United States Cycling Federation

V

Vecchione v. Middle Country Cent. School Dist. 291
vehicles
  accidents with 37-38, 46, 183-184, 186, 191-193, 323-324
  inspection of 111, 117, 365
  insurance for 113-115
  maintenance of 112-113
  operators of 110
ventilation 357
Verni v. Stevens 131-132
vicarious liability 23
viewing areas safety 50, 60
violations
  American football 131-132
  basketball 176
  golf 208-210
  ice hockey 240
  in lawsuits and settlements 131, 176, 208-209, 240, 252-253
  soccer 252-254
violence
  alcohol consumption and 53, 69
  athlete 52, 67-68, 172, 241
  metal detectors and 174
  in risk assessment 52-53
  spectator 52-53, 69
volleyball
  courts 340-342

facilities 238, 340-342
lawsuits and settlements in 337-339
participants 339
safety 337, 339-343

W

waiver 22, 250, 346, 348
warnings 213
warranty, breach of 28
water
  hazards 215
  provision of 105
watercraft
  loss exposures 46
  in triathlons 321-322, 328
weather
  golf and 204-205, 223
  risk control and 81-82, 90
  swimming and 270
weightlifting and weight training
  equipment 346-347, 349-350, 354
  facilities 352-354, 357
  hazards 347
  lawsuits and settlements in 345-349
  medical risk factors for 359
  participants 347
  personnel 347-349
  safety 345, 360-362
  supervision of 349, 356
Weinert v. City of Great Falls 14
White v. Mount Saint Michael High School 251-252
Willett v. Chatham County Bd. of Educ. 172
Williams v. Linkscorp Tennessee Six, LLC 202
witnesses 34-35, 37-38
workers' compensation
  law 15-16
  loss exposures 46-47
workplace harassment 27
Wu v. Sorenson 208

Y

Yarber v. Oakland Unified School District 169
Yatsko v. Berezwick 175-176
Yoneda v. Tom 202-203

PHOTO CREDITS

PART I

page 1—© Human Kinetics

Chapter 1

page 3—© Photodisc/Getty Images
page 5—© Human Kinetics
page 9—© Human Kinetics

Chapter 2

page 13—© Comstock
page 16—© Human Kinetics
page 21—© Human Kinetics
page 26—© Banana Stock

Chapter 3

page 31—© Eyewire/Getty Images
page 34—© Photodisc

Chapter 4

page 43—© Photodisc/Getty Images
page 48—© Mario Tama/Getty Images News
page 51—© SWP, Incorporated 2004

Chapter 5

page 75—© Photodisc/Getty Images
page 78—© Human Kinetics
page 83—© Human Kinetics

Chapter 6

page 91—© Ed Kashi/Aurora Photos
page 94—© Human Kinetics

Chapter 7

page 99—© Jamie McDonald/Getty Images Sport
page 103—© MN Chan/Getty Images News
page 107—© Human Kinetics

Chapter 8

page 109—© Matthew O'Haren/Icon SMI
page 112—© Palm Beach Post/Zuma Press/Icon SMI
page 115—© AP Photo/Fresno Bee, Eric Paul Zamora

PART II

page 121—© Human Kinetics

Chapter 9

page 125—© Human Kinetics
page 128—© AP Photo/Orlin Wagner
page 131—© Shelly Castellano ICON SMI

Chapter 10

page 145—© Human Kinetics
page 150—© Rhona Wise/Icon SMI
page 152—© Human Kinetics

Chapter 11

page 167—© Human Kinetics
page 170—© Comstock
page 173—© Human Kinetics

Chapter 12

page 183—© Eyewire/Getty Images
page 185—© Eyewire/Getty Images

Chapter 13

page 195—© Human Kinetics
page 199—© Human Kinetics
page 205—© Brandon Malone/Action
    Images/Icon Smi

Chapter 14

page 225—© Photodisc/Getty Images
page 226—© Comstock

Chapter 15

page 237—© Human Kinetics
page 239—© Human Kinetics

Chapter 16

page 247—© Eyewire/Getty Images
page 249—© Human Kinetics
page 252—© Human Kinetics

Chapter 17

page 261—© Stewart Cohen/Digital
    Vision

page 263—© iStockphoto/Terence D.
    Healy

Chapter 18

page 289—© Digital Vision
page 292—© Bananastock

Chapter 19

page 299—© Stockbyte
page 302—© Stockbyte

Chapter 20

page 319—© Human Kinetics
page 322—© Human Kinetics

Chapter 21

page 337—© Human Kinetics
page 338—© Photodisc/Getty Images

Chapter 22

page 345—© Andersen Ross/Blend
    Images/age fotostock
page 348—© Bananastock

ABOUT THE AUTHOR

Katharine M. Nohr, Esq, is an attorney with more than 20 years of experience handling negligence cases for insurance companies, including matters involving sport, premises liability, motor vehicles, and coverage. Ms. Nohr has served as per diem judge for the District Court of the First Circuit for the state of Hawaii as well as an appellate mediator and arbitrator. She is also the owner of Nohr Sports Risk Management, LLC, which provides education and consulting.

Ms. Nohr is a certified USA Triathlon official and certified International Triathlon Union official. She currently serves as the Pacific regional coordinator for officials for USA Triathlon and the safety director for the Honolulu Triathlon. Ms. Nohr has served as the chairperson of an appellate panel for USA Triathlon and has taught sport risk management to USA Triathlon race directors.

Ms. Nohr has served on the board of directors and is a former president of the Honolulu Association of Insurance Professionals and former state council director for the National Association of Insurance Women (NAIW). She frequently teaches insurance law seminars and is a certified provider of continuing education credits for property and casualty insurance law and life and health insurance law. She is on the advisory board for the *Risk Management Newsletter for Campus Recreation* and is also the columnist of *The Ball Is in Your Court* for that publication.

As an athlete, Ms. Nohr has participated in triathlon, swimming, running, and cycling competitions. In her free time, she enjoys swimming, hiking, and traveling internationally. Ms. Nohr resides in Kaneohe, Hawaii.

You'll find other outstanding
recreation and sports resources at
www.HumanKinetics.com

In the U.S. call 1.800.747.4457
Australia 08 8372 0999
Canada. 1.800.465.7301
Europe . . . . .+44 (0) 113 255 5665
New Zealand . . . 0064 9 448 1207

HUMAN KINETICS
The Information Leader in Physical Activity
P.O. Box 5076 • Champaign, IL 61825-5076

HOW TO USE THE CD-ROM

SYSTEM REQUIREMENTS

You can use this CD-ROM on either a Windows-based PC or a Macintosh computer.

Windows
- IBM PC compatible with Pentium processor
- Windows 98/2000/XP/Vista
- Adobe Reader 8.0
- 4x CD-ROM drive

Macintosh
- Power Mac recommended
- System 10.4 or higher
- Adobe Reader
- 4x CD-ROM drive

USER INSTRUCTIONS

Windows
1. Insert the *Managing Risk in Sport and Recreation* CD-ROM. (Note: The CD-ROM must be present in the drive at all times.)
2. Select the "My Computer" icon from the desktop.
3. Select the CD-ROM drive.
4. Open the file you wish to view. See the "00Start.pdf" file for a list of the contents.

Macintosh
1. Insert the *Managing Risk in Sport and Recreation* CD-ROM. (Note: The CD-ROM must be present in the drive at all times.)
2. Double-click the CD icon located on the desktop.
3. Open the file you wish to view. See the "00Start" file for a list of the contents.

For customer support, contact Technical Support:

Phone: 217-351-5076 Monday through Friday (excluding holidays) between 7:00 a.m. and 7:00 p.m. (CST).

Fax: 217-351-2674

E-mail: support@hkusa.com